PLATO
Republic

Translated with an Introduction and Notes by
CHRISTOPHER ROWE

PENGUIN BOOKS

PENGUIN CLASSICS

Published by the Penguin Group
Penguin Books Ltd, 80 Strand, London WC2R ORL, England
Penguin Group (USA) Inc., 375 Hudson Street, New York, New York 10014, USA
Penguin Group (Canada), 90 Eglinton Avenue East, Suite 700, Toronto, Ontario,
Canada M4P 2Y3 (a division of Pearson Penguin Canada Inc.)
Penguin Ireland, 25 St Stephen's Green, Dublin 2, Ireland (a division of Penguin Books Ltd)
Penguin Group (Australia), 707 Collins Street, Melbourne, Victoria 3008, Australia
(a division of Pearson Australia Group Pty Ltd)
Penguin Books India Pvt Ltd, 11 Community Centre, Panchsheel Park, New Delhi – 110 017, India
Penguin Group (NZ), 67 Apollo Drive, Rosedale, Auckland 0632, New Zealand
(a division of Pearson New Zealand Ltd)
Penguin Books (South Africa) (Pty) Ltd, Block D, Rosebank Office Park,
181 Jan Smuts Avenue, Parktown North, Gauteng 2193, South Africa

Penguin Books Ltd, Registered Offices: 80 Strand, London WC2R ORL, England

www.penguin.com

This translation first published in Penguin Classics 2012

006

Translation and editorial material © Christopher Rowe, 2012
All rights reserved

The moral right of the translator has been asserted

Set in 10.25/12.25 pt Postscript Adobe Sabon
Typeset by Jouve (UK), Milton Keynes
Printed in Great Britain by Clays Ltd, St Ives plc

ISBN: 978-0-141-44243-3

www.greenpenguin.co.uk

Penguin Books is committed to a sustainable
future for our business, our readers and our planet.
This book is made from Forest Stewardship
Council™ certified paper.

Contents

Chronology

We know as little about Plato's life as we do about most ancient figures. The chronology of his writings – with the exception of the *Apology*, all are in dialogue form – is particularly uncertain. Nevertheless, studies of his style have resulted in a broad division of the works into three groups, which is reflected in the (very rough) chronology below. For this division, see especially Charles Kahn, 'On Platonic Chronology', in Julia Annas and Christopher Rowe (eds.), *New Perspectives on Plato, Modern and Ancient* (Cambridge, MA, 2002), pp. 93–127. (Only certainly genuine works are listed.)

c. **424** BCE Birth of Plato, son of Ariston. The story that the name 'Plato' derived from the adjective *platus*, 'broad' (referring to the width of the great man's shoulders, to his intellectual capacity or the 'breadth' of his style) has been discredited. (The usual date given for Plato's birth is 428 or 427; I have accepted the arguments of Debra Nails for placing the birth some three or four years later: Debra Nails, *The People of Plato* (Indianapolis, IN/Cambridge, MA, 2002).)

404 The defeat of Athens in the great war against Sparta (the 'Peloponnesian' war) signals the temporary end of the democracy which had governed Athens for most of the previous hundred years. It is replaced by a junta of oligarchs, at least two of whom are members of Plato's immediate family. The Thirty Tyrants, as they become known, last only a few months before being overthrown in a civil war and replaced by a revived democracy.

399 Under the new democratic government, Socrates – Plato's mentor and friend for up to ten years previously – is brought to trial on charges brought by private prosecutors. The charges are failing to recognize the gods recognized by the city and of introducing new divinities in their place; also of corrupting the young. Socrates' condemnation and subsequent execution by hemlock poisoning are the last straw: Plato more or less withdraws from the world of practical politics.

390s Plato may have spent some time out of Athens, travelling both in Greece and around the eastern Mediterranean. Meanwhile, he is beginning to publish, i.e., to release works to be copied for and read by others.

390s–380s Plato composes a large and varied group of works, in alphabetical order as follows: *Apology of Socrates* (i.e., *Defence of Socrates*), *Charmides*, *Cratylus*, *Crito*, *Euthydemus*, *Euthyphro*, *Gorgias*, *Hippias Minor*, *Ion*, *Laches*, *Lysis*, *Menexenus*, *Meno*, *Phaedo*, *Protagoras*, *Symposium*. The relative dating of the items in this group is controversial, though it may be that *Cratylus*, *Phaedo* and *Symposium* were among the last written.

389–388 Plato visits Sicily and southern Italy and establishes contact with Pythagoreans in the area.

c. 387 Plato founds the Academy, an institute for research and teaching, adjacent to one of the main gymnasia of Athens, sacred to the local hero Academus.

380s–370s Plato composes the second group of dialogues: *Parmenides*, *Phaedrus*, *Republic*, *Theaetetus*.

367 Plato's second visit to Sicily, at the invitation of Dion, uncle of Dionysius II, tyrant or dictator of Syracuse. Some have supposed that Plato had hopes of making Dionysius an ideal ruler, a philosopher-king; if so, they were soon dashed. Plato evidently had some difficulty getting home.

c. 365 Arrival in the Academy of its most eminent member, Aristotle.

361 Plato visits Sicily once more, for unknown reasons; in any case this visit too seems to have ended badly.

360s–350s Plato composes the third group of dialogues: *Philebus*, *Sophist*, *Statesman*, *Timaeus-Critias*, *Laws* (known to have been Plato's last work; he may still have been working on it when he died).

347 Plato dies.

Introduction

1. *Republic*, or *Constitution* (*Politeia*)

The *Republic* is a large, complex and ambitious work. Along with the *Timaeus* – a work tied to the *Republic* in various ways – it can plausibly claim to be the Platonic masterwork, and has been regarded as such, by Platonists and non-Platonists alike, more or less since it first began to be copied and read some 2,400 years ago. It remains one of the most widely read books in the world: not just because of its historical importance, as one of the ground-works of Western philosophy, even of Western civilization, but because of the richness of its ideas (however shocking some of these may be), the power of its arguments and the virtuosity of its writing.

In the *Timaeus*, the main speaker (one Timaeus of Locri) describes the universe as a rational entity, fashioned by a divinely rational craftsman. In the *Republic*, Plato's Socrates describes how we human beings might best be able to realize our own fundamentally rational nature, or at least the best approximation to it that may be available to us. Whereas according to Timaeus the universe as a whole always functions for the best, we humans are endowed – so the *Republic* repeatedly stresses – with *choice*, so that whether we realize our potential as members of the human race rather than of some less rational species is a matter for us, and depends on our ability to recognize the importance of the choice that faces us about the sort of life we are to live – our ability even to recognize that we have such a choice in the first place, let alone to understand how to make that choice.

The trouble, as the Socrates of the *Republic* suggests, is that we currently do none of this very well; and for good reason, because it requires hard intellectual work. In particular, it requires hard work to establish what the true ends of life are. To live respecting other people, and the gods? To acquire money, fame and power? To live a quiet life? Or what? There are answers to such questions, he proposes, if only we are prepared to spend the time and effort needed to look for them. But most of us are not prepared to do that, and it is in any case unclear how many of us would have either the intellectual qualities or the staying power that would be required for the task. As a result, we live unsatisfactory lives, at best opting to behave piously and justly for the wrong reasons, at worst choosing a life of complete unscrupulousness and injustice. Worse still, when we form communities and cities (i.e., *poleis*, the typical form of political organization in the Greece of Plato's day), we organize these in a similarly unreflective way, so that they merely reproduce, and then reinforce, the habits of mind we have grown up with. The *Republic* describes and sets out to address this situation.

The work is written as a conversation (a 'dialogue'), reported in the first person by Socrates to an unidentified and silent audience: its potential readers, one might suppose – except that the work as a whole tries its hardest to pretend to be spoken rather than written, using first-person narrative and direct speech throughout. 'I went down to the Piraeus yesterday with Glaucon', Socrates begins, 'and we were just turning back when Polemarchus caught sight of us'; the conversation then develops, peppered with 'I said', 'and he said', and so on, right through to the end. Socrates' immediate interlocutors form a mixed collection (as do the bystanders). First, there is a retired businessman, Cephalus, and his son Polemarchus; next a visiting diplomat and expert in rhetoric, Thrasymachus, who has his own theory about the best kind of life; and then the remaining nine tenths or so of the conversation takes place between Socrates and two young men – actually Plato's brothers, Glaucon and Adimantus – who are familiar with, and generally receptive to, Socrates' methods and ideas. So Socrates, the philosopher that everyone knows he is, portrays himself as talking with different kinds of people, with differing degrees of knowledge of and sympathy for the sort of thing – the sort of philosophy – he does. It seems not unreasonable to infer Plato intended the dialogue to be read by a similar audience, including complete non-specialists as well as those who have an inkling of what (true) philosophy might be.

The conversation is genuinely two-way. Socrates finds none of his interlocutors a pushover. Nevertheless, there is no doubt at any point about who the dominant partner in the conversation is: Socrates. Nor is there any doubt that one of the chief purposes of the dialogue is to *persuade* us, its readers, and make a difference to the way we live our lives. From any modern point of view, it is likely to appear an unusual kind of philosophical work. It divides into two main parts, much of the first, shorter part of which is occupied by a lively exchange in which Thrasymachus puts the case for a life of large-scale injustice, and Socrates argues in favour of justice; Glaucon and Adimantus then challenge Socrates to do the job properly, by showing that justice is always to be preferred, in and for itself, whatever the circumstances. Socrates accepts the challenge, but proceeds to try to meet it in an unexpected way. Rather than continuing with direct arguments of the sort he has so far used, against Thrasymachus (and Polemarchus), he gradually builds up a picture of what justice, or goodness more generally, might look like, in a city or society and in an individual, and tries to make his audience see how much more attractive this picture is than any alternatives, up to and including the perfectly unjust society and individual – the tyrant – conjured up by Thrasymachus. The adversarial style of the first part is abandoned completely in favour of persuasive description (albeit combined from time to time with more or less hard argument), culminating in the great story or 'myth' told by Er, who miraculously came back from the dead to inform his fellow human beings about what awaits them after death, and to put the choices they make, and will make, in a context that includes the very structure of the universe itself.

From one perspective, this more constructive turn makes Socrates an odd choice of protagonist, insofar as he disclaims any sort of knowledge: time and time again, in the *Republic* itself, he represents himself as having no more than beliefs, or strong convictions, and as still searching for the answers as much as anyone else. That is the official justification, as it were, for the use of dialogue form, though of course it is transparently clear at every juncture that the author, Plato, knows exactly how the conversation will develop, and where it will end up. But as soon as we begin to understand what the *Republic* is designed to persuade us *about*, the choice of Socrates as main speaker, for the constructive second part as well as for the dialectical opening, makes perfect sense. (For more on Plato's relationship to his Socrates, see section 2 below.) The dialogue is, above all, an exhortation to philosophy, that is, to systematic reflection about our assumptions, attitudes and practices, and – even more fundamentally – about who we are, and what kind of beings we are; and through the way he leads the discussion, Socrates provides an actual example, not just of the importance of such reflection, but of how one might go about it.

At the same time, the character Socrates himself knows the direction in which he thinks such reflection should take us. The last thing he wants is reflection for its own sake; that would be mere dilettantism, playing around at the margins. For one thing, he is entirely convinced in his own mind that injustice is a terrible thing, not only for its victims, but also, and especially, for its perpetrators, and he evidently sees it as a matter of the first importance that we should not only see that this is so, but see why it is. As will already be clear, the case against injustice, and in favour of justice, provides the infrastructure of the whole conversation; indeed, the dialogue could happily enough have carried *On Justice* as its main title, rather than as its subtitle (though that was almost certainly supplied by an ancient editor, or cataloguer). The actual main title that Plato himself apparently chose for it was *Politeia* (the English title '*Republic*' merely reproduces '*Respublica*', the rough Latin equivalent to the Greek term): that is, *Constitution*, a word that refers in the first instance to the ordering and weaving together of the parts of a political community and its members.

But the difference between the two titles, *Constitution* and *On Justice*, turns out in fact to be no more than a matter of emphasis, insofar as Socrates soon begins to argue for treating the individual soul – the motive part, as it were, of that composite thing, the human animal – as itself consisting of different elements that require ordering and weaving together, just like the elements in a political community; and – however surprisingly – justice in both community or city and the individual turns out, at least at first, to consist in one and the same thing, namely, having the right kind of *politeia* or 'constitution' in them. Not only that, but the general arrangement of elements presupposed by that *politeia* in the two cases is the same. If the *Republic* or *Politeia* speaks about *politeiai*, or 'constitutions', then, and about which is the best constitution, it is speaking about individuals at least as much as it is speaking about societies, and probably even more, insofar as Socrates explicitly begins discussing societies in order to get a clear picture of justice, and other kinds of excellence (courage, moderation and wisdom), in the individual. And towards the end of the work, he suggests that even if the good society cannot itself be realized, at any rate we may found it, as it were, in ourselves; that is, even if – to put his political proposals in a nutshell – philosophers never become kings and queens anywhere in any actual community, at least we may set up philosophy as queen of our souls. 'Perhaps [this city of ours] is set up as a paradigm in the heavens,' he says, 'for anyone who wishes to see it, and found himself accordingly' (this is at *Republic* 592b: for the form of reference, see Note on the Text and Translation below).

Just as Socrates, and presumably his author, Plato, are clear about the value of justice, so they are clear about what they are proposing for society. We should not be misled by Socrates' various hesitations and protestations of ignorance – which tend to increase as he moves into wider political subjects – into thinking that he is not serious about suggesting, for example, that most existing poetry be banned from the city, or that individual families and households be abolished, at least for the

upper echelons of society (that is, for the 'guards', including
both the philosopher-rulers and the soldiers who will act as
their helpers or 'auxiliaries'), or that the third class or group,
the producers, be kept under the absolute control of their bet-
ters (the rulers, with the soldier-guards acting as their, or rather
the city's, police-force). Thus far, Plato deserves much of the
criticism that has been levelled against him in the modern
period, particularly in and around the context of the Second
World War, as a proponent of totalitarianism, whether of the
fascist or communist variety. (Such criticisms were articulated
in their most extreme, and beguiling, form, by Karl Popper: see
section 5 of Further Reading.) The political constructions of
the *Republic* are intended to represent the kind of thing that
philosophical discussion will *discover* about what a proper
constitution would look like – or to put it in Platonic terms,
about what the best, or the 'true', constitution actually is. Just
as Plato holds that we can examine the true nature of justice, or
of beauty, or of goodness, or whatever it may be – these being
real entities ('forms': see section 3 below), so he seems to hold
that we can examine, and in principle find a genuine answer to,
the question of how a city needs to be arranged if it is to be said
genuinely to have a constitution, rather than some apology or
makeshift substitute for a constitution. That means going back
to first principles, as the *Republic* does; and the sketch of the
'best' or 'beautiful' city, 'Callipolis', that occupies more than a
quarter of the work, is the result. (For a general outline of the
whole argument of the *Republic*, see below.)

Nevertheless, to focus too much on this sketch, and on the
concrete proposals it contains, in the way that Plato's modern
critics – and also his more misguided modern supporters – have
sometimes done, is to miss a large part of the fundamental
point of the *Republic*. This fundamental point is to attack contemporary value-systems, along with the main engines for the
maintenance and reinforcement of those systems, namely
poetry and music, which Socrates represents as filling the gap
left by the failure of the Muse of philosophy to assert her proper
influence. The real target is not democracy, or any other kind
of political arrangement, even tyranny, 'the fourth and last of

the diseases that affect a city' (544c); and the aim is not to set up actual cities with a Socrates, less still a Plato, in the king's palace. The target is rather the values that Plato sees as underpinning existing societies in all their different varieties – in particular, the value attached to money, power, fame, and the benefits and pleasures that such things supposedly bring. The core of Socrates' criticism is that becoming attached to such things, and making them the focus of one's life, distorts and corrupts the soul, causing reason to become the slave of the emotions and appetites when it should be their master, and thereby reducing the distance that separates the human animal from the brute. Seen from this perspective, the critique contained in the *Republic* has a direct and immediate application to most societies, at most periods, and not least to our own.

2. Plato and Socrates

Plato's Socrates is a fictional version of the real one, who lived and talked in Athens – to Plato, among many others – until his execution for impiety in 399 BCE. This flesh-and-blood Socrates evidently had a distinctive method, and ideas to match. But he himself wrote nothing, which means that our understanding of his method and his ideas depends on what others – and especially Plato – made of them. The difficulty with Plato as a witness, however, is that he never clearly distinguishes between what belongs to Socrates and what is his own; in effect, when he makes Socrates his main speaker, as he does in the *Republic*, and in most of his works, he simply attributes everything to Socrates. But, clearly, much of what he writes *is* his own (how could it not be?). The question is: how much?

In the modern period it has often been supposed that there was a 'Socratic' period early on in Plato's writing career, before he moved on and introduced the ideas that subsequent generations have always regarded as the distinctive features of Platonic thought: above all the 'forms', or 'ideas' (see section 3 below), his political proposals and the introduction of a 'soul' divided into different and potentially – and indeed actually – conflicting parts or elements. On this view, the *Republic* will count as peculiarly Platonic, insofar as it not only includes all three features, but puts them at the very core of its argument; it will itself mark the turning-point, the moment in which Plato finally became his own master. (Dialogues that were apparently written before the *Republic* also mostly differ from it in style – or at least from its second part, after Glaucon and Adimantus have made their challenge; pre-*Republic* dialogues, or at any rate many of them, are much more like the adversarial first part.) But that then raises the question why Plato would have retained Socrates as his protagonist: how is it that he could have kept his teacher on as main character even as he proposed to turn his back on significant parts of what he had learned from him? (The question is regularly, and reasonably, put in a more nuanced form than this, which makes it easier to answer, though not to clear away entirely.)

In fact, as one looks more closely at the features that supposedly mark the *Republic* off from what Plato wrote before it, these features look less and less impressive as pieces of evidence. Thus the Socrates of the *Republic* treats the subject of 'forms', and even of the most important of them, the 'form' of the good, as familiar at least to Socrates' two main interlocutors, Glaucon and Adimantus, if not to the rest of the company present; and the implication of the way he introduces the subject is that it would also be familiar to anyone who had read other Platonic dialogues, including some that tend to be treated – that is, by those who believe Plato had, and then moved on from, a Socratic period – as 'Socratic'. On the political front, too, the Socrates of the *Republic* looks in many respects not so very distant from the Socrates of earlier dialogues – himself markedly critical, especially in the *Protagoras*, of the idea that political expertise could possibly belong to a large number of people (as the institution of democracy, on one reading, might be thought to presuppose); even going so far as to present himself in one context, in the *Gorgias* (521d), as perhaps the only true statesman alive. (His grounds are that he alone concerns himself with the questions that statesmen really *ought* to be interested in, but currently are not; and that already seems to make him a kind of philosopher-king in exile.) Finally, and most significantly, the idea of the divided soul, in the *Republic*, turns out after all not to supersede the Socratic analysis of the soul but rather to be introduced alongside it. This makes a particular difference, because Socrates' understanding of the soul takes us to the very core of his thinking – that is, (at least) as Plato presents it.

For Plato's Socrates, in dialogues written prior to – and sometimes perhaps presupposed by – the *Republic*, the excellences or virtues, like justice, courage and moderation, are reducible to and even identical with knowledge, of a particular sort: knowledge about good and bad, i.e., what is good and bad for the agent. This identification between excellence or virtue and knowledge at first sight looks strange and paradoxical; and Socrates is known for his paradoxes. But *his* paradoxes are intended not merely to surprise or shock. Rather, they are intended as plain statements of the truth. Thus, in this case, he is proposing that courage, for example, or justice actually *is* a matter of knowing – knowing what is really good and what is really bad, i.e., good or bad for oneself. Behind this proposal lie two others: first, that no one actually wants to do what is bad for himself or herself; and second, that all our desires are for the good; that is, for what is really good for us. As another 'Socratic paradox' puts it, 'no one goes wrong willingly': again, Socrates intends this to be taken quite literally. He thus rules out even the possibility of what has come to be known as 'acratic' (un-self-controlled) behaviour, in which our desires and passions get the better of us and cause us to behave contrary to our rational judgements. What matters, for the present context, is that on this theory of Socrates' any mistake we make is the fault of reason, or intellect, and not of desire – desire is always innocent, being always and only for what is truly good for us. Reason interprets our desires, and while it can misinterpret them, by misunderstanding what really is to our benefit, whether in general or in any particular case, it will never be in conflict with them. In short, mental conflict is ruled out. (The special theory of human action of Socrates' that is involved here generally goes under the heading of 'intellectualism', because of the special role given to intellect over against the passions or desires.) So on this account the soul is never, and can never be, divided.

As we have seen, in the *Republic* Socrates starts by treating justice in the individual as a particular ordering or arrangement of different elements of his or her soul, corresponding to the organization of the best city (its constitution or *politeia*). And later in the dialogue, he will go on to give an analogous treatment to the different ways in which souls can go bad. Goodness and badness are both a matter of the interrelation of different elements in us. But in between these two treatments, of the good soul and constitution on the one hand, and bad souls and bad constitutions on the other, is sandwiched a quite different analysis of the different forms of excellence or virtue, namely as deriving – as they do on the assumptions of Socratic psychology – directly from wisdom or knowledge. It is unclear quite how it is that Plato proposes to combine these two different analyses of excellence, and the two contrasting – and indeed incompatible – accounts of the soul that appear to go with them, but combine them he does. The most likely explanation is perhaps that the first variety of justice and the other excellences or virtues, later to be summed up as 'civic' excellence, is an inferior approximation to the second variety, possessed by the philosopher alone, and that the Socratic account of the soul is similarly retained for the ideal case, i.e., as describing the soul as it will be under the best imaginable conditions. (Some such solution may be hinted at in the concluding pages of the *Republic*, as Socrates looks back and reflects on the conversation in general, and the earlier division of the soul in particular: see 611a–612a.) In any case, here too it becomes difficult to establish a clear line between 'Socratic' aspects of the whole and those that are specifically 'Platonic'.

But there is something else, and something even more important, that the *Republic* shares with all the dialogues that came before it, 'Socratic' or otherwise, and indeed with those that will come after it. This is its unfailingly *radical* tone. Socrates may observe conventional forms, and use conventional language, but what he uses that language to express is more often than not distinctly *un*conventional. Whether it is justice

he is talking about, or beauty, or the good, or philosophy, or
the soul, or constitutions; or what it is to be a big city, or a
great one, or to be wealthy and 'have more'; or what it is to be
able to 'do what one wants' (on which, see section 4 below) –
or indeed when he is talking about almost anything, including
even ordinary everyday objects like couches and tables, his take
on them will turn out to be different from that of any Greek of
his time, and indeed from our own. In this sense, he is the same
old Socrates that he always was; that is, the same old Platonic
Socrates – who will in turn, presumably, have borne some kind
of resemblance, unrecoverable by us, to the man himself.

3. On 'forms'

If, as Socrates proposes, philosophers can in principle *discover*
the true nature of justice, courage, the good, or whatever it
may be, then it seems that these things must somehow be there,
in nature, waiting to be discovered. Such things are what Socrates in the *Republic* refers to as 'forms', *eidê* or *ideai*, or 'what
is' (*to on*), or 'the things that are' (*ta onta*, or *ousia*, 'being',
used as a mass noun), or in a variety of other ways. One of the
marks of Plato's writing is that he has very little by way of a
standard technical vocabulary, even when he is discussing technical or semi-technical ideas or concepts. Even the terms *eidos*
and *idea* are widely used for things other than Platonic forms:
they function as ordinary, non-technical and entirely inter-
changeable words for what we refer to quite informally, in
ordinary language, as 'sorts/kinds/forms of thing' ('that sort of
thing', 'those kinds of things', etc.) – for which Plato has other
terms too, like *genos*, *tupos*, or even *phusis*, normally the
standard term for 'nature'.

The key points about Platonic 'forms' are these. Philosophers
systematically talk, as ordinary people sometimes talk, about
things 'in the abstract': justice, goodness, beauty, and so on.
Plato's philosopher, by contrast, will describe such talk as being
about things 'in themselves', or 'by themselves' (or just 'themselves'), where the expression 'in/by itself', in each case, serves
a dual purpose. On the one hand, 'in/by itself' distinguishes the

justice (or whatever it is) being talked about from the things – people, or actions, or whatever – that are just, or have justice 'in' them; on the other, the phrase indicates a kind of completeness and perfection. Just people or just actions may simultaneously be unjust in some respect or other; justice by itself, or justice itself, will always be exactly what it is and nothing else. There may even not be any perfectly just people or just actions at all – but justice (by) itself will continue to exist, perfectly encapsulating (however it may do so) that justice, perfect and entire, to which people will aspire in their actions. In the same way, it may well be that there are no genuine constitutions actually in existence, and never have been, but the form of constitution *does* exist, always has and always will, to be investigated and imitated to the best of our ability. (This is actually an invented example. Plato – Socrates – never specifically mentions a 'constitution itself'. But what he is examining, when he investigates what a constitution needs to be, if it is to do what a constitution ought to do, may as well be a 'form'.) Outside space as well as time, 'forms' exist as paradigms for human life and action. *These* are the things that – whether we know it or not – we are talking about when we discuss things, as we say, 'in the abstract'; but they are anything *but* abstract. If we ask 'but what kind of thing is *that*?', the simplest answer is one that Socrates himself offers in the *Republic* (see, e.g., 510d–e): it is the kind of thing that mathematicians are talking about, even if they don't – fully – realize it, when they talk about the properties of circles, or diameters, or whatever it may be. What they are referring to, unbeknownst to them, is 'the circle', 'the diameter', 'oneness', 'twoness' . . .; 'what a circle/diameter/one/two . . . is'; their *form*.

The *Republic* is interested in forms of things like justice, beauty, goodness, the objects of mathematics (and also, more oddly, couches and tables: see 596a–598c); in dialogues that are more directly interested in the physical world, like the *Timaeus*, or the *Phaedo*, there are also forms of hotness, coldness, sweetness, bitterness, and so on. If forms serve as 'paradigms', this is just one aspect of the general role they play in explanation. The essential thought is that things around us are what they are, however imperfectly and incompletely – just, equal, three, big, cold, or whatever it may be – by virtue of their relationship with the relevant forms: justice, equality, threeness, bigness, coldness . . . Quite what that relationship is, Socrates leaves as an open question, or answers with a metaphor (things around us 'share in' forms, to a greater or lesser extent); he also leaves open how we come to have knowledge of forms, if they are neither part of this world nor, as such, in the things that 'share in' them – and thereby perhaps also leaves it open whether we can ever actually come to have proper knowledge of them at all, unless under some ideal and scarcely imaginable conditions.

4. On reading the *Republic* – and reading Plato

The *Republic* needs to be read as a single whole, for two closely related reasons. First, it is a highly interconnected work, full of forward and backward references, whether implicit or explicit; second, and more importantly, the argument tends to be cumulative in form: rather than being introduced all at once, complex proposals are typically brought in bit by bit, frequently interwoven with others, and developed over long stretches of text – and then perhaps modified again at some later point. In short, we often cannot be quite sure where the argument is going until it is over. We are likely to find the dialogue a long read – a very long read – for a single sitting. But the characters in the dialogue themselves take not a single break, for any purpose, during the whole conversation. Evidently we lack the stamina of Greeks of Plato's time; or perhaps we are supposed to imagine that Socrates, as narrator, thinks such pauses not worth mentioning. In any case, we need to notice the fact that the conversation is actually presented to us as a continuous and uninterrupted whole, and why it is so presented: namely, that the argument is all of one piece. (Even when discussion of a particular subject is described as a 'digression', it turns out after the event to be anything but.) Much of the vast literature on the *Republic*, starting virtually from its first appearance in the fourth century BCE, centres around specific passages, and that is perfectly understandable, not just because of the sheer length of the work, but because it contains so many purple and memorable stretches, and so many individually striking conclusions. But tearing passages from their contexts is of course rarely a helpful method of approaching any work, and in the case of the *Republic* it can be disastrous.

Take as an example the following three statements, each of which is true, but also importantly false or misleading as it stands: (1) 'Plato in the *Republic* divides the human soul into three parts'; (2) 'Plato in the *Republic* defines justice in the individual soul as the "doing of its own" by each of its three parts'; and (3) 'Plato in the *Republic* compares the three parts of the soul respectively to a man, a lion and a many-headed monster.' Plato in the *Republic* does indeed divide the soul into three, but (a) 'part' is only one of several terms he uses in this context, and not even the most prominent; and (b) he also hints, several times over, that a different approach may be needed to get at the full truth about the soul. He does indeed define justice in terms of the relationship between different parts or elements of the soul; but he also, and simultaneously, operates with a quite different conception of justice. And he does indeed compare human beings to a composite of human, lion and monster – but only some human beings; specifically, those who are, or are liable to become, tyrants. If one combines statements (1) to (3), all of which regularly appear in literature about the *Republic*, the outcome is a Plato who subscribes to something like the Christian doctrine of original sin. But there is ample textual evidence, especially from the final pages of the *Republic* itself, that the only baggage Plato's Socrates envisages us as ever carrying with us will be the outcome of choices we ourselves have made. The lesson is clear: the *Republic* is a complex, dynamic text, from which we cherry-pick at our peril. It needs to be swallowed whole, or else piece by piece until we reach the end, and can then safely look back to the beginning again and see how we got there – as Socrates himself does, in his own fashion, over the last few pages of the dialogue (608c–621c).

This connects with another feature that is fundamental to

Plato's way of writing. An earlier section of this Introduction (section 2) emphasized the thoroughly radical nature of the approach adopted by Plato and his Socrates, not just in the *Republic* but in the Platonic corpus as a whole. The dialogues perpetually encourage the reader to think about things in new ways – to think of them as (in Plato's terms) they really and truly are, which is usually quite different from the way ordinary people, including ourselves, are used to thinking about them. The language Plato's Socrates uses is familiar, but he typically uses it in unfamiliar ways. Sometimes he is entirely open about this. Thus justice, for example, is – as we have seen – openly re-defined as a state of the soul, and from that point on, if something or other is said to be just, that will usually need to be understood in terms of the new style of definition, not in the old terms (represented, perhaps, by a list of the types of actions to be done or avoided). But sometimes, too, Socrates is using a term in one way, his interlocutors in another. A central case in point is his conversation, near the beginning of the dialogue, with the rhetorical expert Thrasymachus, which fails because of a total mismatch between the two men's perspectives – or, as Socrates would put it, because of Thrasymachus' total lack of understanding of the real nature of justice and the other things being talked about. Not only has Thrasymachus no inkling of this mismatch, but first-time readers will also only gradually become aware of it. The arguments Socrates mounts against Thrasymachus may look a little bizarre, but on the whole he tends to look as if he is using ordinary terms in ordinary ways. If anyone is the radical, it is Thrasymachus. It is only later, as Socrates' position is progressively revealed, that we can understand the main reason for those bizarre-looking arguments: namely, that while addressing Thrasymachus in familiar, everyday language, Socrates is also, and simultaneously, using this familiar language in a way that reflects his own, and (as he would claim) truer, perspectives on the things it purports to describe.

As the dialogue moves to its conclusion, the final piece of the jigsaw is put in place. Socrates has met the challenge put to him by Glaucon and Adimantus, and established the sovereignty of justice herself without referring to any benefits or rewards she may have to bestow on her possessor. He now requests to be allowed to restore the benefits and rewards she brings. But he then also asks if he can now say about the just what the two brothers had said, for the sake of the argument, about the unjust: 'Then will you allow it if I now say about [the just] what you were saying about the unjust? I'm going to say that when the just become older, they hold office in their own city if they wish, take a wife from whichever family they wish, give their own children in marriage as they wish – everything you said about the unjust, I now say about the just' (613c–d; Glaucon agrees).

Socrates suggests, in other words, that the just person will be able to act exactly as he or she wishes, which was one of the proposed benefits of injustice, at least when accompanied by power. But the just person is now the philosopher; and 'doing what one wants' will have a quite different significance for philosophers from the one it has for the unjust tyrant (or, perhaps, any normal person), because – as philosophers – they will *know* what they want, and that will be something quite different from what the tyrant wants, or rather thinks he wants. And philosophers, as we have learned from the description of the good and beautiful city, if they ever had power, would specifically not want to hold office, would not take wives (or husbands: Socrates has argued that the rulers will in principle include women as well as men) and would not have children to call their own in the ordinary sense at all, let alone be worried about who to marry them off to. Thus, as it turns out, the things ordinarily thought to be good and desirable are actually more or less irrelevant, on Socrates' understanding, to the case for justice. Justice is good for its possessors in itself; any other benefits that there may be from it will derive from the fact that the truly just person is a philosopher, able to make the right choices among the things that present themselves to him or her as good.

How far we have shifted, by this point, from where we may have thought we were starting. All Socrates' interlocutors – not just the businessman Cephalus, his son Polemarchus, and

Thrasymachus the rhetorician, but Plato's brothers Glaucon and Adimantus too – started by taking it for granted that what mattered in life were the usual things: money, power, fame, and so on. And Socrates appeared to be going along with them, or at least made no direct attempt to question their position. Only at the end, after a conversation lasting all night, does it finally become clear that he never accepted it at all. There is nothing good about money, or power, or fame in themselves; indeed, as the case of the tyrant shows, the more we have of them the worse it will be for us – that is, if we lack the knowledge that comes from philosophy, and only from philosophy, of how to put them to good use.

Outline of the Argument
of the *Republic*

what we want depends on our knowing what that – i.e., what we want – really is.

345a–368c: Socrates now expresses his own dissatisfaction about the way the conversation has gone: how can they agree about whether it's the just or the unjust that are happier before they've agreed about what justice actually is? And Glaucon and Adimantus – Plato's own brothers, who now become Socrates' main interlocutors – then both pile in to restate the case for injustice, saying that they need more from Socrates; they accept that justice really is better than injustice, but they want more arguments to prove it. In particular, they want to be shown what justice and injustice are, respectively, and 'what effect each has the capacity to produce, in and by itself, when it's present in the soul' (Glaucon at 358b), with any of the benefits supposedly accruing from them left out of account.

368c–369b: Accepting the challenge, Socrates proposes to examine the nature of justice by establishing first what it, and the other sorts of goodness or virtue, might look like in the case of a good *city*, and then transferring the results to the individual – the thought being that it must somehow be the same thing in both cases, only easier to see in the city, because on a larger scale. He agrees with Glaucon and Adimantus that they should actually create such a city in words (or rather, observe human needs creating it: 369c), so as to be able to observe its justice coming into existence with it.

369b–376c: A first, and basic, city emerges, consisting of specialists, each pooling his labour and products. Glaucon calls it only fit for pigs, even while Socrates protests that it is, in his view, the 'true' city (372e), and so they go on to construct a larger one (which Socrates calls 'luxurious', and 'in the grip of a fever'), with couches, tables, sauces, perfumes, and so on, and the specialists needed to make as well as retail these; and this larger city in turn will need more territory – and so an army, whose members are trained specifically for fighting, and will do nothing but fighting (and policing), to wrest it from the city's neighbours, and protect it. The soldiers – the 'guards' – will need not only to be good physical specimens but to possess a combination of gentleness, towards their own kind, and of spirited aggression towards the city's enemies; they will also need to be philosophical, in order to be able to distinguish what really does and does not belong to them (375e–376b).

376c–412b: How will these paragons be educated, so that they acquire a firm hold on such qualities (and the city acquires them too, through them?)? They will start with stories, tightly controlled to exclude the wrong sorts of content – especially about the gods, and about our fate after death. The poetry and music they listen to as they grow up will be equally tightly restricted, without portrayals of extreme and inappropriate emotion and expression, and always providing the right models for emulation. Narrative will be preferred to the poet's taking on his characters' *personae*, and only the right styles of music and types of instrument will be permitted. Due attention will also be paid both to the guards' material environment, to ensure that they grow up in a context of beauty, and removed from ugliness, and to their physical training and health.

412b–415d: The selection of the future rulers, from these 'guards'. These will be the ones proven most skilful at protecting the city, most committed to it, and best able to retain the lessons they have learned in the course of their education. A foundation myth will be invented, according to which these select few have been born – from the very soil of their land – with gold in their souls; the ordinary guards have silver, the ordinary population, the producers and the rest, iron and bronze.

415d–427c: So now the guards are fully trained and prepared; they march out and pitch camp. No fancy houses for them, or private property of any kind – nothing that will distract them from their proper role, just board and lodging at the city's expense. Glaucon objects: surely they won't be very happy? Socrates: I think they will be, but that is not the point; the only question is what is needed to allow them to do their job as effectively as possible. They'll take and occupy only as much territory as is needed for the city, which will be neither too small nor too great; they – or rather those of them selected for ruling – will see to it that anyone inferior born to the guards is demoted, anyone superior born in the general population promoted to guardship; and above all they'll maintain the standards of the education they themselves have enjoyed. Socrates suggests that the guards will be able to work out for themselves the rules they'll need in relation to 'the acquisition of women ... and the procreation of children', on the basis of the principle 'what friends have, they share' (423e–424a); other kinds of regulation, e.g., for markets, can similarly be left to them.

427c–434c: So the city is founded. The assumption is that it is a good one, and if so, it will contain the different kinds of goodness or excellence: wisdom, courage, moderation and justice. So what are these, and whereabouts in the city are they to be found? Its wisdom will reside in the knowledge about government possessed by the rulers, its courage in the ability of the soldier-guards to preserve the beliefs ingrained in them about what is and is not to be feared, its moderation in the way the desires of the majority are, by agreement, under the control of the wisdom of the rulers; as for justice, Socrates argues that the city will be just by virtue of its adherence to a principle that underlay the whole construction of the city – namely, that each and every individual should be restricted to the single function to which he is best suited. Thus soldiers will fight wars, shoemakers will makes shoes, potters will make pots; and most importantly, rulers – those best suited and qualified to rule – will rule.

434d–445b: The original proposal was to look for justice in the city first, and then to try transferring the outcomes of this search to the individual. Now that justice in the city has turned out to be a matter of the relationship between three different kinds or classes, can justice in the individual be understood in the same sort of way? If it can, that will presuppose that the soul, too, has some kind of tripartite structure. Is this the case? Socrates sets out to show that it is (even while warning that the methods he and his interlocutors are deploying may be lacking in precision: 435c–d): the soul consists respectively of a rational element, a 'spirited' element, responsible for anger and the like, and an appetitive one, where there reside hunger, thirst, sexual desire, and so on. Having produced a complex argument for this, he is then able to define the four kinds of goodness in the individual, on the same lines as he, Glaucon and Adimantus have just defined the four kinds of goodness in the city. Thus justice in the individual turns out to consist in the performance by each of the three elements in the soul, namely, the reasoning element, the spirited and the appetitive, of the single role appropriate to each: a soul, and a person, will be just if reason rules, if spirit does what spirit properly does (which will include supporting reason in the control of the appetites) and if the appetites perform *their* proper functions, i.e., of keeping the person fed, watered, and so on. In short, justice turns out to be 'a sort of health of the soul' (444d) – and in that case, Glaucon suggests, it must plainly be preferable to injustice.

445b–473e: Socrates now tries to move on to a discussion of the various sorts of badness, in cities and in individuals. But Glaucon and Adimantus insist that he must deal with the subject of women and children in the good city, and not treat it, as he had proposed to do, as a simple matter to be left to the guards themselves to decide. Socrates proposes, first, that it would be both perfectly natural, and actually the best thing, for females to share all functions in the city, and therefore also the same education, as the males; second, that it is similarly both possible and best that the nuclear family be abolished, that the women be held by the men – and by implication, the men by the women – in common, and that the children be held in common too. But how on earth could such momentous changes be brought about? After a digression on the rules for war, especially against fellow-Greeks, Socrates is forced to confront this question, which he treats as the most difficult of all. His response is that a society like the one he has sketched could only be realized if power in a city were to be given to *philoso-phers* (thus confirming what was clear all along, that he thinks of the city he has outlined, with the help of the others, as having a rational, philosophical basis).

473e–484d: 'What a hilarious idea!' responds Glaucon. Socrates mounts a defence, which contrasts the state of mind of ordinary people, who identify beauty with the things they see in the theatre, with that of the philosopher, who recognizes that beauty is something that can and must be understood in and by itself. It's the philosopher, he argues, who has the greater claim to knowledge – and who would prefer being ruled by someone without knowledge to being ruled by someone with it, so long as he (or she) has the requisite experience too?

485a–502c: How to find people with the capacity to be like that? They'll be born addicted to knowing about things, i.e., things as they really are, so they'll be by nature less interested in ordinary pleasures – and so, naturally moderate; they won't worry about the things ordinary people worry about, so they'll be naturally courageous, too, and just, and they'll also be quick at learning, have a good memory, be graceful ... How could anyone find fault with a pursuit – philosophy – that required all of these things? But – Adimantus objects – that surely isn't how philosophers actually are? Yes, replies Socrates; real philosophers *are* like that, and people ought to pay them more attention. But for anyone who has a genuinely philosophical nature, there are just too many temptations and sources of corruption. To be truly safe from such corruption, he or she will need to live in the right kind of city; that is, the good one that has been described – and it could, just possibly, come into existence. Who knows, it might already have existed somewhere. Philosophers *could* take control, and they would be no bad craftsmen of 'moderation and justice, and of civic excellence as a whole' (500d).

502c–506c: Having completed the defence of his proposal for rule by philosophers, Socrates now turns to the question how the good city will produce them. They'll not be able to take any short cuts, as he and his interlocutors have done (504b–d; cf. 435c–d), when it comes to understanding the nature of the various kinds of goodness, because if they do they'll miss out on the most important subject of all: the good, or goodness, itself (the 'form of the good'). How will they guard justice and beauty 'if they don't know how just and beautiful things are good' (506a)?

506c–521b: So what is the good? Socrates finally consents to give an idea of his thinking on the subject – in the form of three images: one comparing the good to the sun; one representing different states of mind, from mere conjecture through to knowledge, in terms of sections of a line ('the divided line' image); and one picturing the ascent from ordinary perceptions and assumptions to the knowledge needed for ruling, as a journey from darkness to light. A prisoner is imagined being led up and out of a dark underground cave, where he and his fellow-prisoners could see only shadows, to the sunlit world above, and then going back down again to join the others (the 'cave' image). So too will the newly trained philosophers, each in his or her turn, go back down from enjoying the pleasures of philosophy to take charge of the good city; by contrast, the freed prisoner of the image is merely laughed at when he goes back (as Socrates was, in Athens, especially in the theatre) – but then, in the cave, nothing has changed, whereas in the good city everything will, or would, be different.

521c–541b: Socrates now fills in his account of the further education that will be needed to produce the philosopher-rulers. They will study arithmetic, geometry, solid geometry, astronomy, harmonics and, above all, 'dialectic', i.e., the give-and-take of philosophical argument, which is the means by which we approach the true natures of things, the forms (532a), including the form of the good. A timetable for all these studies is laid out, with study of dialectic beginning at age thirty, and lasting for five years; this is to be followed by fifteen years of experience in minor government roles, and then, at the age of fifty, those who have stayed the course 'must now be led to the end-point of their journey, and compelled to lift the eye of the soul, directing it towards the very thing that illuminates everything else, the good itself, so that once they have seen it they can use it as a paradigm for ordering city, citizens and themselves' (540a–b).

541b–576b: So much for the model city, and the model individual, and the discussion can now go back to the subject – broached but immediately broken off in 445b–449a – of non-correct types of city and individual. (As Glaucon remarks, they have in fact ended up with an even more beautiful model than they had before the digression started: that is, presumably a model of a truly *philosophical* city, and a truly *philosophical* individual, possessing philosophical rather than merely 'civic' versions of the various excellences: 543d–544a; 'civic' excellence as at 500d.) Four incorrect types, each treated as evolving from the one before it, are discussed in succession: the Spartan or 'timo-cratic' city and individual (represented as emerging because of neglect, by the rulers of the good city, of the laws governing mating and of the education system), the oligarchic city and the oligarchic individual, the democratic, and finally the tyran-nical. The primary aim of this long discussion is to find out which is the most unjust type of city and – especially – type of individual, for comparison with that paragon of justice, the philosopher, so that the original dispute, as to whether it is the just or the unjust life that is happier, may be settled.

576b–580c: Judgement is passed: the tyrannical city and individual are most unjust, and also least happy.

580c–588a: Further argument for this conclusion.

588b–592b: On the basis of the results of the whole preceding discussion, Socrates now describes the true awfulness of the claim, as made by Thrasymachus, and then reinforced by Glaucon and Adimantus, that injustice is preferable to justice: it is like recommending us to bring up and feed a many-headed monster – representing the bodily desires and pleasures – within our very selves. Rather, what we must do is try so far as possible to allow what is truly human in us, our reason, to rule over our lives; and those who cannot realize such a goal for themselves should have their lives governed by those who can.

595a–608b: Socrates returns to the subject of poetry, renewing his attack on poetry – especially the tragedians, 'along with their leader, Homer' (598d) – that works through 'imitation', i.e., by mimicking people and their actions and emotions, rather than through narration. Such imitation has a corroding effect on us, because it focuses our minds on the appearance of things rather than their reality. (In effect, it confirms us in a state of mind like that of the theatre-goers described in 475d–484d, and of the prisoners in the cave.)

608b–621d: Socrates now adds in 'the biggest rewards of excellence' – those that derive from the fact that the soul is immortal. He gives a short argument for supposing that our souls will always survive death, then goes on to wonder whether, if the soul is as badly put together as it has apparently turned out (in so many cases?) to be, it would really be something that could last for ever. Perhaps its true condition is different? Everything that was originally taken away from the just and the unjust, for the sake of the argument – in terms of reputation, relationship to the gods, ability to do what they want, and so on – is now given back to them: justice *does* bring rewards, as well as being good in itself, and injustice in fact is punished, if not in life, then after death. The dialogue closes with an account of the judgement of the dead, reported by one Er, who miraculously revived on his funeral pyre, after having witnessed what goes on 'in the other place', i.e., Hades (or Plato's version of it). The main emphasis of the story is on the way our choices, in life, or after it, affect our destiny: if we are to avoid disaster, and descending to the level of brutes, then we must take steps to realize our full rational potential, and allow it to rule over the lion of spirit and the many-headed creature of appetite. 'That way we shall not only be friends to ourselves but loved by the gods, both while we remain here and when we carry off the prizes of justice, gathering them in like victors at the games; and both here and in the thousand-year journey we have talked about [namely, the one "in that other place"], we shall fare well' (621c–d).

Further Reading

Note: The literature on Plato, and on the *Republic* in particular, is vast and increasing. Sections 2–4 below contain a small selection of items that are either relatively new or have stood the test of time; many overlap with one another, and many also contain extensive bibliographies of their own. The collections of essays on the *Republic* listed in section 4.4 provide a particularly useful way both into the dialogue itself, and into the kinds of questions typically asked of it by modern readers, whether philosophical or literary. Items listed in section 3, on Plato in general, will also often include material that relates specifically to the *Republic*.

1. On the cultural and historical background

Paul Cartledge, *Ancient Political Thought in Practice* (Cambridge, 2009): includes some reflections on Socrates' death.

Kenneth Dover, *Greek Popular Morality in the Time of Plato and Aristotle* (Berkeley/Los Angeles, CA, 1974).

D. M. Lewis, J. Boardman, S. Hornblower and M. Ostwald (eds.), *The Cambridge Ancient History* (2nd edn), vol. V: *The Fifth Century* (Cambridge, 1992); vol. VI: *The Fourth Century* (Cambridge, 1995).

Josiah Ober, *Political Dissent in Democratic Athens: Intellectual Critics of Popular Rule* (Princeton, NJ, 1998).

Robert Parker, *Athenian Religion: A History* (Oxford, 1998).

Christopher Rowe and Malcolm Schofield (eds.), *The Cambridge History of Greek and Roman Political Thought* (Cambridge, 2000).

2. A complete English translation of Plato

John M. Cooper, *Plato: Complete Works* (Indianapolis, IN/ Cambridge, MA, 1997).

3. On Plato in general

Julia Annas, *Plato: A Very Short Introduction* (Oxford, 2003).

Julia Annas and Christopher Rowe (eds.), *New Perspectives on Plato, Modern and Ancient* (Cambridge, MA, 2002).

Hugh Benson (ed.), *A Companion to Plato* (Oxford, 2006).

Ruby Blondell, *The Play of Character in Plato's Dialogues* (Cambridge, 2002): thought-provoking on the general issue of the relationship between the philosophical and the literary and dramatic elements in the dialogues.

J. D. G. Evans, *A Plato Primer* (Durham, 2010).

Gail Fine, *Plato I* and *II* (Oxford, 1999): useful general collection of articles on Plato.

Terence Irwin, *Plato's Ethics* (Oxford, 1995): standard modern treatment of its subject.

Charles H. Kahn, *Plato and the Socratic Dialogue: The Philosophical Use of a Literary Form* (Cambridge, 1996).

Richard Kraut (ed.), *The Cambridge Companion to Plato* (Cambridge, 2007).

M. M. McCabe, *Plato and his Predecessors: The Dramatisation of Reason* (Cambridge, 2000).

Debra Nails, *The People of Plato: A Prosopography of Plato and Other Socratics* (Indianapolis, IN/Cambridge, MA, 2002): complete prosopography of the people who figure in Plato's dialogues; indispensable.

Andrea W. Nightingale, *Genres in Dialogue: Plato and the Construct of Philosophy* (Cambridge, 1995): on the intersection between philosophy and literature in Plato.

Catalin Partenie (ed.), *Plato's Myths* (Cambridge, 2009): for a way in to the eschatological myth at the end of the *Republic*, see especially item 2 in this collection, David Sedley's 'Myth, Punishment and Politics in the *Gorgias*'.

Terry Penner, *The Ascent from Nominalism: Some Existence Arguments in Plato's Middle Dialogues* (Dordrecht, 1987).

Terry Penner, 'Socrates and the Early Dialogues', in Richard Kraut (ed.), *The Cambridge Companion to Plato* (Cambridge, 1992), pp. 121–69: a short account of the Socratic theory of desire and action; for a much longer and more complete account, see the following item.

Terry Penner and Christopher Rowe, *Plato's Lysis* (Cambridge, 2005).

Gerald A. Press, *Who Speaks for Plato?* (Lanham, MD, 2000): raises a question, among others, about whether it is legitimate to take Socrates as speaking for Plato, as has traditionally been done, and as it is in the present volume.

C. J. Rowe, *Plato* (2nd edn, London, 2003): a basic introduction to Plato which acknowledges that he wrote *dialogues*.

Christopher Rowe, *Plato and the Art of Philosophical Writing* (Cambridge, 2007): a treatment centred on the *Republic*.

Gerasimos Santas, *Goodness and Justice: Plato, Aristotle and the Moderns* (Oxford, 2001).

Malcolm Schofield, *Plato: Political Philosophy* (Oxford, 2006).

Dominic Scott (ed.), *Maieusis: Essays on Ancient Philosophy in Honour of Myles Burnyeat* (Oxford, 2007): includes several useful pieces on the *Republic*.

Paul Shorey, *The Unity of Plato's Thought* (Chicago, 1903; new impression 1960).

Gregory Vlastos (ed.), *A Collection of Critical Essays*, vol. I: *Metaphysics and Epistemology* (Garden City, NY, 1970); vol. II: *Ethics, Politics, and Philosophy of Art and Religion* (Garden City, NY, 1971).

4. On the *Republic*

4.1. *The Greek text*

Gerard Boter, *The Textual Tradition of Plato's Republic* (Supplements to *Mnemosyne* 107: Leiden, 1989).

John Burnet, *Platonis opera*, vol. I (Oxford [Oxford Classical Texts], 1902).

S. R. Slings *Platonis rempublicam recognovit brevique adnotatione critica instruxit* (Oxford [Oxford Classical Texts], 2003): the 'new Oxford' text.

S. R. Slings, *Critical Notes on Plato's Politeia* (Supplements to *Mnemosyne* 267: Leiden, 2005).

4.2. Commentaries

J. Adam, *The Republic of Plato* (Cambridge, 1902).

Paul Shorey, *Plato, Republic* (Cambridge, MA, Books I–V: 1930; Books VI–X: 1935): not strictly a 'commentary', but a Greek text with facing translation (the 'Loeb' edition); the footnotes are frequently invaluable.

Nicholas P. White, *A Companion to Plato's Republic* (Indianapolis, IN, 1979).

4.3. Introductions

Julia Annas, *An Introduction to Plato's Republic* (Oxford, 1981).

Nickolas Pappas, *Plato and the Republic* (2nd edn, London, 2003).

4.4. Collections of essays

G. R. F. Ferrari (ed.), *The Cambridge Companion to Plato's Republic* (Cambridge, 2007).

Richard Kraut (ed.), *Plato's Republic: Critical Essays* (Lanham, MD, 1997).

Mark L. McPherran, *Plato's Republic: A Critical Guide* (Cambridge, 2010).

Erik Ostenfeld (ed.), *Essays on Plato's Republic* (Aarhus, 1998).

Gerasimos Santas (ed.), *The Blackwell Guide to Plato's Republic* (Oxford, 2006).

4.5. Other books and essays

Myles Burnyeat, 'Utopia and fantasy: the practicability of Plato's ideally just city', reprinted in Fine, *Plato II* (see section 3 above), pp. 297–308.

Myles Burnyeat, 'Culture and society in Plato's *Republic*', *The Tanner Lectures on Human Values* 20 (1999), pp. 215–324.

Myles Burnyeat, 'Plato on why mathematics is good for the soul', in T. Smiley (ed.), *Mathematics and Necessity: Essays in the History of Philosophy, Proceedings of the British Academy* 103 (Oxford, 2000).

G. R. F. Ferrari, *City and Soul in Plato's Republic* (Sankt Augustin, 2003).

Verity Harte, '*Republic* 10 and the Role of the Audience in Art', *Oxford Studies in Ancient Philosophy* 38 (2010), pp. 69–96.

Angela Hobbs, *Plato and the Hero: Courage, Manliness and the Impersonal Good* (Cambridge, 2000).

Christopher Janaway, *Images of Excellence: Plato's Critique of the Arts* (Oxford, 1995).

André Laks, 'Legislation and demiurgy: on the relationship between Plato's *Republic* and *Laws*', *Classical Antiquity* 9 (1990), pp. 209–29.

Jonathan Lear, 'Inside and outside the *Republic*', *Phronesis* 38 (1992), pp. 184–215.

Alexander Nehamas, 'Plato on the imperfection of the sensible world', reprinted in Nehamas, *Virtues of Authenticity* (Princeton, NJ, 1999), pp. 138–58.

C. D. C. Reeve, *Philosopher-Kings: The Argument of Plato's Republic* (Princeton, NJ, 1988).

Gerasimos Santas, *Understanding Plato's Republic* (Oxford, 2010).

Malcolm Schofield, *Saving the City: Philosopher-Kings and Other Classical Paradigms* (London, 1999).

David Sedley, 'Socratic intellectualism in *Republic* 5–7', in George Boys-Stones, Dimitri El Murr and Christopher Gill (eds.), *The Platonic Art of Philosophy* (Cambridge, forthcoming).

5. The later reception of Plato

Anna Baldwin and Sarah Hutton (eds.), *Platonism and the English Imagination* (Cambridge, 1994).

Simon Blackburn, *Plato's Republic: A Biography* (London, 2006).

Melissa Lane, *Plato's Progeny: How Plato and Socrates Still Captivate the Modern Mind* (London, 2001).

Melissa Lane, *Eco-Republic: Ancient Thinking for a Green Age* (Oxford, 2011).

R. B. Levinson, *In Defense of Plato* (Cambridge, 1953).

Iris Murdoch, *The Fire and the Sun: Why Plato Banished the Artists* (Oxford, 1977).

K. R. Popper, *The Open Society and its Enemies*, vol. I: *The Spell of Plato* (first published 1945; 4th edn, London, 1961).

Paul Shorey, *Platonism Ancient and Modern* (Berkeley, CA, 1938).

Leo Strauss, *Studies in Platonic Political Philosophy* (Chicago, IL, 1983).

Nancy Tuana, *Feminist Interpretations of Plato* (Philadelphia, PA, 1994).

Catherine H. Zuckert, *Postmodern Platos: Nietzsche, Heidegger, Gadamer, Strauss, Derrida* (Chicago, 1996).

Note on the Text
and Translation

In order to identify particular passages in the *Republic*, this volume uses – as do all modern translations and editions – the page numbers and page sections as fixed by the 'Stephanus' edition of Plato's text. These are given in the margins, to allow for easy reference. The *Republic* as a whole occupies pages 327 to 621 of the second volume of the Stephanus edition; and each page is typically divided into five sections, marked 'a' to 'e'; thus the text begins at 327a, and ends about two thirds of the way down page 621, i.e., with the second line of 621d. (Line-numbers are less useful than page- and section-markers because the length of a line of text varies between different editions; they are not used in this volume.) 'Stephanus' was the notable Renaissance editor and publisher Henri Estienne (1531–98).

The *Republic* is also usually divided up into ten sections of roughly equal length, known as 'books', and numbered I to X. Thus the full reference for a given passage will usually include the book number as well as the Stephanus page and section, e.g., 'IV, 445a', or 'X, 618d'. (Pages or page sections will occasionally be missing; these will have been occupied by editorial material supplied by Stephanus.) There is also some evidence of a division into six books (let them be 'A', 'B' ... 'F'): see J. Hirmer, 'Entstehung und Komposition der platonischen *Politeia*', *Jahrbücher für Classische Philologie*, Supplement-band 23 (1897), pp. 588–92; and H. Alline, *Histoire du texte de Platon* (Paris, 1915), pp. 14–19. This six-book division may actually have predated the ten-book one, and may even go back to Plato himself. However, ancient divisions between 'books' often have little to do with content, rather being a reflection of what could be contained in a papyrus roll, or of how an author or editor chose to divide the text up among rolls of a necessarily finite length; and the *Republic* itself in fact consists of a single, continuous conversation, broken only momentarily at any point. It therefore seems best to print it accordingly, i.e., as one continuous whole, marking only the few actual pauses for breath that the text seems to indicate. This is the policy of the present volume: that is, the text is not printed, as it usually is, divided up into 'books', and indeed all reference to such divisions – whether the ten-book division or the less certain six-book one – is relegated to the margins, thus: 'Book I begins [Book A]'.

With few exceptions, which are clearly marked in the notes, the translation in this volume follows the text printed in the new Oxford *Republic* (Oxford Classical Texts, 2003). This edition, by Simon Slings, is clearly superior to any of its predecessors, even that of the great John Burnet, and is unlikely to be significantly bettered by any future editor, save in one respect: its punctuation. Punctuation marks were by and large a post-Platonic development, and editors distribute them according to their own sense of the argument and/or the rules and conventions they prefer, or are used to. Thus, for example, Slings had a particular dislike of dashes, which in my view are sometimes indispensable, above all to convey the surely deliberate disjointedness of certain passages, for example when Socrates is especially hesitant, or especially passionate. The translation is accordingly sprinkled liberally with dashes. The reader will also often find question marks in Slings's text turning into full stops in the translation, and vice versa.

The *Republic* contains frequent changes of style, tone and pace. Claiming as it does to be a first-person report of a real conversation, its basic style is informal and colloquial. But the reporter, Socrates, has a tendency to be carried away, especially by the strength of his convictions, and his language can accordingly become more high-flown; he also sometimes needs, and uses, a more formal, precise style when embarking on pieces of close argument. The translation in this volume attempts to be faithful to such stylistic variations, as part of the general aim of achieving the high degree of accuracy that the reader has the right to expect.

Occasionally, the translation spells out things that are only implied in the text. This is acknowledged, in more extreme cases, in the notes, but is generally harmless, except to the extent that it may presuppose particular solutions to controversial issues of interpretation (that is, the particular solutions that the present translator thinks most likely). It is in any case justified by a further aim of the translation, that of achieving at least roughly the degree of readability that the Greek text might have offered to its original readers – or perhaps even a little more: the spelling-out in question occurs particularly in the case of semi-technical phrases and expressions, relating above all to Platonic 'forms', which will no doubt have been as unfamiliar to contemporary readers outside Plato's circle as they are to their modern counterparts. Plato himself helps by introducing more technical terms and ideas in a gradual way – which, incidentally, constitutes another reason for reading the dialogue more or less as a single piece, however long (see section 4 of the Introduction, above).

A final point about readability. The *Republic* contains large numbers of occurrences of 'I [Socrates] said', 'he said', and so on, and a modern reader may sometimes find this intrusive. However, they are there for a reason (that is, to keep up the fiction of a real, live report of a conversation: see section 1 of the Introduction above), and the present translation therefore retains them in nearly all cases. Plato means us to think of the dialogue as a conversation directly reported to us by Socrates, standing there, as it were, in front of us.

The translation and notes owe much to a large number of people, whose help – given in various forms – the translator acknowledges with gratitude (while retaining personal responsibility for any infelicities or errors): Xanthippe Bourloyanni, Amber Carpenter, Verity Harte, M. M. McCabe, Debra Nails, Terry Penner, Heather Rowe, Malcolm Schofield, David Sedley, and my copy-editor, Monica Schmoller. The volume as a whole is dedicated to Siem Slings – as Phaedo said of Socrates, 'best of that generation we'd ever encountered, the wisest, too, and the most just'.

REPUBLIC

I went down to the Piraeus yesterday with Glaucon, son 327a
of Ariston, not just to offer a prayer to the goddess but
also because I wanted to see how they would celebrate
the festival, this being the first time they'd held it. As it turned
out, I liked the procession organized by the locals well enough,
but the one put on by the Thracians appeared to me just as 327b
fine.[1] Well, when we'd offered our prayers and seen what we
came to see, we turned back towards the city. But at that point
Polemarchus, son of Cephalus, caught sight of us heading off
for home, and gave the order to his slave to run over and tell us
to wait for him. The slave duly grabbed my cloak from behind
and said, 'Polemarchus says you're to wait for him.' I turned
round and asked him where his master was. 'Over there,' he
said, 'coming up behind. Please wait.'

Moments later Polemarchus came up to us, with Glaucon's 327c
brother Adimantus, Niceratus son of Nicias, and a number of
others, evidently fresh from the spectacle themselves.

'Socrates,' said Polemarchus, 'it looks to me as if the two of
you are already off, back to the city.'

'Well guessed,' I said.

'Well,' he said, 'do you see how many of us there are?'

'Yes, of course.'

'Then', said Polemarchus, 'you'll either have to outmuscle
our side, or stay with us.'

'Aren't you missing out one option?' I asked. 'What if I persuade you that you need to let us go?'

'What if we're not listening?' asked Polemarchus. 'Would
you be able to persuade us then?'

'Hardly,' said Glaucon.

'Then proceed on the basis that we won't be listening.'

328a   Adimantus intervened. 'I suppose you haven't heard – later on, towards evening, there's going to be a torch-race on horseback, in honour of the goddess.'

'On horseback?' I said. 'That's new. What are you saying – there'll be a horse-race, with the riders handing torches on to each other?'

'Right,' said Polemarchus. 'And that's not all; there'll be festivities all through the night that will be worth watching. We'll get up after dinner and watch them ourselves – we'll be there with lots of the younger crowd, and there'll be plenty of con-
328b   versation. Please stay, and don't make an argument of it.'

'It seems we should,' said Glaucon.

'If you think so,' I said, 'that's what we must do.'

So off we went to Polemarchus' house. There we found Lysias and Euthydemus, Polemarchus' brothers, and Thrasymachus of Chalcedon into the bargain, along with Charmantides of the Paeania deme and Clitophon son of Aristonymus; Polemarchus'
328c   father, Cephalus, was also in the house. Cephalus seemed to me now a very old man; it was some while since I'd seen him. He was sitting there on a chair with a cushion, with a wreath on his head because he'd just been sacrificing in the courtyard of the house. So we sat ourselves down around him, since there were some chairs there arranged in a circle.

As soon as he saw me, Cephalus greeted me and said, 'Socrates, it isn't often you come down to the Piraeus to see us; you should have come before. If I still had the strength to make the
328d   journey easily, up to the city, you wouldn't have needed to come here at all, because we'd have visited you instead; as things are, you need to come here more frequently. I tell you, just as those other pleasures fade away – the ones involving the body – so the desires and pleasures that attach to a good conversation expand to fill the gap. So no arguments: come and spend time with these young people, and visit us here not just as your friends but as if we were family.'

328e   'Cephalus,' I said, 'I really do enjoy talking to the very old; it seems to me we need to treat them like travellers ahead of us on a road that we too will probably have to travel, finding out from them whether it's a rough and hard road or an easy and smooth one. Just so, since you're already at a time of life the poets describe as "old age's edge", I'd be delighted to know from you whether it's a difficult age to be, or what your account of it is.'

'Zeus!' exclaimed Cephalus. 'I'll tell you, Socrates, just how it 329a appears to me. Oftentimes a group of us gets together, as people of a similar age are always supposed to do, and most of the group spends its time together moaning about how they miss the pleasures of youth, reminiscing about the sex, the drinking, the parties and everything else that goes with all that, and complaining as if they'd lost things that were important, and as if they had had a good life then and now have no life at all. Some 329b of them moan about the way their families think they can walk all over them just because they're old, following up with a vivid picture of all the bad things old age is responsible for. But my view, Socrates, is that they're blaming the wrong thing. If old age were responsible, I would have been experiencing the same as them, at least so far as being old is concerned, and so would everyone else who's grown as old as I have. But in point of fact I've encountered others, in the past, who like myself don't feel that way; not least the poet Sophocles. I once witnessed someone asking him, "Sophocles, how is it with you and sex nowadays? 329c Can you still make love to a woman?" "Quiet, man!" he replied. "It's my greatest delight to have got away from all that, like a slave from the raving of a savage master." I thought even then that this was a good answer, and I still do. Old age really does bring a lot of peace from things like sex, a lot of freedom; when our desires slacken off and cease to exercise us, it really is as 329d Sophocles said – we're freed from a whole collection of slave-masters,[2] all of them raving mad. But there's only one thing to blame in all this, and for the trouble with family members, and that's *not* old age, Socrates; it's the way people are. If they're well balanced and even tempered, then old age is not too hard to bear either; if they're not, then for people like that it's not just old age that will be tough, Socrates, but youth too.'

This response of his struck me as admirable; and, wanting 329e him to go on talking, I tried to provoke him: 'Cephalus,' I said,

'I imagine that when you say what you've just said, most people refuse to accept it, preferring to suppose that you so easily put up with being old, not because of the kind of person you are, but rather because of the great wealth you've accumulated; rich people, they say, have plenty to comfort them.'

'True,' said Cephalus; 'people don't believe me. And up to a point they're right, but not as right as they think. Themistocles' famous retort is relevant here – the one he made to the man from Seriphos, who tried to abuse him by claiming that he

330a owed his reputation not to himself but to his city: "Well," said Themistocles, "I wouldn't have got a name for myself if I'd come from Seriphos, but neither would you if you'd been from Athens." The same applies to those that aren't rich and find old age hard to take: for a decent person, old age wouldn't be at all easy if he was poor, but a disreputable one never got to be at ease with himself by acquiring wealth.'

'Tell me, Cephalus,' I said, 'did you inherit most of what you have, or did you create it for yourself?'

330b 'You're asking what sort of businessman I was, Socrates?' he replied. 'I'm somewhere in the middle between my grandfather and my father. My grandfather and namesake inherited pretty much the same as I have now, and multiplied it many times over, while my father Lysanias reduced it to even less than it is now. And I'm happy if I leave these sons of mine here no less than I inherited and just that little bit more.'

'My reason for asking', I said, 'is that you didn't strike me as

330c having a great love for money. This is usually the case with people who haven't made their money for themselves, whereas those who have are twice as attached to it as everybody else: just as poets love their poems, and fathers love their children, so money-makers love their money – as their own handiwork, and then on top of that, like everyone else, they love it for its usefulness. This makes them hard to be with, because they're unwilling to put in a good word for anything but wealth.'

'True,' said Cephalus.

330d 'Indeed so,' I said. 'But I've another question for you: what do you think is the greatest benefit you've enjoyed from possessing great wealth?'

'It's something I probably wouldn't be able to persuade many people of if I told them. The truth, Socrates,' he said, 'is that when a person begins to think he's approaching his end, he's affected by fears and worries that never affected him before. Take the stories told about Hades – that the man who has acted unjustly in this world will find himself paying the penalty for it in that other one: even if he has laughed at such 330e stories before, now the thought begins to torture his soul that they might actually be true. Whether it's just the weakness of old age, or because his closeness to the world below gives him that much sharper a view of it, in either case the effect on him is to fill him with terrified foreboding, so that he starts reckoning things up, and asking himself whether he's treated anyone unjustly. Then if he discovers that he's committed many acts of injustice in his life, he'll keep waking up during the night in terror, like a child, and live expecting the worst. But if he's 331a aware of no injustice in himself, then, as Pindar also said, a sweet and blessed hope stays constantly with him to "nurse his old age". Yes, Socrates, the poet put it quite delightfully when he said that if someone lives out his life justly and piously,

> Sweet hope is his constant companion,
> Warming his heart, nurse to old age;
> Hope, chief guide of mortal minds,
> Ruling our ever-shifting thought.[3]

Wonderfully well said. And this is what I count as the greatest benefit of being wealthy – for the decent person, that is, not just 331b for anyone; because when it comes to avoiding cheating people, even unintentionally, or lying, or failing to pay what one owes, whether sacrifices to a god, or money to a fellow-man, and so going off to Hades with fear in one's heart, being wealthy makes a major contribution. It undoubtedly has many other uses, but weighing one thing against another, I wouldn't by any means count this as the least of purposes, Socrates, for which wealth is most useful.'

'Quite beautifully expressed, Cephalus,' I said. 'Now let's talk 331c about this very thing, *justice*: shall we say, as you've suggested, that it's simply a matter of telling the truth, and of giving back when one's received something from someone; or is it in fact possible to do these very things now justly, now unjustly? Here's an example for you. I imagine everyone would agree that if one borrowed weapons from a friend when he was in a sound state of mind, and he went mad and then asked for them back, they shouldn't be given back to him in such circumstances, and the person who did give them back – or for that matter wanted to tell the whole truth to someone in that condition – would scarcely be just.'

331d   'You're right,' he said.

'Then this is not what constitutes justice[4] – telling the truth and giving back whatever one receives.'

'Oh yes it is, Socrates,' interjected Polemarchus; 'at least if we're to take any notice of what Simonides says.'

'And this is the moment', said Cephalus, 'for me to hand the conversation over to you and Socrates; it's time for me to attend to my rites.'

'And after all,' said Polemarchus, 'aren't I your heir in everything?'

Cephalus laughed and said, 'Certainly you are!', and with that he set off to perform his rites.

331e   'So tell me, Polemarchus,' I said, 'as your father's heir in the conversation, what you claim Simonides says about justice, and gets right.'

'That it's just to give back what one owes in each case,' he said; 'this certainly seems to me to be well said.'

'I grant you it's not easy to disbelieve Simonides,' I said, 'because he's a wise and godlike man; and you probably know what he has in mind by saying this, but I don't. Because, clearly, he can't have in mind what we were talking about just now, giving back something deposited by someone who is not in a
332a sound state of mind when he asks for it. And yet whatever was deposited in this case was surely *owed*. Isn't that so?'

'Yes.'

'But there was to be no giving back, if the person asking for it wasn't sound of mind?'

'True,' he said.

'So Simonides must have something other than this sort of thing in mind when he says it's just to give back what one owes.'

'Zeus! Yes, indeed he does,' said Polemarchus; 'he thinks friends owe it to friends to do them some good, and not any harm.'

'I understand,' I said: 'if someone gives back a deposit of gold to a depositor, it won't count as giving back what is owed   332b if it turns out that the giving and the receiving are harmful, and the giver and the receiver are friends. Isn't that what you claim Simonides is saying?'

'Yes, certainly.'

'What about our enemies? Should we give back whatever happens to be owed to them?'

'Yes, indeed we should give them back what is owed to them,' he said; 'but what's owed, I imagine, by one enemy to another is what's appropriate for an enemy: harm of some sort.'

'So,' I said, 'it seems that Simonides' account of what justice is was a poet's riddle. His thought was, apparently, that *this*   332c was what was just, giving back what was *appropriate* to each person; only he called this what was "owed".'

'What else do you suppose?' he asked.

'Zeus!' I said. 'So if someone asked him: "Simonides, what is the expertise called medicine? What does it 'give back' that's 'owed' and 'appropriate', and what does it give it to?" What answer do you think we'd get from him?'

' "Clearly, it's the expertise that gives medicines, foods and drinks to bodies." '

'And what about the expertise called cookery? What does this expertise "give back" that's "owed" and "appropriate", and to what?'

' "It's the expertise that gives seasoning to dishes." '   332d

'Fine; so what about the expertise that would go by the name "justice"? What does this "give back", and to what?'

'If we're to be at all consistent with our previous answers, Socrates, the answer must be "the expertise that gives benefits to friends and harms enemies".'

'So Simonides is saying that justice is a matter of benefiting one's friends and harming one's enemies?'

'I think so.'

'In that case, who is it that is most able to benefit sick friends and harm sick enemies, in relation to sickness and health?'

'A doctor.'

332e 'How about friends and enemies on board ship, in relation to the dangers of the sea?'

'A qualified steersman.'

'And what of the just person? In what activity is he most able to benefit friends and harm enemies? In relation to doing what?'

'In making war and forming alliances, it seems to me.'

'Very well. But then, my dear Polemarchus, a doctor is of no use to people who aren't sick.'

'True.'

'And a steersman is of no use to people who aren't on board ship.'

'Yes.'

'And is the just person similarly of no use to those who aren't at war?'

'I don't think that at all.'

333a 'So justice is something useful in peace, too?'

'It is.'

'As is farming – right?'

'Yes.'

'For the production of crops?'

'Yes.'

'And shoemaking is useful in peace too?'

'Yes.'

'I imagine you'd say, for the production of shoes.'

'Yes, quite.'

'So now for the same question about justice: justice is a useful thing – for the peaceful use or production of what?'

'It's useful for agreements, Socrates.'

'By "agreements", do you have in mind business associations, or something else?'

'Business associations.'

333b 'Is it the just person that's a good and useful associate when it comes to placing the pieces in a board-game,[5] or is it the expert at playing the game?'

'The expert board-game player.'

'Is the just person perhaps a better and more useful associate than a builder for placing bricks or blocks of stone?'

'Not at all.'

'Well then, in what sort of association will the just person be a better associate to have – say, than the cithara-player, in the same way that the cithara-player will be a better associate than the just person when it comes to striking the right notes?'

'Associations relating to money, I think.'

'Except, probably, Polemarchus, when it's a matter of using money, for example when one needs to make a joint purchase or sale of a horse; in that case, I suppose, it'll be the horse-expert that makes the better associate – right?' 333c

'It appears so.'

'And when it's a ship, we'll need the shipwright or steersman?'

'Apparently.'

'Then for what kind of joint use of our silver or gold will the just person be more useful than all the rest?'

'When we need to set it aside and keep it safe, Socrates.'

'You're saying, when we've no use to make of it at all, and it's to lie idle?'

'Yes, quite.'

'So it turns out that it's exactly when money is unused that justice is useful for it?' 333d

'Likely so.'

'Equally, when a pruning-knife needs to be kept safe, justice will be useful – whether associates are involved, or whether one's acting on one's own; but when the knife's to be used, what we'll need is the expertise of the vine-worker?'

'Apparently.'

'And you'll say the same about a shield or a lyre: when they need to be kept safe rather than being put to any use, justice is useful, but when they're to be used, what's useful is the expertise of the hoplite⁶ or the musician?'

'That's what I'll have to say.'

'So in relation to everything else, too, when it's a question of using anything, justice is of no use, and it's only useful when something is not used?'

'Likely so.'

333e 'Then, my friend, if it's actually only of use for things not in use, justice can't be worth very much! Here's another point to think about. Isn't it the most skilful at landing blows in a fight, whether in boxing or any other similar expertise, that are also most skilled at keeping themselves safe?'

'Yes, absolutely.'

'So too, if someone's clever at keeping people safe from sickness, he'll also be cleverest at making them sick and getting away with it?'

'I think so.'

334a 'Another example: it's the person who's good at keeping an army safe from the enemy who'll also be good at stealing a march on the enemy, anticipating his plans and even his actions?'

'Yes, absolutely.'

'Then the general rule is: if one's clever at keeping something safe, one will be clever at stealing it too.'

'So it seems.'

'In that case, if the just person is clever at keeping money safe, he'll be clever at thieving it too.'

'So the argument suggests, at any rate.'

'Then the just person stands exposed, it seems, as a kind of thief. Quite likely you've got the idea from Homer – Homer
334b himself talks approvingly of Odysseus' maternal grandfather Autolycus, claiming he "outshone all men in thievery and oath-breaking".[7] So justice, on your account and on Homer's and on Simonides', seems to be a kind of expertise in stealing, except that it's stealing to benefit one's friends and harm one's enemies. Isn't that what you had in mind?'

'Zeus, no!' he said; 'I no longer know what I *did* have in mind. All the same, I do still think that justice benefits friends and harms enemies.'

334c 'When you talk about someone's "friends", are these "friends" those that seem to him good men, or those who actually are good men even if they don't seem so – and similarly with "enemies"?'

'It's likely anyone will love those he thinks good, and hate those he thinks bad.'

'Well, don't people make mistakes here, so that they frequently end up thinking someone good when he's not, and vice versa?'

'They do.'

'Then they'll have good men as enemies, and bad men as friends?'

'Yes, certainly.'

'But all the same, it's just in this case for them to benefit the bad and harm the good?'

'Apparently so.'

'But if someone is good, he'll be just, and can be relied on 334d not to act unjustly?'

'True.'

'Then by your argument it's just to harm those who don't act unjustly at all.'

'No, no, Socrates!' he said; 'it looks as if it's the argument that's bad.'

'It's the unjust, then,' I said, 'that it's just to harm, and the just that it's just to benefit.'

'That looks better.'

'So, Polemarchus, it turns out that in all those many cases where people have made a mistake, it will actually be just for 334e them to harm their friends, because they've got bad ones, and to help their enemies, because they're good; and so now we'll be saying the very opposite of what we were claiming Simonides to be saying.'

'Absolutely,' he said; 'that's just how it's turned out. Let's change the way we take "friend" and "enemy"; probably we're making a mistake there.'

'Where's the mistake, Polemarchus?'

'When we take a friend to be the person who *seems* to us to be good.'

'And what's the change you're now proposing we make?'

'We should say,' he said, 'instead, that friends are those who not only seem good but are good; and that those who seem 335a good without actually being good are seeming and not real friends. Similarly with enemies.'

'By this account, then, it's good people who are friends, and bad ones enemies.'

'Yes.'

'So you're saying we should make an addition to our previous account of justice. What we said before was that it was just to do good to our friends and harm to our enemies, whereas now you want us to qualify this, and say that it's just to do good to friends if they're good, and to harm enemies if they're bad.'

335b 'Yes,' he said, 'quite so; I think that would be a fine way of putting it.'

'Then here's another question for you,' I said: 'is it the business of a just person to harm any person whatsoever?'

'Certainly it is: at any rate, those who are bad *and* our enemies should be harmed.'

'But how about horses – if they're harmed, are they made better or worse?'

'Worse.'

'Worse in respect to canine goodness,[8] or equine?'

'The latter.'

'And dogs, too, I suppose, become worse, when they're harmed, in respect to canine goodness, not equine?'

'Necessarily so.'

335c 'And won't we say the same about human beings too – that when they're harmed they become worse in respect to human and not some other sort of goodness?'

'Absolutely.'

'But isn't *justice* human goodness?'

'Again, necessarily.'

'Then, my friend, won't it also necessarily be the case that human beings who are harmed become more unjust?'

'It seems so.'

'Well, can musicians use their musical expertise to make people musically ignorant?'

'Impossible.'

'And what about horse-experts? Can they use their expertise about horses to make people into non-horse-experts?'

'Not possible.'

'And justice? Can the just use their justice to make people 335d unjust? Or in general, can the good use goodness to make people bad?'

'Quite impossible.'

'Right; because, I imagine, it's not a function of heat to cool things, but the opposite.'

'Yes.'

'Nor of dryness to moisten things, but of its opposite.'

'Yes, certainly.'

'Nor, again, of the good to do harm, but of its opposite.'

'Apparently.'

'And the just person is a good person?'

'Yes, certainly.'

'In that case, Polemarchus, it's not a function of the just person to do harm, whether to a friend or to anyone else; that's a function of his opposite, the unjust.'

'I think what you say is absolutely true, Socrates,' he said.   335e

'Then if anyone does claim that it's just to give back what one owes in each case, with the idea in mind that the just man "owes" harm to his enemies and benefit to his friends, it wasn't a wise person who said it – because what he said isn't true. It's become clear to us that in no case will a just person harm anyone.'

'I agree,' he said.

'We'll put up a fight, then,' I said, 'you and I together, if anyone claims Simonides or Bias or Pittacus or any other man of similarly superhuman wisdom has authority for it.'

'I'm certainly ready to join the fight,' he said.

'Do you know whose saying I think this was – this claim   336a
that it's just to benefit one's friends and harm one's enemies?'

'Whose?'

'I think it comes from Periander, Perdiccas, Xerxes, Ismenias of Thebes or some other rich man who thinks he has great power.'[9]

'Very true,' said Polemarchus.

'Well then,' I said, 'since it's become clear that it isn't this, either, that constitutes justice, or what's just, what else could one say it is?'

Even while we were talking, Thrasymachus had attempted   336b
several times to break into the conversation, but had been held back by those sitting by him because they wanted to hear how the discussion would turn out. Now, as we paused with that

last question of mine, he couldn't be contained any longer; gathering himself together like some wild animal, he launched himself at us as if to tear us to pieces, making Polemarchus and myself shake with terror.

336c   'Socrates,' he bellowed out, 'what's got into the pair of you? Such rubbish! And why all this deferring to one another, as if you were a pair of simpletons? If you really want to know what's just, you'll have to do more than asking questions, and playing to the audience by trying to refute whatever answer anyone gives you, safe in the knowledge that it's easier to ask questions than to answer them. Give *your* answer, and say

336d   what *you* claim is just. And make sure you don't tell me it's "what one should do", or "what's beneficial", or "what pays", or "what's profitable", or "what's in someone's interests"; in short, whatever you say, make it clear and precise, because I won't take any drivel like that from you.'

That panicked me, and I looked at him fearfully – I do believe, if I hadn't seen him before he saw me, I would have been struck dumb.[10] But as it was, when the conversation

336e   started to drive him wild I had my eye on him first, so now I was able to answer him. 'Thrasymachus,' I said, 'don't be rough with us; if I and Polemarchus here are going wrong in the way we're conducting our investigation, please be sure that we're not willingly going wrong. Do you think, if we were looking for gold, we'd spoil our chances of finding it by willingly deferring to one another? And here we are, looking for justice, something more valuable than a whole pile of gold; don't for a moment think that we're giving way to each other in the mindless way you suggest, and not striving our utmost to get a sight of what we're looking for. That's what we're doing, my friend, and you'd better believe it. But the truth is, I think,

337a   that we're unequal to the task. So I put it to you that it'd be much more reasonable for clever people like you to pity us than to be severe with us.'

At this Thrasymachus broke into laughter. 'Heracles!' he exclaimed, at his most sardonic. 'Here we go again, Socrates pretending as usual! I knew it would happen – I told these people here you'd refuse to give any answers yourself; you'd pretend not to know anything, and you'd do everything to avoid answering if anyone asks you a question.'

'Yes, Thrasymachus,' I said; 'you're so wise – wise enough to know what would happen if you asked someone how many 337b make twelve, warning him as you did so, "Make sure, my man, you don't tell me twelve is two times six, or three times four, or six times two, or four times three, because I won't take any rubbish like that from you"; asked a question like that, as I think you knew perfectly well, no one would give you an answer. But what if you'd asked your question like that, and the other person had said to you, "Thrasymachus, what do you mean? Am I really not to give you any of the answers you've listed? That would be astonishing – what if one of them was actually the right one? Am I supposed to give you another answer, one that isn't true? Just what *are* you talking about?" 337c How would you have responded to his challenge?'

'Well, well,' he said; 'as if this case were like that one!'

'There's no reason why it shouldn't be,' I said. 'But in any event, even if the two cases aren't alike, and it simply appears to the other person that they are, do you think, whether we forbid him to or not, it'll make him any less likely to answer your question as he thinks fit?'

'So I suppose', he said, 'that's exactly what you're going to do – give one of the answers I told you not to give?'

'I shouldn't be surprised,' I said, 'if that's what I decided, on reflection.'

'In that case,' he said, 'what if I show you a different answer 337d to the question about justice, over and above all these others, and better than them? What punishment will you propose for yourself then?'

'What else', I said, 'but the punishment that's due to the ignorant? And that, I imagine, is to learn from the expert. So I propose that as my punishment.'

'What an innocent you are,' he said. 'On top of your lesson there'll be a fee to pay.'

'When I've got the money, then,' I said.

'You have it,' said Glaucon. 'If it's just a question of money, Thrasymachus, speak on. We'll all chip in for Socrates.'

337e 'Oh yes,' he said, 'I imagine you will; just so that Socrates can go on doing the usual – having someone else give the answers rather than himself, then getting hold of what the other person says and setting out to refute it.'

'And how could a person give any answers, my dear Thrasymachus,' I said, 'if in the first place he doesn't have the knowledge to do so, and doesn't claim to have it – and then, even if he has some thoughts on the matter, he's forbidden to express any of them, and not by just anybody? No, you should
338a be the one to speak; after all, you're the one claiming to be an expert, and able to express what you know. So no more hesitation, please; do me the favour of answering the question in hand – no holding back – and at the same time you'll enlighten Glaucon here, and the others.'

When I said this, Glaucon and the rest echoed my request. Thrasymachus himself was obviously keen to speak, to gain credit with his audience, because he thought he had an answer that was first rate; but he went on making a play of contending
338b I should be the one doing the answering. Still, finally he agreed, and then said, 'There's Socrates' wisdom for you – he refuses to teach anyone himself, and instead goes round learning from everyone else without a word of thanks in return.'

'You're right, Thrasymachus,' I said, 'when you say I go round learning from everyone else, but you're wrong when you say I give them nothing in return, because I give back what I can. Praise is what I'm able to give; money I don't have. Just how ready I am to praise, if I think someone is saying some-
338c thing worth saying, you'll know soon enough, when you've given your answer – because I think you will say something worthwhile.'

'Listen to this, then,' he said. 'What is just, *I* say, is nothing more than what is in the interests of the stronger. Why aren't you applauding? You simply won't, will you!'

'First', I said, 'I need to understand what you're saying, which I don't, so far. You claim that what's in the interests of the *stronger* is just. But what are you saying by that, Thrasymachus? Not, presumably, this sort of thing – that if Poulydamas the pancratiast, say, is stronger than we are, and it's in his interests to eat beef, to build up his body, then it's in the interests of us weaker folk, and just, to eat beef too?' 338d

'You're disgusting, Socrates,' he said. 'You're just taking my proposal in the way you can most easily maltreat it.'

'Not at all, my friend,' I said; 'just tell me more clearly what you're saying.'

'Aren't you aware, then,' he said, 'that some cities are governed by tyrants, while others are democracies, others aristocracies?'

'Of course.'

'And the power belongs, in each city, to the element in it that rules?'

'Yes, certainly.'

'In each case, then, the ruling body lays down the laws with 338e a view to its own interests: a democracy lays down democratic laws, a tyranny tyrannical laws, and similarly with the other forms of rule. Legislation is thus the ruling body's way of proclaiming to those it rules that what is just is what is in *its* interests; those it punishes as lawbreakers and as acting unjustly are the ones who act contrary to those interests. This, my friend, is what I say is just, and it's the same in all cities – 339a namely, what serves the interests of those established in power; and since, I imagine, power is strength, it follows by any correct reasoning that what is just, everywhere, is the same thing, namely, what is in the interests of the stronger.'

'Now I've understood what you're saying,' I said; 'what I still need to understand is whether it's true or not. So, Thrasymachus, you yourself have identified what is just as what's "in someone's interests", even though you were telling me 339b I couldn't; though there is that additional specification, "in the interests *of the stronger*".'

'Yes,' he said; 'just that small addition!'

'Whether it's small, or big, that's not yet clear; it's only clear that we need to inquire whether what you're saying is true. Given the situation – with me agreeing that what is just is a matter of "interests", you wanting to add the specification that these are the interests "of the stronger", and me simply not knowing what to say – an inquiry can't be avoided.'

'Inquire on,' he said.

'That I'll do,' I said. 'Aren't you also claiming that it's just for people to obey their rulers?'

'I am.'

339c 'And are those who rule in any kind of city infallible, or are they capable of slipping up, sometimes, too?'

'I'm sure they're quite capable of slipping up sometimes,' he said.

'Then when they attempt to legislate, some of the laws they set up will be as they should be, and some won't be?'

'I imagine so.'

'And setting up laws "as they should be" will be a matter of setting things up to suit their own interests, while if they don't set them up "as they should be", things will be counter to their interests? Is that what you're saying?'

'Correct.'

'But whatever they lay down, those they rule over must do as they're told, and that is what is just?'

'Of course.'

339d 'By your account, then, it's not only just to do what's in the interests of the stronger, but also just to do the opposite, what's *not* in the interests of the stronger.'

'What's that you're saying?' he asked.

'No more than what you're saying, so far as I can see; but we should take a better look. Haven't we agreed that in telling their subjects what to do, rulers sometimes make mistakes, here and there, about what's best for themselves; and also that whatever the rulers tell them to do, it's just for those they rule over to do as they're told? That was what you agreed, wasn't it?'

'I believe I did agree that.'

339e 'Well then, you'd better also believe you've agreed that it's just to do what's counter to the interests of those in power and stronger. If those in power give orders that are bad for themselves, however unintentionally, and if you claim that it's just for the ruled to do what rulers tell them to do, doesn't it then follow exactly as I say, wisest Thrasymachus: that it's just to do the opposite of what you're claiming is just? After all, it's what's counter to the interests of the stronger that the weaker are going to be ordered to do in this case.'

'Zeus, yes!' said Polemarchus; 'it's as clear as anything.'   340a

'And I suppose you're the best witness,' Clitophon retorted.

'What need is there for witnesses?' asked Polemarchus; 'after all, Thrasymachus himself admits that even if rulers sometimes give orders that are bad for them, it will still be just for the ruled to carry out those orders.'

'Yes, Polemarchus, because Thrasymachus' position is that it's just for the ruled to do what they're told by their rulers.'

'Yes, Clitophon, and it's also part of his position that it's what's in the interests of the stronger that's just. Having pro-   340b posed both of these things, he again admitted that sometimes the stronger party orders those weaker than and ruled by it to do what's counter to its own interests. Given these admissions, it won't be any more just to do what's in the interests of the stronger than to do what's counter to those interests.'

'But', said Clitophon, 'when he said "what is in the interests of the stronger", he had in mind whatever the stronger person *thinks* is in his interests. That's what the weaker person needs to be doing, and that was Thrasymachus' position on what is just.'

'Well,' said Polemarchus, 'that wasn't what was said.'

'It doesn't matter at all, Polemarchus,' I said; 'if Thrasyma-   340c chus is now saying what Clitophon says he is, let's allow him to say it. So tell me, Thrasymachus: *was* this what you wanted to say was just – doing what *seems* to the stronger to be in the interests of the stronger, whether it's actually in his interests or not? Is that what we're to suppose you're saying?'

'No, certainly not,' he said; 'do you suppose that I give the title "stronger" to people who make mistakes, when they're making them?'

'Well, yes,' I said; 'that's what I thought you were doing when you admitted that rulers aren't infallible, and sometimes   340d do make mistakes.'

'Trying to catch people out as usual, Socrates!' he said. 'Here's an example for you: I suppose if someone makes a mistake in treating sick people, you'll call him a doctor, just insofar as he makes that mistake? Or accountants – will you

call someone who makes an adding mistake an accountant, at
the moment that, and insofar as, he's making that mistake? I
think we do talk like that; we do say "the doctor", "the
accountant", or "the writing-teacher" made a mistake; but in
340e fact, I imagine, none of these, insofar as he is what we call him,
will ever go wrong. So, strictly speaking, since speaking strictly
is what you go in for, no expert in any trade makes mistakes.
It's when expertise has failed him – when he's *not* a craftsman –
that he goes wrong. In consequence, no craftsman, no expert,
no ruler ever makes mistakes at the moment at which he *is* a
ruler; even though in fact everyone would say "the doctor
made a mistake", "the ruler made a mistake". Well, take me as
having answered you just now in this other, loose kind of way;
341a but actually the strictest way of putting it is to say that the
ruler doesn't make mistakes, insofar as he's a ruler; that if he
doesn't make mistakes, he lays down what is best for himself;
and that this is what those he rules over need to do. Thus it's as
I was saying all along: what it's just to do, I say, is what is in the
interests of the stronger.'

'So then, Thrasymachus,' I said, 'you think I'm trying to
catch you out?'

'Absolutely right,' he said.

'Because you think I ask you my questions with malice afore-
thought, to have you come off worse in the argument?'

'I'm quite certain of it,' he said, 'and it won't get you any-
341b where; stealth is no good because I know what you're up to,
and a frontal attack to beat me down is beyond your resources.'

'My dear man, I wouldn't dream of trying,' I said. 'But to
prevent us having to go through all this again, tell me once and
for all in which way you're taking "the ruler" and "the stronger":
in the way people tend to speak of them, or in the strict way you
were talking about just now? Which is this "ruler" in whose
interests it's going to be just for the weaker to act?'

'The one who's absolutely strictly a ruler,' he said. 'Take that
and do your worst with it – catch me out if you can; I'm not
341c asking for any quarter. But you won't get anywhere.'

'You think I'm that crazy?' I asked. 'I might as well try to
shave a lion as try to catch Thrasymachus out.'

'Well', he said, 'you tried just now, and you didn't get anywhere then, either.'

'Enough of all this,' I said. 'Answer me this: the doctor you
were talking about just now, the one who's strictly a doctor –
which is he, a money-maker or a healer of the sick? And do
make sure you talk about the real doctor.'

'He's a healer of the sick,' he said.

'And what about the steersman: does the steersman, correctly
so-called, rule over sailors, or is he a sailor?'

'He rules over sailors.'   341d

'We're not, I imagine, to take into account that he sails in the
ship along with the others, and call him a sailor because of
that; it's not in respect to his sailing that he's called a steersman,
but in respect to his expertise, and to the fact that he rules over
the sailors.'

'True,' he said.

'Well then, is there something that is in the interests of each
of these experts?'

'Yes, certainly.'

'And isn't it also the nature of any expertise', I said, 'to seek
out for each[11] what is in his interests and provide it?'

'Quite so,' he said.

'Now is there anything that's in the interests of each expertise beyond its being as perfect as possible?'

'I don't understand the question.'   341e

'Imagine', I said, 'that you were asking me whether it's
enough for a body just to be a body, or whether it needs anything else, over and above that. I would reply "Certainly it
does; that's why we have the invention of medical expertise,
because a body is in bad condition and it's not enough for it to
be like that. So the expertise was put together to provide what
was in the body's interests." Do you think', I asked, 'that would
be the correct answer to give, or not?'

'The correct answer,' he said.   342a

'So what about the art of medicine itself? Is that in bad condition? Is there any kind of expertise at all that needs something
extra, over and above itself, to make it good? Eyes, for example,
need to be able to see well, ears to hear well, so that in those

cases some sort of expertise is needed to seek out and provide
what's in the interests of good sight and hearing; will there
actually be some shortcoming in the expertise itself? Will each
expertise need a further expertise to seek out what is in *its*
interests; and will this further one need yet another, to look out
342b for it, and so on and so on – or will an expertise seek out
for itself what is in its own interests? Or will it actually not
need to call on either itself or another expertise to deal with its
shortcomings and look out for itself? Because no expertise is
afflicted by any shortcoming or error, nor is it appropriate for
any expertise to look out for the interests of anything other
than the thing it is an expertise of, being in itself purely and
simply incapable of inflicting harm, because it gets things
right – for just so long as each expertise really *is*, strictly and
completely, the expertise that it is. Tell me, looking at things in
that strict way, is that how things are or not?'

'That is how they are, apparently,' he said.

342c   'In that case,' I said, 'medicine doesn't look out for its own
interests; it looks out for those of a body.'

'Yes,' he said.

'And horse-expertise doesn't look out for what's in its
own interests but for what's in those of horses. Nor does any
other expertise look out for itself, because it doesn't actually
need anything but itself; it looks out for the thing it's an expertise of.'

'Apparently so,' he said.

'But surely, Thrasymachus, the various sorts of expertise
rule over, and *have power* over, this subject of their expertise.'

He agreed to this, but very reluctantly.

'In that case, there's no expertise that looks out for what's in
342d the interests of the stronger, and prescribes that; every one of
them looks out for the interests of the weaker party, the one
ruled by itself.'

In the end he agreed to this too, though he kept trying to
dispute it. When he did finally agree, I asked him, 'Isn't it true
that no doctor, either, just insofar as he is a doctor, looks out,
and prescribes, for the interests of the doctor, only for those of
the sick person? Because it's agreed that the doctor strictly so-

called is a ruler over bodies, and not a money-maker? That is agreed, isn't it?'

He said yes.

'And that the steersman, strictly understood, is a ruler over sailors and not a sailor?'   342e

'Agreed.'

'Then a steersman and ruler like that won't look out and prescribe for what's in the interests of the steersman, but for what's in the interests of the sailor and subject.'

He agreed, reluctantly.

'So, Thrasymachus,' I said, 'neither does any other sort of ruler, insofar as he is a ruler, look out for or prescribe for what is in his own interests, only for what is in the interests of the subject, the person for whom he exercises his craft; that's what he has in view when he says everything he says and does everything he does – what's in that other person's interests, and is suitable for them.'

When we'd got to this point in the discussion and everybody   343a
could see that his account, of what exactly is *just*, had been stood on its head, well – Thrasymachus, instead of answering, said, 'Tell me, Socrates, do you have a nurse?'

'What's this?' I replied; 'shouldn't you have answered me, instead of asking questions like that?'

'I'm asking', he said, 'because if you can't even recognize sheep for her, or a shepherd, she obviously isn't wiping your runny nose for you as she should.'

'Why exactly do you say that?' I asked.

'Because you think shepherds and herdsmen look out for   343b
what's good for their sheep and their cows – that they fatten them up and care for them with a view to something more than merely what's good for their slave-masters and themselves; and when it comes to rulers in cities, rulers properly so-called, you actually think their attitude towards their subjects is somehow different from the one we'd have towards sheep, and that they spend their days and nights worrying, not about what will bring *them* the greatest benefit, but something else. So far off   343c
the mark are you on the subject of what is just and unjust, and justice and injustice, that it has escaped you that justice and

doing what is just are in fact good for someone else, being what
is in the interests of the stronger and of the ruler, and do harm
to the person who obeys and serves; while it is the reverse with
the opposite, injustice, ruling as it does over those true simpletons, the just. Those who are ruled simply do what is in the
unjust person's interest, since he's stronger than they are, and
343d   make him happy by serving him, while doing nothing whatsoever for their own happiness.

   'My dear, simple-minded Socrates, look at it this way: there's
nowhere that the just man fails to have less than the unjust.
Think first about business dealings: if ever the just and the
unjust are involved together in a joint project, you'll never find
the just person coming away with more than the unjust when
the partnership is dissolved; he'll always be worse off. Or take
relations with the city – when there are contributions to be
made, even if the two of them own property of equal value it's
the just person who'll contribute more, the unjust less; while
343e   if there are handouts to be had, the one will get nothing while
the other makes big gains. And when it comes to holding office,
it's the same story: even if he isn't subject to any other sort of
penalty, the just person not only has his personal affairs suffer
through neglect, but is prevented from benefiting at all from his
public service – because he's just; on top of which he's hated by
friends and acquaintances alike when he refuses to contravene
justice by doing special favours for them. The unjust person,
344a   meanwhile, gets the opposite of all of this. I'm talking, of
course, about the same man I was talking about the other
moment, the one with a capacity for getting the better of others
on a grand scale: it's his case you need to look at if you really
want to assess how much more in one's interests it is, personally, to be unjust than to be just.

   'You'll grasp the point most easily if you go to the perfect
example of injustice, which bestows the greatest happiness on
the doer and the greatest misery on the victims, so long as they
would refuse to do anything unjust themselves. This is tyranny,
which takes away what belongs to others, not bit by bit but
wholesale, whether covertly or by force, whether sacred and
344b   holy, private or public. These are the sorts of actions for which

an offender, if he's found out to have done only one of them, is penalized and incurs the greatest opprobrium; people who commit such crimes piecemeal get called temple-robbers, kidnappers, burglars, swindlers, thieves, and so on. But when someone doesn't merely steal his fellow-citizens' property, but actually kidnaps and enslaves the citizens themselves, instead of being called names like that he is called happy and blessed, 344c not simply by the citizens but by anyone who hears that he's exhausted the whole repertoire of injustice. The fact is that people who revile injustice do so because they're afraid, not of doing it but of having it done to *them*.

'So there it is, Socrates: injustice is a stronger, freer, more masterful thing than justice, if it is done on a large enough scale, and as I was saying from the start, what is actually just is what is in the interests of the stronger, what is unjust being what profits him and is in his own interests.'[12]

After this speech, poured over our ears all at once as if by 344d some attendant at the baths, Thrasymachus was of a mind to leave. But he was prevented from doing so by those present, who forced him to stay and give a proper account of what he'd said. I was particularly insistent. 'Really, Thrasymachus! You throw in that sort of statement, and then propose to go off before you've taught us properly – or learned yourself – whether things are as you say or not? Do you think it's some small thing 344e you're setting out to define, and not how all of us need to conduct our lives in order to live most profitably?'

'Of course not,' said Thrasymachus. 'That's exactly my point.'

'Well,' I said, 'you seem to be denying it; either that, or you care nothing for our welfare, since you seem not to worry at all whether we'll live worse or better lives for not knowing what you say you know. Please, my good man, do have the courage to demonstrate your case to us too; there are enough of us here 345a to make sure you won't do badly out of it, whatever favours you bestow on us. My own position, I have to tell you, is that I'm not persuaded, and neither do I believe that injustice is more profitable than justice, even if one gives it free rein and doesn't try to stop it doing what it wants. Let's suppose, my friend, that your unjust person exists, and that he's able to act unjustly either by not being detected or by brazening it out: still 345b he doesn't persuade *me* that it's more profitable than justice. And perhaps it's not only me – perhaps there's someone else here in the same position as I am; so go on, be a good man and persuade us that we're wrongly advised to be putting a greater value on justice than on injustice.'

'And exactly how', he asked, 'am I supposed to persuade you? If you're not convinced by the things I was saying, what more do you want from me? Am I supposed to knock it into your head for you?'

'Zeus!' I said. 'You keep away from me! The first thing is for you to stand by what you say, or else, if you want to make any 345c changes, to make them openly, and not try to conceal them from us. As it is, you see, Thrasymachus – let's go on looking at what we were talking about before – you started by fixing on the true doctor, but then, later on, you supposed there wasn't any need to keep strictly to his counterpart, the true shepherd; your thinking is that, as a shepherd, he doesn't fatten his sheep with a view to what's best for the sheep, but rather for the sake of having a good time, as if he were a dinner-guest off to a ban- 345d quet, or in order to sell them, as if he were in the business of money-making and not a shepherd. But the expertise of shep- herding, surely, cares about nothing but providing the best for what comprises its proper sphere of concern, since its own needs, if it is to be the best, are already met so long as it is wholly and completely what it is, the expertise of shepherding. In the same way, I was thinking just now that we couldn't avoid agreeing, the two of us, that ruling of any kind, considered just *as* ruling, looks out for what's best for what it rules over and 345e cares for – nothing else, whether we're talking about the polit- ical or the private sphere. Do you really suppose those who rule in cities – that is, true rulers – do so willingly?'

'Zeus!' he exclaimed. 'I don't just think it, I know it!'

'But what about other forms of rule,[13] Thrasymachus? Hasn't it occurred to you that there are no willing volunteers for taking them on? Everybody asks to be paid for it, on the grounds that any benefit accruing from their rule won't come to them

but to those they rule. Tell me this: don't we normally treat 346a
one expertise as differing from another by virtue of the different
capacity it has? And be a good man – don't give me an answer
that's not what you really believe; then we can make some
progress.'

'That's how we say they differ,' he said.

'And each expertise also provides us with some particular
benefit, not a general one: health, for example, in the case of
medicine, safety at sea in the case of steersmanship, and so on
with the other kinds of expertise?'

'Yes, certainly.'

'Then won't the benefit deriving from expertise in fee- 346b
earning be fees? That's what its capacity is for. Or will you call
medicine and steersmanship the same expertise? If you really
do want to tie things down precisely, as you proposed – if
someone is cured while steering a ship, because he's benefited
by a sea voyage, will that make you any more inclined to call
his steersmanship medicine?'

'Of course not,' he said.

'No more, I imagine, will you call fee-earning medicine, if
someone gets his health back while he's earning a fee.'

'Of course not.'

'What about if someone earns a fee while healing – will you
call medicine fee-earning?'

He said he wouldn't. 346c

'And didn't we agree that the benefit provided by each
expertise was particular to that expertise?'

'Let's suppose it is.'

'In that case, clearly, if all expert craftsmen are getting some
common benefit, they must be getting it from their common
use of some one identical thing.'

'It seems so,' he said.

'But we're claiming that the benefit craftsmen get by earning
fees comes to them from their use of the expertise of fee-earning.'

He agreed reluctantly.

'In that case, the benefit in question, the getting of their 346d
fee, doesn't come to any of them from their own particular
expertise. If our brief is to look at things with proper precision,

it's health that comes from medicine, not the doctor's fees; those come from fee-earning. Expertise in building produces a house, but the builder's fee, again, will be the product of fee-earning. And similarly with each of the other kinds of expertise – each does its own particular work, and bestows its benefits on the thing comprising its proper sphere of concern. But if it is not complemented by fees, is there any benefit for the craftsman from his expertise?'

'Apparently not,' he said.

346e 'Well, does he do no good, either, when he works for nothing?'

'No, I'm sure he does.'

'Then isn't it by now quite clear, Thrasymachus, that there's no expertise, and no kind of rule, that concerns itself with what benefits *itself*. It's as we were saying some time ago now – any expertise, any kind of rule concerns itself with what will benefit the *subject*, and gives its orders with that in view, insofar as it looks out for the *subject*'s interests, that is, the interests of the weaker, not of the stronger. That's the reason, my dear Thrasymachus, why I was saying just now that there are no willing volunteers for ruling, and for taking on the business of setting

347a other people's troubles to rights. Rather, as I said, everybody asks to be paid for doing it, because nobody who's going to employ an expertise as it should be employed will do what is best for himself, or give orders with that in view, if he's giving them in accordance with the principles of his expertise; he'll only do what's best for the subject of his expertise – which is apparently why, if people are to be willing to rule, they must be paid for it, whether the pay takes the form of actual money or of honours, or else of a penalty if they refuse.'

'What's that you're saying?' asked Glaucon. 'I recognize two of your ways of paying people, but I haven't understood the third; how would a penalty serve as a form of pay?'

347b 'In that case', I said, 'you don't understand the kind of return the best people receive – the kind that motivates those of the highest quality to rule, when they do so willingly. You do recognize, don't you, that loving honours and loving money both have a bad name, and deservedly so?'

'Indeed I do,' he said.

'Well,' I said, 'that's why good people aren't willing to rule either for money or for honour. They don't want to get paid officially for ruling, and get themselves called hired hands, nor do they want to turn office to profit and be called thieves; and not being honour-lovers, they won't take office in return for honour either. So in their case there has to be compulsion, in 347c the form of a penalty, if they're to be willing to rule; and that no doubt is why it's come to be thought of as shameful to volunteer for office, rather than waiting to be forced to take it on. But actually the severest form of penalty is for someone who refuses to take charge himself to find himself being ruled by someone inferior; it's fear of that, in my view, that motivates people of quality to rule, when they do. And when they do enter office, they don't do so on the basis that they're embarking on something good, and with the expectation of doing well out of it, but as something they're compelled to do, and because 347d they're not able to turn it over to people better than or even equal to themselves. It's very likely, I think, that if there were ever to be a city populated entirely by good men, they would compete as vigorously as people compete now, but for the prize of not ruling, not for that of ruling: clear proof, if it ever came about, that it is not in fact the nature of a true ruler to look out for what is in his own interests, but rather for what is in the interests of the ruled – and anyone who recognized as much would accordingly opt to be benefited by someone else, rather than going to the trouble of benefiting the other person himself. So, anyway, I for one don't agree in the least with Thrasymachus 347e that it's what's in the interests of the stronger that is just. But we'll need to examine that particular proposal again, on another occasion; Thrasymachus is now claiming that the life of the unjust person beats that of the just hands down, which seems to me something altogether more serious. Tell me, Glaucon,' I said, 'how do you choose? Which of the two lives do you think has the truer claim?'

'My view', he said, 'is that it's the life of the just person that's more profitable.'

'So,' I asked, 'did you hear the whole list of good things 348a Thrasymachus just attributed to the life of the unjust?'

'I heard it,' he said, 'but I'm not persuaded.'

'Then do you want us to try to persuade *him* that what he's saying is untrue, supposing we can find a way to do it?'

'Why wouldn't I?' he asked.

'Well now,' I said, 'let's think about how to proceed. If we try matching him claim for claim – if we lay out on our side all the good things contained in the just life, and he then does the same for his side, *we* then come back with another list, and so 348b on, we'll end up having to count the number of good things each of us produces in support of his candidate, and measure them for size; then on top of all that we'll need a panel of judges to decide between us. But if we look at things in the way we were doing just now, by agreeing with one another at each step, we'll be able to do both things ourselves, both making our cases and judging between them.'

'Quite right,' he said.

'So which method do you wish us to use?' I asked.

'The second,' he said.

'Right, then, Thrasymachus,' I said; 'start at the beginning and answer us this. Perfect injustice, you claim, is more profitable than justice, if that's equally perfect?'

348c   'Absolutely,' he said; 'not only do I claim that, but I've told you why I claim it.'

'So come on, what's your answer to the following sort of question about justice and injustice? I imagine you call one of the two things a form of goodness, the other a form of badness?'

'Of course I do.'

'Justice being the goodness, injustice the badness?'

'How utterly delightful! As if I'd say that, when I'm also saying injustice is profitable and justice isn't!'

'So what do you say?'

'The reverse,' he said.

'You're saying justice is a form of badness?'

'No, merely a perfectly well-bred simple-mindedness.'

348d   'So you call injustice deviousness?'

'No,' he said; 'goodness of judgement.'

'Do the unjust also seem to you intelligent and good?'

'Yes,' he said, 'if they have a perfect capacity for injustice, and are able to subject cities, even whole races, of human beings to their rule; you probably think I'm talking about people who go round snatching purses. Well,' he went on, 'that sort of thing is profitable too, if one gets away with it, but it's insignificant, which the things I mentioned just now certainly are not.'

'I'm not in any doubt', I said, 'about what you want to say on that score; what surprised me was your placing injustice with goodness and wisdom, and justice with their opposites.' 348e

'That's where I place them.'

'This is an altogether steeper claim,' I said, 'and it's hard to know how one should respond to it. If you were proposing that injustice was profitable while conceding, still, that it was a form of badness, or something shameful in itself, as others do, we'd have a response ready to hand, in terms of conventional thinking.[14] But as it is, you'll evidently claim that injustice is something fine and strong, and in general you'll attribute to it all the things 349a we attribute to justice, seeing that you've already had the effrontery to put it on the side of goodness and wisdom.'

'You're quite a prophet,' he said.

'But', I said, 'that mustn't make me flinch for a moment from continuing the discussion and finishing the inquiry we've started on – just so long as I understand you to be saying what you think. And you simply don't strike me now, Thrasymachus, as someone who's playing games with us; you seem to me to be saying what you believe the truth to be.'

'What difference does it make to you', he asked, 'whether I believe it or not? Why not just get on with trying to refute my position?'

'No difference at all,' I said. 'So here's a new question for 349b you to answer: do you think a just person would want to outdo[15] another just person?'

'Not at all,' he said; 'if he did, he wouldn't be the charming and simple-minded individual he in fact is.'

'What about the just action? Would he want to outdo that?'

'No, not even the just action,' he said.[16]

'And would he expect to outdo the unjust person, and think it just that he should, or wouldn't he?'

'He'd think it,' said Thrasymachus, 'and he'd expect it, but he couldn't do it.'

349c   'That's not what I'm asking,' I said; 'my question is whether I'm right in saying that the just person doesn't expect or even want to outdo another just person, only the unjust one.'

'Yes, that's right,' he said.

'What about the unjust person? Does he expect to outdo the just – person or action?'

'How could he not,' he asked, 'when he expects to outdo everyone and everything?'

'So not only will the unjust person try to outdo both the unjust person and the unjust action; he'll compete to get the largest share of everything for himself?'

'Right.'

'So let's put it this way,' I said: 'the just person won't try
349d   to outdo his like, only the person who's unlike him; while the unjust person will try to outdo both his like and his unlike.'

'Very well put,' he said.

'But', I said, 'the unjust person is both intelligent and good,[17] the just neither.'

'Well put again,' he said.

'Well,' I asked, 'is it also true that the unjust person resembles the intelligent and good, and the just person doesn't resemble them?'

'Of course!' he said. 'If intelligent and good is what the unjust person actually *is*, how can he fail to *resemble* the intelligent and good as well? And how can the just person even begin to resemble them?'

'Fine. So each of them is of the same sort as the person he resembles?'

'Why on earth not?' he asked.

349e   'Very good, Thrasymachus. Now do you call one person a musical expert and another not?'

'I do.'

'Which of the two do you say is intelligent, and which unintelligent?'

'The musician intelligent, obviously, the non-musician unintelligent.'

'And in the respects in which he's intelligent, you say he's good; in the respects in which he's unintelligent, he's bad.'[18]

'Yes.'

'What about the medical expert? The same with him?'

'The same.'

'Now take the tuning of a lyre: do you suppose, Thrasymachus, in all *your* wisdom, that any one musical person would want to outdo, or expect to outdo, another musical person in the tightening and loosening of the strings?'

'No, I don't.'

'But he would want and expect to outdo the non-musician?'

'He must,' said Thrasymachus.

'And the medical expert? When it's a matter of how much   350a
to eat or drink, do you think he'd want at all to outdo either another medical expert or any action informed by medical expertise?'

'Surely not.'

'But he would want to outdo the medically non-expert?'

'Yes.'

'Think then about any kind of expertise or lack of expertise, and see whether you think any expert whatever would willingly choose either to do or to say more things than another expert would, and not the same things, towards the same action, as his like.'

'Probably', he said, 'that's how it must be.'

'And what about the non-expert? Wouldn't he try to outdo expert and non-expert alike?'   350b

'Probably.'

'And the expert is wise?'

'I say he is.'

'And the wise person is good?'

'I say he is.'

'In that case, the person who is wise and good won't want to outdo his like, only the person unlike and opposite to himself.'

'It seems so,' he said.

'Meanwhile the bad and ignorant person will want to outdo *both* his like *and* the one unlike himself.'

'It appears so.'

'Well, Thrasymachus, does our unjust person try to outdo both the person unlike himself, and his like? Or was that not what you were saying?'

'It was,' he said.

350c 'But the just person won't try to outdo his like, only the one unlike himself?'

'Yes.'

'In that case,' I said, 'the just person resembles the person who's wise and good, while the unjust one resembles the bad and ignorant.'

'Probably so.'

'But we were also in agreement that whichever sort each of the two resembled, that was the sort each of them actually was.'

'We did agree to that.'

'So it's the just person that's been revealed to us as good and wise, and the unjust as the one who's ignorant and bad.'

Well, Thrasymachus did agree to all of these points, but by 350d no means as easily as my present description suggests; he came along only because he was dragged, struggling all the way and sweating in amazing profusion, because it was summer, too – and I'll swear I saw something then that I'd never seen before: Thrasymachus blushing. In any case, when we had agreed that justice was goodness and wisdom, and injustice badness and ignorance, I said, 'So there we are, Thrasymachus; let's count that as established. But there was something else – we were also saying that injustice was something *strong*. Or don't you remember, Thrasymachus?'

'I do remember,' he said. 'But before we get on to that, let me tell you I'm not happy with what you're saying now, and I've something to say on my own account. If I told you what it is, 350e I'm quite sure you'd accuse me of playing the demagogue; so either let me speak at the length I want, or if you want to ask me questions, ask away, and I'll go "Splendid!", as if you were some old woman telling stories, with a nod for yes and a shake of the head for no.'

'No, no!' I said; 'not if it isn't what you think you should do.'

'I will, so as to make you happy,' he said, 'since you prevent me from having my say. Yet I'm wondering – what else do you want from me, if not that?'

'Zeus! Nothing at all,' I said. 'Still, if you're really going to do as you say, then do it, and I'll ask my questions.'

'Ask away.'

'Then I'll put the same question I did just now, so that we go on examining your position in due order. The question is about 351a what kind of thing justice is, by comparison with injustice; because the claim was, I believe, that injustice was a more powerful and stronger thing than justice, whereas now,' I said, 'if justice is in fact wisdom and goodness, I imagine that it'll be easy to show as well that it's stronger than injustice, given that injustice is actually ignorance – as no one could any longer fail to recognize. But I've no desire to take that simple way through, Thrasymachus. Instead, I'd like the inquiry to go in the follow-ing sort of way. You would say that a city can be unjust – it can 351b try to enslave other cities unjustly, have them firmly enslaved, and keep many of them subject to itself having enslaved them?'

'Of course,' he said. 'That's precisely what the best city, being an unjust one, will do most of all, and most completely.'

'I understand that was your position,' I said. 'But the ques-tion I'm raising about it is this: will a city that grows stronger than another one have this capacity in the absence of justice, or will it only have it when combined with justice?'

'If it's justice that's wisdom, as you were just claiming, only 351c when combined with justice; if things are as I was claiming, only when it's combined with injustice.'

'I'm quite delighted, Thrasymachus,' I said, 'that you're not just nodding and shaking your head but actually giving proper answers.'

'I'm doing it to please you,' he said.

'And I appreciate it. Now do something else for me, and answer me this: do you think a city or an army, or pirates, or thieves, or any other group that jointly undertakes some enter-prise in injustice, would be able to achieve anything if they treated one another unjustly?'

'No, I certainly don't,' he said.

351d   'What if they didn't treat each other unjustly? Wouldn't
they be more likely to achieve something?'

'Yes, certainly.'

'Yes, Thrasymachus; I suppose because injustice brings about
factions, hatred, fighting among themselves – things like that,
while justice brings about like-mindedness and friendship. Right?'

'Let's say so,' he said, 'just so that I don't fall out with you.'

'And I do appreciate it, Thrasymachus; very good of you. But
tell me this: if what injustice does is to cause hatred wherever it
occurs, then surely when it occurs in any group, whether of free
351e   men or slaves, it'll make them hate and quarrel with each other
and incapable of taking any joint action among themselves?'

'Yes, absolutely.'

'What if it occurs between two individuals? Won't they fall
out, hate one another and be enemies, rather than friends both
of each other and of the just?'

'They will,' he said.

'And if injustice occurs in *one* individual, my fine friend,
surely it won't lose that capacity it has, or have it to any lesser
degree?'

'Let's say it doesn't,' he replied.

'Then isn't it apparent that it has the capacity for affecting
352a   whatever it occurs in, whether city or family or army or anything else, in the following sort of way: first, it makes that thing
incapable of working with itself because of the faction and falling out it causes; and secondly, it makes that thing both its own
enemy and the enemy of everything that is opposite to it; that
is, the just? Isn't that so?'

'Absolutely, yes.'

'Even when it occurs in one individual, then, I suppose, it will
have these very same effects that it's in its nature to produce:
first, it'll make him incapable of acting because he's in disagreement and not of one mind with himself, and then it'll make him
the enemy both of himself and of the just. Right?'

'Yes.'

'But surely, my friend, it's not only human beings that are
just – the gods are too?'

352b   'Let's say that's so.'

'In that case, Thrasymachus, the unjust person will be the enemy of the gods too; the just person will be their friend.'

'Feast away on your argument,' he said, 'and never fear, I shan't oppose you, in case these people here start hating me.'

'So come on,' I said, 'fill me up with the rest of the banquet; go on answering my questions as you are now. The just are evidently wiser, better and more capable of action, while the unjust are unable to do anything in concert with one another – 352c and indeed, if we say that people have ever to this day achieved any powerful effects by acting jointly with one another, when they're unjust, that isn't entirely true, because if they were unjust through and through they'd be at each other's throats all the time; evidently there must have been some justice in them that made them not treat each other unjustly, as well as the people they were jointly attacking, and allowed them to achieve what they did achieve – they launched into their unjust actions only half-corrupted by injustice, because those who are totally corrupted and perfectly unjust are also perfectly incapable of 352d action. Anyway, as for all that, I'm satisfied that it's as I say it is and not as you were originally proposing. What now needs to be looked into is the question we put forward later in the discussion, whether the just really do live better and are happier than the unjust. In fact, in my own view, it's already clear from what we've said that they are happier, but all the same we should take an even better look at the question. After all, it's not any old issue we're discussing; it's about the way in which a person should live his life.'

'Then do it,' he said.

'I will,' I said. 'Tell me, do you think a horse has a function?' 352e
'I do.'

'And would you identify this function that a horse has, or indeed the function of anything at all, with whatever can be done either *only* with that thing, or *best* with that thing?'

'I don't follow,' he said.

'It's like this: is there anything you can see with except eyes?'
'Surely not.'

'What about hearing – can you hear with anything except ears?'

'Indeed not.'

'So these, we say – and justly – are those things' functions.'

'Absolutely, yes.'

353a 'What about this example: you could cut off a vine-shoot with a butcher's knife, or a leather-cutting tool, or a number of other things – right?'

'Of course.'

'But I imagine you wouldn't be able to do it as well as you could with a pruning-knife, forged for the purpose.'

'True.'

'And shall we identify this as the function in this case?'

'Certainly we shall.'

'Now, I imagine, you'll have a better grasp of what I was after just now, when I asked if the function of anything wasn't to be identified with whatever either *only* that thing could do or it did *better* than anything else.'

'I do understand now', he said, 'and this is what I think the
353b function of each thing is.'

'Splendid,' I said; 'and do you suppose that, for everything that has some function assigned to it, there's a good state for it to be in? Let's go back to the same examples. Eyes, we say, have a function?'

'They do.'

'And is there also a good state for eyes to be in?'

'There is.'

'And ears – we agreed they have a function?'

'Yes.'

'And there's a good way for them to be too?'

'There is.'

'What about everything else? Is it the same?'

'It is.'

'So then here's the point: would eyes ever be able to perform
353c their proper function well if they weren't in the good condition appropriate to them, but were in a bad state instead?'

'How could they?' he asked. 'You're presumably talking about blindness as opposed to seeing.'

'Whatever it is for eyes to be in a good state,' I said; 'I'm not actually asking about that yet, only whether they'll perform the function of eyes well if they're in the appropriate good condition, badly if they're in a bad state.'

'This is certainly true,' he said.

'And will ears, too, perform their proper function badly if they're not in the state ears should be in?'

'Yes, absolutely.'

'So do we assume that everything else follows the same 353d principle?'

'I think so.'

'Come on, then – given all that, think about the following: does a *soul*[19] have some function you couldn't perform with any single other thing there is in existence? For example, caring for whatever it might be, ruling, planning, everything like that – we'd surely be right to assign these functions to soul alone, and regard them as peculiarly belonging to soul?'

'Surely.'

'And what about our being alive? Will we say that's a function of soul?'

'Yes, that more than anything.'

'Well, do we also say that there's a good state for a soul to be in?'

'We do.'

'Then will a soul ever, Thrasymachus, perform its proper 353e functions well if it's not in the state it's appropriate for it to be in, or is that impossible?'

'It's impossible.'

'In that case, anyone with a bad soul must rule and care for things badly, and anyone with a good soul will do all these things well?'

'That's how it must be.'

'And we agreed[20] that a soul was in a good state when it was just, and in a bad state when it was unjust?'

'Yes, we did.'

'In that case, the just soul and the just man will live well, the unjust man badly.'

'Apparently so,' he said, 'according to your argument.'

'But now the person who lives well is blessed and happy, 354a and the person who doesn't is the opposite of these things.'

'Of course.'

'In that case, it's the just person who's happy, and the unjust person who's miserable.'

'Let's say so.'

'But now what profits us is not to be miserable, but to be happy.'

'Of course.'

'And in that case, Thrasymachus, bless you, never will injustice be a more profitable thing than justice.'

'So, Socrates,' he said, 'let that be your entertainment for the feast of Bendis.'[21]

'You're the one who's provided the feast, Thrasymachus,' I said, 'since you've come over all gentle with me and stopped 354b being angry. But actually I haven't dined well, and it's my fault, not yours. I think I'm exactly like a glutton who snatches a taste of each new dish as it comes past him, before he's properly enjoyed the last one: instead of waiting as I should have done till we'd found what we were first looking for – what exactly justice is – I let go of that and went instead for a particular question *about* justice, namely whether it's badness and ignorance or wisdom and goodness. And, then, later on, when the proposal emerged that injustice was a more profitable thing than justice, again I failed to stop myself from moving on to that. So the outcome of our conversation, for me, presently, is 354c a complete lack of knowledge on the subject we've been talking about; since if I don't know what justice is, I'll hardly know whether it really is a kind of goodness or not, and whether possessing it doesn't or does make a person happy.'[22]

357a Well, I thought that with these last words of mine I'd have   Book II
finished with the argument; but actually, as it turned out,   begins
what we'd been through was no more than an introduction.
Glaucon is never one to give up without a fight, and on this
occasion he certainly wasn't going to accept Thrasymachus'
refusal to engage with the argument. 'Socrates,' he said, 'which
do you want: actually to persuade us that it's better in every

respect to be just than to be unjust, or merely to give the 357b
impression of having persuaded us?'

'Actually to persuade you', I said, 'would be my choice, if it
was up to me.'

'Well,' said Glaucon, 'you should know that you're not
achieving what you want. Tell me this: do you think there's a
kind of good that we'd be happy to have, not from a desire for
what we get out of it but because we embrace it for its own
sake – for example, the enjoyment of those pleasures that are
harmless and give rise to no future consequences except con-
tinued enjoyment?'

'I do think', I said, 'that there's a kind of good like that.' 357c

'What about the kind we are attached to *both* for its own
sake *and* for what it gives rise to? Intelligence, for example, and
sight, and health; I imagine we embrace things like this for both
reasons.'

'Yes,' I said.

'And do you see a third kind of good,' he asked, 'one that
includes physical exercise, being healed when we are sick, healing other people, or any other kind of money-making?[23] After
all, we'd count these as burdensome but also beneficial to us;
we wouldn't be happy to have these things just for their own
sake, only for the sake of the wages and all the other things that 357d
we get from them.'

'Yes, certainly,' I said; 'there's that kind too. What of it?'

'In which of these kinds of good', he asked, 'do you place
justice?'

'In my own view', I said, 'it belongs to the finest of the three – 358a
the kind that is to be valued both for its own sake and for what
it gives rise to, if we are to be blessed with happiness.'[24]

'Well,' he said, 'that isn't how it appears to most people;
they think justice belongs to the troublesome kind. It's something to be practised in appearance, for the sake of whatever is
to be got from it in terms of pay-off or reputation, while being
in and by itself a burden to be avoided.'

'I'm aware', I said, 'that this is how justice seems, and for
some time now Thrasymachus has been denigrating it for being

like that, even as he's praised injustice; but it seems I'm somewhat slow to learn.'

358b   'So come on,' he said; 'see if you still think the same when
you've heard me out too. Thrasymachus appears to me to have
succumbed to your snake-charming sooner than he should,
since as far as I'm concerned we haven't yet had a satisfactory
demonstration on the subject of either justice or injustice. What
I'm anxious to hear about is what each of them is, and what
effect each has the capacity to produce, in and by itself, when
it's present in the soul; and I want to leave aside all talk of
"pay-offs" or anything else that we supposedly get from either
of them.

'So this is what I shall do, if you agree: I shall offer a new
358c   statement of Thrasymachus' position, saying first of all what
sort of thing people claim justice is and the origins they claim
for it; next, that everyone who practises it practises it involuntarily, as something they're forced to do and not as something
good; and thirdly, that it's reasonable that they should behave
like that, because in fact the life of the unjust person is much
better than that of the just. Or so they say. Because, Socrates,
that isn't how *I* think it is; all the same, I'm confused, because
while Thrasymachus and any number of others have gone on
358d   pouring this stuff into my ears, I haven't yet heard the case for
justice put as I want it put. What I want is to hear an encomium
of justice for what it is, in and by itself, and that's what I think
I'll get from you more than from anyone else.

'That's why I'm going to talk forcefully in praise of the
unjust life, in order to illustrate how I want to hear you, in your
turn, attacking injustice and praising justice. So see if this proposal of mine is to your liking.'

'There's nothing I'd like more,' I said. 'Is there any subject
358e   an intelligent person would get greater pleasure from talking
and hearing about, any number of times over?'

'You put it beautifully,' said Glaucon. 'So now you're going
to hear about the first subject I said I'd discuss, the nature and
origins of justice. What they say is that doing injustice is naturally a good thing and being a victim of it a bad thing, but that
the badness of having it done to one outweighs the goodness of

doing it; so that whenever people treat each other unjustly and get a taste of what it's like both to do it and to have it done to them, those who aren't able to choose the one while avoiding 359a the other decide that they'll gain by making a contract – to ban the doing of injustice, and so being the victim of it as well. It's from there, so the story goes, that they start establishing laws, as contracts with each other, calling what is prescribed by the law "lawful" and "just"; and that, people say, is the origin and the essence of justice – something in between what's best for us, acting unjustly and getting away with it, and what's worst of all, being the victim of injustice and being powerless to get one's own back. Being in the middle like this, between the two 359b things, what's "just" is something a person is content to live with, not because it's good, but because it makes up for one's lack of strength to do injustice; anyone who *can* do it, they say, and is truly a man, wouldn't ever make this contract, "not to do or to be the victim of injustice", with anybody at all – he'd be crazy to do any such thing.

'So this, Socrates, or something like it, is the nature of justice, as the theory goes, and this is the sort of origin it has. The next point will be to show that people practise it involuntarily, as it's claimed, because they're too weak to do injustice themselves. This is something we can best see if we conduct a thought-experiment like the following: give each of the two individuals, 359c the just one and the unjust, the same licence to do whatever he wants, and then let's follow them round and observe where their desires will take each of them. We'll then catch the just person red-handed, embarking on the same course as the unjust one out of his desire to have more[25] – which is what every nature naturally pursues as a good, even while law forcibly redirects it towards valuing equal shares for all.

'What would especially offer them the licence I have in mind would be if they had the kind of power it's said once belonged 359d to the ancestor of Gyges the Lydian.[26] They say he was a shepherd in the hire of the then ruler of Lydia; there was a heavy rainstorm, the earth shook, and part of it opened up where he was tending his sheep, leaving a chasm. The sight of it astounded him, and he climbed down into it, whereupon the story is that

among the wonders he observed was a bronze horse, hollow, with little doors in it, and when he poked his head inside he saw that it contained a corpse, to all appearances of greater
359e than human size; and the corpse had nothing in its possession except for a golden ring on its hand, which he removed before climbing out again.

'When the shepherds gathered together in their usual way to make their monthly report to the king on the state of his flocks, our shepherd arrived too, wearing the ring. Well, as he sat down with the others, he happened to turn its mounting
360a towards himself on the inside of his hand, and with that he immediately became invisible to those sitting by him, so that they started talking about him as if he had left. He was astounded and, as he fumbled once more with the ring, turning the mounting away from himself, at once he became visible again. Once he had observed this, he tested the ring to see if it really had this power, and found that turning the ring-mounting inwards made him invisible, while turning it outwards had the opposite effect. As soon as he had established
360b this, he arranged to be one of the delegates reporting to the king himself; having arrived in court, he actually bedded the queen, then with her assistance set upon the king, killed him and took over the kingship.

'Now suppose there were two such rings, and suppose the just person put on one and the unjust person the other: no one – or so it would seem – would turn out to be so steely as to stick with his justice and actually keep his hands off other people's property, when he'd be in a position to go out into the market-place, even, and take what he wanted with no fear
360c of comeback, enter people's houses and sleep with anyone he wanted, kill anyone he wanted, get people out of prison, and in general behave among mere mortals with an impunity the equal of a god's.[27] And in behaving like that he would be behaving no differently from the other individual, the unjust one; the direction of travel for both would be the same.

'And someone might well say that this is weighty evidence that no one is voluntarily just, only under compulsion, on the basis that it's not good for him personally; the claim is that

each and every individual behaves unjustly whenever he thinks
he can. For in fact every man in the world believes there is a   360d
greater personal pay-off from injustice than from justice – and
every man will be correct to believe so, as the proponent of this
sort of position will say; because if someone did get the licence
to act as pictured in my story, and never wanted to do anything
unjust, or get his hands on other people's property, he'd be
thought quite miserable by those who saw him, and quite lacking in intelligence, even while in front of one another people
would sing his praises, trying to pull the wool over each other's
eyes because of their fear of becoming victims of injustice themselves.

'So much for that point, then. As for the actual judgement
between the lives of the pair we're discussing, we'll only be   360e
able to get it right if we contrast the *most* just person with the
most unjust one. The way to separate them is by our not sub-
tracting anything either from the unjust person's injustice or
from the just person's justice, but supposing that each of them
has perfected what he practises. Thus, first of all, let's have the
unjust person doing as expert craftsmen – top steersmen, top
doctors – do, when they distinguish between what's impossible
and what's possible within the limits of their expertise, setting   361a
about the second and letting go of the first; and let him also
have the expert craftsman's ability to correct himself if he
somehow slips up despite his skill. In the same way our unjust
person will set about his unjust enterprises correctly and avoid
detection, if he's to have the degree of injustice required. Anyone who gets caught is to be deemed inferior, for the pinnacle
of injustice is to be reputed to be just when one is not.

'So we must attribute to our most unjust person the most
perfect injustice, taking nothing away from it, instead allowing
him to commit the greatest acts of injustice while still success-   361b
fully contriving for himself the greatest reputation for justice,
and making him capable of correcting himself if he slips up
here and there, despite himself, because he'll have the ability
both to speak persuasively, in case any of his injustices becomes
public, and to use force whenever force is required, because he
has both the manliness and the strength to do so, and a ready

store of friends and material resources. And having set up the
unjust individual like this, let's now describe the just, standing
him side by side with the unjust: a simple and noble man whose
desire, to paraphrase Aeschylus, is not to be thought good but
to be good.

361c   'Thus we must deprive him of the reputation for justice,
since if he's to be thought just he'll have honours and material
rewards because of it, and then it'll be unclear whether it's for
justice's sake that he is as he is, or for the sake of the rewards
and honours. So we need to strip him of everything except justice, and put him in a situation opposite to that of his unjust
counterpart: even though he does nothing unjust, let him have
the greatest reputation for injustice, so that he can pass the test
for justice by showing he won't be softened up by a bad reputation and what that gives rise to. Let him continue with his
361d   situation unchanged right up until his death, thought throughout life to be unjust while actually being just, so that both men
can reach their respective pinnacles, the one of justice and the
other of injustice, and we in our turn can judge which of the
two is happier.'

'Wow! My dear Glaucon,' I said, 'how vigorously you clean
up your two men for judgement, like a pair of statues!'

'I do my best,' he said. 'And given that they are as I've said,
I don't imagine it's a hard task to describe the sorts of life that
361e   await them. So let's do it; and even if it does sound crude, don't
think of it as me speaking, Socrates – just those who praise
injustice above justice.

'What they'll say is this – that if that's his attitude, the just
person will find himself being whipped, stretched on the rack,
362a   chained, his eyes put out with red-hot metal, and finally, having suffered in every bad way imaginable, he'll be impaled on a
stake and so come to realize that what's desirable isn't being
just but being thought to be so. It turns out, on their account,
that what Aeschylus says fits the unjust rather better than the
just – they'll say that insofar as the unjust person's practice
reflects the truth of things, and he doesn't order his life according to what people think, he really and truly desires not to be
thought unjust but to be unjust,

> As he follows the furrow deep within the mind
> From which grow the fruits of wisdom won[28]   362b

– first of all acquiring supreme power in the city, because of his reputation for justice, then taking a wife from whichever family he wishes, giving his own children in marriage as he wishes, making contracts with the partners he wants, and over and above all these things benefiting from the profit that comes from being at ease with injustice; thus if he embarks on lawsuits, whether private or public, he defeats his enemies and comes away better off than they do – which in turn brings him wealth, so enabling him to do good to his friends and harm to his   362c enemies, perform sacrifices and make dedications adequately, even magnificently, to the gods, and serve them, as well as which-ever mere mortals he wishes, much better than the just person can, the net result being – so they claim – that in all probability it must be the unjust rather than the just person that is better loved by the gods, too. And that, Socrates, is how they say that the life in prospect for the unjust person, both from gods and from men, is better than the one awaiting the just person.'

When Glaucon had finished this speech of his, I had it in   362d mind to say something in reply, but his brother Adimantus intervened: 'Socrates, you're surely not supposing that the case for injustice has been sufficiently stated?'

'Why should I not?' I asked.

'Something important has been left out,' he said; 'the very thing that needed saying most of all.'

'Well,' I replied, 'the saying is "let brother stand by brother", so if our friend here is falling a bit short, you'd better provide reinforcements – though actually, as far as I'm concerned, what he did say is already quite enough to floor me and render me   362e incapable of coming to justice's aid.'

'You're talking nonsense,' he said. 'Anyway, I've got some new points; hear me out. What I'm thinking is that we need to rehearse the arguments opposing the ones "our friend here" put – arguments praising justice and denigrating injustice; that is, if we're to get clearer about what I think Glaucon wants to say.

'When fathers give advice to sons, and indeed when anyone
363a advises anyone he cares about, I imagine they urge on them the
need to be just, and they do so by singing the praises not of justice, for what it is in itself, but rather of the opportunities that
come from it for earning a good reputation. They suppose that
things like power and a good marriage – all the things on Glaucon's list just now – accrue to a person who's thought to be just,
simply from being thought so, and they want their charges to
have those things; their starting-point is that they're available
to the just person merely from that good reputation he has.

'These people have still more to say on the subject of reputations. They throw in being in good standing with the gods,
too – there's no end to the list of good things they say the gods
363b will give to the pious; just as the noble Hesiod and Homer tell
us, Hesiod reporting that for the just the gods make oaks "Bear
acorns on their topmost branches, honeybees below," while
"The soft wool weighs down their flocks of fleecy sheep;"[29] and
many, many other good things similar to these. Homer says
much the same in these lines:

As when a king unsullied by blame and fearing the gods
363c   Upholds straight judgement, and the black earth bears him
Abundant barley and wheat, and his trees bend, fruit-weighted;
His flocks multiply, and the teeming sea offers him fish . . .[30]

The good things Musaeus and his son give to the just from the
gods are racier than these: in their songs they take the pious off
363d to Hades to recline at a symposium they've specially arranged
for them, providing them with garlands and having them spend
the rest of the time in a drunken stupor, apparently on the basis
that the finest reward for goodness is to be eternally drunk.
Others extend the rewards from the gods even further than
this, claiming that whoever is pious and keeps his oaths "behind
him leaves" children and children of children[31] for generations
to come.

'These and others like them are the encomia they sing to
justice; as for the impious and unjust, these they bury in Hades
in some sort of slime[32] or force them to carry water in a sieve,[33]

even bringing them into disrepute while they're still alive, and   363e
giving the same list of punishments for the unjust that Glaucon
went through for those that are just but reputed to be unjust,
because they can't think of any others.

'So that's how the two kinds, the just and the unjust, are
praised and blamed. And then, Socrates, just think about
another way people talk about justice and injustice – ordinary
people as well as poets. Everybody with one voice sings out that   364a
while moderation and justice are fine enough, they're still hard
and troublesome to achieve; lack of restraint and injustice, on
the other hand, are pleasant and easy to acquire, and shameful
only by convention, because people think them so. They say
that behaving unjustly is for the most part more profitable than
behaving justly, and they're ready and willing to call bad people
happy if they're rich, and give them respect in public and in private, while disrespecting and disregarding those who show the   364b
weakness they associate with poverty, at the same time as they
admit that they're better people than the other lot.

'But of all the things people say about justice and injustice,
there's nothing more astonishing than what they say about the
attitude of the gods to goodness. They actually claim that the
gods themselves allot misfortunes and a bad life to many good
people, and the opposite to those who are the opposite of good.
Beggars and soothsayers go knocking on rich men's doors and
persuade them that they have a special power they're able to call
on from the gods through sacrifices and incantations, enabling
them to cancel out, for the cost of a few nice feasts, any little
injustice that may have occurred, whether their client's own or   364c
their ancestors'; or if the client desires to make an enemy of his
suffer, for a small consideration they'll damage him, no matter
whether he's just or unjust, because, they claim, they have certain binding spells that will persuade the gods to serve them.

'And for all these claims they bring on poets as witnesses,
some quoting them to confirm that being bad is easy, as in

> The ways to be bad are plenty, the choice easy –
> The path is smooth, the destination close;   364d
> But to goodness, the gods ordain, we must sweat our way[34]

along some road or other that they tell us is long, rough and steep. Others cite Homer as confirming that gods can be won over by human blandishments; didn't he actually say that

> Our prayers move the gods themselves;
> By sacrifice we turn them, human though we are,
> Through soothing vows, by pouring wine, the smell of fat,
> If once we overstep the mark and err?[35]

364e

And they produce a whole cacophony of books by Musaeus and Orpheus, descendants – they say – of the Moon and the Muses, using these writings as the basis for their sacrificial goings-on, and managing to persuade not just individuals but whole cities that there really are purifying rites available to release them from their injustices, through sacrifices and play-
365a ful diversions – rites for those still living, rites for the dead too. They call them "initiations", claiming that they spare us the suffering promised by Hades, and threatening terrible out-comes for those who haven't performed their sacrifices.

'When people say all these things, Socrates,' said Adimantus, 'about the respect or lack of it accorded to goodness and to badness – given what they say, and how frequently they say it, what sort of effect do you think it has, when they hear it, on the souls of the young, if as so often they're equipped by nature with the capacity for flitting like bees between all the different things they hear, and drawing their conclusions from them as
365b to what sort of person they should be, and what sort of course they should steer to live the best life? I imagine any one of them would be likely to put that question of Pindar's to himself: "Will straight justice scale the higher wall/ Or crooked tricks?" Which should I use to "shield me through life?"[36] What's prom-ised me if I'm just, they say, is no use to me unless I'm also thought to be just: merely a lot of trouble, and clear losses on the balance-sheet. If I'm unjust, on the other hand, then pro-vided I've secured my reputation for justice I'm promised a life
365c in clover. So, since – as revealed to me by the wise[37] – "to seem outmuscles even truth", and determines our happiness, it's to that I must direct my whole effort; I must create a shadow-

painting of goodness all around me, a front to mask my real identity, with Archilochus' wise old fox,[38] "profit-mad" and shifty, hitched behind all the while.

' "But surely," someone will object, "if one is bad it's not easy to keep it permanently hidden." True, but then no great achievement comes easily; hard though it is, if we're to be 365d happy that's the way we must go – because that's where the track leads, to judge from what I hear. In order to stay hidden, we'll form secret societies and brotherhoods, and there are teachers of persuasive technique who for a fee offer expertise in public and forensic oratory, so we'll ensure there's no come-back for our grabbing what we want by a mixture of sweet reason and force.

' "But the *gods* will notice, and there's no force we can use against them." Well, if they don't exist, or else human affairs are of no concern to them, why should we be concerned about hiding from them? And if they do exist and do care about us, 365e surely the only source of our knowledge, or hearsay, about them lies in the laws and in the poets who have given us their genealogies – the very same authorities that tell us the gods are open to having their minds changed by sacrifices, "soothing vows"[39] and dedications? Which is it to be? Either we have to believe both claims, or neither. Anyway, if we *are* to believe them, it follows that we should live unjustly and sacrifice to 366a the gods from the proceeds. The fact is that if we're just we'll merely avoid being penalized by the gods, while giving up the profits that come from injustice; whereas if we're unjust we'll get the profits and still come away with no penalty by praying as we "overstep the mark and err",[40] so convincing the gods to leave us alone.

' "But surely there'll be payment in Hades for any injustices we've done up here on earth; either we'll pay, or our children's children[41] will." "But my friend," our young spokesman will say as he does his calculations, "there are those initiations and their purifying gods – they have great power, as the greatest 366b cities tell us, along with those children of gods, the poets, who have set themselves up as the gods' mouthpieces, and declare with authority that these things are so."

'So what further argument is there that could be given for our choosing justice over extreme injustice, when combining that with a counterfeit seemliness will allow us to prosper with gods and men exactly as we would wish, whether in life or after death – as most people tell us, and as the top people tell us too?

366c Given everything I've said, is there really any way, Socrates, that anyone with the slightest resources of intellect, physique, money or family would be ready to give respect to justice and not laugh at hearing it praised? I tell you, if there actually is anyone who's capable of demonstrating the falsity of what we've said, and is sufficiently clear that justice is the best thing, I imagine that he himself has a lot of sympathy with the unjust, and isn't angry with them, because he recognizes that no one will hold off from injustice unless either he's endowed by the gods with a natural distaste for it or he's acquired the requisite

366d knowledge; he'll recognize that everybody else is involuntarily just, only attacking injustice because they're unmanly or old or suffer from some other form of weakness and lack the power to do it themselves. That's patently the fact of the matter, because the first of them that moves into power is the first into injustice – as far into it as he's capable of going.

'And the sole cause of all of this is what started Glaucon here and me off on our challenge to you, Socrates: what we

366e want to say to you is, "Come on! Here are all you people claiming to be supporters of justice, but from the heroes whose utterances have survived, from the beginning of history, right down to the men of the present age, there's never yet been a single person who attacked injustice, or praised justice, except in terms of the things they give rise to: reputations, honours, cash in hand. No one, whether in poetry or in ordinary discussions,[42] has ever yet properly described the effect that each of the two things has, by virtue of its own inherent power, on the soul it resides in, even when it goes unnoticed by both gods and men – how one of them is the greatest of all the bad things a

367a soul contains within itself, while justice is the greatest of goods. If only you'd all been telling us that from the beginning, and trying to convince us of it since we were children, then we wouldn't be guarding against each other as we do now, in case one of us behaves unjustly, but instead each of us would be his own best guard,[43] terrified that by behaving unjustly he'd find himself cohabiting with the worst thing of all."

'Those are the points, Socrates, and no doubt there are still others I haven't mentioned, that Thrasymachus or perhaps someone else could make on the subject of justice and injustice; though in my view it would be a vulgar inversion of the pow- 367b ers of the two things. As for me – there's no need for me to hide it from you – it's because I'm so keen to hear you put the opposite case that I've expressed myself as I have, with all the force I could muster. So don't just use your argument to prove that justice is a stronger thing than injustice; show us what each of the two things does to its possessor, in and by itself, to make one of them a bad thing and the other a good thing – and take away the reputations that go with them, in the way that Glaucon urged. Because unless you remove the reputations they truly deserve, and substitute the ones they don't deserve, we'll say that you're praising *being thought to be just*, not *justice*, 367c and directing your fire at being thought to be, not being, unjust, so that you're actually advocating covert injustice, and agreeing with Thrasymachus that justice is good for someone else, being what serves the interests of the stronger, while what's unjust is what is in one's own interests – because it *pays* – and against the interests of the weaker.

'Well now, since you've agreed that justice belongs to the class of the greatest goods, the ones it's desirable to possess not merely for the sake of the things that come from them but much more for their own sake, like sight, hearing, intelligence – health too, of course, and any other good thing that's productive by virtue of its own nature and not simply because people 367d *think* one has it: now you need to speak in praise of this very aspect of justice, through which it benefits the one who has it, in and by itself, while injustice causes harm. Things like rewards and reputations you must leave for others to praise, because whereas I'd put up with listening to anybody else using this way of praising justice and criticizing injustice, lauding or disparaging the reputation or the pay-off one gets from one or the other, from you I won't accept it, unless you tell me I must,

367e because you've actually spent the whole of your life examining
the very matter in question. So as I say, don't only use your
argument to prove that justice is a stronger thing than injustice,
but also show us what each of the two things does, in and by
itself, to its possessor – whether or not gods and men notice –
to make one a bad thing and the other good.'

Now I'd always admired the natural qualities of both Glaucon
and Adimantus, but I was particularly delighted by their show-
368a ing on this occasion. 'You're true sons of your father,' I said;
'the opening line of that elegy fits you beautifully – the one
Glaucon's lover wrote about you because of your distinguished
action in the battle of Megara:[44] "Ariston's sons, godlike scions
to a glorious father." That, I think, my friends, is just how it is:
it's a quite godlike state you're in if you're really not convinced
that injustice is a better thing than justice, and yet can still
speak so powerfully on the subject. And you do seem to me
368b genuinely unconvinced. My evidence for this has to come from
what I know of you independently, because if I had to rely on
your speeches themselves, I wouldn't believe your disclaimers.
However, the more inclined I am to believe you, the more I am
at a loss about what to do. On the one hand, I have no resources
to bring to justice's aid; I think it's beyond me, and a sign for
me of that is that you didn't accept what I said to Thrasymachus, which I thought showed how superior justice was to
injustice. On the other hand, I can't not come to her aid; I'm
368c frightened that it's quite impious to stand by and give up on
justice when she's being abused, instead of trying to defend her
for so long as one has breath and can string words together. So
the best thing is to act as her bodyguard[45] as best I can.'

Well, Glaucon and the others begged me to defend justice by
any means available, and not to give up on the argument; they
said I must track down our two quarries, to find out what each
of them is and what the truth really is about the benefits they
bring. So I said just what I thought: 'It's no mean inquiry we're
undertaking, it seems to me; it's one that requires sharp eye-

sight. So, since we're not experts,' I said, 'I think we should   368d
approach the subject as if we were in the sort of situation where
someone had told a collection of not very sharp-sighted individuals to read something in small letters from a distance, and
then one of them noticed that the same letters were to be found
somewhere else, only bigger and on something bigger – in such
a situation, I imagine, it would be a godsend to read these first
and so be in a position to examine the smaller letters and see if
they really are the same.'

'Yes, certainly,' said Adimantus. 'But what are you seeing
that's like this, Socrates, in the context of the search for jus-   368e
tice?'

'I'll tell you,' I said. 'We talk about justice as belonging to a
single individual; I think we also talk about it as belonging to a
whole city?'

'Certainly we do,' he said.

'Well, is a city something bigger than an individual?'

'It is,' he said.

'Then maybe there'll be more justice in the bigger thing, and
it'll be easier to grasp there. So, if you're both happy with this,   369a
we'll first go looking for the kind of thing it is in cities, and then
on this basis we'll go on to examine it in each individual, that
is, by examining the resemblance to the bigger thing in the character of the smaller.'[46]

'What you're proposing looks fine to me,' he said.

[Book B   'Well then,' I said, 'if we were to describe a city in the pro-
begins]   cess of coming into existence, and watch it as it did so,
would we be able to see its justice coming into existence too,
and its injustice?'

'Maybe we would,' he said.

'Then when our description is complete, we can hope that   369b
what we're looking for will be easier to see?'

'Yes, much easier.'

'So you think we should attempt to carry through this project? I imagine it'll be no small undertaking;[47] so think hard
about it.'

'Consider it done,' said Adimantus; 'no need for delay.'

'Then I'll begin,' I said. 'Cities come into existence, I imagine, because in fact none of us is self-sufficient; taken by ourselves, each one of us is deficient in many respects. Or do you think there's some other origin for the founding of cities?'

'No, I don't,' he said.

369c   'Thus it will be because one person recruits another to fill this or that need, and another another, and so on, and because our needs are many, that we gather many people together to live in a single location as partners and helpers, calling this shared habitation a "city".[48] Right?'

'Yes, certainly.'

'Then one person shares something with another, if he does, or takes his share from another, because he thinks doing so is better for himself?'

'Yes, quite.'

'So come on,' I said, 'let's use our conversation to create a city from scratch. But what will actually be creating it will be our needs, it seems.'

'No question.'

369d   'And the first and greatest of those needs will be for the provision of food, to enable us to exist and live.'

'Yes, absolutely.'

'And the second greatest will be for housing, the third for clothing and things like that.'

'That's right.'

'So tell me,' I said, 'how big will a city need to be to provide for all these needs? Presumably there will have to be one person to do the farming, one for the building, and someone else for the weaving – or shall we add a shoemaker to the list, or someone who looks after some other aspect of the body's needs?'

'Yes, surely.'

'And by this reckoning, at any rate, the minimum number of
369e   men necessary for a city will be four or five.'

'Apparently so.'

'Then here's my next question: should each one of these share what he does with the whole group, so that, for example, the farmer provides food for four, spending four times the effort and four times the number of hours on producing food in order to share it with the others; or should he ignore the others and make a quarter of the food just for himself in a quarter 370a of the time, using the other three quarters to get himself a house, a cloak and some shoes without having the bother of sharing anything with the others, doing his own thing himself by himself?'

Adimantus said, 'Actually, Socrates, the first way is probably easier than the second.'

'There wouldn't be anything the least strange in that,' I said. 'Now that you say it, it occurs to me that in the first place each 370b of us is not born exactly like everybody else, but with different natural capacities, one of us for doing one kind of work, another for another. Don't you think so?'

'Yes, I do.'

'Well, will someone be more effective when he's working as one individual in many different areas of expertise, or when he confines himself to one area?'

'When he confines himself to one,' Adimantus said.

'And I think it's also clear that if someone misses the right moment for doing something, it's ruined.'

'Yes, that's right.'

'Because, I imagine, the job in hand won't wait until the 370c person doing it has the time; he's got to do whatever the job demands, and not just as a sideline.'

'Indeed he has.'

'From which I conclude that more is achieved, and better and more easily, when one person is doing one thing, according to his natural capacities, at the time it needs doing, and when he isn't having to do everything else as well.'

'Yes, absolutely.'

'Well then, Adimantus, we need more than four citizens if we're to provide the things we were talking about. The farmer evidently won't be making his own plough, if it's to be a good one, or his own hoe, or any other farming tool. It's the same 370d with the builder; there are lots of things he'll need – the weaver, too, and the shoemaker.'

'True.'

'And if carpenters, metal-workers and lots of other craftsmen of that general sort become partners in our little city, they already make it quite big.'

'Yes, certainly.'

'Still, it wouldn't yet be *so* big if we added oxherds and shep-
370e herds and other sorts of herdsmen, so that the farmers could have oxen to plough with, and the builders as well as the farmers could yoke them up for fetching and carrying, and the weavers and shoemakers would have skins and fleeces to work with.'

'It won't be a small city, either,' said Adimantus, 'if it has all of this.'

'And there's more to come,' I said; 'it'll be virtually impossible to found the city itself in a place where it won't need imports.'

'Yes, impossible.'

'In that case it'll require still more people, to bring in what it needs from another city.'

'It will.'

'And if our agent goes empty-handed, taking with him none
371a of the things the other side needs in order to fill the gaps in *their* resources, he'll come away empty-handed too. Isn't that so?'

'It seems so to me.'

'When it comes to domestic production, then, our city will need to produce not only enough for its own requirements, but enough of the kinds of things others require too.'

'It will, yes.'

'So it will need more farmers and more craftsmen.'

'Yes, it will.'

'And I imagine it will also need those other "agents" to do the exporting and importing in each case. These are merchants, right?'

'Yes.'

'Then we'll need merchants too.'

'Yes, certainly.'

371b   'Yes, and if this trade is by sea, the city will need lots more people too, experts in working with the sea.'

'Lots of *them*.'

'And how about in the city itself? How will the different

categories of people share the products of their own labour with each other? That, after all, was the point of making the city we're founding a partnership.'

'Clearly', he said, 'they'll share things by selling and buying.'

'So now we'll need a market-place, and a system of tokens,[49] to enable exchange to take place.'

'Yes, certainly.'

'Now if the farmer or another craftsman brings something 371c he makes to the market-place, and doesn't arrive at the same time as people who want to make an exchange for his products, will he spend time sitting in the market-place away from the exercise of his own craft?'

'Not at all,' said Adimantus; 'there are people who see the situation and set themselves up as the agents here: in cities that are founded correctly these will usually be the weakest physical specimens, useless for doing any other sort of work. They have to stay permanently around the market-place, exchanging money 371d for things when people need to sell and things for money when people need to buy.'

'This is the need, then,' I said, 'that causes retailers to come into being in our city. You agree that "retailer" is the name we give to someone who sits in the market-place acting as middle-man in relation to selling and buying, "merchants" being those who move around from city to city?'

'Yes, of course.'

'And there is, I think, yet another category of people who act for us, comprising those whose share in intellectual qualities is 371e not quite enough for it to be worth making them our partners, but who possess sufficient physical strength for manual labour; they sell the physical resources others need, calling what they get for it their "hire", and that, I suppose, is why they're called "hired labourers". Right?'

'Yes.'

'There will apparently be hired labourers too, then, making up the complement of a city?'

'I think so.'

'So, Adimantus, has our city now grown to a point where it's complete?'

'Maybe.'

'So where on earth shall we find its justice or injustice? Of those aspects of the city we've examined, which is the one it will have originated with?'

372a   'I can't think, Socrates,' said Adimantus, 'unless perhaps it's to be found somehow in the mutual need all these categories of people have for each other.'

'Perhaps you're right,' I said; 'we must look and see at once – no holding back. So first of all let's see how our people will occupy their time, now that they're provided for in the way we've described – presumably they'll spend their time producing food, wine, cloaks and shoes. They'll build houses, and in summer they'll work away mostly naked and shoeless, while in 372b   the winter they'll wear whatever clothes and shoes they need to protect them. They'll feed themselves by preparing barley-meal and wheat-meal, now kneading it, now baking it, and serving up noble cakes and loaves on mats of reeds or freshly washed leaves, reclining on palliasses strewn with yew and myrtle; and they'll feast themselves and their beloveds,[50] drinking their wine with garlands on their heads and hymns to the 372c   gods, enjoying the pleasure of each other's company, and taking care not to produce offspring out of proportion to their wealth, in order to protect themselves against poverty or war.'

Glaucon interjected: 'It's a bit lacking in sauce, this feast you're providing for our men!'

'True,' I said. 'I forgot that they'll have their sauce too, and obviously things like salt and olives and cheese; and yes, they'll do as people do in the countryside, and boil up onions and greens. And I imagine we'll provide them with desserts of figs 372d   and chickpeas and beans, and they'll roast myrtle berries and acorns on the fire to a moderate accompaniment of wine. They'll live their lives like this, I expect peacefully and in good health, dying of old age and handing on a similar lifestyle to their descendants.'

And Glaucon said, 'Socrates, suppose you were putting together a city of pigs: would the fodder you'd provide for them be any different from this?'

'So how should I be treating them, Glaucon?' I asked.

'Just in the usual way,' he said; 'anyone who wasn't going to be in discomfort, I imagine, would have couches to recline on, tables to dine from, all the sauces and desserts they have now.' 372e

'Fine,' I said; 'I see what you're saying. Evidently we're not just looking into how a city comes into being, but how a *luxurious* city does so. Well, perhaps that's no bad thing; perhaps by looking at this kind of city, too, we'll be able to observe how justice and injustice take root in cities. Now, I myself think the *true* city to be the one we were describing just now – a healthy kind of city, one might say. But if the two of you want us to examine not just this city, but one that's in the grip of a fever, there's nothing to stop us doing that. It appears that there are 373a some people who won't be satisfied with what we've offered so far, and with the kind of lifestyle we've proposed: there'll have to be couches, tables and other furniture, sauces too, perfumes, incense, prostitutes and pastries, all of them in every variety available. The things we were talking about before, basic necessities like houses, cloaks and shoes, are no longer enough; no, we're to start painting and embroidering, and to get ourselves some gold and ivory and everything like that. Right?'

'Yes,' said Glaucon.

'Then we'll need to increase the size of the city again, because 373b that healthy one won't suffice any longer. We'll have to add to its bulk, multiplying it by adding elements that go beyond the basic requirements of a city, like hunters of all different kinds, and producers of imitations, many of them concerned with shapes and colours, many with music – poets and their underlings, like rhapsodes,[51] actors, chorus-members, contractors; makers of all sorts of manufactured objects, too, not least those 373c used for female adornment. Then again, we'll need more people to do things for us – don't you agree? Child-overseers,[52] wet-nurses, nurses, hairdressers, barbers; people to make those sauces; meat-cooks? Then we'll need swineherds too; we didn't have them in our previous city, because they weren't needed, but the new one will need them on top of everything else[53] – as it will need a whole lot of other domestic animals for people to eat. Right?'

'Of course.'

373d   'Then we'll have much more need of doctors, too, if we live like that than if we lived as before?'[54]

'Yes, much more.'

'And the territory, I imagine, that was adequate to feed the population then will definitely now be small rather than adequate. Am I right?'

'You are.'

'So if we're to have enough land for pasture and ploughing, we must cut off a slice of our neighbours' territory, and if they too abandon themselves to the unbounded acquisition of wealth,
373e   going beyond the limit set by what we can't do without, they must do the same to us.'

'It's quite inevitable, Socrates,' he said.

'So will the next thing be, Glaucon, that we find ourselves at war? Or what do you think will happen?'

'Just that,' he said.

'And let's not say anything at all, yet, about any bad effect war may have, or about any good it does either; let's just say that we've found an origin for war itself, in the very things that are most of all at the root of any of the troubles that befall cities, whether as a result of individual or of communal action.'

'Yes, certainly.'

'Well then, my friend, we'll need to make the city even larger,
374a   and not just a little larger – larger by a whole army, to go out and do battle with the oncoming enemy, in defence of all that wealth and of the things we were listing just now.'

'How so?' asked Glaucon. 'Won't the citizens themselves be up to it?'

'No,' I said, 'not if you and all of us were right in agreeing as we did when we were first moulding our city. What we agreed, I think, was that it was impossible for one individual to work well in many different areas of expertise.'

'That's true,' he said.

374b   'Well then,' I said, 'doesn't it take expertise to compete for victory in war?'

'Very much so,' he said.

'Are you suggesting, then, that we should be more concerned about expertise in shoemaking than in warfare?'

'Not at all.'

'But after all, we weren't in favour of allowing the shoe-maker to try to be a farmer at the same time, or a weaver or a builder; he had to be just a shoemaker, in order for us to have our shoemaking done well, and we similarly assigned to each one of the rest that single function for which his natural capaci- 374c ties fitted him, which he'd work at throughout life, freed from other kinds of work, so that he didn't miss the right moments for doing things and could produce good results. Now take warfare: isn't it of quite the utmost importance that we have good results here? Or is it so easy a thing that an expert in farm-ing, or shoemaking, or whatever it may be will be an expert in soldiering too – when there isn't a person in the world who could become a decent *petteia*-player[55] or dice-player if he did it as a sideline and not as his occupation from childhood on? Do we suppose that someone only has to pick up the tools of the 374d soldier's trade, a shield or a weapon, for him to be transformed immediately into a decent practitioner of hoplite fighting[56] or of any kind of fighting there is in a war? No other tool has that effect – just picking it up won't make someone a craftsman, or an athlete, and indeed it won't even be useful to anyone who doesn't have the relevant expertise and hasn't put in the right amount of practice.'

'Yes,' he said, 'if tools could do that they'd be worth a fortune.'

'So,' I said, 'to the degree that the function of our guards is 374e more important than anyone else's,[57] it will be one that requires that much more freedom from other tasks, more expertise, too, and more attention.'

'That's my view,' he said.

'So it'll also require a nature suited to the activity in question?'

'Of course.'

'Then it'll be *our* task, apparently, if we're really up to it, to pick out which natural dispositions are suitable for guarding a city, and what general types they belong to.'[58]

'Yes, that's our task.'

'Zeus!' I exclaimed. 'It's no small thing we've taken on. Still, we mustn't lose heart, for as long as we have the strength.'

'Quite right,' he said; 'we mustn't.' 375a

'Well then,' I said, 'do you think there's any natural difference, when it comes to being a guard, between a well-bred young dog and a young man of good breeding?'[59]

'What do you have in mind?'

'It's this – presumably both of them need acute senses, the ability to respond nimbly if they do sense something, and also strength in case they catch something and it puts up a fight.'

'They'll certainly need all that.'

'Courage too, if they're going to fight well.'

'Of course.'

375b   'And will we easily find a horse, say, or a dog or any other creature that's brave without being spirited?[60] You must have noticed how irresistible, how invincible, a thing spirit is in a creature; its presence renders any soul that has it fearless and unconquerable in the face of anything.'

'Indeed, I have noticed.'

'It's clear, then, what our guards must be like in relation to their bodily attributes.'

'Yes.'

'And also what their souls must be like,[61] namely spirited.'

'That too.'

'How then, Glaucon,' I asked, 'are we going to avoid their being savage both to one another and to the other citizens,[62] if that's what their natural dispositions are to be?'

'Zeus!' he said; 'it's not going to be easy.'

375c   'But it's surely a requirement that they should be gentle towards those who belong to them and be aggressive only towards their enemies – otherwise they won't need to wait for others to destroy them, because they'll do it for themselves.'

'True,' he said.

'So what shall we do about it?' I asked. Where will we find a disposition that's simultaneously gentle *and* unusually spirited? A gentle nature, presumably, is opposed to a spirited one.'

'Apparently so.'

'Yet surely someone who lacks either of these will never make a good guard. Since combining them looks like an impos-
375d   sibility, the conclusion must be that a good guard is impossible.'

'Likely so,' he said.

Finding myself at a loss, I looked back at what we'd been saying. 'My friend, it's no wonder we're at a loss,' I said, 'because we've lost sight of the analogy we proposed.'

'What's your point?'

'We failed to notice that there actually are natural dispositions of the sort we thought didn't exist – ones that combine the opposites in question.'

'And where do we find these?'

'One can observe them in other animals too, but most of all in the very creature we were comparing to our guard. I imagine you recognize it as a characteristic of well-bred dogs to be as 375e gentle as they could possibly be towards people they are familiar with, and those they know, and the opposite towards those they don't know.'

'Very much so.'

'In which case what we were talking about isn't impossible, and what we're looking for in a guard isn't an unnatural combination.'

'It appears not.'

'Well now, do you think there's a further requirement, if someone's to be fit to be one of our guards, namely, that in addition to being spirited he should be by nature a philosopher?'

'What are you saying?' Glaucon asked. 'I don't understand.' 376a

'Here's something else you'll observe in a dog,' I said, 'something it's truly amazing to find in a beast like that.'

'What's this?'

'A dog is fierce to anyone it sees and doesn't recognize, even without having been badly treated; anyone it does recognize, it fawns on, even without yet having had any good treatment from him. Haven't you ever thought to be amazed by that?'

'I can't say I've paid it much attention up till now,' he said; 'but evidently enough that is how dogs do behave.'

'But it is, surely, a subtle aspect of their nature, and one 376b that's truly philosophical.'

'Explain in what way.'

'Insofar', I said, 'as they divide what they see into friend and enemy just according to whether they've learned to know it or not. And how wouldn't it be a sign of a love of learning to distinguish what belongs to one and what doesn't on the basis of knowledge and ignorance?'[63]

'It must be,' he said; 'that's for sure!'[64]

'But surely', I said, 'loving learning is the same thing as being philosophical – loving wisdom?'[65]

'The same.'

'Then should we be confident about proposing, in the case 376c of humans too, that if they are to be gentle towards those who belong and are known to them, they must have a natural love of wisdom and learning?'

'We should.'

'So the person who's going to be a fine and a good guard of a city will according to us have a nature combining love of wisdom, spirit, speed and strength.'

'Yes, absolutely,' he said.

'So much for him, then, and the basic qualities he'll need. But how shall we have these people brought up and educated?[66] Or will consideration of that topic help us at all to form a 376d view on this question our whole investigation is about, namely, how justice and injustice come into existence in a city? We don't want to miss out things we should discuss; but neither do we want to spin things out longer than necessary.'

Here Glaucon's brother broke in. 'Yes,' he said 'I certainly expect investigating this new topic will help.'[67]

'Zeus!' I exclaimed. 'Dear Adimantus, in that case, we'd better not give up on it, even if it turns out to be a somewhat lengthy investigation.'[68]

'No, we'd better not.'

'So come on, let's imagine we're telling a story, you and I, with all the time in the world; let's talk about how to educate our men.'[69]

'Yes, that's what we should do.'

376e   'What sort of education will it be? It's hard, perhaps, to do better than the one that time itself has discovered, which I suppose is physical exercise for bodies, music for the soul.'

'That's true.'

'So shall we start educating them with music before we start their physical education?'

'Of course.'

'Do you count compositions in words as belonging to music?' I asked.

'I do.'

'There being two kinds of compositions, one true, one false?'

'Yes.'

'And we should educate them in both, but start with the false kind?' 377a

'I don't know what you have in mind,' he said.

'You do know', I said, 'that we begin by telling little children stories – which, presumably, are generally speaking false, even if they contain elements of truth; and we use stories with children before physical education.'

'That's so.'

'So that's what I had in mind when I said that we must start with musical before physical education.'

'Quite right,' he said.

'You're aware, then, that the most important part of any enterprise is the way it's begun, especially when we're dealing 377b with something young and tender? That is when a thing is best moulded, and when it takes on whatever stamp one wants to impress on it.'

'Just so.'

'Then we won't be very ready, will we, to let our children listen to any old stories, crafted by any old story-tellers, and so have their souls take in beliefs that are for the most part opposite to the ones we'll think they should have when their formation is complete?'

'There's no way we'll allow that.'

'So apparently the first thing we must do is to supervise our 377c story-tellers, approving any story they put together that has the required quality and rejecting any that doesn't. We'll induce nurses and mothers to tell children the ones we've approved, and to use stories to mould their souls far rather than their hands to mould their bodies. But most of the stories they currently tell will have to be thrown out.'

'Which ones are they?' he asked.

'If we look at the grander stories,' I said, 'we'll be looking at the less grand ones too;[70] grand or not so grand, they must share the same pattern and have the same effect. Don't you think so?'

377d 'I do,' he said, 'but I don't understand which ones you're calling "grander".'

'They're the ones Hesiod and Homer told,' I said, 'and the other poets. What they do, I presume, is to put together false stories to tell mankind; they did it in the past, and they're still doing it.'

'Which stories are these,' he asked, 'and what's the fault you find in them?'

'The fault we should condemn first and foremost,' I said, 'especially if the falsehood is not a pretty one.'[71]

'What fault is that?'

377e 'When someone uses his story to misrepresent the nature of gods and heroes, like a painter painting a portrait that is nothing like the intended subject.'

'Yes,' he said, 'it's certainly right to condemn that sort of thing. But what do we have in mind here – what sorts of things are we talking about?'

'First of all,' I said, 'there's the greatest falsehood we hear told, about the greatest subjects, which was not at all prettily conceived by its teller: that Uranus did what Hesiod says he did

378a to Cronus, and that Cronus in his turn took his revenge on Uranus. As for what Cronus is supposed to have done and have had done to him by *his* son,[72] even if it all happened to be true I shouldn't have thought we'd be very ready to have it told to the young and silly; at best we'd keep quiet about it, and if for some reason we had to come clean, we'd make sure as few as possible heard about it, under a vow of secrecy, and then only after they'd sacrificed not a pig but some large and unobtainable creature, so that as small a number of people as possible would be in on it.'

'Yes,' he said, 'it certainly causes trouble when people say these things.'

378b 'Right, Adimantus, and they won't be said in our city. Nor will it be said within a young person's hearing that someone who committed the most serious injustices, even down to inflicting all sorts of punishments on an unjust father, wouldn't be doing anything out of the ordinary, merely what the first and greatest of gods themselves did before them.'[73]

'Zeus, no!' he exclaimed. 'I'm with you. Saying such things isn't helpful.'

'Right. Nor in general is it helpful', I replied, 'for it to be said that gods make war, plot and fight against other gods. It isn't 378c true in any case; and if we want those who are going to be guarding our city to think it quite shameful to fall out easily with each other, the last thing we need is to have them being told stories or shown embroidered images of gigantomachies,[74] and all sorts of other fallings-out between gods and heroes and their kith and kin. If ever we're going to persuade our future guards that no one has ever yet fallen out with a fellow-citizen, and that doing so is actually impious, then *that*'s the sort of thing that both the old men and the old women must be saying 378d to little children from the beginning,[75] and the poets too must be forced to compose stories for them along similar lines when they're growing older. Stories like the one about Hera's entrapment by her son, or Hephaestus' father[76] hurling him out of heaven when he made to protect his mother from a beating, or the battles between the gods in Homer's poem[77] – all these will be banned from the city, whether or not they're done with allegorical intent. A young person is not capable of telling the difference between what is allegory and what is not, and whatever someone accepts as one of his beliefs at that age tends to 378e be hard to eradicate or do anything about. All this explains, I hope, why we must make it an absolute priority that what they hear first should be the very finest stories composed for the encouragement of excellence.'[78]

'Yes, that's fair enough,' he said. 'But if someone were to ask us once again[79] what you're referring to – which stories these actually are, which ones would we point to?'

My response to him was to say, 'Adimantus, what you and I are doing presently isn't writing poetry, it's founding a city; 379a and city-founders only have to know the general outlines of what's permissible in the stories the poets compose, or not permissible – they don't have to make up stories themselves!'

'Right,' he said; 'and now for this very point: what *are* these "general outlines" in relation to talk about gods?'

'Something like this, perhaps,' I said: 'whether he is making the gods[80] the subject of epic, of lyric, or of tragic verse, a poet must surely always portray them as they actually are.'

'He must, yes.'

379b   'Then not only are the gods – being gods – in fact good,[81] but they must be said to be so?'

'Of course.'

'And nothing good is harmful, is it?'

'I don't think so.'

'Well, does anything that is not harmful do any harm?'

'How could it?'

'And does what does no harm have any bad effects?'

'Again, no.'

'But what has no bad effects won't be a cause of anything bad, either?'

'How could it be?'

'Another question: what is good – is it beneficial?'

'Yes.'

'So it's responsible for things going well.'

'Yes.'

'So what is good won't be responsible for everything; it will be responsible for things that are as they should be, but not for bad things.'

379c   'Yes, absolutely.'

'So,' I said, 'neither will gods be responsible for everything, as most people say, since in fact they are good; they'll be responsible for a few things in human life, but for many things they won't be. The fact is that the good things we have are far fewer than the bad, and for those good things we must hold no one responsible but gods, while for the causes of the bad things we must look somewhere else, not in the gods.'

'I think what you say is very true,' he said.

379d   'So,' I said, 'we mustn't put up with Homer or any other poet if he makes the mindless mistake of asserting that "two jars"

> stand on the threshold of the hall of Zeus
> Filled full with fates, one good, fearful the other,

and that whoever receives from Zeus a mixture from both jars, to him

> Bad befalls, but tomorrow good will follow,

whereas if someone gets an unmixed portion from the second jar rather than a mixture,

> Foul famine drives him to the corners of the fair earth;[82]

nor will we put up with poets who claim that Zeus is a "lord high steward" who is our dispenser of good things, bad things, all alike.[83] As for Pandarus' oath-breaking and violation of a truce,[84] we won't applaud anyone for claiming it happened because of Athena and Zeus – or for attributing strife and trials of strength between gods to Themis[85] and Zeus; and we shan't allow our young people to hear it said, as Aeschylus says,[86] that

> it's god who plants the cause in mortal men
> If ruin, utter ruin, he wishes upon a house.

If anyone composes a play about the sufferings of Niobe that includes these lines, or writes about what happened to the offspring of Pelops[87] or in the Trojan War or anything like that, then either we should prevent them from saying it was the gods' doing, or if they are going to say that, then they'll have to devise a story along the sort of lines we're looking for, and say that the gods were only doing what was just and good to people who in fact benefited from being punished; nor must we allow the poet to say that those who were punished were miserable and unhappy, and it was gods who made them so. If they said that the bad were unhappy because they needed punishing, and that in punishing them the gods were doing them good, we'd permit that, but saying that gods are responsible for causing

379e

380a

380b

bad things to happen to people, when they are good – a person must use every method he can to resist *that* either being said in his city, if it's to be well governed, or being heard by anyone, whether young or old, and whether the story's being told in verse or not, since the telling of it, were it to be told, would not only be impious and contradict our purposes as founders, but would leave the teller even contradicting himself.'

'I'm voting with you on this law,' he said; 'I like it.'

'So this', I said, 'will be one of the outlines, laid down in law, for what people must say and poets compose about the gods: "The gods are not responsible for everything, only for good things."'

'Very satisfactory,' he said.

'And here's a second. Do you think gods are sorcerers, and likely to make themselves appear now in one shape, now in another – now actually passing into many different forms by changing their appearance,[88] now deceiving us and merely making us think that's what they're doing? Or do you think their nature is simple and unitary, making them least likely of all to depart from their own proper form?'

'I can't say,' he said; 'not just like that.'

'Think of it this way. If a thing were to exchange its own form for another, either it must do the changing itself, mustn't it, or something else must do it?'

'Necessarily so.'

'And isn't it things that are in the best condition that are least subject to alteration and change from outside? As for example a body is subject to alteration by things like food, drink, physical labour, and every plant by the heat of the sun, wind and other similar external factors; isn't it in both cases the healthiest and strongest specimen that's altered least?'

'No question.'

'And with souls – won't it be the bravest and wisest that are least disturbed and altered by any outside factor?'

'Yes.'

'And I imagine the same is true of all artifacts too, whether tools or buildings or clothing: those that have been well put together and are in good condition are the ones that will be least altered by time and other factors.'

'That's right.'

'Thus anything at all that is in good condition, by virtue of 381b either its nature or expert intervention, or both, is most resistant to change from outside.'

'It seems so.'

'But *gods*, surely, and everything that belongs to gods, are in every respect in the best condition possible.'

'Of course.'

'So from this point of view[89] gods will be least liable to shape-shifting.'

'Indeed so.'

'And will they change or alter themselves, by themselves?'

'Clearly they must,' said Adimantus, 'if they really do change.'

'Well, do they change themselves into something better and more beautiful than they are, or into something worse and less beautiful?'

'It must be into something worse, if they really do change; I don't imagine we'll want to claim that gods are actually defi- 381c cient in beauty or excellence.'

'Quite right,' I said. 'And do you think, Adimantus, that in that situation anyone would willingly make himself worse in any respect, whether he was a god or a man?'

'Impossible,' he said.

'In that case', I said, 'it's impossible even for gods to wish to change themselves. Each of them, being the finest and best possible, retains his own proper form, one and the same, forever.'

'I think that's a quite unavoidable conclusion,' he said.

'Let none of the poets tell us, then,' I said, 'my excellent 381d Adimantus, that

the gods disguise themselves, resembling strangers,
Becoming who they will as they wander the city streets,[90]

and let none of them say false things about Proteus or Thetis,[91] or bring Hera on in tragedy or any sort of poetry in the shape

of a priestess collecting alms for "the life-providing sons of
381e Inachus, Argive river."⁹² Nor are these the only falsehoods
they should avoid; there are many more. And neither should
mothers be persuaded by these into frightening their little
children with story-telling of a pernicious sort, saying that
certain divinities really do go around at night looking like a
collection of outsiders of every shape and size; that's nothing
short of blasphemy against the gods, at the same time as making
children too afraid.'

'You're right,' he said; 'they shouldn't do that.'

'But here's the other possibility:⁹³ if their nature prevents
them actually changing in themselves, do they nevertheless
behave like sorcerers, deceiving us into *thinking* they're appearing to us in exotic guises?'

'Maybe,' he said.

382a   'But think about it,' I said: 'would a god want to say or act
out something false like that, offering us mere appearances?'

'I don't know,' he replied.

'You don't know', I said, 'that the true falsehood – if I can
call it that – is something hated by every god and every man?'

'What are you saying?' he asked.

'What I'm saying', I explained, 'is that being deceived in what
I suppose is the most important aspect of ourselves, about the
most important things, is something no one willingly chooses;
we fear more than anything to have falsehood lodged there.'

'I'm not seeing it even now,' he said.

382b   'That's because you think I'm saying something deep. All
I'm actually saying is that the last thing anyone will accept is
being deceived in his soul about how things really are. To have
been deceived, and be ignorant, with the falsehood lodged
there in the soul, is when people hate it the most.'

'Yes, much the most,' he said.

'And this ignorance, in the soul of the person deceived,
would surely be rightly described as "true falsehood", as I
put it just now. Falsehood as spoken or written is a kind of
382c representation of falsehood as experienced in the soul – an
after-image, as it were, not falsehood pure and simple. Isn't
that so?'

'Yes, quite.'

'Real falsehood, then, is hated not just by gods but by men too.'

'I think so.'

'What should we say about spoken or written falsehood? The reason why it doesn't merit our hatred is that it's sometimes useful, and for some people. But when, and for whom? Isn't it when we're dealing with enemies, or even with people we call our friends, who've gone mad or somehow lost their minds, and are up to no good: on such occasions this other kind of falsehood can be used, can't it, like a drug, to stop them? 382d And also in the sorts of story-telling we were discussing just now, because we don't know the truth about the distant past we make the false resemble the true as far as we can, and so it comes to be useful here too.'

'That's very much the way it is,' he said.

'So then tell me for which of these purposes the gods would find falsehood useful. Would they use it because they don't know about the distant past, and need to make up something that resembles it?'

'That would be totally absurd,' he said.

'So the gods have nothing in them of the poet and his falsehoods.'

'I think not.'

'Would they need falsehoods for fear of their enemies?' 382e

'They wouldn't need them for *that*.'

'What about dealing with friends who've gone mad or otherwise lost their minds?'

'But nobody who's out of his mind or mad is loved by the gods.'[94]

'In that case, there's no purpose for which the gods would use falsehood.'

'None.'

'Whichever way you look at it, then, no divinity or god will have anything to do with falsehoods.'[95]

'Absolutely not,' he said.

'The gods, then, are wholly themselves and wholly truthful in everything they do and say. They neither change their form nor deceive others, awake or asleep, whether by the way they appear, or what they say, or the signs they send.'[96]

383a   'That's how it appears to me, too,' he said, 'as I listen to your argument.'

'So,' I said, 'do you agree to this as the second of our outlines[97] for what people are to say and poets compose about gods: "The gods are neither shape-shifting sorcerers themselves, nor do they lead us astray by telling us or acting out falsehoods?"'

'I agree.'

'So while there are many things we'll praise in Homer, we won't praise him for having Zeus send that dream to Agamemnon,[98] nor will we praise Aeschylus for that moment in his
383b   play[99] when Thetis claims that Apollo sang at her wedding "to count the blessings of my offspring" – how they would

> Live out their lives in happiness, unknowing of disease.
> In sum, I was the darling of the gods, my future was secure.
> He sang his paean, and my heart was gladdened by the prophecy –
> I was in hope: no god speaks false, and it was a god who spoke,
> Phoebus himself, arch-prophet, brimming with the mantic art.
> So there he was himself, a god there with us at the feast:
> Himself he said those things, himself he killed my son.[100]

383c   If ever anyone says such things about gods, we'll be angry with him and refuse to give him a chorus;[101] we'll also forbid teachers from using such things to educate the young. Otherwise our guards will not grow up in awe of the gods, or godlike themselves to the highest degree that's possible for mere men.'

'I'm completely in agreement with these outlines of yours,' he said, 'and I'd make them the law.'

386a   'So much for the subject of the gods,' I said: 'these, it   Book III
seems, are the sorts of things our people should and   begins
shouldn't hear said about them, from childhood on, if they're going to honour not just the gods but their parents as well, and place the right value on their friendship with each other.'

'Yes, and I think we're taking the right view.'

'What about if they're going to be courageous?[102] We'll need to ensure, won't we, that they not only hear the things we've just been talking about, but the sorts of things that will make them least afraid of death? Or do you suppose that anyone will ever be courageous if he has in him a fear of dying?' 386b

'Zeus! No, I don't,' he said.

'And do you think anyone will be fearless in the face of death, and choose it in preference to defeat and slavery, if he believes that Hades is a real and terrifying place?'

'There's no way he will.'

'So it looks as if there's another aspect of story-telling that will need supervision. We'll have to ask those who take it on themselves to write stories on this subject not to present so consistently gloomy a picture of Hades and what awaits us there, but rather to talk it up; what they presently say about it, we'll tell them, is neither true nor helpful to people whose job it will be to fight.' 386c

'We certainly will,' he said.

'Then we'll strike out everything like that, beginning with these verses:

I'd rather work the fields above for someone else,
A serf to a man with nothing who works all day to live,
Than lord it over all the bloodless dead assembled here,[103]

and these:

The halls of the dead break open, revealed to god and man, 386d
Dank, mouldering, horrible to the immortal gods themselves,[104]

and

Alas, then, it is true: there in the halls of Hades roam
Mere wraiths and phantoms, of all mind and thought bereft,[105]

and

Alone possessed of mind, the rest mere passing shadows,[106] and

> Straight off to Hades flew his soul, his limbs abandoning,
> Lamenting as it went youth lost and manhood gone[107] –

387a these too,

> Like smoke his soul beneath the earth
> Was gibbering gone,[108]

and

> As when in the distant corner of an echoing cave the bats
> Gibber and flutter, as one falls from the hanging cluster
> On the rocky roof where they cling fast to one another,
> So flitted the shades, gibbering, together.[109]

387b We'll ask Homer and the other poets not to be angry if we draw a line through these verses and any others like them – not because they're not poetic, or pleasant for ordinary people to listen to, but because the more poetic they are the less they should be heard by those – children and adults – whom we need to be free and more afraid of slavery than of death.'

'Yes, I quite agree.'

387c 'So we should also get rid of all those terrible names that strike fear into everyone, names like Cocytus and Styx,[110] "the dead and buried", and all names along these lines that send a shiver through anyone who hears them.[111] They may have their purposes in other connections, but we're afraid for our guards, and the possibility that a reaction like that will make them too unstable and soft for our needs.'

'Yes,' he said, 'it's right to fear that.'

'So we're to remove these names?'

'Yes.'

'And have them replaced in ordinary speech and in poetry with names along opposite lines?'

'Clearly so.'

'Then shall we also take out passages where famous men   387d
grieve and lament?'

'Inevitably,' he said, 'given what we've already taken out.'

'Well, see whether or not there's a reason for it. A good person, we say,[112] will suppose that for another like himself, even
someone whose comrade he is, dying is not such a terrible
thing.'

'We do.'

'In that case, he won't grieve, at least for his comrade's sake,
as if something terrible *had* happened to him.'

'He certainly won't.'

'But then we also say that a person like this is most self-   387e
sufficient, so far as concerns living a good life, setting the
standard for others by being least reliant on another.'

'True,' he said.

'Least terrible for him, then, to be deprived of a son, or a
brother, or of money, or anything else like that.'

'For him least of all.'

'Then we're saying that he also grieves least when any such
misfortune befalls him, bearing it in the most even-tempered
way.'

'Yes, much the least.'

'So we will be justified in taking out the scenes where famous men wail, and give them to women, so long as they're not
women of a superior sort, along with the inferior men, so that   388a
the people we claim to be bringing up to guard the country will
turn up their noses at behaving as people like *that* do.'

'Yes, we will.'

'And we'll have another request to make of Homer and the
other poets, not to have Achilles, son of a goddess,

> Lying now on his side, now twisting his body and turning
> Face up, then down,

and "then raising himself straight" only to

> Drift there, distraught, on the shore of the unforgiving sea;[113]   388b

nor should he be shown "with both hands grasping the soot-black dust, streaming it down from his head",[114] or weeping and wailing in all the various other ways the poet describes. Nor should we have Priam, near relative of gods, "begging and entreating" and

> rolling there in dirt and filth,
> Calling on each man by name, appealing to them one by one.[115]

And we'll put in a still more urgent request, that *gods* really mustn't be portrayed as grieving and saying,

388c   Oh! What a wretch am I, unhappy mother of the best of sons![116]

– and if gods mustn't be portrayed like that, certainly a poet should never take it on himself to represent the very greatest of them so inaccurately as to have him declaring

> Alas, dear man to me, in flight around the city walls:
> With my eyes I see you run, and my heart it grieves within,[117]

or

> Ah me! That fate should say Sarpedon, most beloved of men,
388d   Must by Patroclus, Menoetius' son, be tamed and killed.[118]

After all, my dear Adimantus, should our young people take portrayals like this seriously, rather than laughing at them as unworthy of their subjects, then they'd hardly be likely to think such things unworthy of mere mortals like themselves, or reproach themselves if it ever occurred to them to talk or behave like this. They'll show no trace of shame or resolve, singing copious dirges and laments at slight mishaps.'

'Very true,' he said.

388e   'But they certainly mustn't do that, as our argument indicated just now – and we'd better stick with that, until someone produces a better argument to convince us otherwise.'

'No, I agree, they mustn't behave like that.'

'On the other hand, they mustn't be over-fond of laughter, either. Usually when someone gives in to violent laughter it goes along with violent changes in him too.'

'That's my view,' he said.

'So we mustn't put up with any man being portrayed as overcome by laughter, if he's worthy of any note; still less with gods being portrayed like that.' 389a

'Much less!' he said.

'Then there are more things we won't put up with Homer's saying about gods, such as

And now there rose a mirth unquenched among the blessed gods
To see Hephaestus busy, bustling through the hall[119]

– these we certainly mustn't put up with, by your argument.'

'If you want to attribute it to me,' he said, 'that's fine; either way, there'll be no putting up with things like that.' 389b

'But then again we must place a high value on *truth*. If what we were saying just now is right,[120] and falsehood, while being actually of no use to gods, has its usefulness for human beings as a kind of medicine, then clearly anything like that needs to be put in the hands of medical experts and kept away from laymen.'

'Clearly so.'

'Falsehoods, then, will be a matter for the rulers of our city,[121] if it's for anybody, as a means of dealing either with enemies or citizens to the benefit of the city as a whole; everybody else must keep strictly away from anything of the sort. If any private citizen tells or acts out a falsehood[122] towards the rulers, of all people, we'll declare it to be a mistake equal to or greater than a patient's or an athlete's not telling the truth to a doctor or trainer about his current physical state, or someone's not telling the steersman the actual condition of the ship or the sailors, and his own or any of his fellow-sailors' fitness to perform their roles.' 389c

'Very true,' he said.

'So if the ruler catches any other of "those who work their craft" in the city engaging in falsehoods, whether they're 389d "skilled in prophecy or healing of sickness or the working of wood",[123] he'll punish the offender as someone importing a practice that will overturn and sink a city like a ship.'

'At any rate,' he said, 'if there's to be action backing up all that talk.'

'Next, what about moderation?[124] Won't our young men need to be moderate?'

'Of course.'

389e 'The chief elements of moderation, as it occurs in the generality of people, will be these, won't they: being obedient to their rulers, and being rulers of their own desires in relation to things like drink and sex, and food?'[125]

'I think so.'

'I imagine, then, that we'll count as well said the sort of thing that Homer's Diomedes says:

Sit, my friend, keep your silence, listen hard to what I say,[126]

and the similar

On went the Achaeans, their spirits aflame;
Silence they kept, fearing their captains' wrath;[127]

and anything else like that.'

'We will.'

'What about a line like

You wine-sack, you, with the eyes of a dog and the
heart of a deer,[128]

390a and the ones that follow – are you happy with these, or with any insubordinate remarks uttered by the rank and file to their superiors, whether in verse or not?'

'No, I'm not.'

'Because I don't think they're suitable for young people to hear, at any rate from the point of view of developing moderation in them; there's no denying that they are also enjoyable in their way. What's your view?'

'The same as yours,' he said.

'And what if the wisest of men is portrayed as thinking that the finest thing of all is when

> there beside us tables stand
> Filled full with bread and meat, the wine mixed in its bowl;   390b
> The pourer draws it off, and fills the waiting cups[129]

– do you think these are suitable lines for a young person to hear if he's to achieve control over himself? Or what about

> To die of hunger: what more pitiable way to meet one's doom[130]

or the portrayal of Zeus, alone awake while the other gods and all mankind are asleep, planning and then forgetting his 390c plans, just like that, out of a desire for sex – so overcome at the sight of Hera that he refuses even to go into the bedroom, preferring to have her right there on the ground, and telling her he's gripped by desire greater than "when first they used to come" to each other "their dear parents all-unknowing"?[131] And then there's the same sort of scenario with Hephaestus' entrapment of Ares and Aphrodite;[132] that won't be suitable material either.'

'Zeus, no!' he said. 'Not suitable at all, to my mind.'

'But any examples there are, in the speeches or actions of 390d famous men, that show them putting up with whatever sort of provocation it may be, these should be put before our young people to watch and hear; for example,

> He smote his breast, and with these words reproved his heart:
> "Hold hard, my heart; more shameful a thing you bore than
>   this." '[133]

'Yes, absolutely,' he said.

'We certainly mustn't let our men be corruptible by bribes, or be lovers of money.'   390e

'No indeed.'

'And we mustn't let anyone sing them the line that goes

"Gifts sway the minds of gods; gifts sway respected kings";[134] we mustn't praise the advice Achilles' tutor Phoenix gave him, either, when he told him to come to the aid of the Achaeans if they gave him gifts, and not to relent from his wrath
391a if they didn't.[135] It wasn't sound advice, and in any case we won't believe Achilles himself capable of any such thing; we won't accept that he loved money so much as to accept Agamemnon's bribes, or for that matter refuse to release a corpse except in return for payment.'[136]

'It would be quite out of place', he said, 'to praise advice like that.'

'I hesitate to say it,' I went on, 'out of respect for Homer, but it's actually impious to say these things against Achilles or believe it when other people do; to say that he told Apollo

> Far-shooter, deadliest of all the gods, you did me harm;
> Had I the power, I swear I'd pay you back in full,[137]

391b or that he refused to listen to the river – a god – and was ready even to fight him, or again that he promised those locks of his, already dedicated to that other river, Spercheius: "This hair I'd give the noble Patroclus to carry as his spoils"[138] – when Patroclus was already a corpse. Nobody should believe he *did* do it, either. As for stories like the dragging of Hector's corpse around Patroclus' tomb, or the massacre of war-prisoners[139] on his pyre, all of these we'll deny were true. We won't allow our
391c people to believe that Achilles of all people – not only the son of a goddess and of Peleus, supremely moderate, and grandson of Zeus, but brought up under the supreme wisdom of Chiron[140] – was so completely disturbed an individual as to have two opposing sicknesses in him: illiberality combined with a love of money on the one hand, a sense of superiority over gods and men on the other.'

'Quite right,' he said.

391d 'So,' I said, 'let's not believe and let's not allow it to be said, either, that Theseus son of Poseidon and Perithous son of Zeus launched on those terrible abductions,[141] or that any other son of a god, or hero,[142] could have brought himself to do the ter-

rible and impious things that people nowadays falsely attribute
to them. Let's force the poets to say either that the heroes did
not do these things or that they were not sons of gods, and not
allow them to have it both ways, which would be to give them
licence to try to persuade the young that gods are begetters of
bad things, and heroes no better than mere men – the sort of
thing we were saying before was both impious and untrue; we   391e
showed earlier, I think, that it's impossible for bad things to
come from the gods.'

'Yes, of course.'

'What's more, things like this are damaging to anyone who
hears them, because he'll be inclined to forgive himself for
being a bad person, encouraged by the thought that, after all,
this is what even "those near of kin to gods" do,

> Those close to Zeus, for whom on Ida's rock
> There sits a cloudy altar to ancestral Zeus,
> The gods' blood flowing still potent in their veins.[143]

That's why we must put a stop to stories of this sort; we need
to avoid spawning a ready and easy-going acceptance of bad-   392a
ness[144] in our young people.'

'Yes, absolutely,' he said.

'So,' I said, 'what area have we left out of this discussion of
ours, of what we should and should not permit to be said in
our city? We've dealt with how gods should be talked about,
and demi-gods, and heroes, and the underworld.'

'That's so.'

'What's left, then, will be how poets and others should talk
about human beings?'

'Evidently.'

'That, my friend, is something it's impossible for us to lay
down at the present time.'

'How so?'

'Because I imagine we'll say that in fact both poets and
story-tellers make fundamental mistakes when they talk about   392b
human beings, by saying many unjust people are happy, many
just ones miserable, acting unjustly pays if you get away with

it, justice is good for someone else, a loss to oneself; we'll forbid them to say such things, and order them to say the opposite
in the songs they sing and the stories they tell. Don't you think
so?'

'I don't just think we will,' he said; 'I know.'

'Well, if you agree I'm right about this, I'll put you down,
shall I, as having conceded to me on the subject we were discussing all along?'[145]

392c   'Quite correct – it's too early to do that,' he said.

'So the time for us to agree about the kinds of things that
poets and story-tellers should say about human beings is when
we find out both what justice is and that it is something naturally beneficial to its possessor, whether he's thought to have it
or not?'

'Very true,' he said.

'So that's enough about *what*'s to be said; what we need to
consider next, I think, is *how* it's to be said, and then our
inquiry into the whole subject, the what and the how, will be
complete.'

And Adimantus said 'This I don't understand. What are you
saying?'

392d   'We can't have you not understanding,' I said. 'Perhaps
you'll grasp my point better this way. Everything that story-
tellers or poets say is by way of narration, isn't it – narration of
the past, or the present, or the future?'

'What else would it be?' he said.

'Well, don't they proceed by using either pure narrative, or
narrative effected through imitation, or a mixture of both?'

'Here again,' he said, 'I need you to make things clearer
for me.'

392e   'I seem to be a ridiculously poor teacher,' I said; 'so, like bad
public speakers, instead of trying to get my point over in general terms, I'll separate off a bit of it and use that to show you
what I have in mind. You know the beginning of the *Iliad*,
where the poet says that Chryses begged Agamemnon to let his
daughter go, Agamemnon got angry, and Chryses, because he
393a   wasn't getting what he wanted, prayed to his god[146] to pay the
Achaeans back?'

'I do.'

'So you'll know that until the following two verses:

> and he beseeched the Achaeans, all together,
> But the two sons of Atreus most of all, leaders of their peoples,[147]

the poet speaks in his own person and doesn't even try to fool us with the idea that anyone but him is speaking; but after that he speaks as if he was actually Chryses himself, and tries as 393b hard as he can to make us think that it isn't Homer who's speaking but the old priest. And practically the whole of his narrative, both of the events at Troy and of what happened on Ithaca and in the entire *Odyssey*, is composed like that.'

'Yes, certainly,' he said.

'Well, it's all narrative – both the speeches, when he puts them in, and the parts in between the speeches?'

'Of course.'

'But when he does put in a speech, as if someone else were speaking, won't we say that he makes his own delivery so far as 393c possible resemble that of the person he tells us is going to speak?'

'We will, of course.'

'And this making oneself resemble someone else, whether in his voice or his appearance, is a matter of imitating the person one's making oneself resemble?'

'Obviously.'

'So it seems that in cases like this Homer and the other poets are using imitation to put their narrative together.'

'Yes, clearly.'

'Whereas if a poet didn't try to conceal himself at any point, his poetry, and his narrative, would have been done entirely without imitation. I'll give you an illustration of how this might 393d happen, to prevent your telling me once more that you don't understand. If Homer started as he does by saying Chryses came with a ransom for his daughter to supplicate the Achaeans, especially the kings, but after that went on not by becoming Chryses but remaining as Homer, you'll see at once that it wouldn't any longer be imitation but pure narrative. It would go something like this – I won't try putting it into verse, because I'm no poet:

393e   The priest came and prayed the gods would grant them a safe return home with the capture of Troy, but that they would accept the ransom and release his daughter out of reverence for his god. When he had spoken, the rest of the Greeks showed him respect and were for taking his side, but Agamemnon was in a savage mood and told him to go away and not come back, because if he did his staff and the god's wreaths wouldn't be enough to save him; as for his daughter, he said she'd grow old with him in

394a   Argos before she'd ever be released, and Chryses had better go away and not provoke him if he wanted to get home in one piece. The king's words terrified the old man, and he left in silence, but as soon as he was out of earshot of the army he prayed repeatedly to Apollo, calling him by his various names, reminding him of any gifts that might have found favour with him in the past, whether from temple-building or the sacrifice of victims, and asking for the favour to be returned; he prayed that the Achaeans should pay back for his own tears with the god's arrows.

394b   That's the way, my friend, that we get pure narrative, without imitation.'

'I understand you,' he said.

'Well, understand another point,' I said: 'the opposite occurs when one takes out the poet's bits in between the speeches, and leaves the to and fro of dialogue.'

'I understand this as well,' he said; 'this is the sort of thing you find in tragedies.'

'That's exactly what I had in mind,' I said; 'and I think you're now clear about what I wasn't able to make clear to

394c   you before, namely, that some poetry and story-telling works wholly through imitation – tragedy, as you say, and comedy – whereas some is a matter of the poet's own utterance throughout; that I imagine you'll find most of all in dithyrambs.[148] The sort that employs a combination of both imitation and the poet's own voice will be found not just in epic but in lots of other places too – if that helps you.'

'I have now grasped what you were originally saying,' he said.

'And don't forget what came before that, when we said we'd covered *what* should be said, and still had to consider *how* it's to be said.'

'I do remember.'

'This, then, was the point I was making, that we needed to 394d agree whether we'd allow our poets to compose their narratives using imitation, or in part using imitation and in part not, and if so what they should and should not imitate; or whether we'd stop them imitating anything and anyone at all.'

'My guess is', he said, 'that you're considering whether we're going to allow tragedy and comedy into the city, or ban them both.'

'Maybe,' I said; 'and maybe also my question is even broader than this – I don't yet know myself. Let's treat our argument like the wind, and follow whichever way it blows us.'

'Yes,' he said; 'a good proposal.'

'Well, Adimantus, see what you think about this point: 394e should our guards be good imitators or not? Or does the answer to this question follow from what we said before,[149] to the effect that each individual will only be good at one activity, not many, and that if he tries his hand at it he'll dabble in many things but fail to achieve distinction in any?'

'Yes, clearly.'

'Then the same will hold of imitation: one and the same individual is not as good an imitator of many things as he is of one.'

'No, that's right.'

'In that case, he'll hardly be able to combine any sort of 395a worthwhile activity with multiple imitations and skill as an imitator; it's my impression that the same people can't simultaneously excel even at two forms of imitation that apparently border on one another, for example simultaneously excelling in comedy and tragedy.[150] You were just calling these forms of imitation, weren't you?'

'I was, and yes, you're right, the same people can't do both.'

'Nor can they be good rhapsodes and good actors at the same time.'

'True.'

395b 'But neither will a good tragic actor also be a good comic actor – and all the things we're talking about are forms of imitation, right?'

'Right.'

'In fact, Adimantus, it seems to me that human nature is cut up into still smaller pieces even than this, so as to make it incapable either of imitating many things well, or of doing in real life the things those imitations represent.'

'Very true,' he said.

'So if we're going to save our original principle, that our guards need to be released from the activities of all other crafts-

395c men to be true craftsmen of freedom for the city, and are to be barred from any activity that does not conduce to this end, then they must do absolutely nothing except fulfil this function of theirs, nor imitate anything else. Any imitating they do, from childhood on, will be of what is appropriate to their function: courageous people, people who are moderate, pious, free, and everything like that; anything unfitting a free person, anything whatever that is shameful, they will neither do nor be clever at imitating, to avoid their ending up being what they imitate.

395d Haven't you noticed that imitations carried on too long from a young age become a person's habits, even his nature, whether physically and in the way he sounds, or in the way he thinks?'

'Very much so,' he said.

'Then', I said, 'those we claim to care about, and insist must turn into good men, we'll certainly not permit, since they *are* men, to imitate a woman, whether young or old, whether ranting at a man, setting herself up in competition with gods,

395e boasting because of her supposed good fortune, or gripped by misfortune, grief, lamentation and the like; still less will we permit imitation of a sick woman, a woman in love or a woman in labour.'[151]

'Absolutely right,' he said.

'There'll be no imitation of slave-women, either, or of slaves, doing what slaves do.'

'No, not that either.'

'Nor again of bad men, evidently; men who are cowards and

behave in ways opposite to the ones we were talking about just
now, insulting and making fun of each other, calling each other
foul names when they're drunk or even when they're sober, or   396a
going wrong in all the other ways people do in what they say
or what they do towards themselves or towards others. And I
don't think we'll want to get them used to talking or acting like
madmen. They'll certainly need to be able to recognize mad
people, and bad ones, whether men or women, but they won't
do any of the things they do, or imitate them.'

'Very true,' he said.

'What about imitating metal-workers, or craftsmen of any
similar sort, or rowers on triremes, or those who shout out
the time to the rowers, or do anything else connected with all   396b
that?'

'How can we let them do that', he said, 'when they won't
have our permission to pay notice to such things in the first
place?'

'How about stallions whinnying, bulls bellowing, rivers
sounding, seas roaring, claps of thunder and so on and so
forth – will they imitate any of those?'

'Hardly,' he said, 'given that they're forbidden either to be
mad or to play the madman.'

'In that case,' I said, 'if I understand what you're saying,
there's one form of narrative that the truly fine and good per-   396c
son would use to express himself whenever he had to say
something, and another form, unlike this one, that someone
would always rely on if he had the opposite nature and upbringing to our man's.'

'So what are these two forms of narrative?' he asked.

'It seems to me,' I said, 'that when a man of the right quality
arrives at a point in the narrative when a good man is saying or
doing something, he'll be ready and willing to report it as if he
really were that other person himself; he won't be ashamed at
that sort of imitation, which he'll take on most of all when the   396d
good man is acting resolutely and in full possession of his senses,
less fully and readily when he is undone by sickness or passion,
or indeed drunkenness, or some other misfortune. When he
comes to someone unworthy of himself, on the other hand, he'll

refuse any serious attempt at assimilating himself to the inferior individual, except perhaps for brief moments when the other person does something worthwhile, and will be ashamed at undertaking it both because he is a beginner when it comes to imitating people like that, and because he holds his nose at 396e shaping himself to fit the mould of those inferior to himself – unless it's merely for amusement, the thought of it disgusts him.'

'That's reasonable,' he said.

'Then will he use a narrative of the form we described just now by reference to Homeric epic, so that his mode of expression will combine both things, imitation and non-imitative narrative, but with the former representing only a small element in proportion to the rest of what he is saying? Or am I making no sense?'

'You're making very good sense,' he said; 'that must be the pattern for this sort of speaker.'

397a   'As for the one who's not like this,' I said, 'the worse he is, the readier he'll probably be to put in everything and think nothing unworthy of himself, with the result that he'll set about imitating anything whatever, in full seriousness and before a mass audience; even the things we were talking about just now, like claps of thunder and the noises of wind and hail, axles and pulleys, the sounds of trumpets, pipes, Pan-pipes – every kind of instrument, not to mention dogs barking, sheep bleating, 397b birds twittering. Will this person's delivery in fact be wholly through imitation, by voice and gesture – or will it have a small element of plain narrative in it too?'

'It must have that too,' he said.

'These, then,' I said, 'were the two forms of delivery I had in mind.'

'Yes, I recognize these,' he said.

'Well now: are the variations in one of them small, so that if the speaker endows his delivery with an appropriate arrangement of notes and an appropriate rhythm, the outcome, when he gets it right, will be speaking that corresponds to – is actually in – one and the same musical mode,[152] just because the variations are small, and matches a single musical rhythm in a similar way?'

'Quite obviously that's how it is,' he said.   397c

'But what about the other form of delivery? Doesn't it require the opposite – every kind of mode and every kind of rhythm, if it too is to be done in the appropriate way, insofar as it contains variations of every shape and kind?'

'Yes, very much so.'

'So do all poets, and in general all speakers, hit upon either one or the other of these two forms of delivery, or some mixture they make up out of the two?'

'They must,' he said.

'So what shall we do?' I asked. 'Which of these shall we let   397d
into the city? All of them, or one of the unmixed ones, or the mixed one?'

'If it's up to me, the unmixed form that imitates the good person.'

'But look here, Adimantus, the mixed form surely has its pleasures, and in fact the one that brings most pleasure to children and their overseers is the opposite of the one you're choosing – and the same goes for most ordinary people.'

'Yes, it does.'

'But perhaps,' I said, 'you'll say that it's not appropriate to   397e
the political arrangements we ourselves are proposing,[153] because we have no two-sided men among us, or many-sided ones; each does just one thing.'

'No, it's not appropriate.'

'And is this the reason why it's only in a city like ours that we'll find shoemakers being shoemakers and not steering a ship as well as making shoes, farmers being farmers and not sitting as judges as well as farming, soldiers being soldiers and not making money as well as soldiering, and so on with everyone else?'

'True,' he said.

'Then it seems that if there was a man with the skill to turn   398a
himself into all sorts of shapes and imitate anything that exists, and he brought himself and his poems to our city to display them to us, we would fall down before him as if he were some sacred figure, a wonder and a pleasure to listen to, but we would tell him that we have no men like him in our city and we

are not permitted to have any; we'd pour myrrh over his head, give him a chaplet of wool and send him off to another city, while for ourselves we'd go on employing the more austere and less pleasing poet and story-teller, to our benefit, because he'd imitate the good person's way of expressing himself, and he'd say what he says according to the outlines we laid down for poets and story-tellers in our original legislation, when we were first setting out to educate our soldiers.'

'That's certainly what we'd do,' he said, 'if it were up to us.'

'At this point, my friend,' I said, 'we've probably completed our treatment of the part of music that relates to speech and to stories, since we've talked about both what is to be said and how it is to be said.'[154]

'That's my view too,' he said.

'There remains, then, after this,' I said, 'the subject of melody – what tunes people should sing?'

'Clearly so.'

'Well, wouldn't all and sundry be able to work out what we should say these tunes ought to be, if we're going to be in harmony with what we said before?'

Glaucon laughed and said, 'Then I fear I can't be one of your "all and sundry", Socrates; I'm not at this moment sufficiently able to propose by myself what we should be saying on the subject, although I have my suspicions.'

'Well,' I said, 'you're certainly sufficiently able to say this much to begin with, namely, that a song is composed out of three things: speech, arrangement and rhythm?'

'Yes,' he said, 'that much I can say.'

'Well then, the requirements we'll lay down for the part of it that consists of speech will surely be no different from those we laid down for unsung speech; the same outlines of what can be said, and how, will apply.'

'True,' he said.

'And then the words will dictate the arrangement of the notes and the rhythm.'

'Of course.'

'But we said there was no call for lamentation and wailing in spoken speech.'

'So which of the musical modes express grief? You tell me; 398e
you're the musical expert.'

'Mixed Lydian,' he said, 'and Intense Lydian, and a couple
of others like that.'

'So should we remove these from the city?' I asked. 'After
all, they're no use even to women, if they're to be of the right
quality, let alone to men.'

'Yes, absolutely.'

'And again, drunkenness is something least appropriate for
guards, and similarly with softness and idleness.'

'Of course.'

'So which modes go with softness and drinking-parties?'

'Ionic modes,' he replied; 'and some Lydian ones too, are
called relaxed.'

'So, my friend, can you see any use in these for soldiering men?' 399a

'No use,' he said. 'Probably you've only got the Dorian and
the Phrygian left.'

'I've no knowledge of modes,' I said; 'just leave us the one
that will appropriately mimic the tones and variations of pitch
of a courageous person engaged in military action or any other
role involving force; someone who, whether he has failed and
is now marching towards mutilation or death, or whether he 399b
has met with some other misfortune, stands up to all that is
happening to him with discipline and endurance. And besides
this one, leave us another mode that will do the same for such
a person engaged in peaceable activity relying on consent rather
than on force, as he tries to persuade someone of something, or
ask for something, whether he's praying to a god or teaching
or admonishing a man, or whether it's the other way round,
and he's the one submitting to someone else who's asking *him*
for something or teaching him or trying to change his mind –
and coming out of all of this as he would have wished, with
no arrogance, just consistently moderate and measured behav- 399c
iour and willing acceptance of the outcomes. These two modes,
violent and peaceable, that come closest to mimicking the ar-
ticulations of men failing, men succeeding, moderate men and
courageous men, are the ones I need you to leave when you've
taken away the rest.'

'They're exactly the ones I mentioned just now,' he said.

'In that case,' I said, 'the tunes our people sing won't require a large number of strings, or anything exploiting the whole range of modes.'

'It doesn't seem so to me,' he said.

399d 'So we won't give sustenance to craftsmen who make triangular harps or finger-harps or any other multi-stringed or pan-modal instrument.'

'It seems we won't.'

'What about makers and players of pipes? Will you welcome them into the city? Or isn't their kind of music more "multi-stringed" than any, so that pan-modal compositions really imitate pipes?'

'Evidently so,' he said.

'Then all you have left', I said, 'are the lyre and the cithara, which will be useful in the city; in the countryside there'll be some sort of Pan-pipe for the herdsmen.'

'So our argument suggests, at any rate,' he said.

'What we're doing here, my friend, is really nothing new,' I 399e said, 'putting Apollo and Apollo's instruments before Marsyas and his.'[155]

'Zeus! No,' he said, 'I don't think it is.'

'By the Dog!'[156] I exclaimed. 'This city of ours that we were calling "luxurious"[157] – without noticing, we're actually giving it a thorough cleaning up.'[158]

'And very sensible that is of us,' he said.

'So come on,' I said, 'let's go on and clean up the bits that are left. Following on from the subject of modes, there'll be the matter of rhythms. We won't go for complicated rhythms, or for the whole range of metres; we'll just look to see which ones 400a belong to a well-balanced and courageous life,[159] and when we've spotted them[160] we must make the metre, and the tune, follow the speech of someone like that, rather than making the words follow metre and tune. I leave it to you which the relevant rhythms are, just as I did with the modes.'

'Zeus!' he said. 'I really can't tell you what they'd be. What I *can* say, from observation, is that there are three forms[161] of rhythm out of which the various metres are combined, just as there are four in the case of musical notes, making up all the modes. But which imitates which sort of life, that I can't tell you.'[162]

'That', I said, 'we'll discuss when we're with Damon[163] – which metres go along with slavishness and excess, or madness and badness generally, and which rhythms must be preserved for people of the opposite sort. But I think I've heard him, none too clearly, naming some sort of marching rhythm "composite" and "dactylic" – and, yes, calling it "heroic", somehow or other turning things upside down by making shorts equal longs as the foot rises and falls;[164] and he also called one "iambic", I think, and another sort "trochaic", assigning each of these their long and short quantities. With some of these, I think he was as much concerned with praising and finding fault with the design of the foot as with the overall rhythm itself, or else with both together – I'm not capable of telling. But as I said, let's put all this off, for Damon, because the discussion needed to settle the issues won't be a short one. Or do you think it will?'

'Zeus, no, I certainly don't!'

'But this much, at any rate, you are capable of settling, namely, that in general seemliness and the lack of it follow from the presence and absence of good rhythm?'

'Of course.'

'But then good rhythm follows from what is well said, by assimilating itself to it, lack of rhythm from the opposite; and similarly with harmony and its absence – that is, if rhythm and concord really do follow on from speech, as we were saying just now, and not the other way round.'

' "But then"[165] these must follow on from speech,' he said.

'What about the way things are said,' I asked, 'and what is said? Don't these follow from the disposition of the soul?'[166]

'Of course.'

'And the rest follow on from what is said and the way it is said?'

'Yes.'

'Goodness of speech and concord and seemliness and good rhythm then all follow on goodness of disposition – not what we call "having a good disposition" by way of a pretty name for silliness, but a state of mind that is truly equipped with a good and fine disposition.'

'I absolutely agree,' he said.

'So mustn't our young people pursue these things in everything, if they're going to fulfil the function that belongs to them?'

'They must.'

401a 'And I imagine that the paintings and other similar products of art that they find around them will be full of these things; so, too, the woven fabrics, the decorations, the buildings and everything else produced for everyday use, as well as the bodies nature herself produces, and the plants – for in all of these we may find seemliness or unseemliness. Unseemliness, lack of rhythm, lack of concord: these are close relatives of badness in speech and in disposition, while their opposites are close relatives, in fact imitations, of the opposite, a disposition that is moderate and good.'

'I completely agree.'

401b 'So is it just the poets we must stand over, compelling them either to portray the image of a good disposition in their poems or not compose in our city at all; or should we be standing over the craftsmen too, and forbidding them to reproduce this thing we're calling a bad disposition – unrestrained, unfitting a free person, and unseemly – whether in paintings of living creatures or in buildings or in any other product of their crafts, or else, if they can't comply, telling them they won't be allowed to practise in our city, so that we can prevent our guards from being brought up among images of badness, like animals in a bad pasture, taking in a little from here, a little from there as they 401c graze, day after day, not noticing that they are putting together one big thing, and a bad one, in their own souls? Should we look for those craftsmen with the natural ability to track down what the nature of the fine is, and the seemly, so that the young may live as if in a healthy place where everything that affects their eyes and their ears is from things finely done, like a breeze bringing health from wholesome places, bestowing on them 401d from childhood on, without their noticing, an affinity to as well as friendship and harmony with fineness in speech?'[167]

'That', he said, 'would be much the finest way for them to be brought up.'

'So, Glaucon,' I said, 'is this why it's so important to bring them up exposed to music? Rhythm and concord, after all, penetrate deeper down inside the soul than anything else; they take the most powerful hold on it, causing it to share the seemliness they bring with them – provided, that is, that its owner is being brought up exposed to the correct music, because if he isn't, the effect will be the opposite. Again, the person who's been brought up with the right kind of music will have the sharpest eye for things that are deficient, either because they are not well crafted or because nature has left them lacking; he'll show a correct distaste for such things, and turn to praising and taking pleasure in the things that possess the requisite fineness, receiving them into his soul and taking nourishment from them, so becoming fine and good himself. He'll correctly reproach and hate what is shameful even at a tender age, even before he's capable of understanding speech; when he can understand it, he more than anyone will welcome it, recognizing it from its affinity to himself,[168] if he's been brought up musically like this.'

'It seems to me, at least,' he said, 'that this is the sort of thing a musical upbringing is for.'

'So,' I said, 'it's the same, is it, as when we were learning to read and write? The crucial moment came when we began to recognize that there were just a few letters that kept recurring in all the words they were in, and no longer told ourselves we needn't bother reading them because the word they were in was too small or too big – now we were keen to recognize them wherever they were, in the belief that we'd never be expert readers and writers until we got to that stage.'

'True.'

'It's true, too, isn't it, that we'll never recognize images of letters, supposing that these showed up on the surface of liquids or in mirrors, until we recognize actual letters; we need the same skill, and the same practice, to do both?'

'Absolutely so.'

'Then – by the gods![169] – this is what I'm saying: will it be the

402c same with music, so that we won't be experts at music either –
we ourselves or the people we say we've got to educate, our
"guards" – until we recognize the forms of moderation, courage, liberality, high-mindedness, all the close relatives of these,
and their opposites as well, as we encounter them everywhere
around us,[170] observing their presence where they are present –
not just them, but any images of them, and giving them full
attention whether in small things or in big ones, on the basis
that it's all a matter of the same skill and the same practice?'

'There's no getting away from it,' he said.

402d 'Well,' I said, 'if ever there happen to be fine dispositions
present in someone's soul, and those dispositions have a form
matching the things I just mentioned – if they're in tune with
them and share the same general outline, this would be the
most beautiful[171] of sights for anyone capable of seeing it?'

'Much the most.'

'And what is most beautiful is most lovable?'

'Of course.'

'Then the person who knows about music will be in love
with those of his fellow-humans who are most like that; if
someone were out of tune,[172] he wouldn't be in love with him.'

'Not if it were his soul that was deficient,' said Glaucon; 'but
if the defect were physical, he'd be ready to welcome him into
his arms all the same.'

402e 'I gather you've a beloved like that,' I said, 'or have had one
in the past; and I agree with you. But tell me this: is there anything in common between moderation and extreme pleasure?'

'How could there be?' he said. 'Extreme pleasure makes one
lose one's mind[173] as much as extreme pain does.'

'Does it have anything in common with any other excellence?'

403a 'It can't.'

'What about excess and lack of moderation?[174] Does it have
anything in common with them?'

'With *them* most of all.'

'And can you think of any pleasure that is greater and keener
than the one we get from sex?'

'I can't,' he said; 'nor can I think of one that's more manic.'

'But love that's of the correct sort is by nature a matter of loving what is well balanced and beautiful in a moderate and musical way?'

'Very much so,' he said.

'So nothing manic, or akin to lack of restraint, must be involved in correct loving?'

'Nothing.'

'So the pleasure of sex mustn't be involved, and lover and 403b beloved mustn't have anything to do with it, if they're to love and be loved in the correct way.'

'Zeus, no, Socrates!' he said. 'It certainly must not!'

'That, then, it seems, will be the law you'll lay down in the city you're founding: "A lover is to kiss, be with, touch a beloved as if he were a son, for fine ends,[175] if he can persuade him; in all other respects, association with any person who is the object of serious attention must be such as never to suggest any connection beyond this. Anyone failing to observe this rule 403c is to be subject to the accusation of unmusicality and boorishness."'

'That's how it will go,' he said.

'Well then,' I said, 'do you agree that our discussion of music has reached an end? At any rate, it's ended up where it should end; the proper place for talk of music to end, I imagine, is with talk of love of the beautiful.'

'I agree,' he said.

'After our young men's musical upbringing, then, comes its physical counterpart.'[176]

'Naturally.'

'It's imperative that the same close attention be paid to this 403d aspect of their upbringing, starting from childhood and continuing through life. Matters stand something like this, I think – see if you agree: it seems to me not to be the case that any body that's in good condition makes a soul good through the excellence it has; it's rather the other way round, that a good soul through *its* excellence makes for a body that is as good as it is capable of being. How does it seem to you?'

'I agree with you,' he said.

'So now that we've looked after the mind[177] well enough,

would it be the correct way to proceed if we handed over to *it*
the precise details of how to look after the body – provided, of
course, that we offer enough by way of general outlines? That
way we'll avoid a long treatment of our own.'

'Certainly.'

'One thing we said[178] was that our young men must keep
themselves from getting drunk; I imagine a guard is the last
person to need to get drunk and not know where on earth
he is.'

'Yes,' he said, 'it would be absurd for someone who was a
guard to need a guard himself.'

'What will we say about their food? Our men are athletes in
the greatest contest of all – right?'

'Yes.'

'So will the condition of trained athletes be suitable for our
people?'

'Perhaps it will.'

'On the other hand,' I said, 'it does tend to make for sleepi-
ness, and to pose a risk to health. Haven't you noticed how
trained athletes sleep their lives away, and the serious and
violent reactions they suffer if they diverge just a little from
their prescribed regime?'

'I have.'

'So it's a more refined sort of training that will be needed for
our warrior athletes, if they're to match up to what's required
of them: that is, if they're to be as wide awake as guard-dogs,
to have the sharpest sight and hearing possible, and aren't to
be quick to fall sick under the constantly changing conditions
that affect military campaigns, whether it's the water, or the
food, or extremes of heat or cold.'

'That's how it seems to me.'

'So will the best physical training be one closely related to
the musical training we were describing just now?'

'What do you have in mind?'

'It'll be training of a simple and well-judged sort, especially
when it comes to preparing for war.'

'How's that?'

'Things like this one can actually get from Homer,' I said.

'You'll remember that on campaign, when the heroes are feasting, he doesn't give them fish to feast on, even though they're   404c
on the sea, in the Hellespont, nor does he give them boiled,
only roast, meat, which is actually what is most convenient for
soldiers on the move; from practically every point of view it's
more convenient for them to roast things on the fire than to
carry pots and pans around with them.'

'Very much so.'

'Nor, I think, did Homer ever mention sauces and season-
ings. Or does anyone in training know without needing to be told
that a body that's going to be in good condition has to be kept
away from everything like that?'

'Yes,' he said, 'they know and they keep off it, quite correctly.'

'In that case, if you think that's right, it seems you won't   404d
approve of Syracusan cooking and the Sicilians' inventiveness
with sauces.'

'I think not.'

'Then you disapprove, too, of Corinthian girls[179] being a
favourite with men if the men are to be in good physical shape.'

'Yes, absolutely.'

'So you similarly disapprove of what people think of as the
delights of Attic pastries?'

'Yes, I must.'

'Yes, because, in my view, we'd be right in comparing that
kind of eating and that kind of regimen to the songs and tunes
that are put together using every mode and every rhythm.'[180]   404e

'No question.'

'There, we said, variety breeds lack of restraint, here it
breeds sickness; just as simplicity in music breeds moderation
in souls, so in physical training it breeds health in bodies.'

'Very true,' he said.

'And when lack of restraint and illnesses burgeon in a city,   405a
don't lawcourts and doctors' surgeries open up all over the
place, and the arts of lawcourt speaking and medicine start giving themselves airs, as many people, even free ones, start to
take such things really seriously?'

'Yes, that must be what happens.'

'Nor, I think, will you find a surer sign of a city that educates its citizens badly and shamefully than when it's not merely the inferior sort of people, people who work in manual trades, who require top doctors and advocates, but those who pretend

405b to have been brought up in the manner of free men. Or don't you think it shameful, and a sign of a lack of education, for a person to be forced to rely on a justice imposed by others, acting as his masters and judges, because of a lack of resources of his own?'

'Yes,' he said, 'that's most shameful of all.'

'Or do you think there's something more shameful than this?' I asked. 'It's when someone doesn't just spend most of his life in lawcourts, whether defending or prosecuting, but is persuaded by boorishness to pride himself on the very fact, because

405c he thinks he's so very clever in the matter of committing crimes, and knowing every dodge, every way out, every twist and turn he needs to avoid being caught and punished – all this for the sake of small things worth nobody's attention; he has no idea how much finer and better it is to organize his life for himself so as to have no need of a juryman nodding off in front of him.'

'I was wrong,' he said; 'this is more shameful still.'

'And where doctors are concerned,' I said, 'it's reasonable

405d enough to need their skills for healing wounds, or because one happens to have caught some seasonal disease; what is shameful – don't you think so? – is filling oneself with fluids and gases, as if one were some sort of lake, through the kind of lazy regimen we've just described, thus compelling those clever sons of Asclepius[181] to invent names for diseases like "flatulence" and "flux"?'

'Very much so,' he said; 'these really are new and strange names for diseases.'

'I don't think such names existed in Asclepius' time,' I said. 'My evidence for saying this is that his sons did not reprimand

405e the woman who gave the wounded Eurypylus at Troy a drink of Pramnian wine,[182] sprinkled amply with ground barley

406a and grated cheese, which is nowadays considered liable to cause inflammation; nor did they take issue with Patroclus, who was in charge of the treatment.'

'Actually,' he said, 'it is a strange drink to give someone in that condition.'

'Not so, in fact,' I said, 'if you bear in mind that Asclepius' sons never used to follow the contemporary fashion in medicine for mollycoddling diseases, that is, until Herodicus arrived on the scene. But Herodicus, who was a physical trainer, when he fell ill managed to mix up training with medicine, and tortured   406b first and foremost himself, then lots of other people as well.'

'How so?' he asked.

'By spinning out his death,' I said. 'As he continually tracked the disease that killed him, though he couldn't find the cure, I think he still lived out his life looking for it, at the cost of dropping everything else, and suffering torture if he diverged at all from his usual regimen; thanks to his expertise he died a bad death all the way to old age.'

'He got a fine reward, then,' said Glaucon, 'for his skill.'

'One that he or anyone deserves', I said, 'for not knowing   406c that Asclepius failed to reveal this form of medicine to his offspring, not out of a lack of knowledge or experience but because he knew that in the case of everyone who is well governed there is a single function assigned to each individual in the city, which he is bound to perform, leaving no time for anyone to live permanently ill and under treatment. It's absurd that we see the truth of this in the case of craftsmen, but we don't see that it also holds for the rich and supposedly fortunate.'

'How so?' he asked.

'If a carpenter is ill,' I said, 'he expects the doctor to give him medicine to drink to make him vomit up the disease, or else   406d something to purge the bowels, or else cautery, or surgery, and then to be done with it; and if someone prescribes him an extended regimen, with compresses to the head and everything of that sort, the carpenter is quick to say that he doesn't have time to be ill, and it doesn't pay him to live in that way, giving his attention to his ailment and neglecting the work that's set before him. He soon dispenses with that sort of doctor, embarks on the regimen he was used to before, regains his health and lives doing the job that belongs to him; or if his body is not strong enough for that, death puts an end to his troubles.'

'That', said Glaucon, 'seems the appropriate way for someone like him to approach medical treatment.'

407a   'Is that because he had a job to do, and if he didn't do it, it
wasn't worth his being alive?' I asked.

'Clearly so,' he said.

'Whereas the rich person, we generally say, has no such job
waiting for him, nothing that would make his life unliveable if
something forcibly kept him away from it?'

'People generally say not.'

'Evidently', I said, 'you don't pay attention to Phocylides'
advice,[183] that as soon as a man has enough to live on he should
practise at excellence?'

'Yes,' he said, 'but I think he should do it even before that.'

'Let's not get into a fight with him about it,'[184] I said; 'let's be
our own authorities as to whether that's what a rich person
407b   should practise at, and life is unliveable for anyone not practising at it; or whether nursing diseases is a hindrance when it
comes to paying attention to carpentry and other manual
crafts, whereas it's no hindrance to doing what Phocylides
exhorts us to do.'

'Zeus! Yes it is,' he said; 'practically the greatest hindrance
of all is this excessive attention to the body, which goes beyond
any ordinary physical regimen. It's a nuisance for everything
from managing a household through military service to sitting
and holding public office in the city.'

'But actually the most important consideration is that it is
407c   bad for learning of any kind, and having ideas or going over
things with oneself, because it's always on the lookout for some
sort of headache or dizziness which it then says is caused by
doing philosophy, the result being that it puts a complete block
on excellence being practised and tested in this way;[185] it makes
a person think all the time that he is ill and never stop agonizing about his body.'

'Yes, that's likely enough,' he said.

'So shall we say that Asclepius too recognized all this? People
who had naturally healthy bodies and a healthy regimen, but
407d   who had some isolated disease in them – shall we say it was for
people in this condition that he revealed the art of medicine,

removing their ailments through drugs and surgery before prescribing a return to their more usual regimen, so as not to
interfere with the smooth running of the city; whereas in the
case of bodies that were wholly and completely diseased, he
didn't employ a regimen involving a bit of draining off here and
a bit of topping up there to try to make their owners' lives long
and bad, in the course of which they'd probably father more
sickly bodies like their own into the bargain – his thought being   407e
rather that people who weren't able to cope with the normal
round of life oughtn't to be treated, since they brought no profit
either to themselves or to the city?'

'You're making Asclepius quite a political expert,' he said.

'Clearly he was,' I said; 'and don't you see how this rubbed
off on his sons, who managed simultaneously to show them-   408a
selves excellent fighters at Troy and practise medicine in the
way I'm describing? Don't you remember how from Menelaus'
wound, too, the one that Pandarus inflicted on him, "They
sucked clean the blood, and upon it sprinkled soothing
balms,"[186] without prescribing what he should drink or eat
afterwards, any more than they did for Eurypylus[187] – on the
basis that medical remedies are sufficient to cure men who
before they are wounded are healthy and have a well-balanced   408b
regime, even if they happen to go on at once to drink something unsuitable, whereas they thought that for someone
naturally sickly and lacking in restraint staying alive was of no
profit either to him or anyone else, nor should their skills be
used for such people, who ought to be left untreated even if
they were richer than Midas.'

'By your account, the sons of Asclepius were exceedingly
clever people,' he said.

'That's fitting,' I said, 'even though the tragic poets and
Pindar take a different view from us, claiming in the same breath
that Asclepius was a son of Apollo, and that he was bribed with
gold to cure a rich man who was already as good as dead, for   408c
which they allege he was struck by a thunderbolt. We, in accordance with what we said before,[188] refuse to accept both claims:
if he was the son of a god, he wasn't a money-grubber, we'll say,
and if he was a money-grubber he wasn't the son of a god.'

'That much', he said, 'is absolutely correct. But what do you say to the objection that there must, surely, be good doctors available in the city? And I imagine good doctors will especially be ones who have applied themselves to the largest number not
408d just of healthy people but also of sick ones; similarly, good jurymen will be those who have actually dealt with all sorts of different types of people.'

'I do have good ones in mind,' I said; 'very much so. But do you know which I regard as good?'

'I'll know if you tell me,' he said.

'I'll try,' I said; 'but you've mixed two different cases in the same question.'

'How so?' he asked.

'Doctors', I said, 'will be most skilful if, from childhood on, they've not just learned the rules of their art but have also had
408e experience of the largest number of bodies possible, in the worst condition possible, and have also had every disease themselves, having been born with a somewhat sickly constitution. It's not their bodies they use to treat other bodies, I imagine, because if it were, these couldn't be allowed ever to be or to come to be in bad condition; what they use is their souls, which can't become bad and be bad if they're to treat anything well.'

'Correct,' he said.

409a   'But jurymen, my friend, use their souls to rule over other souls, and these can't be allowed to have been brought up, from childhood, in close familiarity with souls that are bad, and to develop a sharp inner eye for the injustices of others by having gone through and actually committed the whole range of possible injustices themselves. Rather, they must from the first have had no experience of bad dispositions, and be uncontaminated by them, if they are to be fine and good themselves and make judgements about what is just in a healthy fashion. This is the reason why the better sort of young people appear
409b silly and easily duped by the unjust ones – they simply don't have models in themselves for the way the bad are affected.'

'Yes,' he said, 'they really do suffer like that; very much so.'

'So that', I said, 'is why the good juryman must be an old man and not a young one, someone who has learned late in life what injustice is, and not by having identified it there in his own soul, as his own, but by having practised over many years at seeing its peculiar and innate badness in others' souls, and as belonging to others – through knowing about it, that is, and not through relying on his own personal experience.'

'That certainly seems the noblest kind of juryman,' he said.   409c

'Yes, and the good kind, which was what you were asking me about; because the person who has a good soul is good. The cunning and suspicious kind, who's done many unjust things in his time, and thinks he's wise in a smart sort of way – he looks clever when he's with people like himself, because he knows from consulting the models in himself that he needs to be extra-cautious, but when he's in the company of good people and people older than himself, he immediately looks stupid, suspecting people when he doesn't need to and not recognizing a   409d healthy disposition when he sees it, because he has no model of such a thing available to him. But because he more often encounters bad people than good ones, he seems more wise than foolish, both to himself and to others.'

'That's absolutely true,' he said.

'Then if we want a good and wise juryman,' I said, 'it's the other kind of person we should be looking for, not this one; because badness will never recognize goodness or itself, whereas goodness, as education is added to natural endowment, will, in time, acquire a knowledge that is at once of itself and of bad-   409e ness. So it's this latter person, in my view, not the bad one, who turns out to be wise.'

'And that's my view too,' he said.

'So will you make legal provision in the city for a doctor's art of the sort we described, along with this kind of juryman-ship? And will they, together, look after those of the citizens   410a that are born well formed in their bodies and their souls, while refusing to treat those who are not – allowing them to die if the malformation is in their bodies, and if it's in their souls and is incurable, taking steps themselves to kill them off?'

'That has appeared as the best solution,' he said, 'both for those unfortunates themselves, and for the city.'

'And clearly,' I said, 'our young people will respond to that simple music we claimed would breed moderation, and will be on their guard against being in need of the juryman's skills.'

'Naturally.'

410b   'And won't a truly musical person follow the same tracks in pursuit of the right physical training, and capture it at will[189] – one that spares him any need of a doctor, except when he can't avoid it?'

'It seems so to me.'

'In fact, when he's working out in the gymnasium he'll be doing it with the spirited aspect of his nature[190] in view, and by way of arousing that rather than developing bodily strength. Ordinary athletes undertake diets and workouts for the sake of their physique; not our man.'

'Quite correctly.'

'Then surely, Glaucon,' I said, 'it's not the case, as some suppose, that educators who prescribe a combination of music and
410c   physical training do so in order to have the one look after the body, the other the soul?'

'Why do they, then?' he asked.

'Very probably', I said, 'they have both in mind mostly for the sake of the soul.'[191]

'How so?'

'Haven't you noticed', I said, 'what effect it has on the mind when people devote their whole lives to physical exercise, and don't have anything to do with music? Or indeed, when it happens the other way round?'

'What effects do you have in mind?' he asked.

410d   'In the one case, fierceness and harshness; softness and gentleness in the other,' I said.

'I have indeed noticed', he said, 'that those who've devoted themselves to physical exercise, and not watered it down with anything else, turn out fiercer than they should be, while those who are the same with music turn out softer than is good for them.'

'And the fierceness', I said, 'will come from their nature as spirited – which, if it's correctly nurtured, will be courageous, but will most likely become harsh and difficult to handle if it's strained further than it should be?'

'I think so,' he said.

'Whereas isn't it their philosophical nature that will bring   410e
gentleness?[192] When that's too slack, it will be softer than it
should be, but when it's nurtured well it will be gentle and well
balanced.'

'That's so.'

'But we say[193] that our guards must possess both of these
natures.'

'They must.'

'So the two must be made to be in tune with each other?'

'Of course.'

'And the soul of the person thus in tune is moderate and   411a
courageous?'

'Yes, absolutely.'

'Whereas that of the person not attuned is cowardly and
crude.'[194]

'Very much so.'

'So when someone surrenders himself to music to charm him
with its pipes, pouring in over his soul through his ears, like a
funnel, those sweet, soft, dirge-like modes we talked about,
and he spends his whole life humming in tuneful delight, he at
first softens up the spirited aspect in him, if he had one, as if he
were tempering iron, making it useful instead of useless and   411b
inflexible, but when instead of stopping he keeps on pouring,
and puts it under a spell, the next moment he melts it into
liquid, until finally he dissolves his spirit clean away, so excis-
ing the very sinews of the soul and creating Homer's "softest of
spearsmen".'[195]

'Certainly so,' he said.

'And if he's naturally endowed from the beginning with
a spiritless soul, it doesn't take long for him to achieve this
result; if he has a spirited one, through weakening the spirit in
him he makes it unstable, quickly roused by small things and   411c
equally quickly dying down. People like that are already quick-
tempered and irascible instead of being spirited, and are full of
peevishness.'

'Yes, exactly so.'

'And what about somebody who puts in a lot of hard work

in the gymnasium and lives high on the hog, as high as he can go, without contact with music and philosophy? Doesn't his good physical condition at first fill him with self-confidence and high spirits, and give him more courage than he had before?'

'Yes, very much so.'

411d 'But what about if he does nothing else, and has nothing to do with music whatsoever? Even if there was some love of learning in his soul, since it has no taste of actual learning or inquiry, and takes no part in discussion or music in general, doesn't it become weak, deaf and blind – because it has nothing to wake it up, or nurture it, or give its perceptions the thorough cleansing they need?'[196]

'That's so,' he said.

'And such a person, I think, comes to hate discussion, and have nothing of the musician in him. He no longer has any use
411e for verbal persuasion, substituting the savage use of force in everything, like some wild animal, in order to achieve his ends, so living a life of ignorant ineptitude, devoid of rhythm and grace.'

'Absolutely so,' he said.

'So there being these two things, it seems, the spirited and the philosophical, I'd say that the gods[197] have given us two arts, that of music and that of physical training – not for soul and body, except incidentally, but for this other pair, to enable
412a them to be brought into concord with each other by the appropriate degrees of stretching and slackening.'[198]

'Yes, it seems so,' he said.

'In that case, the person we'd be most correct to call the most perfect musician and the most perfectly expert in concord won't be the one who attunes strings to each other; much more will he be the one who best mixes physical with musical training and applies them to the soul in the most measured way.'

'Likely so, Socrates,' he said.

412b 'And shall we not always need some such person as this in our city, Glaucon, to oversee its arrangements,[199] if these are to be preserved?'

'Yes we shall, and there couldn't be any higher priority.'

'These, then, will suffice as the outlines of their education and

upbringing. Why should anyone need to discuss the arrangements people like this will make for dancing, for hunting, with
and without dogs, for athletic competitions or competitions with
horses? It's pretty clear they must follow the pattern we've outlined, and by this stage discovering them won't be a difficult
matter.'

'Probably it won't,' he said.

'Well then,' I said: 'what is it we'll need to establish next?   412c
Won't it be which of these same people of ours will rule, and
which will be ruled?'

'Naturally.'

'Clearly, the ones who rule should be older, and the ones
who are ruled should be younger?'

'Clearly.'

'Clearly, too, the ones who rule should be the best of them.'

'That's clear too.'

'Now the best among farmers turn out to be best at farming,
don't they?'

'Yes.'

'But in our case, since we're looking for the best among
guards, mustn't these be those best at guarding a city?'

'Yes.'

'So they must be intelligent and capable in this regard, and
they must also care for the city?'

'That's so.'   412d

'But a person will care most for something he really loves.'

'Necessarily.'

'And he will most love something when he thinks the same
things are in its interest as in his own, and when he supposes
that he is doing well if it is, and if it's not, neither is he.'

'Just so,' he said.

'That means we need to pick out from the guards as a whole
those who most appear, to our observation, completely com-   412e
mitted to doing whatever they think is in the interests of the
city, and unwilling under any circumstances to carry out anything they think not to be in its interests.'

'They'd be the ones we want,' he said.

'Then it looks to me as if we'll need to watch them at all

stages of their lives, to see if they're able to guard this commitment against any sorcery or assault that may lead them to
forget, and jettison this belief of theirs, about the need to do
what is best for the city.'

'How would they "jettison" it, exactly?' he asked.

'Let me explain,' I said. 'It seems to me that a belief will exit
the mind either voluntarily or involuntarily: voluntarily, when
a belief is false and one has learned better, involuntarily in the
case of any true belief.'

'I understand about the voluntary sort, but I need you to tell
me about the involuntary.'

'What's that?' I said. 'Don't you think, as I do, that if it's
good things human beings are deprived of, it's involuntary,
whereas if it's bad things it's voluntary? Or perhaps it isn't a
bad thing to be cheated out of the truth, and a good thing to
possess it? – or don't you think believing what is the case is to
have the truth?'

'No,' he said, 'you're right; I do think being deprived of true
belief is something involuntary.'

'So when it happens to people, it'll be a case of theft, or sorcery, or assault?'

'You've lost me again,' he said.

'It's probably because I'm using metaphors like a tragic poet,'
I said. 'The people I have in mind as victims of "theft" are those
who have been persuaded to change their mind, or who forget;
in the second case it's time that robs them without their noticing
it, in the first it's talk. I imagine you understand now?'

'Yes.'

'My victims of "assault", then, will be people made to
change their belief by some physical pain or suffering.'

'I've got that too, and you're right.'

'As for the victims of "sorcery", I think you'll say yourself
that they're the ones who change their belief either out of pleasure, which charms them into it, or out of fear, because there's
something that frightens them.'

'Yes,' he said, 'when anything deceives people it does resemble sorcery.'

'So, as I was saying just now, we must look for those among

413a

413b

413c

our people who are best at guarding this commitment they
have in them, to doing whatever they think at any time is best
for them to do in the interests of the city. We must observe
them even while they're still children, setting out for them the
sorts of tasks in which someone is most likely to forget ideas
like that, or be tricked out of them; anyone who remembers his
lessons well and proves hard to trick we'll put on our list, and   413d
anyone not like that we'll cross off it. Right?'

'Yes.'

'And we must also set them assignments that will make them
work hard, cause them pain and have them competing with
each other – we'll be looking for the same qualities here too.'

'Right,' he said.

'And finally,' I said, 'we'll need to create a contest of a third
kind, so that we can see how they respond to sorcery: just as
horse-trainers expose colts to noises and commotions to see if
they are easily spooked, so we must take our young guards and
face them with terrors of some sort, then confront them with
pleasures instead, testing them far more severely than smiths   413e
test gold in the fire – to see if any of them shows himself hard
to spook and able to maintain his composure in everything, by
virtue of his excellence as a guard of himself and of the musical
education he set out to acquire, displaying himself as a person
of true rhythm and concord in all the tests we set him: if he's
like that, he'll be of the greatest service both to himself and the
city. And the one who always passes the test, whether as a
child, a young person or an adult, and emerges from the fire   414a
with no blemish, is our man – he's the one we must set up as
ruler, and guard, of the city, giving him honours not just while
he's alive but when he's dead, awarding him the greatest privileges in the allotment of tombs and other memorials; anyone
who doesn't come out like that, we will reject. That, Glaucon,'
I said, 'seems to me the sort of way we need to select those to
be put in place as rulers and guards; of course it's only an outline, not a detailed treatment of the subject.'[200]

'I too think it must be something like that,' he said.

'So will it actually be most correct to call these people, the   414b
ones we've selected, the complete and finished guards, watching

over both hostile elements outside the city and friendly elements within it, in order to prevent the latter from wishing harm to it, the former from being able to cause harm; while the young ones that we were calling guards up till now we should rather call auxiliaries, supporting the decisions of the rulers?'

'I think that's right,' he said.

'So,' I said, 'what can we devise from among those falsehoods we were talking about just now, the ones that could be used when the occasion required it[201] – can we produce some
414c single noble falsehood that will convince the rulers too, if that can be managed, but if not,[202] all the rest of the city?'

'What sort of thing do you have in mind?' he asked.

'Nothing so new,' I said; 'something with a Phoenician flavour[203] – the sort of thing that once happened all over the place, or so the poets say and have induced many to believe, but hasn't happened in our time, probably never could, and would take a lot of persuading to make people believe it.'

'You seem to be hesitating about telling us,' he said.

'And you'll see that I have good reason for hesitating,' I said, 'when I do tell you.'

'Go on, tell us,' he said; 'there's nothing to be afraid of.'

414d 'I shall. But I don't quite know where I'll find the audacity, and the words, to try to persuade first the rulers and the soldiers, and after them the rest of the city, that really and truly all the time we were bringing them up and educating them,[204] they only *thought* this was being done to them, and it was all a kind of dream; in fact, all this time they were actually under the ground being moulded and nurtured within the earth, and their weapons and other equipment were being crafted with them, until the time
414e came that they were completely finished, and the earth, their mother, released them into the world above, so that now they plan for the land in which they have their existence as for a mother and nurse, defending her if anyone attacks her, and taking thought for other citizens as their brothers, born with them from the earth.'

'Quite barefaced,' he said; 'no wonder you hesitated so long about telling us.'

415a 'Yes,' I said, 'I had good reason. All the same, let me tell you the rest of the story. "All of you in the city are brothers," goes the story we'll tell them, "but as the god was moulding you, for those of you fitted to rule he used gold as part of the mixture in the process of generation, which is why you are the most valued, while for the auxiliaries he mixed in silver, and iron and bronze for the farmers and the craftsmen. And because you are all akin to each other, though for the most part you'll have 415b children like yourselves, there are times when silver offspring will be generated from gold, or gold from silver, and so on with the other permutations. So the first and most important instruction given by the god to the rulers is that they must guard over nothing as well or as watchfully as they do over each new generation, looking to see which metal it is that is mixed into their souls. And if their very own offspring turns out to be touched 415c with bronze or iron, they won't in any way feel sorry for it, but instead accord it the honour its nature deserves, transferring it to the craftsmen or the farmers; correspondingly, if one of these is born touched with gold, or with silver, they'll honour it and bring it up to join the ranks of the guards, or of the auxiliaries, saying that there is an oracle that the city will fall when the guard that guards it is iron or bronze." Can you think of any way of contriving that they believe this story?'

'No, none,' he said, 'at any rate so far as the first generation is concerned; their sons, maybe, and later generations, and the 415d rest of humanity after that.'

'I see what you're saying,' I said, 'and even that much will help encourage them to care for the city and each other. Let's leave our story to its fate, as it is told by succeeding generations; as for ourselves, let's arm these earthborn scions of ours and lead them out, with the rulers at their head. When they arrive at the city, let them look and see what the best location will be for them to pitch their camp, one that would make it easiest for them both to keep those inside the city in check, 415e should anyone refuse to obey the laws, and to fight off those outside the city, should an enemy come like a wolf to prey on a flock. And having pitched their camp, and made sacrifices to the appropriate recipients, they should make themselves places to sleep. Or what do you think?'

'Just so,' he said.

'Places adequate to protect them from both winter and summer weather?'

'How not?' he said. 'I imagine you're talking about their houses.'

'Yes,' I said; 'that is, ones suitable for soldiers, not for people who make money for a living.'

416a   'Once again, I need you to explain,' he said; 'what's the difference?'

'I'll try to tell you what it is. I imagine there would be nothing more terrible or shameful than if shepherds brought up dogs to act as auxiliaries for their flocks, and deliberately encouraged just those traits in them that would make the dogs themselves set out to harm the sheep, whether because of simple lack of restraint or hunger or some other bad trait in them, and become like wolves instead of dogs.'

'Of course that would be terrible,' he said.

416b   'We must guard, then, mustn't we, in every way we can against our auxiliaries' behaving like this towards the ordinary citizens, just because they are stronger than ordinary citizens are, and becoming like savage slave-masters instead of well-intentioned allies?'

'We must,' he said.

'And would they themselves be provided with the surest of guarantees against that, if they've really been well educated?'

'But they have been well educated,' he said.

To which I replied, 'That we shouldn't insist on, my dear Glaucon.[205] But what we should certainly insist on is that they
416c   must receive the correct education, whatever it is, that being the most important factor in ensuring that they are gentle both to each other and to those guarded by them.'

'Yes, and rightly,' he said.

'Well, and any intelligent person will say that in addition to their having this education, the arrangements for their housing and possessions generally must be such as neither to interfere
416d   with their fulfilling their role as guards as well as possible, nor to incite them to do harm where the other citizens are concerned.'

'Yes, and it'll be true.'

'So,' I said, 'see if the following mightn't be the sort of way

they should live and be housed, if they're going to turn out like
that. First of all, none of them should have any private property
whatsoever, except where it can't be avoided. Second, none of
them should have a house or store-room that isn't open to
everyone who wants to go in. The necessaries of life, in the
quantities required for men who are athletes for war, at once
moderate and courageous, they should receive from the other   416e
citizens as pay for guarding them, to an agreed amount such
that they will neither have a surplus in any year, nor go short;
and they'll frequent common messes, living a shared life like
soldiers on campaign. Gold and silver, we should tell them, they
always have, divine and god-given, in their souls, and they
don't need the human sort as well; besides, it's impious to mix
and defile the possession of divine gold with possession of the
mortal – the currency of the many has been the occasion of   417a
many an impious act, whereas theirs is unsullied. Indeed, for
them, and for them alone in all the city, it is solemnly forbidden
to handle, even touch, silver and gold. They mustn't even come
under the same roof, let alone wear silver or golden jewellery,
or drink from silver or gold. That way, they'll save themselves
and save the city. When they acquire land, houses and currency
as their own private property, that's when they'll be householders
and farmers instead of guards, and will become slave-masters   417b
and enemies instead of allies of the rest of the citizens, so spending their lives hating and being hated, plotting and being plotted
against, more frightened and more fearful of enemies within
than of enemies without, running already a hair's breadth from
shipwreck and from taking the rest of the city down with them.
For all these reasons,' I said, 'let's declare, shall we, that this is
how the arrangements for the guards must be, in relation to
housing and all the rest, and legislate accordingly? Or not?'

'Yes we shall,' said Glaucon.

Book IV   At this point Adimantus interjected: 'So what will your   419a
begins   defence be, Socrates, if someone says you're not making
[Book C]   these men of yours very happy? And it's nobody's fault but
their own, since the city truly belongs to them, yet having it

doesn't do them any good. Normally, people in such a position would own land, build themselves fine mansions and acquire furniture to match; they'd make private sacrifices to the gods, they'd have guests to stay, and, yes, they'd do what you were talking about just now, and own gold and silver, and everything else that's thought to be required for happiness – but here you are, our objector will say, apparently making your people no more than hired auxiliaries[206] who sit there and do nothing except keep watch.'

'Yes,' I said; 'and what's more, they'll do it for their rations alone, and won't get pay as well, as ordinary people would;[207] so they won't even be able to go on private trips abroad if they want to, or give anything to prostitutes, or spend money on anything else they want in the way that people usually do who are thought to be happy. You need to add these points to the charge-sheet, and lots more like them.'

'Consider it done,' he said.

'So you're asking what our defence will be?'

'Yes, I am.'

'If we follow the same path as before,' I said, 'I think we'll find what we need to say. We'll say that it would be no surprise at all if these men of ours weren't in fact happiest being as they are, but that actually what we're aiming for in founding our city isn't to make any particular group of our people exceptionally happy, but rather to achieve happiness so far as possible for the city as a whole. Our thought was[208] that it was in that kind of city that we'd be most likely to find justice, and injustice in the city that was worst governed, so that having identified them both, we could come to that judgement between them that we've been seeking to make all along. So now we're shaping the happy city, as we think, not separating off a few people in it and supposing them to be happy, but rather the city as a whole; and shortly we'll be examining the opposite kind of city.[209]

'Imagine we're painting a statue, and someone comes up and criticizes us for not applying the most beautiful colours to the most beautiful parts of the figure, because the eyes are the most beautiful thing and they've not been coated with purple but with black. It would be perfectly reasonable for us to say to him, "Strange that you think we should give the eyes so beautiful a colour that they no longer look like eyes at all. It's the same with the other parts too; just look and see whether by applying the appropriate colour to each, we're not giving beauty to the whole thing." In just the same way, you shouldn't force us to attach a kind of happiness to the guards that will make them anything *but* guards. We could if we wanted give 420e our farmers the same treatment – dress them up in elaborate robes, put gold round their necks and tell them to work the land when they felt like it. We could have the potters reclining on couches, left to right[210] before the fire, drinking and feasting to their hearts' content, their wheels to one side to use just so much as they wish. We could give everybody else the same sorts of blessings, and make the whole city happy that way. But don't advise us to adopt that course, because if we do as you say, 421a farmers won't be farmers, potters won't be potters, and in general all those types needed to make up a city will tend to merge into one another. Now if this happens with most of them it doesn't matter so much: if shoe-stitchers are corrupted and turn bad, so that they only pretend to be good at stitching shoes, a city has nothing to fear from that. But if those who guard the laws and the city are not what they seem to be, you see for yourself that it spells the complete ruin of any city; equally, excellence in those who guard us is the sole measure of good government and of happiness. So if we, for our part, are making our guards true guards, who least of all threaten harm 421b to the city, whereas that critic of ours just wants to make some collection of farmers happy, as if they were feasters at a communal banquet, not members of a city – well, it's something else he's talking about, not a city.

'The question must be, then, whether we should be establishing our guards with the aim of providing them with the greatest possible happiness, or whether we shouldn't rather be looking to see whether this comes about for the city as a whole, compelling and persuading these auxiliaries and guards of ours[211] to make it their aim to ensure that they are the best possible 421c craftsmen in relation to their own specific function;[212] similarly with all the rest. With the city as a whole growing along these lines, and being governed well, it must be left to each separate group to share in happiness in the way assigned to it by its nature.'[213]

'Yes,' he said, 'I think you're right.'

'I wonder, then,' I said, 'whether you'll think my next point too is reasonable; it's closely related to the last one.'

'What is it?'

'See if you think these are the things that destroy other sorts of craftsmen too, and make them actually bad at what they do.'

421d   'What sorts of things are "these"?'

'Wealth,' I said, 'and poverty.'

'How's that?'

'I'll tell you. Do you think a potter will still want to devote himself to his craft when he's rich?'

'Hardly,' he said.

'He'll become idler and more careless, compared with his old self?'

'Yes, much.'

'So becoming a worse potter?'

'Much worse.'

'And again, if he's prevented by poverty from providing himself with the tools or anything else he needs for his craft, 421e not only will the work he produces be worse, but his teaching of his sons, or anyone else he teaches, will result in inferior craftsmen.'

'Of course.'

'Both things, then, wealth *and* poverty, make not only for inferior products of a craft, but inferior craftsmen.'

'Evidently so.'

'So we've found another set of things, it seems, that our guards must guard against, in case they ever slip past them into the city unnoticed.'

'What things?'

422a   'Wealth', I said, 'and poverty. Wealth turns people into lovers of luxury and idleness, poverty makes them illiberal and bad at what they do;[214] either makes them look for political change.'

'Absolutely so,' he said. 'But here's something for you to

consider, Socrates: how will our city be able to go to war, when it won't have acquired any money – especially if it finds itself having to fight a large and wealthy city?'

'Clearly,' I said, 'it'll be harder to fight one city like that, but easier against two.'   422b

'What are you saying?' he asked.

'Well,' I said, 'I imagine the first point is that if it comes to a fight, it may be against rich men, but they themselves will be trained athletes in the business of war.'[215]

'That much is true,' he said.

'So tell me this, Adimantus,' I said: 'don't you think a single boxer, who's been prepared as well as he could possibly be just for this, boxing, can easily fight two men who aren't boxers at all but wealthy and flabby?'

'Probably not at the same time,' he said.

'Not even', I said, 'if he could feint at giving ground to whichever of them came at him first, then turn and strike, and   422c
go on doing the same over and over again in the stifling heat? Wouldn't a boxer like him actually see off more than two such opponents?'

'That wouldn't be in the least surprising,' he said.

'But don't you think the wealthy have more knowledge and experience of boxing than of fighting wars?'

'I do,' he said.

'In which case we'd reasonably expect our warrior athletes easily to take on forces two or three times the size of their own.'

'I'll give you that,' he said; 'I think you're right.'   422d

'What if they sent representatives to one of the opposing cities, to say what is actually true: "We don't use gold ourselves, or silver, because we're not allowed to, as you are; so what the others have is all yours if you come and fight with us"? Do you think anyone who heard that would prefer to go to war against a pack of lean and mean dogs, rather than fighting with them against a flock of soft and flabby sheep?'

'I don't think so,' he said. 'But all the same, if just one city acquired the combined wealth of all the others, watch out that it doesn't spell danger for one that isn't wealthy.'

'How innocent you are', I said, 'if you think that there's   422e anything worth calling "a city" apart from the sort of one we're constructing.'

'What *should* I call them?' he asked.

'Every other city', I said, 'needs to be referred to in the plural. Any of them you like will be a whole collection of cities, not *a* city – it's like one of those puzzles people like to play 423a with.[216] There are anyway two at war with each other, the one consisting of poor citizens, the other of wealthy ones; and then within either of these two there is a whole collection of others. You'll achieve nothing at all if you treat these as a single city, but if you treat them as many different ones, handing over the money and privileges of one group, or indeed the members of that group, to another, then you'll always have plenty of allies and few enemies. And if you find a city governed in the moderate sort of way we've arranged for ours, it will be greatest, not as measured in terms of reputation, you understand, but truly greatest, even if it can only deploy a thousand to fight for it. 423b Real greatness like this in a single city you won't easily find among either Greeks or non-Greeks, though you will find many with a reputation for greatness that are many times the size of our little one. Or do you take a different view?'

'Zeus! No,' he said.

'So,' I said, 'will this also be the best criterion for the rulers of our city when it comes to determining what size to give it, and accordingly how much land needs to be marked off for it, any beyond that being treated as of no interest?'

'What criterion is that?' he asked.

'I think it's this,' I said: 'they should go on increasing the size of the city for so long as that is compatible with its being a single city; no further than that.'

423c   'Yes, that'll be a good way of proceeding,' he said.

'So shall we lay this further injunction on our guards, too? They must watch out for all they're worth to prevent the city from either being small or merely appearing great – it must be sufficient in size, and one, not many.'

'A simple task, of course,' he said.

'And there's another task for them that's even simpler,' I said, 'something we've talked about before, when we said that

if someone inferior is born to the guards, he must be sent off
to join the ordinary citizens, and if these should give birth to   423d
someone of quality, he must be promoted to the rank of guard.
This was an illustration of the point that even in the case of the
ordinary citizens, the general rule still applies: namely, that
each individual must be matched with the single function for
which nature has fitted him, so that by performing the single
role that belongs to him, each and every citizen may become
one person, not many people at once, and the whole city may
thus grow as one city and not many.'

'Yes,' he said, 'even simpler to manage!'

'Actually, my good friend Adimantus,' I said, 'one might
think that we're giving the guards a long list of big things to do,   423e
but in fact they're all straightforward so long as they keep their
eye on the proverbial one big thing – or perhaps I should say
big enough rather than just big.'[217]

'What's that?' he asked.

'Their education,' I said, 'and their upbringing; because if
they're well educated and grow up into decent adults, they'll
easily see for themselves all the requirements we're discussing,
as they will other things too – everything that we're now leaving to one side, such as the acquisition of women and things   424a
like marriage and the procreation of children; they'll see that
these all have to be done as much as possible in accordance
with the saying, "What friends have, they share".'

'Yes,' he said, 'that would be best.'[218]

'What's more,' I said, 'when once a city starts off well, its
progress from there describes a kind of circle:[219] good natures
are produced within it by an upbringing and education that's
kept sound, while in turn sound natures, by acquiring an education to match, become even better than those that came
before them – and especially in relation to breeding; it's the
same with other animals.'

'Yes,' he said, 'that's probably so.'   424b

'So to put it briefly, those charged with caring for the city
must keep a firm hold on this education and make sure that it
is not corrupted when they're not looking, guarding it through
thick and thin against revolutionary innovations, whether in

physical training or in music, and keeping it as much as possible as it is – fearing that moment when someone tells everybody it's "the song the singer latest sings/ Men heed the
424c more",[220] in case possibly someone supposes the poet to be talking not about new songs but about a new way of singing, and thinks this is something to approve of. One mustn't either approve of such a thing or suppose it to be what the poet had in mind. We must beware of adopting a new form of music, as potentially risking everything; for styles of music never change without the foundations of political harmony being affected too – so Damon[221] says, and I believe him.'

'You can put me down as a believer too,' said Adimantus.

424d   'So it's here or hereabouts that our guards must build their guard-house,' I said: 'in music.'

'It's true,' he said; 'rule-breaking there easily slips by unnoticed.'

'Yes,' I said, 'on the grounds that it's only play, and won't do any harm.'

'And neither will it,' he said, 'except by gradually inserting itself and encroaching quietly upon people's dispositions and behaviour – and from there emerging stronger, affecting first
424e their contracts with one another, then the laws and the city's institutions, Socrates, until finally its brutal violence overturns everything, both private and public.'

'Very good,' I said; 'that's how it is?'

'It seems so to me,' he said.

'So as we were originally saying, *our* children must start off at once with play of a more tightly rule-governed sort, the argument being that if it breaks the rules and the children become rule-breakers too, there's no way that they'll grow up
425a to be good and rule-governed adult men themselves?'

'Quite right,' he said.

'So when children do make a good start to their play, and have been imbued with law and order through their musical education, the effect is exactly the opposite of what it was in the other case – rule-*keeping* is their companion in everything, helps them to grow, and if the city was falling down in any respect before, sets it to rights.'

'True enough,' he said.

'Then these are people who'll also discover the apparently trivial rules of life for themselves, all of which their predecessors abolished.'

'What are they?'

'Things like younger people not talking out of turn in the 425b presence of their elders, giving up their seats for them, standing up for them, looking after their parents; not to mention having their hair cut right, wearing appropriate clothes and shoes – the whole way they carry themselves, and so on and so forth. Don't you think so?'

'I do.'

'It's silly, I think, to put it all into law. Telling people to do such things or writing them down doesn't make them happen, and they're soon forgotten.'

'Yes, inevitably.'

'At any rate, Adimantus,' I said, 'whatever direction a person is given by his education, what follows will surely be more 425c of the same. Like always encourages like, doesn't it?'

'Of course.'

'And finally, I think we'd say, it'll turn into a single complete and vigorous whole, whether good or the opposite of good.'

'It must do.'

'So given these considerations,' I said, 'I for one wouldn't try to legislate for such things.'

'That's reasonable enough,' he said.

'But for goodness' sake!' I exclaimed. 'What about the regulation of the market-place? All those contracts people make with one another in the market, or with workmen, if you will; 425d mutual insults, assault, bringing lawsuits, setting up juries; even, I suppose, the exaction and payment of market-fees or harbour-tolls, if we can't do without them – I'm thinking of market or city or harbour regulations in general, whatever these may be: shall we take it on ourselves to legislate for these?'

'It's not worth laying them down,' he said, 'for men who are already good and fine; most of these things, those that require 425e legislation, I imagine they'll easily think out for themselves.'

'You're right, my friend,' I said, 'provided only that the gods[222] grant them preservation of the laws we discussed before.'

'Yes,' he said; 'otherwise they'll spend their lives perpetually writing and rewriting a whole raft of regulations like that, thinking they'll finally get to the best solution.'

I said, 'What you're saying is that such people will be living like sick patients too lacking in restraint to want to give up a bad regimen.'

'Yes, absolutely.'

426a 'And what a charming way they go on! For all the attention they get from the doctor they get nowhere, unless it's to make their illnesses worse and more exotic; and all the time they're hoping some new drug they're recommended will make them healthy again.'

'Yes,' he said; 'that's a good description of what happens to patients like that.'

'And isn't it a particularly charming feature of theirs,' I said, 'that they regard it as the most hateful thing of all if someone tells them the truth: that until someone stops getting drunk, 426b gorging himself, sleeping around and lying about, no kind of treatment – no drugs, no cautery, no surgery, no incantations, either, or amulets, or anything else like that – will do him any good at all?'

'Not very charming,' he said; 'getting angry with someone who says the right thing isn't charming at all.'

'I gather you're not an admirer of men like that,' I said.

'Zeus! No, I'm not.'

'So you won't admire a city, either, that collectively behaves in the same sort of way. Don't you think that cities are doing the same thing as these patients of ours, when despite being 426c badly run they first of all proclaim to the citizens that they mustn't try to change the city's constitutional arrangements as a whole, threatening anyone who does so with execution, and then proceed to honour the man who – when they're run like that – looks after them most delightfully, man for man, insinuating himself into their favours, anticipating their wishes and showing himself adept at fulfilling them? A good man,

they'll call him, one who's wise about what matters, and they'll
honour him accordingly.'

'Yes,' he said, 'it is the same thing, and I haven't the least
admiration for it.'

'And what about those who are willing to look after cities in   426d
this condition, and are even eager to do it? Aren't you in awe
of their courage and adaptability?'

'Yes, I am,' he said, 'except for those who've been deluded
into thinking that they're true political experts, just because
they receive praise from ordinary people.'

'What are you saying?' I asked. 'Don't you feel for them?
If someone doesn't know a thing about measuring, and lots
of other people in the same position say that he's four cubits
tall,[223] do you think it's possible for him not to think he is?'   426e

'I'm with you here, too,' he said; 'I don't think it is possible.'

'So don't be cross with them. People like that are surely the
most charming examples of humanity, continually writing and
rewriting laws about the sorts of things we were discussing just
now, and always supposing they'll discover some way of
putting an end to criminality in business dealings and the other
areas I was just mentioning, when in actual fact they're cutting
off the head of a Hydra.'[224]

'Yes, right,' he said; 'that's exactly what they're doing.'   427a

'So for my part,' I said, 'I wouldn't have thought the true
legislator needed to occupy himself with laws and political
arrangements of that form, whether he's operating in a city
that's run badly or in one that's run well; in the first because it's
useless and gets nobody anywhere, and in the second because
some of the rules in question anyone could find out for himself,
and others will follow automatically from our previous recommendations.'[225]

'So what is there left for us to legislate about?' he asked.   427b

To which I replied, 'For us, nothing, but for Delphic Apollo
there remain the greatest and finest and first of subjects for
legislation.'

'Which are?' he asked.

'The founding of temples, sacrifices and other forms of
service to gods and demi-gods and heroes; then, for the dead,

the proper forms of burial, and all the other things that must be done for those in Hades to keep them favourable to us. We don't know anything about such things ourselves, and in found-427c ing a city, if we've any sense, we won't listen to advice from anyone, or use anyone as our guide, unless it's the one our ancestors used; for this god is surely *the* ancestral guide in such matters for all mankind, sitting there on the navel-stone at the centre of the earth[226] and giving us the benefit of his guidance.'

'You're right,' he said; 'that's how it's to be done.'

427d 'There, son of Ariston,' I said, 'consider the city now founded. The next thing will be for you to look in it – you'll need to get yourself a good enough light from somewhere, and call in your brother to help you, along with Polemarchus and the others – in case we can somehow see exactly where justice will be in the city, and injustice too, what the difference is between the two things, and which of them a person is to get for himself if he's to be happy, whether all gods and men fail to observe him or not.'

'Nonsense,' said Glaucon. 'You promised *you*'d do the 427e looking – because, you said,[227] it wouldn't be pious for you not to come to justice's aid as best and in whatever way you could.'

'You're right to remind me,' I said. 'Yes, I must do as you say, but I'll need you all to help me.'

'We'll be there,' he said.

'Well,' I said, 'I expect to find what we're looking for in the following way. I imagine, if our city has been properly founded, that it is completely good.'[228]

'It must be,' he said.

'Clearly, then, it has wisdom in it, courage, moderation and justice.'

'Clearly.'

'Well, whichever of these we find in it, what will be left will 428a be what we've not found?'

'Of course!'

'Then take any four things: if we were looking for just one of them in anything, and we happened to recognize it first, then we wouldn't need to go any further; but if we'd started by recognizing the other three, by that very fact we'd have recognized the one we were looking for – since there clearly wouldn't be anything else for it to be except the one that was left.'[229]

'You're right,' he said.

'So since in fact we are dealing with four things, should we carry out our search in just this way?'

'Evidently.'

'Yes, and actually the first thing I think is clearly visible, as we look at it, is wisdom – and there's evidently something a bit odd about it.' 428b

'What's that?' he asked.

'The city we described does genuinely seem to me to be wise; because it's able to make good decisions – right?'

'Yes.'

'And clearly the ability to make good decisions is in itself a kind of knowledge; I imagine, at any rate, that it's through knowledge, not ignorance, that people decide well.'

'Clearly.'

'But there are all sorts of different kinds of knowledge in the city.'

'Of course.'

'So is it because of the knowledge of its carpenters that the city deserves to be called wise and good at decision-making?'

'Hardly,' he said; 'that would make it good at carpentry.' 428c

'Then a city shouldn't be called wise because of its knowledge about wooden products, and the way it decides how these will be best.'

'Certainly not.'

'What about its knowledge of metal-working, or anything like that?'

'All ruled out.'

'Nor is it because it knows about producing crops from the soil; that makes it good at farming.'

'It seems so to me.'

'So then,' I asked, 'is there any kind of knowledge in the city we've just founded, residing in some particular citizens, through 428d which it reaches decisions, not about some particular concern of the city, but about the city as a whole, and the way in which it will best relate both to itself and to other cities?'

'Indeed there is.'

'What is it,' I asked, 'and which of the citizens has it?'

'It's this knowledge about guarding, and it belongs to these rulers of ours that we were just now naming as *complete* guards.'[230]

'So what do you call the city because of this knowledge?'

'Able to make good decisions,' he said, 'and genuinely wise.'

'Well,' I said, 'do you think there'll be a greater number of
428e   metal-workers in our city or of these true guards?'

'Far more metal-workers,' he said.

'And in fact, of all those groups whose names mark them out as having knowledge of some sort, the true guards will be the smallest.'

'By far.'

'In that case, it's by virtue of its smallest group or part, and the knowledge residing in this, the part that's set over it and rules it, that a city will be wise as a whole, if it's founded
429a   according to nature; it seems to turn out that this is by nature the smallest category of people – the one that properly shares in the only kind of knowledge in the city that deserves the name of wisdom.'

'Very true,' he said.

'So here we are, I'm not sure how, having found one of our four; and not just that – we've found where it's situated, too.'

'I certainly think it's been found quite satisfactorily,' he said.

'But actually it's not too hard to see courage in our city either – courage itself and what it resides in, which is what earns the city its title as courageous.'

'How so?'

429b   'If someone had to decide whether to say a city was cowardly or courageous,' I asked, 'what would he do but look at that part of it that defends it and marches out on its behalf?'

'No one would be silly enough to look at anything else,' he said.

'Right,' I said, 'because whether or not everybody else in it was cowardly or courageous wouldn't, I imagine, be responsible for the city's being the one or the other.'

'No, it wouldn't.'

'In that case, a city is courageous too through a part of itself, by virtue of having in that part the capacity to preserve under any circumstances the belief that the things that are to be feared are the very same or of the same sorts that the lawgiver told them about in the course of their education. Isn't this what you call courage?'   429c

'I didn't entirely understand what you said,' he replied. 'Please say it again.'

'I'm saying that courage is a sort of preservation.'

'*What* "sort of preservation"?'

'Of the belief that has come about in them, thanks to the law, and through their education, about what, and what sorts of thing, are to be feared; and what I had in mind by preservation "under any circumstances" was their successfully preserving this belief in the face of pains or pleasures, desires or fears, and never dispensing with it.[231] I have what I think is an apt comparison to offer, if you're willing.'   429d

'I'm willing.'

'Well,' I said, 'you're aware, aren't you, of what dyers do when they want to dye wool and make it purple? They first of all choose, out of so many colours, the wools whose single natural colour belongs to the whites, and then they give them a preliminary treatment, preparing them carefully so that they'll take on the hue as well as possible; only then do they dip them in the dye. Whatever wools are dyed in this way become colourfast, and washing them either without soaps or with them won't remove their hue; any that aren't – well, you know what happens to them, whether someone's trying to dye other colours of wool, or even these white ones without the preliminary treatment.'   429e

'Yes, I know,' he said; 'they're ridiculously easy to wash out.'

'Well,' I said, 'that's the sort of thing I want you to suppose we were trying to do when we selected our soldiers and educated them with music and physical exercise. What we were trying to contrive was precisely that they should be persuaded into taking up our laws as well as they possibly could, just like a dye, so that through their having combined the right nature   430a with the right education, their beliefs – about what is to be feared or about anything else – might come to be colour-fast, immune from being washed out by those soaps, so fearful for 430b their capacity to wash away: pleasure, more fearful than Chalestrian lye; pain, and fear, and desire, more to be feared than any.[232] That sort of capacity to preserve, under all circumstances, the correct belief, as prescribed by law, about what is and is not to be feared – that's what I'm calling courage, and what I'm taking it to be, unless you have something else to suggest.'

'No, nothing,' he said. 'I think you're supposing that if correct belief about these same things has come about independently of education, as in the case of animals and slaves, it isn't at all reliable, and should be called something else, not courage.'

430c   'Very true,' I said.

'So I accept that this[233] is what courage is.'

'Yes, do,' I said; 'and you'll be right – just so long as you're accepting it as an account of *civic* courage.[234] But we'll be discussing the subject again, if you want, and even better than we have now; for the moment it's justice, not courage, that we were supposed to be looking into. We've done enough with courage, I think, for that purpose.'

'You're right,' he said.

'Well now,' I said, 'there are still actually two things left for 430d us to identify in our city: moderation, or moderateness,[235] and what our whole inquiry is for – justice.'

'Yes, quite.'

'How shall we find justice, then – so as not to bother ourselves any more with moderateness?'

'I have to say I don't know,' he said, 'and in any case, I wouldn't want justice to show up first, if that means we're to give up on moderateness. If you're willing to indulge me, please look at that first.'

'But of course I'm willing,' I said; 'I certainly should be.'

'You look, then,' he said.

430e   'That I must,' I said. 'And as I view it from here, it looks more like a kind of concord or attunement than the previous two did.'[236]

'How so?'

'Moderateness, I suppose, is a kind of order,' I said; 'an inner control over certain pleasures and desires, as people put it, when they talk about someone as being "stronger than himself", however *that* might come about; and it has left its traces in other similar expressions. Right?'

'Very much so.'

' "Stronger than himself" – isn't this a ridiculous expression? The person who's stronger than himself will surely have to be weaker than himself as well, and the weaker stronger, since it's always the same individual who's being talked about.' 431a

'Obviously.'

'But actually,' I said, 'what's behind this way of talking appears to me to be the idea that there are different elements within the individual person, in relation to his soul, one better and one worse, and that when the naturally better element is in control of the worse – well, that appears to me to be what's intended by "stronger than himself", at least to go by the way it's used as a term of praise; when a bad upbringing or keeping a certain sort of company causes the better element, which is also the smaller, to be overpowered by the sheer mass of the worse one, that's being "weaker than oneself", used as a reproach for someone's 431b being in that condition, which they call a lack of restraint.'

'Yes, very likely,' he said.

'Well,' I said, 'if you look at our new city, you'll surely find the first of these two things in it: you'll say "stronger than itself" is a just description of it, that is, if in fact we're to call "moderate" and "stronger than itself" what has its better element ruling over the worse.'

'I'm looking,' he said, 'and you're right.'

'And again, the many and various ordinary desires, and pleasures and pains – these you'll find especially in children and 431c women and slaves, as well as in the ordinary, inferior men who make up the majority of those who are called free.'

'Yes, absolutely.'

'Whereas the simple and measured ones, guided by reasoning together with intelligence and correct belief, are to be found in just a few people; the ones with the best natures and the best education.'

'True,' he said.

'And do you see these features cropping up in your city, too – the desires in the inferior majority being controlled, there and then, by the desires and the wisdom that reside in those who are fewer and superior?'

'I do,' he said.

'So if any city deserves to be called stronger than pleasures and desires, and stronger than itself, this one certainly deserves it.'

'Yes, absolutely,' he said.

'Then won't it also deserve to be called moderate, in all these respects?'

'Very much so.'

'Yet again, if there's any city where rulers and ruled have in them the same belief about who it is that should rule,[237] it will certainly be in ours, don't you think?'

'Very much so,' he said; 'absolutely.'

'So in which of the two groups of citizens will you say the moderateness resides when they are like this? In the rulers, or in the ruled?'

'In both, I imagine,' he said.

'So you see, it was a good prediction we made just now, about moderateness resembling a sort of attunement.'

'Why?'

'Because it is not like courage or wisdom, which worked their effect on the city by residing in a part of it, the one making it courageous, the other making it wise; moderateness works by being spread literally through the whole of the city, causing everyone – the weakest, the strongest, the middling, whether in wisdom, in physique, or for that matter numbers, wealth, or any other similar measure you like – to sing the same song from high to low in unison. The outcome is that we'd be quite right to declare this unanimity to constitute moderateness, a concord between naturally worse and naturally better as to which of them should rule, whether in a city or in each individual citizen.'

'I'm completely in agreement,' he said.

'So there we are,' I said; 'we've spotted three of the things we were looking for in our city, or so it seems; as for the remaining form of excellence still needed to make the city good – what, I wonder, will that be? It's justice I'm talking about, obviously.'

'Obviously.'

'Now's the time, then, Glaucon, for us to be like sharp-eyed hunters and surround the thicket, making sure justice doesn't slip out somewhere and vanish from sight. It's evidently some-   432c
where hereabouts – keep your eyes peeled, and see if you can spot it; perhaps you'll see it before I do and point it out to me.'[238]

'I only wish I could,' he said. 'You'd be better off treating me as a hunt-follower, who can see what's pointed out to him; that's quite enough for me to manage.'

'So follow me,' I said, 'and pray with me for a good out-come.'

'I'll do that,' he said; 'just lead on.'

'Actually,' I said, 'the place we're in seems particularly impenetrable and full of shadow; at any rate, it's dark and dif-ficult to hunt in. Still, on we must go.'

'Yes, we must!' he said.   432d

Then I spotted something. 'Aha!' I exclaimed. 'Glaucon, I do believe we're on to something! It seems it's not going to get away from us altogether.'

'Good news,' he said.

'Oh dear,' I said, 'we've been behaving like slackers.'

'How?'

'My dear man, all this time it's apparently been running around right under our feet, and we didn't see it. We've made ourselves look quite ridiculous, like people who go looking for something when they've actually got it there in their hands; we   432e
did the same, failing to see it and looking off into the distance instead, which is probably why we missed it.'

'What are you saying?' he asked.

'Just this,' I said: 'it seems to me that all along we've been talking and hearing about justice without understanding that we *were* actually talking about it, in a way.'

'That's a long introduction,' he said, 'for an eager hearer.'

'So hear me,' I said, 'and see if perhaps I'm making sense.   433a

Justice, I think, is the universal rule we laid down at the beginning, when we started founding our city – either this, or else some form of it. What we laid down, I believe, and frequently asserted, if you recall, was that each individual should practise the single role to which his nature is most suited, among those relevant to the city.'

'Yes, we did.'

'And actually there's something we've not only heard others saying but have often said ourselves:[239] that to behave 433b justly is to mind one's own business, not meddle in others' affairs.'

'Yes, we've often said it.'

'Well, my friend,' I said, 'justice is very likely this, minding one's own business, if "minding one's own business" is understood in a particular way. Do you know my reason for thinking so?'

'No,' he said; 'do tell me.'

'It seems to me', I said, 'that what's left, in our city,[240] after the three things we've looked at,[241] namely, moderateness and courage and wisdom, is what makes it possible for all of them to come about in the city, and preserves them in existence for 433c so long as it too is present.[242] And we did say[243] that if we found the three and took them away, justice would be what was left.'

'Yes, there's no getting round that.'

'Well,' I said, 'if one had to decide which of these things contributes most to the goodness of our city by its presence, it would certainly be a hard decision: whether it was the unanimity between the rulers and the ruled, the preservation of beliefs about what is and is not to be feared, ingrained by law in the 433d soldiers, or the wisdom to guard the city present in the rulers – or whether it was actually *this* that most contributed to making the city good, when present in child, woman, slave, free man, craftsman, ruler and ruled, namely, that each single individual was doing the job that was his, and not meddling in what should be done by others.'

'Yes, it certainly would be hard to choose,' he said.

'So vying for the prize in relation to a city's goodness, alongside its wisdom, its moderateness and its courage, will be the capacity we identify as the doing of what belongs to him by each individual within it.'

'And would you propose what vies with *these* for the prize, in relation to a city's goodness, to be justice?'

'Yes, absolutely.'

'See what you think about the following point too. Will you assign to the rulers in the city the task of judging legal disputes?'[244] 433e

'Of course.'

'And in making their judgements will they put anything before the goal of ensuring that no set of people either has what belongs to others or is deprived of what is their own?'

'No, that will be their chief goal.'

'Because it's just?'

'Yes.'

'So in a way this point, too, will support the view that having and doing what is one's own – what naturally belongs to us – is justice.' 434a

'That's so.'

'Then see if you agree with me about this. If a carpenter tried to do the things a shoemaker does, or the other way round, whether they were exchanging their tools or social positions with one another, or the same person was actually trying to do both jobs, and everything else was switched round accordingly,[245] does it seem to you that it would do great harm to the city?'

'Not too much,' he said.

'However, if someone who is a natural craftsman or some other sort of money-maker[246] gets puffed up by wealth, the number of his supporters, his sheer physical strength or anything else of that kind and tries to gain entry to the category of war-fighter, or else if someone in the latter category tries to get into that of guard and decision-making expert when he's not qualified – if ever *these* swap their tools and social positions, or someone tries to do all these things at the same time, I think you agree with me that this interchange between them and this meddlesomeness of theirs is death to the city.' 434b

'Yes, absolutely.'

'So when there are three groups, their meddling in each
434c   other's functions and changing into each other is most harmful
to the city, and would be quite correctly described, more than
anything, as criminality?'[247]

'Exactly so.'

'But won't you say that doing the worst one can to one's
own city is injustice?'

'Of course I will.'

'So this is injustice. And let's agree to the converse: when the
money-making group, the auxiliary group and the guarding
group do what belongs to them, that is, when each of these
groups performs its proper role in a city, as they fail to do in the
other case, that will be justice, and will be what makes the city
just.'

'This seems to me precisely the way it is,' he said.

434d   'Let's not be too firm about it quite yet,' I said; 'but if we find
that this pattern[248] extends to each individual person as well,
and will happily be justice there too, then we'll go along with
it – why not? If it doesn't, we'll have to try another line of
inquiry. For now, let's complete the strategy we originally
embarked on, our idea being that if we tried to get a view of
justice first in something that had justice in it but was bigger
than the individual, it would then be easier to spot the kind
434e   of thing it is in the individual himself. The bigger thing, we
decided, should be a city, and so we set about founding the best
city we could, because we could be confident that if it was good
we would find justice in it. So now let us refer what we've discovered in the case of the city back to that of the individual, and
if they fit, all will be well; if things turn out to be different in the
435a   individual, we'll go back to the city and test our new findings
there, and so perhaps, by comparing the two with each other
and rubbing them together, we'll make the flame of justice shine
out as if from a pair of fire-sticks – and once it's become visible
this way we'll be able to confirm it in our own minds.'

'That sounds the way to go,' he said; 'let's do it.'

'Well,' I said, 'if a thing can be called the same whether it's
larger or smaller, is it actually unlike in the respect in which it's
called the same, or like?'

'Like,' he said.

'In that case, a just man won't differ at all from a just city in   435b
respect of the form itself, justice, that they have in them;[249] in
that respect he'll be like it.'

'Yes, like,' he said.

'But now, a city appeared to be just insofar as each of three
kinds of natures in it performed its own role; and again it
appeared to be moderate and courageous and wise through
these same three kinds' being affected or disposed in certain
other ways.'

'True,' he said.

'This means, then, my friend, that we shall expect the individual too to have these same kinds[250] within his own soul, and   435c
to merit the same epithets as the city through these kinds being
affected in the same ways as the city's.'

'That must be right,' he said.

'Oh dear,' I said; 'that's another really simple question we've
landed ourselves with – whether the soul contains these three
kinds in itself or not.'

'Not at all a simple question, it seems to me,' he said; 'the
old saying probably has it right, that nothing good comes
easily.'

'Evidently,' I said. 'And I have to tell you, Glaucon, that
in my view we shall never get a precise hold on this matter   435d
by using methods like the ones we're using in our present
exchanges – it's another road that leads there, and it's longer
and more challenging.[251] But no doubt we'll do as well in
answering this new question as we've done in our preceding
discussions.'

'Shouldn't we be content with that?' he asked. 'It would certainly be enough for me, at least for the moment.'

'Well, certainly,' I said, 'for me it'll be quite sufficient.'

'No flagging, then,' he said; 'on with the question.'

'Well,' I said, 'do we have any choice but to agree to this
much, that there are the same kinds and dispositions in us as   435e
individuals as there are in the city? I don't imagine they could
have got there from anywhere else. It would be ridiculous to
suppose that spiritedness in cities doesn't originate in individual

citizens – who do actually get the credit for it, as for example in Thrace or Scythia, or pretty generally in the northern regions; and there could hardly be any other source for the love of learning that would be associated especially with our region, or for the love of money one would attribute most of all to the Phoenicians and the inhabitants of Egypt.'

436a

'Quite so,' he said.

'That's how it is, then,' I said; 'nothing difficult about seeing that.'

'No indeed.'

'But what *is* difficult to see is whether we perform each of these three activities with the same thing, or with three things, one for each – do we learn with one element in us, feel anger with another and use some third element for desiring the pleasures of nourishment, procreation and everything related to these? Or in each of these cases, as we set ourselves in motion, are we acting with the whole soul? That's the question it will be difficult to settle properly.'

436b

'I think so too,' he said.

'So here's a way we can try to settle our question, whether it's the same thing we're acting with in each case, or different things.'

'What is it?'

'Clearly, it's a general rule that the same thing won't act or be acted on in opposite ways simultaneously, at any rate in the same respect or in relation to the same thing. So if we do some-how find this happening in the present case, we'll know that it wasn't one and the same thing we were dealing with but more than one.'

436c

'So far so good.'

'Now think about what I'm saying.'

'Say on,' he said.

'Is it possible', I said, 'for the same thing to be simultan-eously at rest and in motion in the same respect?'

'No way.'

'Well, let's be even more precise about what we're agreeing, to prevent our falling out as we go on. Imagine a person stand-ing still but moving his hands and his head: if someone claimed

that this was an example of the same person being at rest and
in motion at the same time, we'd object that that wasn't the   436d
right way to put it; rather, we'd say, one bit of him is at rest,
another in motion. Isn't that so?'

'It is.'

'Then even if our respondent were to extend the joke with
the further subtlety that tops, at any rate, do rest and move at
the same time, as wholes, when they have their base fixed in
one place as they go round, as likewise does anything else that
goes round in a circle on the same spot – even then we'd not
concede the point, because in such cases the resting and the
moving weren't going on with respect to the same bits of them.
We'd prefer to say that there's both a straight and a circular in   436e
them, and they're at rest with respect to the straight bit, because
they're not leaning in any direction, but there's circular movement with respect to the round bit; if any of them leans where
it's straight, whether to right or left or front or back, and moves
round at the same time, then it's not at rest in any way.'

'Yes, and we'd be right to say that,' he said.

'Then if we hear anyone saying things like that, we shan't be
rattled, nor shall we be any readier to believe it possible for
anything, if it's still the same thing, to have done to it, or to be,
or to do both of two opposite things at the same time, in the   437a
same respect and in relation to the same thing.'

'I won't be, anyway,' he said.

'All the same,' I said, 'to prevent our having to confront
every single objection of this sort and waste valuable time confirming that they aren't true, let's proceed on the simple
assumption that they *aren't*, on the understanding that if the
assumption turns out to be wrong, everything we've concluded
on this basis will come undone.'

'Yes, we must do that,' he said.

'Well now,' I said, 'assenting and dissenting, striving to get   437b
a thing and rejecting it, drawing something to one and pushing
it away: would you count all these kinds of things as being
opposites – whether actions or passions, it will make no difference?'[252]

'Yes, I count them as opposites,' he said.

'So,' I said, 'what about being thirsty and being hungry – the appetites[253] in general, wanting, too, and wishing? You'll count all of these, I imagine, somewhere among the kinds just men-
437c tioned; for example, you'll say, won't you, that the soul of the person with any sort of appetite is either striving for the thing he has an appetite for, or drawing to itself what he wishes to have, or indeed, insofar as its owner wants to be provided with something, assenting to that, to itself, as if something was ask-ing "Do you want it?", and the soul was reaching out to get it?'
'I shall.'

'And wishing not to have, and not wanting, or not having an appetite for something? These I think you'll count as cases of the opposite – the soul's rejecting something, pushing and driv-ing it away from itself.'
'Of course.'

437d 'Given all of this, shall we say that the appetites form a dis-tinct category,[254] and that the most conspicuous of these are the one we call "thirst" and the one we call "hunger"?'
'We shall,' he said.
'The one being a desire for drink, the other for food?'
'Yes.'

'Now will thirst, insofar as it is thirst, be for anything more than what we say it is a desire for, in the soul? For example, is thirst thirst for hot drink or cold drink, or for a sizeable drink or a small one, or in general for drink of any particular kind? Or is it rather, that when an element of heat is present together
437e with the thirst it will produce the desire for cold as well, and similarly coldness will produce the desire for hot; if the thirst is sizeable because size is present in it, it'll produce desire for size, and if it's small, for smallness? As for thirst by itself, that will never become a desire for anything except that very thing it is its nature to be a desire for, namely drink, and similarly with hunger and food.'

'Just so,' he said; 'when taken by itself, each of the appetites is exclusively for what it is its nature to be for, by itself; the extra bits belong to the thing desired as qualified in this or that way.'

438a 'So let's not have someone catch us off our guard, and throw us into disarray with the objection that no one in fact desires just drink, or food; it's good drink we desire, and good food. Everybody, after all, desires good things – don't they? So if thirst is a form of desire, it will be for a good something, whether it's a drink or whatever it's a desire for, and similarly with other desires.'

'Yes,' he said, 'and one could perhaps think this objector had a point.'[255]

'But look here,' I said. 'Of things that are such as to be related to something, those that are qualified in some way have 438b a correlate that's qualified too, while others are just themselves and so is their correlate.'

'I don't understand,' he said.

'You don't understand', I said, 'that the greater is greater in relation to something?'

'Certainly I do.'

'In relation to the less?'

'Yes.'

'Whereas the much greater is much greater in relation to the much less – right?'

'Yes.'

'And the greater at some time is so in relation to the less at some time; what will be greater relates to what will be less?'

'Of course!'

'And again the greater in number relates to the fewer in number, the double to the half, and so on; the heavier relates to 438c the lighter, the quicker to the slower; the hot to the cold, too, and similarly with everything like that?'

'Absolutely.'

'And what about the different kinds of knowledge – isn't it the same with them? Knowledge, taken by itself, is knowledge of learning – or whatever we should suppose it *is* of[256] – similarly taken by itself, whereas a particular knowledge, one of a particular kind, is of some particular thing of a particular kind. Let me illustrate what I'm saying: isn't it when knowledge 438d becomes, say, knowledge of house-building that it differs from other kinds of knowledge, thus acquiring the specific name "house-building-knowledge"?'

'Obviously.'

'Isn't that through being a particular kind of knowledge, distinct from any other?'

'Yes.'

'And isn't it because it's knowledge of some particular thing that it, too, becomes a particular kind of knowledge – and similarly with the other varieties of expertise and knowledge?'

'That's so.'

'That, then,' I said, 'if perhaps you understand me now, is what I'd like you to take me as having wanted to say when I was claiming that with things that are such as to be related to something, if they're taken alone by themselves their correlates are also just themselves alone, whereas if they're qualified in some way so too are their correlates. I'm not at all saying that they'll be of the same sort as whatever their correlates are – that would make the knowledge of things healthy and unhealthy itself healthy and unhealthy, and the knowledge of bad things and good things itself bad and good; rather, my point was that as soon as knowledge becomes knowledge of something of a certain sort, for example of the healthy and unhealthy, and not just of *something*, unqualified, then it turns out itself to be knowledge of a certain sort, with the result that it's no longer called "knowledge", simply, but its particular object is added in, and it's called "*medical* knowledge".'

'I understand,' he said, 'and I think this is a fair statement of the matter.'

'Going back to thirst, then,' I said, 'wouldn't you count it as one of the things that is what it is in relation to something – "what it is", presumably, in this case, being thirst.'

'I would,' he said; 'and it's for drink.'

'So if the drink is of a certain sort, then so too is the corresponding thirst, but as for thirst itself, this isn't for either a big drink or a little one, or for a good or a bad one, or in general for a drink of any specific sort; it's the nature of thirst by itself to be for drink by itself alone?'

'Yes, absolutely.'

'In that case, to the extent that the soul of the person with

the thirst is thirsty, it wants nothing else except to drink. That's 439b
what it's reaching out for; that's the object of its impulse.'

'Clearly so.'

'So if there's ever anything that drags it in the opposite
direction when it's thirsty, it'll be something else in it, not what
actually has the thirst, and is pulling it like some wild animal
drawing it towards drinking? We're saying, after all, that the
same thing won't simultaneously behave with one bit of itself
in two opposite ways in relation to the same thing.'

'It certainly won't.'

'Just so, I imagine, in the case of the archer, it's unhelpful to
say that his hands are simultaneously pushing the bow away
and dragging it back; better to say that one hand pushes it
away, the other draws it to him.'

'Yes, absolutely,' he said.   439c

'Are we to say, then, that there are people who refuse to
drink, sometimes, when they're thirsty?'

'Yes, very much so,' he said; 'lots, and often.'

'So what should one say about these people?' I asked. 'Isn't
it that there's something in their souls telling them to drink, but
that there's also something in them getting in the way of their
drinking – a different something, which overpowers the other?'

'I think so,' he said.

'Now doesn't what gets in the way of such things, when it
does, originate in rational calculation, whereas the things that 439d
drag or draw the soul in such directions[257] come about either
through external factors or because of sickness?'[258]

'Apparently so.'

'Then it won't be unreasonable of us', I said, 'if we claim the
things in question to be twofold and distinct from one another,
calling the bit of the soul with which it reasons its reasoning
element, and the bit with which it experiences lust, or hunger,
or thirst, or is all a-quiver with any of the other appetites, the
unreasoning and appetitive element, going with certain ways of
being filled up and getting its pleasures.'

'No,' he said, 'it would be a likely thing for us to suppose.'

'Let these two kinds of thing, then,' I said, 'count as laid 439e down by us as being present in a soul. But now what about spirit, and the bit of us we get angry with[259] – will this be a third kind, or will it be the same in nature as one of the other two?'

'Probably', he said, 'the same in nature as the second of them, the appetitive.'

'On the other hand,' I said, 'there's a story I once heard that I'm inclined to believe, about how Leontius, son of Aglaion,[260] was coming up from the Piraeus along the outside of the northern wall when he saw dead bodies lying there beside the public executioner, and found himself simultaneously wanting to look at them and feeling disgust with himself for doing so, and trying to turn himself away; for a while, it's said, he put up a fight and covered his face, but in the end, overpowered by the desire, he ran up to the corpses, forced his eyes wide open and said, "There's a lovely sight for you, you wretches! Take your fill!"'

440a

'I've heard the story too,' he said.

'And this account, surely,' I said, 'indicates that anger is sometimes at war with the appetites, as one distinct thing with another.'

'Yes, it does,' he said.

440b

'Aren't there also many other cases', I asked, 'where we see someone cursing himself, when his appetites force him to go against his reasoning, because he's angry at the bit of him that's forcing him on? It's as if there were two factions at war with one another, with spirit stepping in on the side of reason. As for its making common cause with the appetites, when reason shows there must be no acting against *its* demands, I don't imagine you'll have observed that sort of thing happening in your own case, or I think in anyone else's.'

'Zeus, no!' he said.

440c

'What if someone thinks he is acting unjustly?' I asked. 'Isn't it the case that the nobler he is, the less capable he is of anger at being made to suffer hunger or cold or anything else like that by anyone he thinks is inflicting these things on him justly? The spirit in him won't readily be roused in such a case – that's my point.'

'True,' he said.

'How about when a person thinks someone's treating *him* unjustly? Doesn't he seethe with anger in such a case – as well as because of the hunger or cold or whatever it is he's being made to suffer? Doesn't he go into battle on the side of what seems just, enduring until he wins, not ceasing from noble actions until he either succeeds or dies, or else he is called back and calmed by the reason in him, like a dog by a herdsman?' 440d

'That's an excellent parallel for what you're talking about,' he said. 'And in our city we did specify that the auxiliaries should be like dogs serving rulers ruling like shepherds.'

'Yes,' I said, 'you've a good notion of what I want to say. I wonder if you're also noticing another point.'

'What's that?'

'That it's apparently the opposite of what we were thinking just now about the spirited element. Then we were thinking of it as something appetitive, but now we're claiming that far from being that, if the soul is in conflict it will much rather deploy its weapons in the service of the reasoning element.' 440e

'Absolutely,' he said.

'Does it do that as something that's distinct from this too,[261] or as a kind of reasoning element itself, so that there are not three kinds of thing in a soul but only two, one rational and one appetitive? Or just as in the case of the city the different elements holding it together were three,[262] money-making, soldiering[263] and decision-making, so too in the soul does the spirited element constitute a third, making a natural ally for the reasoning element – unless it is corrupted by a bad upbringing?' 441a

'It must be a third,' he said.

'Yes,' I said, 'provided it's shown to be distinct from the reasoning element, just as it was from the appetitive.'

'It's hardly difficult to show,' he said; 'after all, you can see it in children – spirit is something they're full of as soon as they're born; as for reason, most of them seem to me to acquire it somewhat late, some of them never.'

'Zeus! Yes, you're quite right,' I said; 'and one can see the same phenomenon in animals.[264] And there's that evidence from Homer as well, in the shape of the verse we cited in that other context:[265] "He smote his breast, and with these words reproved his heart"; clearly there Homer has represented what has made the calculations about the better and the worse as 441b

441c something distinct, chiding something else that is experiencing irrational anger.'

'You're quite right,' he said.

'So it's been hard going, but we've safely swum our way through this far,' I said: 'there's reasonable agreement between us that the same kinds of elements, and the same number of them, are contained both in the city[266] and in the soul of each individual person.'

'That is so.'

'Well then, doesn't this much necessarily follow, that the way in which the individual is wise, and the element with which he is wise, will be the same as they were in the case of the city?'

'Naturally.'

441d 'And also that the city will be courageous with the same element in it, and in the same way, as the individual is courageous; and that in all other respects, in regard to goodness, it will be the same for both?'

'Necessarily.'

'Then I imagine, Glaucon, that we'll say that a man is *just* in the same way that a city was.'

'This too entirely follows.'

'And I don't suppose we're likely to have forgotten that we said a city would be just if each of the elements in it, there being three of them, performed the role that belonged to it.'

'I don't think we've forgotten,' he said.

441e 'Then we must keep in mind that each of us, too, will be just, and performing the role that belongs to us, when all the three elements in us perform *their* own roles.'

'Keep it in mind we must,' he said.

'Well, doesn't it belong to the rational element to rule, if it's wise and exercises forethought on behalf of the soul as a whole, and to the spirited element to be its subject and ally?'

'Yes, absolutely.'

'And isn't it, as we said,[267] a mixture of musical and physical training that will bring them into accord with each other, 442a stretching and nourishing the one with beautiful words and beautiful lessons, and slackening the other by soothing it, taming it with harmony and rhythm?'

'Quite so,' he said.

'Then, when they've been looked after like this, and have truly learned and been educated in their proper roles, they will take charge of the appetitive element, which is the most populous element of the soul in each person and by its nature the most insatiable when it comes to money,[268] and they'll watch over it so that it doesn't become big and strong by getting its fill of the so-called pleasures relating to the body and so cease to perform *its* own proper role, instead trying to enslave under its rule what it's not fitting for its kind to rule over, and turn the whole of life upside down for everyone.'

'Yes, quite right,' he said.

442b

'And also', I said, 'won't the two of them be best placed to stand guard on behalf of the whole soul against external enemies, one of them making the decisions, the other doing the fighting as decided by the ruling element, and using the courage it has to carry out those decisions?'

'That is so.'

'I imagine, then, that we'll also call each individual person courageous because of this part of him,[269] that is, when despite any pains or pleasures the spirited in him keeps to what's been pronounced fearful or not by the words it has heard.'[270]

442c

'Yes, and rightly so.'

'But then we'll call him wise because of that small part, the one we said would rule in him, and therefore hand down these pronouncements; it too will have knowledge[271] in itself of what is in the interests both of each part and of the whole community made up by the three of them together.'

'Yes, quite.'

'What about moderateness? We'll call the individual moderate, won't we, because of the friendship and harmony of these very things – when the ruling element and the two that are ruled share the belief that the rational should rule, and don't fight like opposing factions against it?'

442d

'Moderateness, certainly,' he said, 'is precisely that, whether in city or individual.'

'And again the individual will be just by virtue of the feature – and in the manner – we've so often talked about.'[272]

'That really must be so.'

'Well now,' I said: 'we're sure the outlines of justice aren't somehow blurred? It's still precisely what we saw it to be in the case of the city?'

'It seems so to me,' he said.

'Yes,' I said, 'and if anything in our souls still disputes the 442e conclusion,[273] we can provide complete confirmation by applying the vulgar tests to it.'

'What are these?'

'For example, if we had to reach agreement about that city of ours and the man who resembled it in nature and upbringing, and whether it's likely someone of that sort would walk off with a pot of gold or silver he'd received for safe keeping, 443a would anyone suppose, do you think, that he'd be more likely to do it than people who weren't like him?'

'No one would,' he said.

'And he'd have nothing to do with things like temple-robbery either, or theft, or betrayal, whether private betrayal of friends or treason against one's own city?'

'Nothing.'

'Nor would he be in any way untrustworthy, whether it was a matter of oaths or of any other sort of agreement.'

'Of course not.'

'And things like adultery, neglect of parents, disrespect to the gods – he'd be the last sort of person we'd expect to go in for these?'

'The very last.'

443b   'And isn't the explanation in every case that each of the elements that he has in him is performing its own proper role in relation to ruling and being ruled?'

'That is what explains it, nothing else.'

'So are you still looking for something else to be justice, rather than the power that produces men of this sort, as well as cities?'

'Zeus! No, I am not,' he said.

'Our dream, then, has become reality – we said we had an idea, immediately we started founding the city, that we were

probably stumbling, with a bit of divine help, into some pre- 443c
liminary outline of what justice might be.'

'Yes, absolutely.'

'Yes, Glaucon; so it was after all – and that's why it's useful
for us – a kind of image of justice, this rule that the shoemaker
by nature should do shoemaking, nothing else, the carpenter
carpentry, and so on and so forth.'

'Evidently.'

'But the truth, it seems, was that while justice was indeed
something like that, it wasn't at all a matter of a person's external actions, but rather of what he did inside, in relation to his 443d
true self and what is truly his own, preventing each element[274]
in him from doing what belongs to others, and stopping them
from meddling in one another's roles – in the true sense putting
his own affairs in order, ruling over himself and setting himself
straight, becoming a friend to himself[275] as he fits together the
three elements in him, just like three defining sounds of musical
attunement, highest, lowest and middle, along with any others
there are in between;[276] binding all these together, so becoming 443e
moderate and well adjusted, completely one instead of many.
Then and then only is it a matter of his acting, whether in relation to the getting of money, or looking after the body, or
perhaps it'll be a matter relating to the city, or private contracts
with individuals; and all the time he'll be thinking, and calling,
"just" and "fine" whatever action preserves and helps to bring
about this disposition of his, and "wisdom" the knowledge
that presides over such action; "unjust" is what he'll think and 444a
call whatever action undoes his disposition, "ignorance" the
belief that presides over that.'

'Absolutely true, Socrates,' he said.

'So there we are,' I said. 'If we claimed we'd discovered the
just man and the just city, and what justice in them really is, I
don't think we'd be thought to be saying something totally
false.'

'Zeus!' he said. 'I should think not!'

'Are we to make the claim, then?'

'We are.'

'Then so be it,' I said, 'because after this, I think, we need to consider injustice.'

'Clearly.'

444b 'Mustn't it be a state of faction, as it were, among the three elements, a tendency to meddle or interfere in each other's roles – one part of the soul rising up against the whole with a view to imposing its own rule on it, contrary to its own nature, which fits it rather for enslavement, and to enslaving the kind whose nature is to rule?[277] These are the sorts of things we'll say, I think, and in general that it's the confusion of these elements in the soul, and their straying from their proper roles, that constitutes not only injustice but lack of restraint, cowardice, ignorance – in brief, every form of badness.'

444c 'That', he said, 'is precisely what we'll say.'

'Then,' I said, 'given that we're clear about injustice and justice, isn't it already patently clear, too, what it really is to do unjust actions and behave unjustly, and to do just things?'

'How so?'

'What's clear', I said, 'is that there really is no difference between them and doing what's healthy or unhealthy: they are to the soul what healthy or unhealthy actions are to the body.'

'In what respect?' he asked.

'Healthy actions, I imagine, produce health in a body, and unhealthy ones disease.'

'Yes.'

444d 'Well, don't just actions produce justice in a soul, unjust ones injustice?'

'Necessarily.'

'And producing health is setting up the elements in the body so as to control and be controlled by one another according to nature, while producing disease is setting them up to rule and be ruled one by another contrary to nature?'

'Yes, it is.'

'Well then,' I said, 'won't producing justice similarly be a matter of setting up the elements in the soul so as to control and be controlled by one another according to nature, and producing injustice a matter of setting them up to rule and be ruled by one another contrary to nature?'

'Surely,' he said.

'In that case, it seems that goodness will be a sort of health of the soul, a state of beauty and well-being; badness will be 444e disease, ugliness, weakness.'

'That is so.'

'So won't it also be true that fine and beautiful practices lead to the acquisition of goodness, ugly and shameful ones to that of badness?'

'Necessarily.'

'What now remains for us, it seems, is to inquire whether 445a what pays is to do just actions and follow fine and beautiful practices, and be just, whether one is seen to be so or not, or rather to do unjust actions and be unjust, provided one doesn't pay the penalty for it, and isn't made a better person by being punished.'[278]

'But see here, Socrates,' he said, 'by this point the question appears to me to be becoming absurd. If people think life not worth living when the natural condition of the body is being ruined, even supposing they had all the food and drink and wealth and power in the world, are we really to imagine it to be worth living when the natural condition of the very thing that gives us life[279] is being turned upside down and ruined, just on 445b condition that we can do whatever we wish *except* what will enable us to rid ourselves of badness and injustice, and acquire justice and goodness in their place – given that they've each been shown to be as we have described them?'

'Yes, it's absurd,' I said; 'even so, now that we have come this far, we mustn't draw back from doing what we need in order to see as clearly as we possibly can that all this really is as we say.'

'Zeus!' he said. 'Drawing back is the very last thing we should do.'

'Come over here now,' I said, 'if you want to see how many 445c forms badness takes, or so it seems to me – the ones worth observing, at any rate.'

'I'm here with you,' he said; 'go on.'

'Very well,' I said. 'The way it appears to me, as it were from my vantage-point, now that we've got this far up in our discussion, is that there's one form of goodness and a limitless number of forms of badness, but only four or so that are actually worth mentioning.'

'How do you mean?' he said.

'Take those types of political regime that are clearly distinct in form, and there'll probably be a corresponding number of types of soul.'

445d   'How many is that?'

'Five,' I said; 'five types of political regime, and five of souls.'

'Which are you saying these are?' he asked.

'One, I'm saying, is this type of regime that we've been describing, and it could be called by either of two names: if one of the rulers turned out to be exceptional, it would be called a "kingship", and if more than one, an "aristocracy".'[280]

'True,' he said.

'So this', I said, 'is one form I have in mind. Whether there were a number of such men[281] or only one of them, they

445e   wouldn't change any of the laws of the city that matter, having had the upbringing and education we described.'

'No, that's unlikely,' he said.

449a   'This, then, is the sort of city, and the sort of political   Book V
regime, that I call good, and also correct; so too this sort of   begins
man. And given that this city of ours is correct, I call other sorts
mistaken, both in relation to the general management of cities
and in relation to the way they manage the disposition of individual souls in the city. These other cities exhibit four types of
badness.'

'Which are these other sorts of city?' he asked.

I was about to talk about these, following on from our city,

449b   and how they seemed to me to evolve from one another, when Polemarchus, who was sitting a little way from Adimantus, stretched out his hand and took hold of Adimantus' cloak at the top by the shoulder, leaning forward and drawing him close; putting his head down next to his, he said some things which we didn't catch, except for this much:

'Shall we let it go, then, or what shall we do?'

'Certainly not!' said Adimantus, now raising his voice.

To which I responded, 'What exactly is it you're not "letting go"?'

'You,' he said.

'For what, exactly?' I asked.   449c

'We think you're shirking,' he said; 'depriving us of your take on one whole area of our discussion, and one of the most important – you seem to imagine you can get away without talking properly about women and children, and just saying, "well, obviously, it'll be a case of 'what friends have, they share'".'[282]

'Was that not right, Adimantus?' I asked.

'Yes,' he replied. 'But saying the right thing isn't enough, in this or any other context; we need to be told *how* the sharing will be done, since it could be in lots of different ways. So 449d oblige us by saying which one you have in mind, because we've been waiting here for some time, thinking that at some point you'd mention the subject of how they'll organize the procreation of children, and bringing them up once they're born – in general, this whole subject of, as you put it, "sharing" women and children; we think that getting this right or failing to get it right will make all the difference to the kind of regime it is. So seeing that you're proposing to move on to a quite different kind of regime before you've dealt with any of this, we've now decided, as you heard, not to let you go until you've discussed 450a this whole subject as you've discussed others.'

'And you can all put me down as voting the same way,' said Glaucon.

'Quite,' said Thrasymachus; 'take that as unanimous, Socrates.'

'Look what you've done to me,' I said, 'ambushing me like this! What a big subject it is that you're raising – one that practically takes us back to the beginning of the arrangements for our city; just when I was feeling pleased with myself for getting through them, and content if people would accept what I'd said 450b on the subject of women and children and let any more detailed discussion of it go. You have no idea what a swarm of arguments you've stirred up by egging me on in this way; it was only because I could see it coming that I put it aside, to avoid a major commotion.'

'Come on,' said Thrasymachus. 'Do you think these good people have come all this way to be fobbed off now with fool's gold? It's arguments they want!'

'Yes,' I said, 'so long as there aren't too many of them.'

'When it comes to the kind we're asking to hear, Socrates,' said Glaucon, 'an intelligent person wouldn't think them too many if they filled his whole life. But don't worry about us; you just get on with talking through the things we're asking about, in the way you think fit – the mode of sharing that our guards will use in relation to children and women, and the part of their upbringing that's regarded as most troublesome, when they're still small and it's not yet time for them to begin their education. Try and say how it needs to be done.'

'You're lucky', I said, 'that it isn't you that has to try to explain it, because there's a lot that's hard to believe, even more than with what we were talking about before. Not only might one not believe my proposals possible; even if they were entirely possible, there'll still be doubts as to whether they're for the best. That's why one hesitates to get involved with it all, in case it looks like mere wishful thinking.'

'No need for hesitation,' he said. 'The audience you'll have won't be lacking in sense, or belief, or good will.'

And I said, 'Thanks very much! I suppose you're saying that to try to reassure me?'

'Indeed I am,' he said.

'Well,' I said, 'you're having exactly the opposite effect. If I believed I knew what I was talking about, your reassurances would be in order; it's a safe and unthreatening prospect for someone to say what he knows to be true about the most important subjects, and ones that are dear to him, among dear and sensible friends. But for someone to talk when he doesn't believe he knows, but looks for the truth as he talks, which is exactly what I'm doing now, is both frightening and dangerous. The fear isn't of being laughed at, which would be a childish thing to be afraid of, but rather of falling down in my pursuit of the truth and dragging down my dear friends with me, so ruining them as well as myself in relation to things we most need to get right. Glaucon, I bow to Adrasteia,[283] and accept my punishment for what I'm going to say – because I really do suppose it a lesser mistake to kill someone without intending it than to deceive fine and good people in matters of justice and law.[284] Better to run that risk among enemies, then, than among friends; so you do well to reassure me.'

Glaucon laughed and said, 'Socrates, if anything outrageous 451b happens to us because of what you say, we let you off any charge of homicide – your hands are clean, and you're no deceiver as far as we're concerned. So carry on, you've nothing to fear.'

'Right,' I said: 'a person acquitted in court, the law says, is clean and pure; if it's true there, likely enough it'll be true here.'

'So that's cleared up,' he said; 'nothing there to stop you speaking.'

'We need to go back again,' I said, 'and talk about things we 451c probably should have talked about at the time, in the proper order. Maybe, though, it'll turn out right to do as we're doing now, going through women's roles only after we've completely finished going through the men's,[285] especially when you yourself are challenging us to do just that. For actually in a society of people born and brought up as we've described, in my view the only correct way of getting, and generally dealing with, women and children will be one that goes in the same direction we gave at the start. Our aim, I believe, was to set the men up, in our fictional city, like guards of a flock.'

'Yes.'

'So now let's go on and assign them the mode of reproduc- 451d tion and upbringing that goes with this, and see whether we think it's suitable or not.'

'What's that?' he asked.

'It's like this: do we think the females among our guard-dogs ought to share in all aspects of guarding with the males, hunt with them and partner them in everything else, or do we think they are incapacitated by bearing and bringing up their pups and should stay indoors, while the men take on the whole labour of looking after the flocks?'

'I think they should partner the males in everything,' he said; 'except that we should treat them as weaker, by comparison with the males.'

451e 'Well, is it possible to employ any creature for the same purposes as another if you don't give it the same upbringing and education?'

'No, it's not.'

'So if we're going to employ the women to do the same things as the men, we need to teach them the same things.'

452a 'Yes.'

'Music was what we gave the men, and physical training.'

'Yes.'

'Then we must assign both these kinds of discipline to the women too, along with what's needed for fighting wars, and treat them in the same way as we do the men.'

'It looks like it,' he said, 'from what you're saying.'

'There'll probably be many aspects of what we're now proposing', I said, 'that will appear ridiculous, if they're done as we say, in contrast to what we're used to.'

'Very much so,' he said.

'What do you see as most ridiculous about it all?' I asked. 'Isn't it obviously the picture of the women exercising naked in 452b the wrestling-schools alongside the men, and not just the young ones but the older ones too – like old men in the gymnasium who love to strip and train despite the wrinkled and unpleasant sight they present?'

'Zeus, yes!' he said. 'That would appear ridiculous, at least from where we are now.'

'Well,' I asked, 'now that we've started out along this line, we shouldn't be afraid, should we, of all the various jibes the wags would make about this sort of change if it happened in 452c the gymnasia, in music, and most of all when it came to carrying arms or riding horses?'[286]

'You're right,' he said.

'And since we've begun, we must press on to where the legislative going gets rough, having first requested the wags *not* to do what they always do but be serious instead, while reminding

them that it's not long since Greeks thought it quite as shameful
and ridiculous as most non-Greeks do now for *men* to be seen
naked, and that when first the Cretans and then the Spartans
started stripping off to exercise, the wits of the time would have   452d
had their chance to make fun of it all. Don't you think so?'

'I do.'

'However, I imagine that when they did start the practice,
and found it better to strip for all such things than to cover up,
its ridiculousness in their eyes melted away as their arguments
proved it best. It showed them that it's idle to suppose anything
ridiculous but what is bad, or try to raise a laugh by treating
anything as ridiculous because of the way it looks unless it's the
mindless and bad; or conversely, to try to be serious by reference to any other mark of beauty than a thing's goodness.'   452e

'Absolutely right,' he said.

'So mustn't our first task in all these things be to reach agreement as to whether they're possible or not? Mustn't we give an
opportunity to anyone who wishes to dispute with us – no matter if he's a joker, or someone more serious – whether human   453a
nature of the female variety is capable of sharing with the male
in all tasks, or in none at all, or can perform some and not
others, and whether this particular one, fighting wars, falls into
the former or the latter category? Isn't that likely to be the best
way of starting, to ensure our finishing in the best way too?'

'Much the best,' he said.

'So,' I said, 'do you want us to have the dispute among ourselves, on behalf of the other side, so that their claims won't be
left undefended against our assault?'

'There's nothing to stop us.'

'Then let's start with the following point, on their behalf: 453b
"You've no need of anyone else to dispute your case with you,
Socrates and Glaucon! Didn't you yourselves agree, when you
started founding this city of yours, that every single individual
must fulfil the single function that belongs to them by nature?"'

'We did agree to that, I think; why wouldn't we?'

' "Well, can there fail to be a world of difference between a
woman's nature and a man's?"'

'They must be different.'

' "Shouldn't the function we assign to them also be different, then – the one that accords with their nature?" '

'Of course.'

453c   ' "So how can it not be a mistake for you now to claim that the men and the women should do the *same* things, when there's this huge gulf between their respective natures? You're contradicting yourselves." Will you have any clever defence to make against that?'

'It's not very easy to think of one,' he said, 'on the spur of the moment. In fact I shall be asking you – I *am* asking you – to explain what the argument is on our side, too.'

'I saw these difficulties coming some time ago, Glaucon,' I said, 'and lots of others just as terrible; that's why I was so 453d hesitant all along to involve myself in all of this, trying to legislate for the getting and bringing up of women and children.'

'Zeus!' he said. 'It doesn't look a simple subject – not simple at all.'

'No indeed,' I said. 'But the truth is that it's all the same: you fall in, you have to swim, whether it's a little diving-pool or the middle of the biggest sea.'

'Yes, absolutely.'

'So should we start swimming, and try to save ourselves from the argument we've got ourselves into? We'll have to hope for a dolphin to pick us up, or some other unlikely form of rescue.'

'It seems so.'

453e   'Come on, then,' I said, 'and let's see if we can somehow find a way out. Here goes. We agree that different natures must be assigned different pursuits, and that a man's nature and a woman's are different; now we're saying that these two different natures must share the same pursuits. That's what we're accused of?'

'Exactly that.'

454a   'What a noble power it is, Glaucon,' I said, 'that antilogic[287] has!'

'How so?'

'Because a lot of people seem to me to fall into it unintentionally, and think they're having a discussion when they're really only point-scoring. It's because they lack the ability to analyse what's being said by distinguishing different kinds of thing; they set their sights on contradicting what's been said, in a purely verbal way, thus engaging in competition with one another rather than in dialectic.'[288]

'Yes, that certainly does happen to many people,' he said, 'but surely your description doesn't apply to us, and what we're doing now?'

'Yes, it certainly does,' I said; 'the first part, at any rate – we   454b
really are in danger of engaging in antilogic, unintentionally.'

'How?'

'We're overly keen to score a point by insisting on the idea that the same nature shouldn't be assigned to the same pursuits,[289] on a purely verbal basis, without having paused even for a moment to think about what kind of difference and sameness in nature we had in mind when we proposed to assign different pursuits to a nature that was different, and the same ones to one that was the same – difference and sameness with reference to what?'

'No, we didn't think about that,' he said.

'Apparently, then,' I said, 'it's open to us to ask ourselves if   454c
bald people and people with hair are the same in nature, not opposed, and then, when we agree that actually they are opposed, to stop people with hair from making shoes if bald people are doing it, or conversely to stop bald people if hairy ones are.'

'That would be ridiculous,' he said.

'Would it be so for any other reason', I asked, 'than that we weren't thinking then about sameness and difference in nature in each and every respect? No, we were looking out solely for the kind of diversity or likeness that was relevant to the per-   454d
formance of the tasks in question themselves. What we were saying was that, for example, two people who both had an aptitude for medicine would share the same nature.[290] Or do you not think so?'

'I do.'

'But someone with a medical aptitude would have a different nature from someone with an aptitude for carpentry.'

'I imagine, certainly.'

'So,' I asked, 'shall we declare that if the male or the female sex turns out to be outstandingly adapted to one of the crafts, or to some other pursuit, that's what must be assigned to it? If, on the other hand, they turn out to differ just in the respect that the female gives birth while the male mounts the female, we shall declare that we haven't yet been given anything to show that a woman differs from a man in the respect that matters to us, and we'll go on thinking that our guards and their women must do the same things.'

'Yes, and we'll be right to think so,' he said.

'Next, then, do we insist that our opponent should say precisely for which craft, or which pursuit, among all those that go to make up a city, a woman's nature isn't the same as but different from a man's?'

'That's fair.'

'Well, perhaps you'd find someone else giving the response you yourself gave only a little while ago, that it's not easy to say on the spur of the moment, but given time it would be no problem.'

'Yes, someone might.'

'So how about if we ask an opponent like that if he'll go along with us while we see if we can't show him that in fact there is no pursuit, relating to the way a city is run, that is peculiar to women?'

'By all means.'

'So come on, we'll say to him, answer us this: when you claimed that one person was fitted by nature for something while another was not, was it the basis for your claim that one of them picked things up quickly and the other only did so with difficulty; that the quick learners were generally good at finding out for themselves about the subject they'd learned, while those who'd had repeated lessons and practice didn't retain even what they'd learned; and that whereas in the case of the former their bodily faculties were reasonably subservient to the needs of the mind, in the case of the latter body positively opposed mind? Did you have some other criteria in mind for distinguishing someone fitted by nature for something from someone not fitted for that thing?'

'No one would claim there are any others,' said Glaucon.

'Well, do you know of anything at which human beings practise in which the male sex isn't superior to the female, in all the respects mentioned? Or are we to waste time talking about things like weaving, or looking after pancakes or stews, where the female sex does seem to count for something, and there's nothing more ridiculous than if a woman comes off second best?' 455d

'You're right', said Glaucon, 'that if you compare the two sexes with one another, women come a long way behind men in practically everything; yet many women are better than many men, in many things. Still, the general position is as you say.'

'In that case, my friend,[291] among those pursuits appropriate to people running a city none belongs to a woman because she's a woman, or for that matter to a man because he's a man. The requisite natures are similarly scattered among both types of creature,[292] so that woman naturally shares in every pursuit and so does man, though in all of them a woman is a weaker thing than a man.' 455e

'Yes, absolutely.'

'So shall we assign all of them to men, and none to women?'

'How could we do that?'

'But actually, I imagine, and this is what we'll claim, one woman is naturally fitted to doctoring, too, while another isn't; and similarly one will be naturally musical, another unmusical.'

'Of course.'

'And won't one be naturally fitted for physical training and 456a war, while another is naturally unwarlike and disinclined to physical exercise?'

'I imagine so.'

'Again, will one be a natural wisdom-lover,[293] another a wisdom-hater? And one spirited, another lacking in spirit?'

'That's true too.'

'Then one woman will have an aptitude for guarding too, another not. Or weren't those the very aptitudes we selected for our male guards?'

'They were.'

'A woman's nature, then, and a man's will be the same when

it comes to the guarding of a city, with the single proviso that one of the two is weaker, the other stronger.'

'Evidently.'

456b 'So women of this sort must be selected to live, and share the guarding, with men of the same sort,[294] given that they will be up to it, and are akin to them in nature.'

'Yes, absolutely.'

'And mustn't we assign the same pursuits to the same natures?'

'We must.'

'In that case we've come round in a circle, back to where we were before:[295] we agree there's nothing contrary to nature about assigning music and physical training to the women guards.'

'Absolutely right.'

456c 'So there was nothing impossible about the law we proposed to lay down, and it wasn't mere wishful thinking, given that what we were laying down was actually in accordance with nature; it seems it's what we do now, contrary to what we're proposing, that's unnatural.'

'It does seem so.'

'Now didn't we set out to look into whether we were proposing things that were both possible and best?'

'We did.'

'And we're agreed that they're possible?'

'Yes.'

'The next step, then, is for us to agree that they're best.'

'Clearly.'

'If we're thinking about how a woman turns into a guard, women won't need a different kind of education from the men,
456d will they, especially given that it'll be starting from the same set of natural aptitudes?'

'No, they won't.'

'Well, I wonder how you stand on the following question.'

'What's that?'

'Whether you yourself hold that *men* are different, one being better, another worse – or do you think they're all much of a muchness?'

'I certainly don't.'

'Well, in the city we were founding, do you think it was our guards that have been made the better men, by the education we described for them, or the shoemakers by their education in shoemaking?'

'What a ridiculous question,' he said.

'I see,' I said. 'And aren't these men of ours the best of all the citizens?'

'Yes, much the best.'

'What about the women? Won't our women guards be the best of all the women?' 456e

'Again, much the best.'

'And is there anything better for a city than that there should come to be in it both women and men who are as good as possible?'

'No, there is not.'

'And this will result from musical and physical education being applied in the way we've described?' 457a

'Certainly.'

'In that case, the change to custom we were proposing wasn't merely possible, but best for a city.'

'Just so.'

'The women of the guards must strip, then, since their goodness will serve to cloak them; they must share in the fighting of wars, and do everything involved in guarding the city – and nothing else; though at the same time they'll be assigned lighter duties than the men because of the weakness of their sex. The man who laughs at the idea of women naked, stripping for the 457b sake of what is best, harvests laughter's fruit "by wisdom unmatured",[296] and evidently has no notion of what he's laughing at, or what he's doing. It's a most beautiful saying, and one that will always hold, that what is beneficial is beautiful, and what is harmful is ugly.'

'Yes, absolutely.'

'Then can we claim that we're surviving this first wave, as it were,[297] by what we're saying about the law relating to women – well enough, at least, not to have been totally washed away? Our proposal is that both our guards and our guardesses 457c should share all their pursuits in common: can we claim that somehow or other our argument is hanging together, that this is something that's both possible and beneficial?'

'That's certainly no small wave you're escaping,' he said.

'You'll not say it's big', I replied, 'when you see the next one.'

'So go on,' he said; 'let me see it.'

'The law that follows on the one we've just proposed, and all the previous ones,'[298] I said, 'is this –'

'What is it?'

'That these women, all of them, should belong in common to all these men, and that none of the women should cohabit exclusively with any one man; the children, too, should be held in common, so that neither will any father know his own offspring, nor any child his father.'

'This', he said, 'is *much* bigger than the last one, if you really expect us to believe either that it's possible or that it's beneficial.'

'I don't think', I said, 'that there'd be any dispute on the second count – surely no one would deny that for women to be held in common would be highly advantageous, and children too, if only it could be managed. But on whether it is possible or not, I think there would be very considerable dispute.'

'No,' he said, 'there'd be plenty of dispute on both counts.'

'So there are two arguments ganging up on me,' I said. 'There I was thinking that I'd be able to get away from one of them; if you thought what I was proposing was beneficial, all I'd have had to do was talk about whether it was possible or not.'

'We saw you trying to get away,' he said; 'you're going to have to give an account of yourself on both.'

'I'll take my punishment,' I said. 'But grant me this much: let me indulge myself in the way lazy thinkers do when they're out walking on their own. I imagine people like that leave to one side any question of how something they want will actually come about, not wanting to tire themselves out with deciding whether it's possible or not; they simply assume they already have what they're wishing for, going straight for arranging the

details, happily describing to themselves the kinds of things
they'll get up to when it's really happened to them, and so making a soul that was anyway lazy even lazier. Well, I'm presently   458b
feeling a bit soft myself, and I want to put off for later discussion
whether the things I'm proposing are possible – for now I'm
going to assume they *are* possible, and on that basis, with your
permission, I'll be looking into how the rulers will arrange the
details when it all comes about, along with my suggestion that it
would be more than anything in the interests both of the city
and of the guards if it did. These are the issues I'll look at with
you first, leaving the others for later – with your permission.'

'You have my permission,' he said; 'do carry on.'

'Well,' I said, 'I think that if the rulers in the city are going to
be worthy of the title, and similarly if those serving as their   458c
auxiliaries are worthy of theirs,[299] then the latter will be ready
to carry out the orders given them, and the former will issue
those orders, in some things obeying the laws we have given
them, and in others, where we hand over responsibility to
them, imitating those laws.'

'That's reasonable,' he said.

'It will be for you, then,' I said, 'as their legislator, to use the
same methods you used for selecting the men to select women,
as similar to them in nature as possible, to hand over to the men;
and because they will share living-quarters and common messes,
and no one will have private possessions of that sort, they'll   458d
all be together; and once they've thoroughly mingled in the
gymnasia and in the course of their bringing-up in general,
they'll be driven, I imagine, by the necessity born in them, to
couple with each other. Or perhaps you don't think that's the
necessary outcome?'

'Necessary, not by the laws of geometry,' he said, 'but by the
laws of sexual attraction[300] – probably more potent sources of
persuasion, and compulsion, when it comes to the majority of
the population.'

'Very much so,' I said. 'But when we've said that, Glaucon,
unregulated coupling, or unregulated anything, is not permis-   458e
sible in a city of happy people, and the rulers will forbid it.'

'Right; it wouldn't be just,'[301] he said.

'Clearly, then, the next step will be for us to make mating a sacred matter, to the very best of our ability; and it's the most beneficial kind that will be sacred.'

'Absolutely right.'

459a 'So how will mating be arranged in the most beneficial way? Tell me this, Glaucon, because I notice you keep hunting-dogs and a striking number of fine-bred birds at home: there's something about their mating and their production of offspring you surely must have attended to?'

'What's that?'

'For a start, while they're all fine-bred, won't some of them either be, or turn out, better than the rest?'

'They will.'

'So do you breed from all of them alike, or are you keen to breed so far as possible from the best?'

'From the best.'

459b 'And from the youngest, the oldest, or so far as possible from those in their prime?'

'From those in their prime.'

'And if they're not bred like that, do you think your stock of birds and dogs will be of much lower quality?'

'I do,' he said.

'What about horses,' I asked, 'or any other kind of creature? Do you think it will be any different with them?'

'It would be odd if it were,' he said.

'Wow!' I exclaimed. 'My dear friend, what extraordinary demands our rulers will face; if it's the same with humankind 459c too, the rulers will need to be top-class!'

'It is the same with humans,' he said; 'what of it?'

'Because', I said, 'they're going to have to use plenty of medicine. Presumably, for bodies that don't require medicines but will respond to a change of regimen, we suppose that even an inferior doctor will suffice; but when there's a need for medicines as well, we know that we'll need the doctor to be bolder.'

'True, but what's your point?'

459d 'It's this,' I said: 'our rulers are probably going to have to use a great deal of falsehood and deceit for the benefit of the

ruled. I believe we said that the productive use of such things
fell into the category of medicine.'[302]

'Yes, and we did right to say so.'

'Well, in the matter of mating and the production of children
its rightness seems especially apparent.'

'How's that?'

'From what we've agreed,' I said, 'it follows that the flock
will only be of the topmost quality if the best males sleep with
the best females in as many cases as possible, the worst with the
worst in the fewest, and the offspring of the first kind of union   459e
are reared, those of the second not; and all this has to be
achieved without anybody except the rulers knowing, if we're
to meet the further requirement that our guarding group should
be as free from faction as possible.'

'Quite right,' he said.

'So we'll need to legislate for special festivals, at which we
can bring together the brides and bridegrooms. There'll be sacrifices too, and our poets will have to compose hymns suitable   460a
for the matings that result.[303] We'll leave it to the rulers to
decide how many of these there will be, to allow them to keep
the number of men as constant as it can be, taking into account
wars, diseases and everything like that, and so, as far as possible, prevent our city from becoming either a big city or a
small one.'[304]

'Right,' he said.

'So I imagine we'll need to devise lotteries of some sophisticated sort, to ensure that our inferior men blame chance, at
each mating, and not the rulers.'

'Very much so,' he said.

'And the young ones that stand out, I imagine, whether they   460b
prove themselves in war or in some other sphere, will have to
be given honours and prizes, including, especially, greater
opportunities for sex with the women, so that not only will as
many children as possible be fathered by men like that, but
there'll be an official explanation why that should be so.'[305]

'Right.'

'Next, any resulting offspring will be taken over by officials

appointed for the purpose, whether these are men or women –
or indeed a mixture of both, since public offices will presumably
be shared by both women and men.'

'Yes.'

460c   'They'll take the offspring of the good ones, I think, and
carry them off to the rearing-pen, where they'll be under the
care of special nannies living apart in a designated quarter of
the city. Offspring of inferior parents, together with any of the
better sort that may be born with some defect, they'll hide
away as appropriate, in a secret location not to be divulged to
anyone else.'[306]

'That's what would need to happen,' he said, 'to keep the
breed of the guards pure.'

'These officials will also look after the rearing – they'll take
the mothers to the pen when their breasts are full of milk, all
460d the time using any device available to prevent them recognizing
their own offspring; if the mothers don't have enough, it'll be
the job of the officials to provide others with milk for the
infants. They'll take care of all of this in such a way as to ensure
that our women aren't breast-feeding for too long, and can
pass on the sleepless nights and all the rest of the hard work to
wet-nurses and nannies.'

'By your account,' he said, 'the women of the guards are
going to have a pretty easy time of being mothers.'

'And that's how it should be,' I said. 'Let's move on to the
next point on our list: we said that the offspring should be from
parents who were in their prime.'

'We did.'

460e   'Would you agree on twenty years as a fair estimate of the
span of a woman's prime, thirty for a man's?'

'Which twenty, and which thirty?' he asked.

'The law will be: a woman shall give birth for the city from
her twentieth to her fortieth year; a man shall breed for the city
from the time his "sprinter's edge" is past its sharpest,[307] until
his fifty-fifth year.'

461a   'That's certainly the prime for both,' he said, 'in body and in
mind.'[308]

'So if anyone older or younger than this encroaches on the

official breeding arrangements, we'll declare the offence both impious and unjust: we'll say that he or she is creating a child which, if it goes undetected, will be born from a conception unsanctified by sacrifice, or by the prayers that priestesses and priests, indeed the whole city together will make at every mating festival, that from the good there will be born better, from those who benefit the city always still greater benefactors; instead, such a child will have been conceived in the shadows, together with a fearsome lack of restraint.'[309] 461b

'You're right,' he said.

'And the same law will apply', I said, 'if anyone still of the right age for fathering has relations with women of the right age without the involvement of a ruler; we'll count him as foisting an illegitimate, uncertified and unsanctified child on the city.'

'Quite right,' he said.

'But I imagine that when the women and the men are past breeding age, we'll leave them pretty well free to sleep with anyone they want, except not with daughters and mothers, in the case of the men, or daughters' daughters or mothers' moth- 461c
ers, and not with sons, fathers, and so on down or up in the case of the women. But this freedom will be subject to the proviso that they must make every effort, ideally not to bring into this world at all any child conceived under such circumstances, if it is, but if a birth cannot be avoided, to make arrangements for it on the basis that rearing such a child is not an option.'

'All this, too, is reasonable enough,' he said. 'But how will they tell one another's fathers or daughters apart, or make any of the distinctions you were attributing to them just now?'

'They won't,' I said. 'It'll be like this: counting from the day 461d
on which he becomes a bridegroom, a male guard will address any male born in the tenth, or indeed the seventh, month after as his son, and any female as his daughter, and they'll address him as father, so that in turn he'll call their offspring his grandchildren, and they him and his generation their grandfathers and grandmothers; those born in the period when their mothers and fathers were procreating will call each other their sisters and brothers – all of which will bring about the result we were 461e
looking for just now, that they won't try copulating with each

other. However, the law will allow brothers and sisters to "marry",[310] if the lot so falls and the Pythia adds her consent.'[311]

'Quite right,' he said.

'You asked, Glaucon, how the guards of the city would share women and children: this, or something like it, is the way they'll do it. What we need to do next is to get confirmation from our argument that it's both consistent with our other arrangements for the city, and best by a long way. What do you think?' [Book D begins]

462a   'Zeus, yes!' he exclaimed. 'I think that is the thing to do next.'

'If we're going to agree on this, won't the first step be to ask ourselves what we'd say the greatest good is, in relation to city-building, that lawgivers must have in their sights when establishing their laws, and what is the worst of all bad things, and then go on to consider whether we think the proposals we've just been going through match the footprint of the good, not that of the bad?'

'That above all.'

'Well, can we think of anything worse for a city than the 462b thing that pulls it apart and makes it many cities instead of one? Or of any greater good than what binds it together and makes it one?'

'We can't.'

'Doesn't the sharing of pleasure and pain bind it together, when so far as possible all the citizens are similarly delighted or distressed by the same gains or losses?'

'Yes, absolutely,' he said.

'Whereas making such things private has a dissolving effect – when some are highly distressed at things that are happening to the city and those in it, while others are just as delighted by the same things?'

462c   'Naturally.'

'And doesn't this sort of situation come about as a result of people's failing to use expressions like "mine" or "not mine" in unison? And likewise with "someone else's"?'

'Yes, surely.'

'Then the city that's best run is the one where more people say "mine" and "not mine" with reference to the same thing, and in the same respect, than in any other city?'

'By far the best.'

'Is it also the one that is closest to the state of a single individual? Imagine one of us is hit on the finger: the whole common structure extending through the body as far as the soul, arranged together as one by the ruling element in it – that's what perceives the blow; all of it feels the pain together, the whole responding to the suffering of a part, which is why we say that it's the *person* who has the pain, in the finger. The same will apply whatever part of the body is involved, and whether it's pain, because the part's suffering, or pleasure because it's getting better.' 462d

'It will,' he said; 'and as for your question, the best-run city comes closest to your example.'

'So when something happens to one of its citizens, whether good or bad, I imagine that it's a city like this that's most likely to say that the affected part is one of its own, and join with it in its joy or distress, all as one.' 462e

'It must,' he said, 'if it's to be well governed.'

'Time now', I said, 'to go back to our city, and consider whether it's this or some other kind of city that will most embody the characteristics we've just agreed on in principle.'

'Then shall we do that?' he asked.

'So here's a question. Other cities, I take it, contain both rulers and ordinary people, as will ours.' 463a

'They do.'

'And both the rulers and the people will address each other as fellow-citizens?'

'Of course.'

'But at the same time as calling them fellow-citizens, what else do the people in other cities call their rulers?'

'In most, they call them slave-masters; in cities with democracies, they use this very term, "rulers".'[312]

'And what about the people in our city? How will they describe their rulers, apart from calling them their fellow-citizens?'

'As their saviours and helpers,'[313] he said.

463b   'And how will these describe the ordinary people?'

'As the ones who pay them and keep them fed.'[314]

'What do rulers in other cities call their populations?'

'Slaves,' he said.

'What do rulers in other cities call each other?'

'Fellow-rulers.'

'And ours?'

'Fellow-guards.'

'Now can you tell me if any ruler in other cities is ever in the position of describing some of his fellow-rulers as belonging, others as not belonging?'

'Yes, lots of them do that.'

'And in thinking and talking of them as "belonging", presumably he's saying they belong *to him*; similarly, those who don't "belong" don't belong *to him*.'

'Right.'

463c   'What about your guards? Will any of them be able to think of, or address, any of his fellow-guards as "not belonging"?'

'Certainly not,' he said; 'after all, if ever he meets someone, he'll think of himself as meeting either brother, sister, father, mother, son, daughter, or some descendant or progenitor of one of these.'

'Very good,' I said; 'but answer me this as well – will you lay down merely that they must use the *language* of kinship, or that

463d   all their actions must conform to it? In relation to their fathers, for example, will you insist on their observing all those customary rules about respecting fathers, and caring for them, and the need for obedience to one's parents, telling them that otherwise they'll win no favours from gods or from men, because if they break the rules they'd be doing something that was neither pious nor just? Will these be the sentiments you want ringing in their ears from birth, sung in unison by their fellow-citizens, not

463e   just about those pointed out to them as their fathers, but about all their other relatives as well? Or perhaps not?'

'Exactly these,' he said. 'It would be ridiculous to have them merely mouthing the language of kinship, without the corresponding behaviour.'

'In this city, then, more than in any other, the citizens will use the expressions we were talking about just now – "Mine's doing well!", or "Mine's doing badly!" – in harmony, when things go well or badly for one of their number.'

'Very true,' he said.

'And we said, didn't we, that along with this way of think-   464a
ing and talking went shared pleasure and distress?'

'Yes, and we were right.'

'Well, more than any others, *our* citizens will share, won't they, in one and the same thing, to which they'll give the label "mine"? And by the very fact of their sharing in this, won't they then share their distress and pleasure more than any?'

'Much more.'

'Well, won't the cause of this be the guards' "sharing" women and children[315] – along with the other arrangements we've proposed?'

'That much more than anything else,' he said.

'And we actually agreed that such harmony was a greater   464b
good for a city than any, comparing a well-run city to the body and its relationship to the pain and pleasure of one of its parts.'

'And we were right to agree on that,' he said.

'So in fact the sharing by the auxiliaries of children and of women has been shown to be the cause of the greatest good for a city.'

'Very much so,' he said.

'And we're also agreeing with what we said before;[316] because I think we said they shouldn't have private houses or land or any other sort of possession, but should be paid for   464c
their guarding by being fed by everybody else, and spend this "pay" of theirs together, if they were to be guards worthy of the name.'

'We were right,' he said.

'What I'm saying is, won't our previous proposals and our present ones make them still more into true guards, by having them not pull the city apart by calling different things "mine" instead of the same one – one of them hauling off into his house whatever he's managed to acquire without the others, another hauling off *his* stuff to *his* separate house, along with a separate   464d wife and separate children, thus bringing into the city private pleasures and pains for private individuals? Won't all our proposals have the guards so far as possible experiencing pain and pleasure together, insofar as they share a single idea of what "belongs" to them and have a common goal in view?'

'Quite so,' he said.

'What's more, since the only thing they have that's private to them is their body, and everything else is shared, won't lawsuits and accusations, pitching one guard against another, be practically non-existent? And that means they'll be free from all the dissensions that typically arise in human societies because people have their own money or children or other family.'

464e

'They're certainly going to be rid of all that,' he said.

'Nor, again, will there be justification for any suits for aggression, or assault, between them; we'll declare that it's fine and just for people of the same age to defend themselves against one another, thus imposing on them the need to keep their bodies in condition.'

'You're right,' he said.

465a

'Yes,' I said, 'and another thing that's right about this law is that if anyone were to be angry with someone, and satisfied his anger in this immediate way, he'd be less likely to move on to greater commotions.'

'Yes, quite.'

'As for older people, they'll have responsibility for controlling and restraining all the younger ones.'

'Clearly.'

'Equally clearly, a younger person probably won't ever try to constrain an older one, unless it's on official orders, let alone strike him; and I imagine he won't dishonour him in any other way either. Those two guards, fear and shame, will be sufficient to prevent it: shame, because it stops him attacking those he counts as parents, and fear that others will come to the aid of the victim, whether as sons, or brothers, or fathers.'

465b

'Yes,' he said, 'that's the way it happens.'

'On all sides, then, our men will be at peace with one another, thanks to the laws?'

'Yes, profoundly so.'

'And if there's no dissension between them, there's no fear that the rest of the city will ever be at odds with them either, or with each other.'

'No, indeed not.'

'As for the pettiest of nuisances they'll be rid of, their very   465c
unseemliness makes me hesitate even to talk about them –
things like being poor and having to toady to the rich, all the
problems and pains involved in rearing children, and making
enough money to feed the household, borrowing a bit here,
defaulting there, using any device to get enough together, then
handing it over to wives and slaves to manage: well, my friend,
just what and how people have to suffer for all this is plain
enough, it's ignoble, and it's not worth talking about.'   465d

'Plain enough even to the blind,' he said.

'All of this, then, our guards will be rid of, and they'll live a
life more blessed than the so-called blessed life Olympic victors
live.'[317]

'How so?'

'It's for a fraction, I hazard, of what our men have that the
victors at the games are called happy. The victory won by our
men is finer, and the sustenance they receive from the public is
the more complete. What they win is the safety of the entire
city, and they are crowned with the wreath of sustenance and
all the necessities of life, they and their children;[318] they receive   465e
honours from their own city during their lifetimes, and are
accorded a burial worthy of them when they die.'

'Fine rewards indeed,' he said.

'Well,' I said, 'do you recall someone complaining earlier on
in the conversation – I don't know who it was[319] – that we   466a
weren't making our guards happy? After all, they have the
power to take everything their fellow-citizens have, and yet
they have nothing! To this I think we replied that we'd consider
the point again, should the occasion arise, but for the time
being we said our concern was to make our guards into guards
and to make the *city* as happy as we could; we weren't looking
at just one group of people in it and fashioning happiness for
them.'

'I recall.'

'So what do you think now? If it's true that we've shown the life of our auxiliaries to be much finer and better than that of 466b Olympic victors, surely we don't need to compare it with the life of a shoemaker, or other sorts of craftsman like that, or the life of a farmer?'

'I don't think so.'

'All the same it's fair to repeat here what we said then, that if a guard sets out to become happy in a way that makes him no sort of guard at all – if he is not content to live the life of a guard, measured, stable and, as we declare, best, and instead some mindless, adolescent idea of happiness takes hold of him and impels him to start appropriating everything in the city for 466c himself, just because he can, he'll soon learn how truly wise Hesiod was when he said there was a way in which "the half is more than the whole".'[320]

'If he takes my advice,' said Glaucon, 'he'll stay with the life we've given him.'

'You agree, then, with our description of the sharing of the women[321] with the men, in relation to education, children and guarding the rest of the citizen-body: whether at home in the city or marching to war, they must guard and hunt with them, just as bitches do with the dogs, and share in everything and in 466d every way, so far as possible? And you agree that in doing all this they'll not only be doing what is best, but doing nothing contrary to the nature of the female in relation to the male, insofar as both sexes are naturally adapted to partnership with one another?'

'I agree,' he said.

'It remains, then, doesn't it,' I said, 'to establish whether this kind of sharing can in fact come about in a human society, as it does among other creatures, and if so, how?'

'I was just going to suggest that,' he said.

466e 'Yes,' I said, 'because I imagine the subject of wartime, and how they'll go about making war, is clear enough.'

'How's that?' he asked.

'Clearly they'll march out together, women and men, and they'll also take as many of their children to war with them as are grown up enough, in order for these to observe, as the chil-

dren of other craftsmen do, the work that will fall to them as
adults and craftsmen in their own right; but as well as observ-   467a
ing, they'll also help by playing all the supporting roles required
in war, as well as taking care of their fathers and mothers.
You've surely noticed this happening among artisans – how
long a time potters, for example, have their children spend
helping and observing before they actually put their hands to
the wheel?'

'Very much so.'

'So should they take more care than our guards in educating
their children, through the appropriate first-hand experience
and observation?'

'That would be quite ridiculous,' he said.

'And besides, every creature puts up a different sort of fight   467b
when its own offspring are on the scene.'

'That's true. But if they're defeated, Socrates, something that
happens all the time in war, there's no small danger that they'll
lose their children as well as themselves, and make it impossible for the rest of the city to recover.'

'That's true,' I said. 'But first of all, do you suppose things
should be arranged so as to avoid any risks?'

'Certainly not.'

'Well, if risks *are* to be run, shouldn't it be under circumstances where people will be better for overcoming them?'

'Clearly so.'

'And do you suppose it makes only a small difference, and   467c
one not worth any risk, whether our future fighting men have
the opportunity to observe, as children, what it is to fight a war?'

'No, for the purpose in question it does make a difference.'

'So when there's war, the children must be there as observers, but this will only be a good thing if we can also devise
some means of keeping them safe – right?'

'Yes.'

'Well, first of all', I said, 'their fathers won't be unprepared
in these matters, as human beings go, and they'll have a pretty
good idea, won't they, of which campaigns will or won't be
particularly dangerous?'

'That seems likely.'

467d   'So they'll take the children on some, but be careful about taking them on others.'

'Right.'

'And when it comes to appointing their officers,' I said, 'I imagine they'll put in charge of them not those of the lowest quality but people suitably qualified by their experience and their age to be leaders and guides for children.'

'Yes, that would be appropriate.'

'And yet, we'll say to ourselves, things turn out unexpectedly for people all the time.'

'Very much so.'

'To guard, then, against that sort of eventuality, my friend, we'll need to give the children wings from the start, even when they're little, so that if the need arises they can fly off and make their escape.'

'What are you saying?' he asked.

467e   'We must mount them on their horses', I said, 'at the earliest possible age, teaching them to ride first, and only then taking them to watch the fighting, not on spirited mounts, or ones trained for battle, but the fleetest and most responsive. That way not only will they be in the best position to observe what their role will require of them in the future, but they'll be most assured of getting safely away, should that be necessary, following the lead of their older guides.'

468a   'That seems right to me,' he said.

'And what about the conduct of war itself?' I asked. 'How will your soldiers comport themselves, towards each other and towards their enemies? I wonder if my thoughts on this are right or not.'

'Tell me what they are,' he said.

'As for their conduct towards each other,' I said, 'any of them who through cowardice has deserted his post, thrown down his weapons or done anything of that sort must, surely, be made into a craftsman of some sort, or a farmer?'[322]

'Yes, absolutely.'

'And anyone taken alive by the enemy should be made a
468b   present of to his captors, shouldn't he, for them to put their catch to whatever use they wish?'

'Yes, quite.'

'What of the one who has distinguished himself by display-ing outstanding valour? Do you think he should be crowned with wreaths there and then on the battlefield by the youths and children on campaign with him, each in turn? Or not?'

'I do think so.'

'What about their shaking his hand?'

'That too.'

'But', I said, 'I imagine you wouldn't go as far as suggesting –'

'What?'

'That he should kiss and be kissed by each of them.'[323]

'That more than anything!' he said. 'And I further add this rider to the law, that for the duration of that campaign *no one* be permitted to refuse his kisses, whoever it may be, which will have the additional benefit that if anyone is actually in love with someone else, whether male or female, he'll be that much more eager to carry off the prize for valour.' 468c

'That's fine,' I said, 'because we already said that if he's good at what he does he should have more opportunities for mating than the rest, and will be selected for such purposes more often than the others are, so that as many children as possible may be born from someone like that.'[324]

'Yes, we did,' he said.

'And in fact Homer too agrees that it's just to honour the young in such ways when they prove their excellence. Didn't he have Ajax rewarded "with the choicest cuts"[325] for having dis-tinguished himself in the war, thus showing he thought this an appropriate honour for those in the prime of youth and cour-age, one that would simultaneously increase their strength?' 468d

'Quite right,' he said.

'Then we'll go along with Homer this far,' I said. 'When there are sacrifices, and on all such occasions, we ourselves will hon-our the good and brave, to the degree that they have shown themselves such, both with hymns and with the privileges we were talking about just now, and with more besides – "with the best seats, and the best meats, and cups filled full with wine" – so that we can train our good men and women[326] even as we hon-our them.' 468e

'All very fine,' he said.

'Right, then; and as for those who die on campaign, won't our first act be to declare, in the case of anyone who has died exceptionally well, that they belong to the golden race?'[327]

'Very much so,' he said.

469a 'And shall we not believe Hesiod when he says that whenever any of those of such a race die, actually they "holy demi-gods become, here on the earth,/ Noble, defenders against the bad, guards of merely mortal men"?'[328]

'Yes, we shall.'

'So we should ask the god[329] how one should bury the semi-divine or divine, in order to distinguish them from the rest, and bury our noble dead in accordance with his guidance?'

'No doubt about it.'

469b 'And for ever after we shall tend and revere their tombs as those of demi-gods. We'll follow the same observances, too, whenever anyone dies, whether from old age or in some other way, if their lives are adjudged of exceptional excellence.'

'Yes, that's only just,' he said.

'And how will our soldiers behave towards their enemies?'

'What sort of thing do you have in mind?'

'First of all there's the question of enslavement: does it seem just for Greeks to enslave Greek cities, or should they rather try, even, to prevent others from doing it, so far as possible, and accustom them to sparing those of Greek descent, so as to guard against their becoming slaves to non-Greeks?'

469c

'Sparing Greeks is the best and only option,' he said.

'Then they're not to own a Greek as a slave themselves, either, and they'll advise other Greeks to follow their lead?'

'Absolutely,' he said; 'that way they'll be more inclined to turn their attention to the non-Greek, and hold back from attacking each other.'

'What about stripping the dead, when the battle's been won,' I asked; 'apart from their weapons, is that a good thing? Or doesn't this rather offer cowards an excuse for not going after an enemy who's still fighting – as if they're doing something essential by poking about on a dead one? Many an army has been lost because of that sort of pilfering.'

469d

'Indeed so.'

'And don't you think it illiberal and money-grubbing to plunder a corpse? Isn't it the mark of an effeminate and petty mind to treat the body of the dead person as hostile, when in fact the enemy in it has flitted off,[330] leaving the mere instrument of its hostilities behind? Do you imagine there's any difference between doing that and the way bitches snarl and worry at the stones that have hit them, and don't bother with the person throwing the stones?' 469e

'No difference at all,' he said.

'So we must abandon the practice of stripping corpses, and of preventing the enemy from taking up his dead.'

'Zeus! Yes, we must,' he said.

'Nor, I imagine, shall we take their weapons off to our sanctuaries to dedicate them to the gods, especially if their owners were Greeks, if we're concerned at all with fostering good will towards our fellow-Greeks. In fact, we'll be afraid that it may bring pollution of some kind, to take things to a sanctuary in this way, from our kin, unless of course the god gives some indication to the contrary.' 470a

'You're quite right,' he said.

'How about the practice of ravaging Greek territory, and burning Greek homes? How will your soldiers act here towards their enemies?'

'I'll be happy to hear you give your view,' he said.

'Well,' I said, 'my view is that they should do neither; they should simply deprive the enemy of the annual harvest. Shall I tell you why?' 470b

'Yes, do.'

'It appears to me that just as we use two words "war" and "faction", so they are in fact two, and distinct, applying to disputes in relation to two distinct things. The two things I have in mind are, firstly, what belongs to and is akin to ourselves, and secondly what belongs to someone else and is alien. Hostilities with regard to the first category are labelled "faction", hostilities with regard to the second are labelled "war".'

'That's all quite reasonable,' he said.

'So see if the following suggestion is reasonable too: namely, 470c that those of Greek descent belong to and are akin to each other, but alien and not belonging to the non-Greek.'

'Well put,' he said.

'So when Greeks fight with non-Greeks and non-Greeks with Greeks, we'll say they are at war, and inclined by nature to be so, "war" being applied as the name for hostilities for this sort; but when Greeks do anything like this to each other, we'll

470d say that their nature is to be friends, and insist that such behaviour is called "faction" because it betrays a Greece[331] that is sick and divided.'

'I agree we should think that way,' he said.

'Now observe', I said, 'what happens with faction as it's currently understood – wherever something like this happens, and a city splits up into opposing sides, if they both ravage each other's fields and burn their houses, how entirely abominable this sort of faction is thought to be! Evidently neither side loves the city, since if they did they'd never dare raze her like that, their nurse and mother. A measured response, people think, is

470e for the winning side to deprive the losers of their crops, and act on the basis that they'll be making up their differences and won't always be at war with each other.'

'That's a much gentler approach than the other,' he said.

'Well then,' I said, 'this city you're founding will be Greek, won't it?'

'It had better be,' he said.

'Won't its citizens also be good and gentle?'

'Very much so.'

'And will they not be Greek-loving? Will they not think that Greece belongs to them, or share the same sacred places as other Greeks?'

'They will; very much so.'

471a 'They'll think of a dispute with Greeks as faction, then, because it's with their kin, and they'll not call it war?'

'They will not.'

'And so they'll dispute with them on the basis that there will be reconciliation?'

'Absolutely.'

'So they'll bring them to their senses in a kindly fashion, not

punishing them in order to enslave them, or destroy them; their
role is to make them see sense, not make war on them.'

'Just so,' he said.

'Being Greeks themselves, then, neither will they raze Greece,
or burn down Greek homes, or act as if everyone – men, women
and children – in a city is hostile to them; rather, they'll suppose   471b
only a few are so, who'll always be the ones that started the
dispute. So for all these reasons, they'll refuse to raze their land
or wreck their homes, bearing in mind that most of them are
their friends, and they'll continue the dispute only until the
guilty few are compelled to face justice by the innocent who are
doing the suffering.'

'I accept', he said, 'that this is how our citizens must
approach their opponents; as for non-Greeks, they should be
treated as Greeks presently treat each other.'

'So shall we establish this law, too, for our guards: "no   471c
ravaging of territory, and no burning of homes"?'

'Let's do that,' he said; 'all of this is fine enough, and so is
everything that went before it. But here's something on which
you're not doing so well. It seems to me, Socrates, that if one
allows you to go on talking about things of this sort, you'll forget
altogether to deal with the subject you earlier pushed to one side
in favour of these other ones: namely, the possibility of the realization of these political arrangements of ours, and exactly *how*
their realization would be possible. To be sure, if they were realized, everything would be fine and dandy for the city lucky
enough to enjoy them. I'll even add in the things you're leaving   471d
out: that the soldiers would be best at fighting their enemies
because they'd be the last to abandon each other, recognizing and
saluting one another by these names we've given them –
"brothers", "fathers", "sons"; if the female element went on
campaign with them as well, whether as part of their formation
or posted in the rear, to frighten the enemy and provide reinforcements should the need for these be compelling, I'm sure all this
would make them an irresistible force; I also see all the advantages you're missing out that would accrue to them at home. But
please take me as accepting that there would be all these benefits,   471e
and thousands of others too, if this regime of ours came about,

and don't go on giving us more detail about it. Instead, let's now set to persuading ourselves about the point at issue, that and how it's all possible, and say goodbye to everything else.'

472a   'I hadn't expected this sudden attack on my argument,' I said; 'I see you've no sympathy for my hanging back. Perhaps you don't realize that just when I've barely escaped out from under the first two waves that were threatening me,[332] you're now bringing on the third, the biggest and hardest of them to overcome; when you see it and hear it, then you'll completely feel for me, and understand my fear and hesitation about trying to discuss, or even mentioning, so unlikely sounding an idea.'[333]

'The more of this sort of thing you say,' he replied, 'the less
472b   likely we are to let you off having to tell us how this regime of ours is capable of being realized. So get on with it, and no more beating about the bush.'

'Well,' I said, 'shouldn't we begin by recalling that we've arrived at this point in the course of examining what sort of thing justice, and injustice, is?'

'We should; but what of it?' he asked.

'Nothing. But if we do discover the answer to our question about justice, shall we expect the just man himself not to differ
472c   at all from justice itself, and to be such as justice is, in every respect? Or will it be enough for us if he comes as close as possible to it, and shares in it in more respects than the rest?'

'That will be enough,' he said.

'Then it was a paradigm we wanted', I said, 'when we started looking for the sort of thing justice is in itself, and the perfectly just man, were he ever to come into existence – what *he* would be like, if he did; similarly with injustice and the most unjust man. Our aim was to use the perfectly just and the perfectly unjust man as reference points, so that however these two did in relation to happiness and its opposite, we'd be compelled to accept that whichever of ourselves resembled them as closely as
472d   was possible would have a portion of happiness most like theirs. We weren't aiming to show that what we were describing was possible as such.'

'That much is certainly true,' he said.

'Well then, do you think a painter is any less good a painter if he paints a paradigm of what the most beautiful human being would be like, and manages to render every detail in his painting accordingly, but isn't able to demonstrate the possibility of such a man's coming into existence?'

'Zeus! No, I certainly don't,' he said.

'Well, weren't we too creating a paradigm – in speech, of a good city? That's what we're claiming, isn't it?'

'We certainly are.'   472e

'So do you think that what we've been saying is any less well said just because we may not be able to show it possible to found a city as we were proposing?'

'No indeed,' he said.

'So that's the truth of the matter,' I said. 'But if I've got to try my hardest even so, for your sake, and show how best, and under what conditions, it would all be most possible, I ask you to make the same concessions to me, as I make my attempt, that you agreed to just now.'

'What concessions?'

'Is it possible for anything to be realized in practice as it is   473a described in words, or is it rather in the nature of things for actions to be further removed from the truth than words are, even if some deny it?[334] How about you? Do you accept it?'

'I do,' he said.

'Then don't make me have to prove that the sorts of things we've been describing would be realizable in practice, in every detail. If we're able to show how a city might be governed in a way that comes closest to our description, that should be enough for you to declare that we've discovered how the things   473b you yourself are prescribing[335] are possible. Won't you be content to achieve this much? I certainly would.'

'Me too,' he said.

'The next step, it seems, is for us to try to search out and identify precisely what it is that's done badly in cities as they currently are, and what accounts for their not being run in the way we want. What is the smallest change needed to introduce this kind of regime into a city? Preferably, it would be one thing that changed, or if not one, two; and if not two, the minimum number possible, and the smallest and least disruptive.'

473c 'Quite so,' he said.

'Well,' I said, 'there is one change that I think we can show would transform a city. It isn't a small one, I grant you, and it wouldn't be easy to bring about, but it would be possible.'

'What is that?' he asked.

'I am at that very moment', I said, 'that we were comparing to the biggest of waves. Never mind; I've got to say it, even if it's about to swamp me, just like a gurgling wave, in laughter and contempt. Listen hard to what I'm going to say.'

'Say on,' he said.

473d 'Unless', I said, 'either philosophers rule in cities as kings, or those now called kings and princes not only do genuine philosophy but do it sufficiently well – *unless* there is this coming together of political power and philosophy, and all the many types of people currently trying to move into either without the other are forcibly debarred, there is no respite from troubles, my dear Glaucon, for cities or, I think, for the human race; nor, until that time, will this regime that we've so far only talked 473e about ever come into existence, insofar as it can, and see the light of the sun. This is what has all along been making me so hesitant to speak out, because I could see how very unlikely a proposal it would sound; it's no easy thing to see that there's no other way for anyone to be happy, whether in private or in public life.'

To which he said 'Socrates, that's some statement you've let 474a fly at us! It's the sort of proposal to make a whole collection of worthless types immediately throw off their cloaks, so to speak, grab any weapon available and rush at you, stripped and ready to do wonderful mischief to you; if you don't have the arguments to fend them off and get away, you'll pay for it, and find out what it's really like to be mocked.'

'And aren't you to blame for that?' I asked.

'Yes, and I make no apology for it. But you can be sure I shan't abandon you; I'll be there beside you with the resources I have – good will, encouragement and responses that are prob-
474b ably more in tune with you than another person's might be.[336] So now you know you've a helper like that behind you, go

ahead and try to demonstrate to doubters that things really are
as you say.'

'I must,' I said, 'if you're offering an alliance as impressive as
that! What we absolutely have to do, I think, if we're to escape
from the people you're talking about, is to respond to them by
identifying which philosophers we have in mind when we dare
to propose that philosophers should rule. That way, and when
we've made plain which type of individual we're talking about,
our proposal can be defended by showing that it's to them that   474c
engagement in philosophy and leadership in a city naturally
belong, while the rest are fitted neither for the one nor for the
other, and are born followers, not leaders.'

'This will be the moment to do it,' he said.

'Come on, then,' I said, 'follow me – there may be a way
through, somewhere hereabouts, to an exposition that will
serve.'

'Lead on,' he said.

'Do you need to be reminded – or perhaps you yourself
recall? – that it won't ever be correct for us to declare someone
a lover of something[337] if it's clear that there's only one part of
it he loves, and another he doesn't; he must be passionate about
all of it?'

'It seems I need a reminder,' he said; 'I don't entirely recall
the point.'

'I wouldn't have expected that response from you, Glau-   474d
con,' I said; 'a man skilled in love ought hardly to be unaware
that all boys of the right age have the capacity to provoke passion in the expert boy-lover, and to seem worthy of being
embraced and cherished. Isn't that how you people behave
towards beautiful boys? One with an upturned nose you'll
praise as "charming", a down-turned nose will be "regal", one
between the two "just right"; dark-skinned boys you'll praise   474e
for their "manly" aspect, light-skinned ones you'll pronounce
"sons of gods", and as for the very term "honey-pale" – what's
that, do you think, if it's not the cooing coinage of a lover
happy to put up with a boy's pallid skin provided only he's of
a ripe young age? In short, there's no pretext you won't use,   475a

and nothing you won't say, so as not to deprive yourselves of anyone in the bloom of youth.'

'If you want to use me as your example of how love-experts behave,' he said, 'I agree for the sake of argument.'

'What about wine-lovers?' I asked. 'Don't you see them doing exactly the same thing – using any pretext to say yes to any wine?'

'Yes, very much so.'

'And I imagine you observe the same happening with people addicted to honours: if they can't be generals, they'll be captains, and if they can't be honoured by great and important 475b people, they'll make do with honour from lesser and less important ones; which goes to show that it's honour they're after, in any shape or form.'

'Quite so.'

'Yes or no to my question, then: if we say anyone has a real appetite for something, shall we declare his appetite to be for the whole of the kind of thing in question – or only for some part of it, not for another?'

'For the whole of it,' he said.

'So we shan't say of the philosopher either, the lover of wisdom, that his appetite is only for one part of wisdom, not another; it's the whole of it he's after?'

'True.'

475c   'If someone is picky about what he learns, then, especially if he's still young and can't yet give a reasoned account as to what is and isn't worthwhile, we'll not say he's a lover of learning, or a lover of wisdom, any more than we say the person who's picky about what he eats is hungry and has an appetite for food, or is a food-lover, because by our reckoning he's more like a food-hater.'

'Yes, and we'd be right.'

'Whereas if someone is ready and willing to sample any and every kind of study, and approaches the business of learning with an insatiable appetite for its pleasures, *him* we'll justly declare a wisdom-lover[338] – right?'

475d   To this Glaucon responded, 'In that case, your philosophers will be a broad and strange collection of people. It seems to me it will include anyone who loves seeing sights:[339] doesn't that involve delight in learning? And then there are those who love listening – a very strange set of people to count as philosophers, when they'd never willingly attend a discussion or involve themselves in any activity of that kind, but rush around at the Dionysia as if they'd hired out their ears to listen to every chorus that's put on,[340] not missing a performance in town or country. Shall we be counting all *these* as philosophers, along with other similar enthusiasts for things, lovers of similarly inconsequential arts?'   475e

'Not at all,' I said; 'though they bear a resemblance to philosophers.'

'And which do you have in mind as the true philosophers?' he asked.

'Those', I said, 'who love the sight of truth.'

'That's another right thing to *say*,'[341] he replied; 'but what does it amount to?'

'It wouldn't be at all easy', I said, 'to explain to anyone else; but you, I think, will concede me this –'

'What, exactly?'

'That since beautiful is opposite to ugly, beautiful and ugly are two.'   476a

'Of course.'

'And that since they are two, each is one?'

'That too.'

'It's the same story with just and unjust, good and bad, and so on with every kind of thing:[342] each of them is, by itself, one, but because they show up everywhere, by virtue of being associated with actions, and bodies, and each other, each of them appears many.'

'You're right,' he said.

'Well, it's here that I make my division, between your sight-lovers, your lovers and doers of the arts, on the one hand, and on the other those the argument is about, the ones, and the only ones, who will rightly be called philosophers.'   476b

'What are you saying?' he asked.

'I imagine', I said, 'that while those who love to listen, or to see sights, embrace beautiful sounds, colours, figures, and everything that is crafted out of these, their minds are incapable of seeing, let alone embracing, the nature of the beautiful by itself.'[343]

'Yes indeed,' he said, 'that's how it is.'

'But those who are capable of going and seeing the beautiful by itself[344] and in itself – won't they be few and far between?'

'Very few.'

476c 'Then what do you think of the life of someone who recognizes that there are beautiful things, but doesn't recognize a beauty by itself, and isn't capable of following if someone else tries to guide him to a knowledge of it?[345] Do you think he lives in a dream, or with his eyes open? Think of it this way: isn't a dreaming state one in which a person thinks – whether in his sleep or when he's awake – that something that's like something else isn't just *like* but actually *is* the thing it resembles?'

'That's a fair description of dreaming, in my view,' he said.

'What about the person in the opposite situation, who not only thinks that there is something that's beautiful by itself,[346] 476d and is capable of seeing both it and the things that share in it, but doesn't think either that these things *are* it or that it *is* the things sharing in it? The question is the same as in the other case: does this person live his life with his eyes open, or in a dream?'

'Very much with his eyes open,' he said.

'And would we be correct in describing the latter person, on the grounds that he knows, as having *knowledge*, and the former as having *belief*, on the grounds that he merely believes?'[347]

'Yes, absolutely.'

'So what if the person we're saying has belief and not knowledge gets angry with us, and disputes the truth of what we're 476e saying? Will we have any way of calming him down and gently bringing him over to our side, yet concealing from him that he is not in a healthy state?'[348]

'We certainly ought to try,' he said.

'So come on, think what we'll say to him. Or do you want us to ask him a series of questions, while telling him that nobody begrudges him any knowledge he does have, and that we'd be delighted to find that there are things he knows? "Tell us this," we might say to him: "When someone knows, does he know something, or nothing?" Glaucon, you answer me on his behalf.'

'I'll answer that he knows something.'

'Something that is, or something that is not?'[349]

'Something that is; how could something that *is not* be known?'[350]   477a

'Do we then have a sufficient hold on this point, however many times we might want to look at it, that what is, entirely, is entirely knowable, whereas what is not in any way at all is wholly unknowable?'

'Most sufficient.'

'Fine. So if there is in fact something in such a condition as *both* to be *and* not to be, it will lie, won't it, between what is, purely and simply, and its opposite, what is not in any way.'

'It will.'

'Then since we're agreed that knowledge is for what is,[351] and that nothing but non-knowledge[352] can correspond to what is not, for this something in-between we'll need, won't we, to look for something that's itself in between ignorance and knowledge?'   477b

'Yes, absolutely.'

'Well, do we say there's such a thing as belief?'

'Of course we do.'

'And do we say it's a different capacity from knowledge, or the same one?'

'A different one.'

'In that case, belief and knowledge are assigned to different things,[353] according to their differing capacities.'

'Just so.'

'Knowledge, then, is naturally assigned to what is – to knowing, in relation to what is, that it is?[354] Or rather, before we proceed, I think we need to make the following clarification.'

'What's that?'

'Capacities, we'll say, constitute that category of things in the world by virtue of which not only we can do the things we can do but everything else can do whatever it is capable of. For example, I count sight and hearing as capacities – if you understand the type of thing I have in mind.'   477c

'I do.'

'So here's what I think about capacities. When I distinguish one capacity from another, I'm not seeing it as having a particular colour, or shape, or any of the sorts of features many other things have, to which I can then refer as grounds for saying to myself that one set of things is different from another. When it comes to a capacity, I only look at what it's for and what it does, and that's how I come to call each of them a capacity, labelling it the same one if it is assigned to the same thing and does the same, and as a different capacity if it is assigned to a different thing and does something different. What about you? What's your practice here?'

477d

'The same as yours,' he said.

'Then let's go back, my fine friend,[355] to where we were,' I said. 'Knowledge – do you say it's a certain sort of capacity, or do you put it into some other category?'

477e

'No, into the same one you put it in,' he said; 'in fact, it's the most powerful of all capacities.'

'What about belief? Shall we count that as a capacity – or as some other type of thing?'

'It must be a capacity,' he said. 'What else makes us capable of believing, if not belief?'

'But you were agreeing just a little while ago that knowledge and belief were not the same thing.'

'Right,' he said; 'how would any intelligent person treat what is infallible as the same as what is not infallible?'

478a

'Well said,' I replied; 'we're clearly in agreement that belief is different from knowledge.'

'We are.'

'Being different capacities, then, each is for something different.'

'Necessarily so.'

'Knowledge, I suppose, being for what is, as a capacity for knowing, in relation to what is, that it is?'[356]

'Yes.'

'And belief, we say, is a capacity for believing?'

'Yes.'

'Believing the same thing knowledge knows?[357] Will what is known be the same as what is believed, or is that impossible?'

'It's impossible,' he said, 'given what we've agreed; if it's true that different capacities are naturally for different things, that both of the two things in question, belief and knowledge, are capac- 478b ities, and that they're different capacities, it follows that there's no room for what's known to be the same as what's believed.'

'So if what's known is what is, what will be believed will be something other than what is?'

'Right.'

'Will it be what is *not*? Or is it impossible even to believe what is not?[358] Look at it this way: if someone has a belief, doesn't he direct his belief to something? Or again, is it possible to believe, and believe nothing?'

'No.'

'The person believing believes some one thing?'

'Yes.'

'And if that something *is not*, it would be strictly called no-thing rather than some one thing?'   478c

'Yes, quite.'

'To what is not, in fact, we assigned a state of ignorance, as we had to, and knowledge to what is.'

'Right,' he said.

'So it isn't what is that's believed, nor is it what is not?'

'No.'

'So belief won't be either a state of ignorance, or of knowledge?'

'It seems not.'

'Well, does it lie outside the limits of these, surpassing either knowledge in clarity or ignorance in the lack of it?'

'Neither.'

'Alternatively, perhaps,' I said, 'belief appears to you something that is darker than knowledge, and brighter than ignorance?'

'Yes, much.'

'And it lies within the limits set by both of these?'   478d

'Yes.'

'So belief will be in between them.'

'Quite so.'

'And weren't we saying earlier that if there turned out to be something that both is and is not simultaneously, as it were,[359] the place for such a thing was between what is, purely and simply, and what wholly is not, and that it wouldn't be either knowledge or ignorance that corresponded to it, but rather what turned out similarly placed between ignorance and knowledge?'

'And we were right.'

'But now there's turned out to be, between them, the very thing we're calling belief?'

'There has.'

478e   'So it seems it remains for us to find the thing that shares in both being and not being, and couldn't be labelled as either, purely and simply; then, if it does turn up, we'll be justified in labelling it as what is believed, assigning extremes to extremes and the in-between to the in-between. Right?'

'Right.'

479a   'Given all this, then, I'll demand an answer from this splendid fellow who thinks there's no such thing as the beautiful taken by itself, any nature[360] that belongs to beauty, by itself, remaining forever exactly as it is, but at the same time supposes that beautiful things abound – that fellow who loves to be a spectator, and won't put up with it for a minute if someone says the beautiful is *one* thing only, and similarly with the just, and so on: "Tell me this, fine fellow that you are," we'll say: "of all these many beautiful things of yours, surely there's not a single one of them that won't appear as ugly?[361] Or of the many just things, that won't appear as unjust? Or of the many pious things, that won't appear as impious?"'

'No,' said Glaucon, 'they must always appear as in a way both
479b   beautiful and ugly, and similarly with your other examples.'

'What about the many doubles? Do they appear any less as halves than as doubles?'

'No.'

'And big things, small things, light things or heavy things – they won't be called by whatever names we give them, will they, any more than by the opposites of these?'

'No,' he said; 'they'll always keep both.'

'So is it the case with any of these many things of yours that it is whatever anyone claims it to be more than that it is not?'

'It's like with those double meanings people play with at parties,' he said, 'like the children's riddle about the eunuch 479c hitting the bat, playing on what he hit it with and what it was sitting on;[362] they too seem to go both ways, so that it becomes impossible to grasp any of them firmly in the mind as either being or not being both or neither.'

'So do you know what to do with them,' I asked, 'or any better place to locate them than in between being and not being?[363] I don't suppose they'll turn out to be darker than what is not by outdoing it in not being, or brighter than what is by outdoing it in being.'

'Very true,' he said. 479d

'Then it seems we've discovered that the many things ordinary people think about beauty and the rest tumble around somewhere between what purely and simply is not and what purely and simply is.'[364]

'We have.'

'But we agreed in advance that if something of this sort turned up, it must be declared something that was believed, not known – the wanderer in between, captured by the in-between capacity.'

'That we have agreed.'

'Those spectators of many beautiful things, then, who at the same time fail to see the beautiful itself, and aren't capable of 479e following, either, if someone else tries to lead them to it;[365] those people who see many just things, but not the just itself, and similarly with everything else – we'll declare that all of it is a matter of believing, and that none of the things they believe do they know.'

'There's no avoiding it,' he said.

'And what about those who are spectators of each and every thing by itself, remaining as it does forever exactly as it is? Won't we declare that they're knowing and not believing?'

'There's no avoiding that conclusion either.'

'Then shall we also declare that this latter sort of spectator

480a embraces and loves the things for which there's knowledge, the former sort the things for which there's belief? We recall saying, don't we, that it's beautiful sounds, colours, and so on, that these lovers love to witness, and that they can't bear even to think of there being such a thing as the beautiful by itself?'

'We do.'

'We surely won't be striking a false note, then, if we call them philodoxers rather than philosophers?[366] Will they really be so very angry with us for saying so?'[367]

'Not if they take my advice,' he said; 'there's no call for getting angry about the truth.'

'It's as philosophers, then, and not philodoxers, that we must address those who embrace "what is", by itself, in each case?'

'Yes, absolutely.'

484a 'So, Glaucon,' I said, 'after a somewhat lengthy discus-   Book VI
sion, and quite a bit of difficulty, we're finally clear about   begins
who are to count as philosophers and who are not.'

'Yes,' he said; 'and it probably couldn't have been done briefly.'

'Evidently not,' I said. 'My own view is that an even better explanation would have been possible if this were the only sub-
484b ject we needed to talk about, and there weren't so many other things awaiting discussion if we're to see how a just life differs from an unjust one.'

'Then what's our subject after this?' he asked.

'What else', I asked, 'but the one that comes next? Given that philosophers are those capable of getting a hold on that which remains forever exactly as it is, and those who have no such capacity, lost and wandering as they are in a multiplicity of things that are now this and now that, are non-philosophers, which of these should lead a city?'

'So', he asked, 'what would be a reasonable response to the question?'

'To make guards of whichever of them appear capable of guarding a city's laws and practices.'

'You're right,' he said.

'And when we need someone to look after anything for us, 484c
if the choice is between a blind person and a sharp-sighted one,
isn't it clear which one we'll need?'

'Of course it is!' he said.

'Well, do you think it differs at all from blindness if a person
is really and truly deprived of knowing each thing as it really
is – if he has no paradigm in plain view in his soul, nothing to
which he can refer, like a painter, as the truest guide, always
looking to that and observing it as accurately as possible, so as
to equip himself to lay down, if there's a need for it, what is to
be thought in the here and now about what's beautiful or just 484d
or good, and to guard and preserve it when it is laid down?'[368]

'Zeus, no!' he exclaimed; 'they're not much better than the
blind.'

'So shall we make them our guards, in preference to those
who not only have knowledge of each thing as it is, but also
have just as much experience as the others, and don't lag behind
them in any other part of excellence[369] either?'

'It would be very strange', he said, 'to prefer anyone else to
those with knowledge, provided that they're up to the mark in
other ways; if they have knowledge, they'll be ahead of everybody else in what is pretty much the most important thing of all.'

'Do we need to say, then, how the same people will come to be 485a
qualified in both respects?'

'We certainly do.'

'It's as we said when we were starting this part of the discussion,[370] namely, that we must first establish what natural
dispositions will be required in them. When we're sufficiently
agreed about that, I think we'll also be in a position to agree
not only that the same people can possess all the qualifications
in question, but that these are the only people who should be
leaders in a city.'

'And how shall we do that?'

'Well, let's assume that these philosophical types of ours are 485b
always in love with any subject of study that will reveal to them

anything at all about the kind of thing that always is, and doesn't wander this way and that because of coming to be and passing away.'[371]

'Yes, let's assume that.'

'And furthermore, that they're in love with everything about this kind of thing, and don't willingly let go of any part of it, small, larger, more valuable or less valuable, just like the people we discussed before[372] who were addicted to honours or to loving.'

'You're right,' he said.

485c   'Well, consider next whether there's another natural quality someone must possess if he's to be the sort of person we were describing.'

'What's that?'

'An aversion to what is false – an unwillingness ever to accept falsehood, which he'll hate as much as he loves truth.'

'Probably so,' he said.

'There's no "probably" about it, my friend; if someone's naturally passionate about anything, there's no way he can fail to be attached to everything akin to or belonging to his beloved.'

'You're right,' he said.

'And will you find anything more akin to wisdom than truth?'

'How would I do that?' he asked.

'So is it possible for the same nature to be both a lover of
485d wisdom and a lover of falsehood?'

'Not at all.'

'The person who is really and truly a lover of learning, then, must reach out as much as he can for all that is true, from childhood on.'

'Yes, absolutely.'

'But I imagine we recognize that if someone's appetites incline heavily towards one particular thing, those he has for other things are that much weaker; it's as if a stream is being diverted off into another channel.'

'Obviously.'

'So I think that if the flow of a person's appetites is directed towards learning and everything like that, they'll centre on the pleasure a soul has in and by itself, and they'll ignore the pleas-

ures that come through the body – that is, if his love of wisdom
is true and not faked.'   485e
    'That's more than necessary.'
    'In fact a person like that is moderate, and has no love of
money at all, since the things that make people eager for money
and lavish expenditure will be of less interest to him than to
anyone else, because of the way he is.'
    'Just so.'
    'And there's surely another point you need to consider if   486a
you're to distinguish a philosophical from a non-philosophical
nature.'
    'What's that?'
    'Watch out that it has no trace of the illiberal in it; small-
minded, surely, is the last thing a soul needs to be if it's always
to be reaching out for the whole of everything there is, divine
and human.'
    'Very true,' he said.
    'Do you suppose, then, that to such an elevated mind, spec-
tator of all of time and of all there is,[373] human life can seem at
all important?'
    'Impossible,' he said.
    'Will such a person think even death frightening, then?'   486b
    'Hardly,'
    'So a true love of wisdom apparently won't go with a cow-
ardly and illiberal nature.'
    'I think not.'
    'Well, is there any way that someone who is orderly and is
not a lover of money, who is not illiberal, is not a charlatan and
is not a coward, will turn out to be a breaker of contracts, or
unjust?'[374]
    'No.'
    'So this is another thing you'll consider when determining
whether a soul is philosophical or not, from earliest childhood – whether it's just and gentle, or unsociable and savage.'
    'Yes, certainly.'
    'And there's another consideration still that I imagine you   486c
won't leave out.'
    'Namely?'

'Whether someone finds it easy or difficult to learn. Would you expect anyone to have the right kind of passion for anything if doing it causes him distress and even small progress with it costs him a lot of effort?'

'I'd say it would be impossible.'

'And what about if someone were filled full with forgetfulness, and couldn't retain anything he'd learned? Could he fail to be devoid of knowledge?'

'Scarcely.'

'And when he's labouring away to no profit, don't you think he's bound to end up hating himself, what he's doing and anything like it?'

'Of course.'

486d 'Then if you're looking for souls that have a sufficient love of wisdom in them, never include one that's forgetful. Let's seek for a good memory to be made a requirement.'

'Yes, absolutely.'

'And we'll certainly agree that the only effect of an unmusical and unseemly nature is to pull a soul down into a lack of measure.'

'No question.'

'And do you think truth is akin to lack of measure, or to its presence?'

'To a presence of measure.'

'Then in addition to our other requirements, let's look for a mind that's naturally measured and graceful, whose inborn qualities will render it easily led to grasp the nature of each thing as it really is.'[375]

'Of course.'

486e 'What do you think? Don't the qualities we've listed – all of them interconnected – somehow seem like requirements for a soul that's going to share, adequately or even completely, in the truth of things?'

487a 'Absolute requirements,' he said.

'So are you going to find fault with a pursuit that no one could follow properly unless he naturally possessed good memory, quickness at learning, high-mindedness, grace and a love for and affinity to truth, justice, courage and moderation?'

'Not even Momus[376] himself could find fault with a pursuit like *that*!' he said.

'And isn't it to people like this,' I asked, 'and to them alone, that you'd turn over your city, once they'd been rounded off by education and adulthood?'

At this point, Adimantus broke in. 'Socrates, no one could 487b argue with you about any of this. But here's the sort of reaction people have every time they hear the things you're saying now: they think that because they're not experienced enough in question-and-answer, at each question the argument leads them a little bit astray, and then when all the little bits are collected together at the end of the exchange, they come down to earth with a bump and find they've contradicted what they said at the beginning. It's like playing a board-game against experts: just as beginners at *petteia* end up being closed off and unable 487c to move, so they too find themselves ultimately hedged in and reduced to silence by this newfangled kind of *petteia* that uses words instead of pieces, even though the truth is still just as much on their side. I say this with an eye to the present situation: someone might well say that he has no way of arguing against you as you put each question to him, but nevertheless he can perfectly well see that if people take up philosophy, not just in order to complete their education, and as something to be abandoned before they've grown up, but rather as some- 487d thing to spend their time on even after that, they mostly become downright peculiar, not to say totally corrupted, and even the ones that seem the most respectable, when they're subjected to this kind of treatment[377] by the pursuit you praise so much, turn out to be of no use to their cities.'

When I heard him say this, I asked him, 'Well, do you think those who say this are saying something false?'

'I don't know,' he said; 'I'd be glad to hear what you think.'

'What you'll hear from me is that *I* think what they're saying is true.'

'In that case,' he asked, 'how can it be right to say that 487e "troubles won't cease for cities" until they're ruled by

philosophers[378] – the very people we're now agreeing are useless to them?'

'That', I said, 'is a question that needs to be answered by
means of a verbal image.'[379]

'And I suppose you never talk through images!' he exclaimed.[380]

'Fine,' I said; 'so you're going to poke fun at me, just when
488a you've got me into something as difficult to prove as this is?
Well, here it is, anyway – yes, one more illustration of my
addiction to images. Actually, so difficult is the situation of
these "most respectable" types of yours, in relation to the cities
they live in, that there's no single thing anywhere that will provide an analogy; one needs to put together lots of different
elements to produce the sort of image needed to defend them,
like the goat-stags and other composite creatures pictured by
painters.[381] Think of a scenario like the following, on board
either a fleet of ships or a single ship on its own. The ship-
488b owner[382] is bigger and stronger than everyone else on board,
but a bit deaf, somewhat short-sighted too, and with a knowledge of seamanship to match; meanwhile, the crew are in
dispute with one another over control of the steering, each of
them thinking *he* should steer, even though none of them has so
far learned how to do it, or can give either the name of his
teacher or the dates of his apprenticeship. On top of that, they
declare that it can't be taught anyway, and will happily cut
488c down anyone who says it can. Perpetually milling around the
ship-owner, they beg him to turn over the steering-oar to them,
and will do anything to force him; sometimes, if they don't suc-
ceed in persuading him and others have better luck, they'll kill
the others or throw them overboard. Then, when they've incapacitated the noble owner with drugs, or drink, or whatever it
may be, they become the ship's officers, making free with its
cargo, and as they drink and feast they sail the ship – well, just
488d as you'd expect sailors like that to sail it. And as if this weren't
enough, they're full of praise for anyone clever enough to help
them persuade or force the ship-owner to let them take control,
calling him a real sailor and steersman, and a master of naut-
ical expertise, and castigating anyone not like that for being

useless. They don't understand enough about the true expert
in steersmanship even to know that he must give his attention
to the seasons of the year, to the heavens, to the stars, to the
winds, and everything that belongs to his art, if he is really and
truly to become an expert in running a ship; as for his steering
whether some people want him to or not, they think it's no   488e
more possible to acquire a skill in that, or to practise for it,
than it is to acquire the art of steersmanship in the first place.[383]
If this sort of thing happened on board ship, don't you think
the genuine expert in steersmanship would truly be called a   489a
"stargazer" and a "babbler"[384] by those who sailed in ships
that were set up like that?'

'Very much so,' said Adimantus.

'I think you understand the point', I said, 'without close
examination of the image; the resemblance to the attitude cities
have towards the true philosophers is clear enough.'

'Very much so,' he repeated.

'The first thing for you to do, then, with that critic who's surprised by the lack of honour accorded to philosophers in cities,[385]
is to teach him this image, and to try persuading him that it   489b
would be much more surprising if cities did honour them.'

'I'll do that,' he said.

'And say to him as well, "You're right when you say the
most respectable people in philosophy are useless to ordinary
people", but tell him he shouldn't be blaming them for it; the
blame belongs to those who fail to put good men to good use.
It's unnatural for a steersman to be begging ordinary sailors to
let him give them orders, or for the wise to go knocking on the
doors of the rich – the wit who said otherwise was wrong.[386]
The true and natural order of things is that if a person is ill, no
matter whether he's rich or poor, he should go knocking on the   489c
doctor's door, and that everyone who needs orders from someone else should go to the person capable of giving them; it's not
for the ruler, if he's truly good for anything, to beg the ruled to
be ruled. In short, you won't go wrong if you compare the political types currently ruling over cities to the sailors we were
just describing, and the people they call useless stargazers to
the true steersmen.'

'Quite right,' he said.

'These are the reasons, then, and these are the circumstances,
489d that explain why it is so difficult for the best pursuit of all to
acquire good standing, among people who pursue just the
opposite. But by far the greatest and most powerful slander on
philosophy comes about because of those who claim to be
doing the things philosophers do – the people you were referring to when you described the charge against philosophy,
which I accepted, that most of those who went in for it were
totally corrupted, and the most respectable merely useless. You
did, didn't you?'

'Yes.'

'Well, have we explained the reason for the "uselessness" of
the good ones?'

'We certainly have.'

'Would you like us next to explain the corruption of the
489e others, and why it's so inevitable? Should we try to show, if we
can, that philosophy isn't to blame for this either?'

'Yes, absolutely.'

'Well, let's begin our exchange on this subject by recalling
where we started from when we were describing the endow-
490a ments our shining example of excellence would need to be
born with.[387] What guided his progress, if you recall, was truth,
first and foremost, which we said he had to pursue in all things
and all ways, on pain of proving a charlatan with not the slightest trace of a true love of wisdom.'

'Yes, that was what we were saying.'

'Isn't this one thing that runs emphatically counter to the
views currently held about him?'

'Yes, indeed,' he said.

'So won't it be a reasonable defence for us to make on his
behalf that if someone really and truly loved learning, he'd
have been born, as we said, to struggle towards what really is,
490b and wouldn't spend time dallying over the many things people
believe in; on he'd go, losing none of his sharpness, none of his
passion, until he'd grasped the nature of each thing as it really
is, in itself, with the part of the soul that is peculiarly suited for
grasping such a thing; using that to come near to and genuinely

couple with what is,[388] spawning intelligence and truth, he'd
live a true life, truly nourished, only then ceasing from his
birth-pangs, and not before?'

'That would be the most reasonable defence possible,' he
said.

'And will this person have any share in loving falsehood, or
will it be quite the contrary – he'll hate it?'

'He'll hate it,' he said.   490c

'With truth there as guide, then, I think we say no chorus of
troubles could ever follow on behind.'

'How could it?'

'What we say *will* follow is a just and healthy disposition,
itself followed by moderation.'

'Correct,' he said.

'As for the rest of the chorus that constitutes a philosophical
nature, do we really need to go back and make them line up all
over again? I'm sure you remember the other things that turned
out to go with these, namely courage, high-mindedness, quickness at learning, a good memory. Then you objected that even
if everybody found themselves forced to agree with what we   490d
were saying, if they set aside the arguments, and actually looked
at the people we were talking about, they'd say they could *see*
that apart from the useless few they were totally bad. It's the
search for what was to blame for this slander on philosophy
that's brought us to where we are now, to the question why it
is that most of them are in fact so bad; that's why we've picked
up the subject of the truly philosophical nature again, and laid
down what it has to be.'

'That is so,' he said.

'What we need to do, now,' I said, 'is to observe how this   490e
kind of nature comes to be corrupted in many cases, leaving
only a small element to escape, and turn into those few they say
aren't actually corrupted, merely useless. After that, we need to   491a
look in turn at the natures that mimic this one and set themselves up in its territory: what types of souls are these that
usurp an activity so far beyond their capacities, and by going
wrong in so many ways end up giving philosophy the universal
reputation you describe?'

'What sorts of corruption have you in mind?' he asked.

'I'll try my best to describe them to you,' I said. 'One point, I think, we'll find everyone ready to accept, which is that the sort of person who fits all the requirements we laid down just now for becoming the complete philosopher is a rare creature, 491b rarely born to human parents. Don't you think so?'

'I certainly do.'

'And just think of all the many powerful influences there are to corrupt these rare specimens.'

'What are they?'

'What will sound the most surprising of all is the way each of the very features of a philosophical nature we were picking out for praise – courage, moderation, and all the rest – actually works to corrupt its owner's soul, pulling it away from philosophy.'

'That does sound strange,' he said.

491c   'And, moreover,' I said, 'the same corrupting effect is worked by all the so-called good things – beauty, wealth, physical strength, a politically powerful family, and everything like that; you'll grasp the type of thing I have in mind.'

'I do,' he said, 'and I'd be grateful if you'd say more precisely what you're talking about.'

'Well,' I said, 'get the correct hold on the general idea, and you'll find it's all quite clear; these introductory remarks of mine won't seem so strange.'

'So what is it you're telling me to get a hold on?' he asked.

491d   'With any seed or growing thing,' I said, 'no matter whether it's a plant or an animal, we know that if it hasn't had the particular nourishment that's appropriate to it, or the right weather, or location, the more vigorous a specimen it is the greater the number of ways it will fail; bad, I think, is more opposed to good than it is to something that's merely not good.'

'Obviously.'

'It stands to reason, then, I think, that the best nature will come off worse than one that lacks quality, if the nurture it receives is that much further from the one it deserves.'

'It does.'

'Well then, Adimantus,' I asked, 'shall we declare that with 491e souls, too, it's the ones born with the best natures that come to

be outstandingly bad, if they receive a bad education in childhood? Or do you imagine that behind great crimes, and
unmitigated badness, there lies an inferior nature, rather than a
vigorous one that's been destroyed by its nurture? Do you
really suppose a weak nature would ever be capable of great
things, good or bad?'

'No,' he said; 'it's as you say.'

'So this philosophical nature, as we've set it out, can go in   492a
either of two ways: if it receives the learning appropriate to it, I
think it will inevitably go on, as it grows up, to every form of excellence; but if it is sown in the wrong soil, and then sprouts and
is nourished there, it will end up in quite the opposite way, unless
there's some god on hand to help it out. Or do you suppose, as
ordinary people do, that there are young men out there being
corrupted by sophists, and that individual sophists do any corrupting that's worth mentioning, when actually it's the very same   492b
people that paint this picture who are themselves the sophists-in-
chief, providing the perfect education for making anyone, young
or old, man or woman, exactly as they want him to be?'

'When do they do *that*?' he asked.

'Whenever they sit down in large numbers together,' I said,
'whether it's in the assembly, the lawcourts, the theatre, an
army-camp, or on any other public occasion where a mass of
people get together in a great hubbub in order to disparage or
praise what's being said or done, and overdoing it either way,   492c
bawling at the top of their voices and clapping their hands, the
noise of their boos and applause doubled, as if it weren't
already loud enough, by the echo from the rocks or the space
around them. What heart do you think a young man will have
left, as they say, in the face of all that? What kind of education
would he need beforehand, if it's not to be overwhelmed by
such torrents of disparagement and praise, and carried away
with them whichever way they happen to go – so that he ends
up labelling the same things "beautiful" and "ugly" as *they*
do,[389] doing what they do and being as they are?'

'Yes,' he said; 'there's just no way he can avoid it.'   492d

'And we haven't even mentioned the most powerful compulsion on him.'

'What's that?' he asked.

'It's the one these educator-sophists[390] apply on top of the talking, if he's still not won over. You're aware, surely, that if anyone doesn't do as they say they punish him with loss of citizen rights, or fines, or death?'

'All too aware,' he said.

'So what individual sophist do you think could compete against them? What could he possibly say, in private, and win?'

492e   'I imagine, nothing,' he said.

'No,' I replied, 'and it would be quite mad even to try. There is not, there never was, nor will there ever be an education for excellence capable of countering theirs,[391] and producing a character of a different kind – so long, my friend, as we're talking about the merely human: the divine, as they say, is another matter. There is no getting away from the fact that if anything

493a   is saved and turns out as it ought to be, given regimes of the sort we're talking about, it can only be said to have been saved by divine dispensation.'[392]

'And that's what I think too,' he said.

'Well,' I said, 'there's something else you should be thinking.'

'What's that?'

'That the education offered by each of these fee-earning individuals that ordinary people call sophists, and think of as their competitors, consists in teaching nothing but the opinions that these same ordinary people express when they get together – *that* is what their "wisdom" consists in. It's as if someone were rearing a large and powerful beast, and spent his

493b   time learning its moods and appetites – how best to approach it and handle it, when it was at its most awkward, or indeed its gentlest, and what made it so; the occasions for the various sounds it would utter, what sorts of voices would calm it or send it wild – and when he'd acquired all this knowledge, by spending so much time with the beast, decided to call it wisdom, and turned to teaching, claiming to have established a body of expertise; when in truth he would have no idea about any of the opinions and desires he was dealing with, and what

493c   in them was beautiful or ugly, good or bad, just or unjust, but would simply apply all these names after the beliefs of the great

beast, labelling what gave it pleasure as good and what upset it
as bad. He'd have no other account to give of such things: what
was merely necessary, he'd call just and beautiful, and the distance that truly separates the natures of the necessary and the
good[393] he'd neither have seen for himself nor be able to demonstrate to anyone else. Zeus above! If there were someone like
that, don't you think he'd make a strange educator?'

'Yes, I do,' he said.

'Well, do you think he's any different from someone whose
idea of wisdom, whether in the sphere of painting, or music, or
indeed politics, is a familiarity with the temper of ordinary,   493d
motley people when they get together, and what gives them
their pleasures? Clearly, if anyone goes to them to show off his
poems, or some other piece of craftsmanship, or services he's
performed for the city, and gives ordinary people more power
over him than he has to, then it's as sure as sure can be[394] that
he'll be forced into composing things they approve of, whatever these may be; and have you ever yet heard anyone trying
to explain why such things are genuinely good and beautiful,
and not ending up as a laughing-stock?'

'No,' he said, 'and I don't suppose I ever will.'   493e

'Well then, with that in mind, recall what we said[395] about
the following question: beauty by itself, as opposed to the many
things that are beautiful, or anything by itself as opposed to the
many whatever it is – are there a large number of people that   494a
will put up with being told that there are such things, or think
it for themselves?'

'Hardly,' he said.

'It's impossible, then,' I said, 'for a large number of people to
be philosophically minded.'

'Impossible.'

'It's also inevitable, then, that those who do philosophize
will be disparaged by the majority.'

'Inevitable.'

'And by all those private individuals, too, who like to mix
with a crowd and crave its approval.'

'Clearly so.'

'So, given all this, do you see any way of preserving a born

philosopher, so that he stays true to his nature and becomes what
494b his nature fits him to be? Think of it in terms of what we said
before: we agreed that quickness at learning, a good memory,
courage and high-mindedness were all parts of a philosophical
nature.'

'Yes.'

'Won't someone with those qualities stand out even as a
child above all his peers, especially if the body he's born with
matches his soul?'

'Of course,' he said.

'I imagine his family and his fellow-citizens will want to
make use of him, then, when he gets older, for their own purposes.'

'Naturally so.'

494c 'So they'll lay siege to him with their requests and their com-
pliments, anticipating with their flattery what he'll be able to
do for them in the future.'

'That's how it usually happens,' he said.

'And how do you think such a young man will respond,' I
asked, 'especially if he happens to belong to a large city, stands
out as wealthy and of good family, and is good looking and tall
as well? Don't you suppose he'll be full of impossible expecta-
494d tions, thinking to himself that when he grows up he'll be up to
running things, not just for the Greeks but for non-Greeks
too – flying high already, then, in his own mind, its intelligence
crowded out by posturing and empty pride?'

'Very much so,' he said.

'And if someone should come up to him when he's developing this condition, and gently tell him the truth, that there's no
intelligence in him, that there should be, and that there won't
be unless he becomes a slave to acquiring it, do you think it will
be easy for him to listen, in the midst of everything that's besetting him?'[396]

'Far from it,' he said.

'And further,' I said, 'if a good natural disposition and an
affinity for what is being said to him[397] allow him to feel the
494e pull of philosophy and be drawn towards her, what do you
think will be the reaction from those who think they're losing

his usefulness to them as well as his friendship? Won't they do and say anything both to prevent him from being persuaded and to stop the person doing the persuading from being able to do so, hatching private plots and instigating public court-cases against him?'

'That's absolutely bound to happen,' he said.   495a

'Is there any chance, then, that such a person will become a philosopher?'

'None whatsoever.'

'So you see,' I said, 'we weren't wrong when we said that in a way it was the very parts that go to make up a philosophical nature, when subjected to a bad upbringing, that are responsible – along with the things people call good, like wealth, and all that sort of baggage – for its *abandoning* philosophy.'

'No,' he said, 'it was the right conclusion.'

'This, then,' I said, 'my fine friend, is the way the best natures – already rare enough, as we say ourselves – are, sadly, ruined for the finest of pursuits; that's how many, and how   495b powerful, the corrupting factors are. It's these few men who turn out either to have the most destructive effects on cities and on individuals or, if by chance the stream in them has flowed that way,[398] to work the greatest benefits for both – small nature never did anything big either to individual or to city.'

'Very true,' he said.

'And when they do abandon philosophy, the very pursuit that suits them best, so leaving it bereft and unconsummated,   495c not only do they themselves go on to live an unsuitable life, and with no truth in it,[399] but other unworthy suitors then move in and take the orphan over, left as it is with no kin to defend it, shaming it and causing people to make the very reproaches against philosophy that you say they make, to the effect that if anyone spends time with it he's either worthless or, most likely, worth a good beating and more.'

'Well, yes,' he said, 'that is what they say.'

'And with good reason,' I said. 'When other people, little people, see this space abandoned by its rightful owners, and full of fine words for dressing up in, those of them who happen   495d to be cleverest, at whatever tiny thing it is they do, leap joyfully, like escaped prisoners running off to a sanctuary, straight from their own trades and into philosophy. The truth is that despite its parlous condition philosophy still retains a greater prestige in comparison with other areas of expertise, a prestige which is sought after by many whose natures lack the necessary comple-tion, and whose souls are actually as broken and crushed by the physicality of their occupations as their bodies have been deformed by the performance of their trades.[400] Isn't that inev-itably so?'

495e

'It certainly is.'

'And do they look any different to you from a bald little metal-worker who's come into some money, and just as soon as he's had his chains taken off,[401] had a good wash at the baths and dressed himself up in a brand-new cloak, presents himself as a suitor for the hand of his master's daughter because she's poor and on her own?'

496a

'There's not a lot of difference,' he said.

'And what sort of children would one expect parents like that to produce? Illegitimate ones, presumably, of no quality.'

'Yes, inevitably.'

'What about these people we're talking about, undeserving of an education, who get close to philosophy and consort with it, quite contrary to what they deserve? What sort of thinking and what sorts of beliefs shall we say they'll breed? Surely what it's true to call "sophisms" – nothing genuine, nothing to do with true wisdom?'

'Quite so,' he said; 'absolutely.'

'It's a very small portion, then, Adimantus,' I said, 'that remains, of those who consort with philosophy and deserve to do so: maybe it will be some noble and well-brought-up char-acter, his decline arrested by exile, remaining true both to his nature and to philosophy for lack of those who'll corrupt him; or else a great soul will be born in a little city, and find its affairs too small for his attention. A few, because of their nat-ural gifts, might migrate from other fields of expertise, having justly come to look down on them.[402] Or else there's what reins in our friend Theages:[403] everything else with Theages is just right for him to abandon philosophy, but the sickly state of his

496b

496c

body prevents him, by debarring him from a political career. My own case – my divine sign[404] – isn't worth mentioning; there may possibly have been someone who had the same experience before me, but then again there may not have been. Those who have joined this small band have tasted how blessedly sweet a possession philosophy is, and at the same time they have seen enough for themselves of the madness that grips ordinary people – that in the running of cities virtually nothing is done by anyone that is conducive to political health, nor is there a single ally with whom one might go to the aid of justice 496d and still remain alive; it would be a case of a solitary human among wild animals, neither wanting to join in their depredations nor able to stand alone against their collective savagery, dead before he'd done any good to his city or friends and useless both to himself and everybody else. Once a person has made all these calculations, he keeps his peace and minds his own business, like someone withdrawing from the prevailing wind into the shelter of a wall in a storm of dust or rain, and as he sees everyone else filling themselves full of lawlessness he is 496e content if he himself can somehow live out life here untainted by injustice and impious actions, and leave it with fine hopes and in a spirit of kindness and good will.'[405]

'To go like that would not be the smallest achievement,' he 497a said.

'But neither would it be the greatest, if he's not had the fortune to live under a regime that's suited to him; for under such a regime not only will he grow in stature himself, but he will save the common cause along with his own. – Well, in any case, I think we've given a fair account of the reasons for the slanders against philosophy, and of why she doesn't deserve them – unless you've anything to add.'

'No,' he said, 'I've nothing to add on that subject. But when you talk about a "suitable" regime, which of the current types do you have in mind?'

'Not a single one of them,' I said; 'that's just my complaint, 497b that none of the current ways of organizing a city is up to the requirements of a philosophical nature. That is why such a nature becomes warped and altered – just as an imported seed,

sown in alien soil, tends to have its own properties overwhelmed and go native, so under present conditions the
philosophical nature isn't able to maintain its own proper
powers, but rather falls away, taking on a character not its
497c own; whereas if it's under the best regime, as it too is best, then
it will be revealed that it was all along really and truly divine,
and all the rest were merely human, whether in terms of natural
capacities or of what they spend their time doing. And now,
clearly, you're going to ask me which this best regime is!'

'You're wrong,' he said; 'what I was actually going to ask
was whether it's the city we've founded in our discussion, or
some other one.'

'In all respects but one it is the city we've talked about,' I
said; 'and actually we did say even then what I have in mind to
say now – that there must always be one element in the city
497d that has the same understanding of its arrangements as you, the
legislator, had when you were laying down its laws.'[406]

'Yes, we did say that,' he replied.

'But it wasn't adequately shown,' I said, 'for fear of the
objections you people have made, which show just how long
and difficult a demonstration it will be. I have to tell you that
what remains isn't the easiest subject in the world to deal with.'

'What is it?'

'How a city will be able to practise philosophy without
being destroyed. For all great enterprises are risky: what is fine,
they say, is never easy.'

497e 'All the same,' he said, 'let's have it out in the open, and get
the demonstration done.'

'If I don't manage it,' I said, 'it won't be because I don't want
to, just because I can't; you'll see for yourself my own enthusiasm for getting the job done. And just note the eager abandon
in what I'm going to say even now: that the way the pursuit of
philosophy needs to be handled is the opposite of the way it's
handled now.'

'How so?'

498a 'As things are, those who do engage with philosophy do so
as they move from childhood and adolescence, in the interval
before they start taking charge of a household and making

money; then, just when they've got up to the hardest part of it, which is the one to do with arguments,[407] they give it up – and these are the types that are treated as most philosophical. After that, they regard it as a big thing if they're merely willing to go along and hear others swapping arguments, because from their point of view it's no more than a sideline; and as they approach old age, apart from a few noticeable exceptions, their fires are extinguished more surely than Heraclitus' sun, never to be kindled again.'[408]

'And what should happen?' he asked.   498b

'Quite the opposite. Young people – adolescents and children – should embark on a young person's education, and a young person's version of philosophy, meanwhile taking very good care of their bodies, as these sprout and mature into manhood, to serve the needs of philosophy; only then should the soul be exercised harder, at that age of a man's life when it begins its own process to completion. Finally, when their physical strength goes, and they are no longer candidates for political   498c or military service, they should roam free, like sacred animals,[409] and do nothing except philosophy, unless it's as a sideline – that is, if they're to live happily and reserve a destiny for themselves in that other place,[410] when they die, that befits the life they have lived here.'

'It seems to me you're talking like a true enthusiast, Socrates,' he said. 'But I imagine most of your listeners are even more enthusiastic about opposing you, and won't in the least be convinced, starting with Thrasymachus.'

'Don't try and start a quarrel between Thrasymachus and   498d me,' I said, 'just when we've become friends – not that we were enemies before. We're not going to give up trying until either we convince both him and everybody else, or we do something for them that will help them when they've been reborn, in some future life, and they encounter discussions like this again.'[411]

'You're looking at a short time, then,' he said.

'No time at all, in fact,' I said, 'when it's compared with the whole of time. But it's no surprise if most ordinary people aren't convinced by what's being said, because they haven't ever seen realized what's now been theorized. What they're

498e   much more likely to have seen is wordplay like that,[412] words
deliberately made to chime with one another, not combining
spontaneously as ours do; a man not just rhyming but chiming
with excellence, as completely as could be, in work and word,
499a   and holding princely power in a city structured like himself,
that they've never once seen, let alone more than once. Or do
you suppose they have?'

'Certainly not.'

'Nor, again, my friend, have they had sufficient exposure, as
you have, to the kind of fine and free discussion that stretches
every sinew to search for the truth, for the sake of knowledge,
and bids the wariest of welcomes to all the self-justifying
subtleties and point-scoring of legal disputes and day-to-day
conversations.'

'No, they haven't had that either,' he said.

499b   'So those were the problems we foresaw back then,' I said,
'when for all our trepidation we found the truth compelling us
to say that no city or regime, and equally no individual man,
would ever achieve completion until some chance brought it
about that these philosophers of ours – the few, currently
described as useless, that have not gone to the bad – are compelled, whether they wish it or not, to take charge of a city, and
to put themselves at the city's service, or else the sons of those
presently wielding princely or kingly power, or those kings and
499c   princes themselves, come by some sort of divine inspiration to
be possessed by an unfeigned passion for true philosophy. I
myself declare that I have no reason for declaring either or both
of these outcomes impossible; if they were, we'd justly be
laughed at, for mere empty and wishful thinking[413] – right?'

'Right.'

'So if something either has happened, in the endless reach of
past time, or is now happening in some region far beyond the
ken of us Greeks, or else will happen at some time in the future,
499d   to compel top philosophers to take charge of a city, on this
point we're ready and willing to fight our corner: that the
regime we've described has come into existence, and exists, or
will exist, only when the Muse, herself,[414] takes control of a
city. It's not impossible for her to do so – we're not talking

about something that's impossible; just difficult – that much
we're agreed about.'

'I think so, too,' he said.

'But most ordinary people won't think so,' I said; 'is that
what you're going to say?'

'Maybe,' he replied.

'My fine friend,' I said to him, 'don't write off ordinary
people so completely. They'll surely think differently if you   499e
take on a soothing instead of a combative tone, and try to free
them from their prejudice against the love of knowledge by
pointing out to them who it is you have in mind by "philosophers" – describing their true nature, as we did just now, and   500a
what they typically do, so that they don't imagine you're talking about the same people they are. If they're given this new
perspective, you really will find them taking a different view,
and giving different answers to your questions.[415] Or do you
really think anyone will be harsh and malicious to someone
who is neither the one nor the other to them, when in himself
he's gentle and lacking in malice? I'll get in before you and say
that I think responding like that to gentleness requires a natural
harshness you won't find in the mass of the people, only in a
few individuals.'

'I certainly agree with you there,' he said.

'And do you also agree with me on this other point I'm mak-   500b
ing, that the responsibility for the harsh view ordinary people
take towards philosophy lies with that disorderly collection of
outsiders that has burst in on it uninvited, spending their time
in slanging matches, making themselves as unpleasant as possible and perpetually directing their talk at individuals[416] – the
last thing philosophy is for?'

'Yes, by a long way,' he said.

'Right, Adimantus; because I imagine that if someone truly
has his mind on things as they really are, he will not have time   500c
to look down at the preoccupations of mere mortals and fight
with them, filling himself full of malice and ill-will. Instead, as
he turns his eyes towards an ordered array of things that forever remain the same, and observes these maintaining their
harmony and rationality in everything, and neither behaving

unjustly nor being treated unjustly by each other,[417] he will imitate these and model himself after them so far as he can. Or do you think anyone can avoid imitating a thing he spends his time with, and in awe of?'

'He can't,' said Adimantus.

500d 'So if the philosopher spends his time with the divine and ordered, he'll achieve such order and divinity as is possible for man; though there's always a chance, for anyone, of being slandered.'

'There certainly is.'

'If, then,' I said, 'he finds himself somehow compelled to apply what he sees there to humankind, not just to mould himself but to arrange the dispositions of others at the level of both individual and city, do you suppose he'll turn out a bad craftsman of moderation and justice, and of civic excellence as a whole?'[418]

'Hardly!' he exclaimed.

'And if ordinary people grasp that what we're saying about him is true, will they maintain their harsh attitude towards 500e philosophers, and will they go on disbelieving us when we say that there's no other way that a city could ever be happy, that is, unless it was painted by artists using the appropriate divine paradigm?'[419]

'No, they won't be so harsh', he said, 'if they actually do 501a grasp it. But what mode of "painting" would this be, exactly?'

'It would be', I said, 'as if the city, and the dispositions of those in it, were a wooden board they'd start by wiping clean. That's not at all easy, but in any case you'll recognize this as one way in which our artists would immediately differ from all others: they would refuse to do anything with either individual or city, or write laws, before either they'd received a clean slate, or they had cleaned it themselves.'

'And rightly so,' he said.

'And after that, do you think they'll set about sketching the outline of its political arrangements?'

'Naturally.'

501b 'Then, I imagine, as they worked away, they would glance repeatedly both at what justice, beauty, moderation and everything else of that sort are in nature and at what they are in human beings, and fill in the details of their sketch accordingly,[420] mixing and blending together from the various pursuits available to them the likeness of a man,[421] all the time basing themselves on what Homer himself described, when it appeared in human beings, as the image or likeness of a god.'

'Right.'

'And I imagine from time to time they'll rub something out 501c and replace it with something else, until they've done all they can to make human dispositions as acceptable to the gods as it is possible for them to be.'

'The painting, certainly,' he said, 'would be very beautiful.'

'So,' I asked, 'are we doing anything to convince the people you claimed[422] were so intent on attacking us that *this* is the kind of regime-painter we were praising to them before, the one who evoked their harsh response to us when we proposed to hand cities over to him? As they listen to our case, are they softening at all?'

'I should think they will,' he said; 'if they have any sense.'

'Yes, because what grounds will they have for disputing it 501d with us? Will they claim that philosophers are not lovers of what is, and of truth?'

'That would be a strange claim,'[423] he said.

'Or will they claim that the philosopher's natural disposition, as we have described it, is not akin to what is best?'

'They can't claim that either.'

'Or that such a disposition, if any, when it's been reinforced by the appropriate pursuits, won't be completely good, and philosophical? Will they claim to prefer the ones we ruled out?'

'Indeed not.'

'So will they still respond so savagely to our proposal that, 501e until control of a city comes to be in the hands of people of a philosophical kind, there will be no respite from troubles either for that city or for its citizens, nor will the regime whose story we're telling in theory reach completion in practice?'

'Perhaps,' he said, 'less savagely.'

'Well,' I said, 'would you be happy if we said not just that

502a they'll be less savage to us, but that they'll be totally gentle, because they'll have been totally won over, so that if nothing else they'll be shamed into agreeing with us?'

'Yes, absolutely,' he said.

'So let's count them as persuaded by our case thus far. And will anyone dispute that the children of kings and princes could actually come to be born with the requisite philosophical natures?'

'No one at all,' he said.

'And if they are born like that, can anyone claim that they must inevitably be corrupted? We ourselves grant that it's hard for them to survive,[424] but could anyone claim that in the whole
502b of time not a single one out of all of them could ever be saved?'

'How could they?'

'But if there turned out to be just one,' I said, 'no more would be needed, if he had a city that listened to him, to bring about everything that is presently thought impossible.'

'No, you're right,' he said.

'Because if he did rule somewhere,' I said, 'by establishing the laws and modes of behaviour that we've described, it's surely not impossible that the citizens would be willing to follow.'

'Not impossible at all,' he said.

'And would it be at all surprising, or impossible, for others to have the same ideas as we do?'

502c 'I for one don't think so,' he said.

'Moreover, that our proposals are best, if they really are possible, is something I imagine we covered well enough earlier on.'

'I agree.'

'Our conclusion, then, it seems, is that our legislative proposals are best, if they could be put into practice, and that while putting them into practice would be difficult, it would certainly not be impossible.'

'Yes, that's our conclusion,' he said.

'Now that we've finally dealt with that point, should we go
502d on to the remaining question – how are there going to be these saviours of ours in the city,[425] preserving the regime? What

studies and pursuits will they need to shape them, and at what sorts of age should they embark on each of these?'

'That definitely needs discussing,' he said.

'My clever ruse did me no good at all', I said, '– putting off as I did the troublesome subjects of acquiring women, producing children and putting the rulers in place, because I knew just how badly the full truth about this would be received, and how difficult it would be to put into practice; it's done nothing to spare me having to go through it all anyway. Well, the topic of women and children is over and done with, and now we need to tackle that of the rulers, as if we were starting all over again. If you recall, we said[426] that they had to show that their love of the city would survive the test of pleasures and pains, and that this commitment of theirs would not be cast aside because of any hardship or fear or any change of fortune; if one of them was incapable of showing *that*, he was to be excluded, but the one who came through without a mark on him, like gold tested in the fire, was to be established as ruler, and given privileges, and prizes, both in his lifetime and after his death. Those were the sorts of things we were saying back then, while our argument tried to slip past unseen, with its face veiled, for fear of stirring up the subject we're now embarked on.'

'Quite right, that's what was said; I remember,' he replied.

'Yes, my friend,' I said; 'because we were reluctant to say what we've now finally dared to admit to. But now let our daring proposal stand: those to be appointed as the truest guards[427] must be *philosophers*.'

'That's where we stand,' he said.

'Notice how few of them you're likely to find. The different elements of the nature we said they would need tend to be found together only rarely; for the most part, a bit of it appears here, a bit there.'

'How so?' he asked.

'Those born quick at learning, with a good memory, shrewd, sharp, and so on, as you surely know, don't tend also to be born with the youthful high-mindedness that would be needed[428] for them willingly to live an orderly, quiet and stable

502e

503a

503b

503c

life. Their very sharpness carries that sort heaven knows where, and anything stable in them is quite squeezed out.'

'True,' he said.

'On the other hand, those stable characters that don't easily 503d change and are more dependable may be hard to move when it comes to the fears of war, but aren't they the same when it comes to learning anything? They're as hard to move and to teach as if they'd been numbed, and they do nothing but nod off and yawn whenever they're set anything that stretches their minds.'

'That's true,' he said.

'And what we said[429] was that they had to be well and truly endowed with both sets of qualities, or else they could be given no share either in education, of the truest sort, or in honour, or in ruling.'

'And we were right,' he said.

'Don't you think it will be rare to find such a blend?'

'Of course.'

'Then we must test their natural endowment not just in the 503e ways we said before, by exposing it to hard work, to fear and to pleasure, but in another way that we omitted to talk about then, by exercising it in a range of intellectual subjects, all the time looking to see whether it will have the capacity to bear the 504a weight of even the weightiest subjects, or whether it will shrink from these as people do from physical challenges.'

'That's certainly an appropriate sort of test,' he said; 'but what exactly are these "weightiest subjects" you're talking about?'

'You probably remember', I said, 'that after distinguishing three kinds of element[430] in the soul we tried to reach conclusions about justice, moderation, courage and wisdom, and say what each of them is.'

'If I didn't remember that,' he said, 'I'd deserve not to hear the rest.'

'So do you also remember what we said before that?'

'What was that?'

504b   'I think what we were trying to say[431] was that in order to achieve the finest view that was possible of the things in question, we'd need to take another and longer way round, and then they'd become clearly visible to us, but that meanwhile it would be possible to apply proofs that were on the same level as the things we'd been saying up to that point. You people said that was enough for you, and it was on this understanding that we said what we said then – to me, it seemed to lack precision; whether you were happy with it is for you to say.'

'It seemed to me to deal with the subject in due measure,' he said, 'and so it did to the others, too.'

'My friend,' I said, 'if your measure in such cases falls even   504c
to the slightest degree short of what a thing really is, there's no "due measure" about it at all. Nothing incomplete is a measure of anything – even though people sometimes do think they've got as far as they need, and that they don't need to inquire any further.'[432]

'Quite so,' he said; 'that does happen to a lot of people, out of laziness.'

'And *that*', I said, 'is the last thing we want to find in someone guarding a city and its laws.'

'Probably so,' he said.

'So, my friend,' I said, 'someone like that needs to go round by the longer route, and work just as hard at his studies as he   504d
does in the gymnasium, or else – to come back to what we were talking about just now – he'll never get to the end of the weightiest subject, and the one that is most appropriate to him.'

'Didn't we already deal with that when we talked about justice and the rest?' he asked. 'Is there something still more important than they are?'

'Yes, there is,' I said; 'and it's not a mere sketch of them, either, that we should be looking at, in the way we're now doing, instead of going for the full-blown portrait. Wouldn't it be ridiculous to put every effort into ensuring that other, unimportant things are as precise and unblemished as they can be,[433]   504e
and meanwhile not assign the greatest importance to precision in the most important things?'

'Highly ridiculous,' he said. 'But do you really think anyone's going to let you go without asking you what this "most important" subject *is* – what exactly you're referring to when you use language like this?'

'I don't think so at all,' I said. 'Go on, *you* ask me! Anyway, it's something you've heard about on more than a few occasions.

505a Either you don't remember, or you're deliberately attacking me just to make trouble. I think the second is the more likely, because you've heard often enough that it's the form of goodness[434] that is the most important subject, since it is what brings about the goodness and usefulness both of just things and of everything else. And you pretty much know that's what I'm going to say now – as you know I'll go on to say that we don't have sufficient knowledge of it; and if we don't, even if we had the greatest knowledge possible of everything else, and not of

505b *this*, you know that it's of no more use to us than possessing anything if good doesn't come of it. Or *do* you think it takes us any further on, to have made any acquisition you like, but not a good one? Or to be wise about anything and everything else, but with the good left out, and have no wisdom about anything beautiful and good?'

'Zeus! I certainly don't,' he said.

'And there's something else you know: ordinary people think the good is pleasure, whereas the more sophisticated think it's wisdom.'

'Of course!'

'And further, my friend, you know that people who think it is wisdom can't show us what it is wisdom about, but ultimately they're compelled to declare that it's about – the good.'

'How ridiculous is that!' he exclaimed.

505c 'Yes indeed,' I said, 'if they blame us for not knowing what the good is, and then turn round and address us as if we did know. After all, they're saying it's being wise about what's good, as if we already understand what they're talking about when they utter the word "good".'

'Very true,' he said.

'And what about those who make pleasure the good? Surely they're just as much at sea as the other lot. Don't they in their turn have to accept that there are pleasures that are bad?'

'They most certainly do.'

'It looks, then, as if they're left having to accept that the same things are good and bad. Right?'

'Obviously.'   505d

'So, plainly, there are big disputes about the subject, and lots of them.'

'Of course.'

'And isn't it also plain that whereas many would choose to do, or possess, or think things that seemed to them just and beautiful, even when they were not so in fact, they draw a line when it comes to *good* things? They won't be satisfied with getting things that merely seem good; they'll insist on seeking out what really is good. This is one sphere in which nobody needs to be told to scorn mere appearances.'[435]

'You're quite right,' he said.

'What every soul pursues, then, the very thing for the sake of   505e
which it does everything it does – divining that there is such a thing, but puzzled and unable to get an adequate grasp on what exactly it is, or come to any stable conviction about it as it can about everything else, and so missing any benefit there might have been in anything else: are we going to say that the best of the citizens ought to be similarly in the dark on a subject like that, and a subject of such importance, when we're going to   506a
put everything in their hands?'

'That's the last thing we want,' he said.

'At any rate,' I said, 'I imagine that if it's not known exactly how just things and beautiful things are good, these won't have acquired a guard for themselves who's worth anything very much, that is, if he lacks that knowledge; and it's my guess that without it no one will properly know about just and beautiful things either.'

'That's a fair guess,' he said.

'So will the arrangements for our city be completely in order if it's a guard like this who oversees it – one who does know   506b
how the just and the beautiful are good?'

'Surely. But what's your own view, Socrates?[436] Do you say the good is knowledge, or pleasure? Or something else again?'

'What a man!' I exclaimed. 'It's been quite clear all along that you wouldn't be satisfied with what other people think about the matter.'

'No,' he said, 'and it doesn't seem to me to be right, either,

Socrates, for somebody to be willing to talk about other people's views but not about his own, especially when he's been busying himself for so long with it all.'

506c

To which I said, 'And I suppose you think it's right for someone to talk about things as if he knew about them, when he doesn't?'

'No,' he said, 'not as if he knew about them, just as someone thinking what he thinks. That's what he should be willing to say.'

'What's that?' I asked. 'Haven't you observed what ugly things all beliefs are without knowledge? The best of them are blind – or do you think those who believe something true, but mindlessly, are any better than blind men going down the right road?'

'No better,' he said.

'So do you really want to look at ugly things – blind, lame things – when you could be hearing nothing but brightness and beauty from others?'[437]

506d

'For goodness' sake, Socrates,' said Glaucon, 'don't stand aside just when you're at the finish, as it were. Even if you only discuss the good in the same way as you discussed justice, moderation and the rest, it'll be enough for us.'

'Yes, my friend,' I said, 'and more than enough for me too. I'm afraid I won't be able to manage it; I'd cut a sorry figure, eager though I'd be to do it, and you'd laugh at me. What I hope you might agree to, my friends, is to leave aside the question of what the good itself is, for now, because to get as far as

506e

my present thinking on the subject – which is what you're asking for – seems to me out of proportion to the purposes of the present discussion. What I *am* willing to talk about is something that is clearly the offspring of the good, and bears a very close resemblance to it – if you're happy for me to do that; if not, let's pass on it.'

'Yes, do as you say,' said Glaucon. 'You'll owe us a description of the father, but you can give us that another time.'

507a

'I wish I could pay up now and you could take it away with you, not just the interest payments. Anyway, you'll have to make do with the interest, in the shape of my "offspring" of the good.[438] But watch out that I don't somehow defraud you all,

unintentionally, by paying the interest on my account in counterfeit coin.'

'We'll be watching out,' he said, 'as best we can. Just give us
what you have to say.'

'I will,' I said, 'now that I've agreed on the interest I'm to
pay – and as soon as I've reminded you of the things we've said
not only earlier in the present conversation[439] but over and over
again on other occasions too.'

'What are they?' he asked.

'When we talk,' I said, 'we talk about there being many   507b
beautiful things, and there being many good things, or whatever it may be, distinguishing between them in what we say.'

'Yes, we do.'

'And we also talk about there being a beautiful itself, and a
good itself, and similarly with everything we treated as many
earlier on – now, by contrast, treating each thing in terms of a
single form of each, on the basis that each *is* a single form, to
which we apply the label "what is", in each case.'[440]

'That's so.'

'And we say that the first set of things is seen, not grasped by
intellect, whereas the things we're calling "forms" *are* grasped
by intellect and not seen.'

'Absolutely.'

'And with which aspect of ourselves do we see what is seen?'   507c

'Our sight,' he said.

'And we hear what's heard with our hearing,' I went on,
'and generally perceive anything we perceive with one of our
senses?'

'Of course.'

'Well,' I said, 'have you noticed how much more extravagant the craftsman of our senses was when he made this
capacity we have for seeing and being seen?'

'Not exactly,' he said.

'Look at it this way: do our hearing and our voice need any
further kind of thing if they're to hear and be heard, such that
if it – this third thing – is not present as well, there'll be no   507d
hearing and no being heard either?'

'No, they don't,' he said.

'And I don't think many of our other capacities need any such third thing, which is not to say that none of them does. Can you think of any?'

'No, I can't,' he said.

'And the capacity for seeing and being seen – you haven't noticed that it needs one?'

'How so?'

'If the capacity for sight is there in a pair of eyes and their owner tries to use it, then there may be colour in them,[441] but unless sight and colour are joined by a third kind of thing, specifically adapted for this very context, you recognize that sight won't see anything and the colours will also be unseen.'

507e

'What *is* this third thing you're talking about?' he asked.

'What you call light,' I said.

'Good,' he said.

'There's nothing small, then, about the kind of thing that yokes together our sense of sight and the capacity of being seen; no yoking was ever more valuable – I'm assuming light is not without value.'

508a

'Right,' he said, 'hardly valueless!'

'Well, which of the gods in the heavens do you take to be in charge of this? Whose light is it that causes sight to see as best it can, and things that are being seen to be seen?'

'The same god as you and everybody else take it to be,' he said; 'obviously what you're asking about is the sun.'

'Well, do you think as I do about the relationship of sight to this god?'

'How do you think about it?'

'Neither sight itself nor the container in which it comes about, what we call the eye, actually *is* the sun.'

508b

'No indeed.'

'But of all the instruments relating to the senses it is, I think, the one that most *resembles* the sun.'

'By a long way.'

'And the capacity it has for seeing, too, flows into it, as it were, through the sun's dispensation.'

'Yes, absolutely.'

'Again, while the sun is not sight, is it not seen by it – the very thing it is cause of?'

'Just so,' he said.

'So that's what you need to take me as calling the "off-spring" of the good – the sun, which the good fathered[442] in proportion to itself: as the good itself is, in the sphere of the 508c intelligible, in relation to intellect and the things that are grasped by intellect, so the sun is in the visible sphere in rela-tion to sight and the things that are seen.'

'How so?' he asked. 'I need more explanation.'

'You'll recognize', I said, 'that when our eyes are no longer turned to things with colours bathed in daylight, but to things lit by the lamps of night-time, they're weakened and seem no better than blind men's eyes, as if they had no untrammelled capacity for sight in them?'

'I do indeed,' he said.

'But when they're turned to things lit by the sun, they see clearly, and sight is plainly present in those same eyes.'   508d

'Of course.'

'Well, think of the case of the soul along the same lines. When the soul directs itself towards something lit by the rays of truth, and towards what *is*,[443] it grasps and recognizes it at once, and appears to possess intelligence; but when it directs itself at what comes into being and passes away, mingled as that is with darkness, it can manage no better than beliefs, its power weakening as these move up and down, this way and that, just like something of no intelligence at all.'

'A fair comparison.'

'Well, what provides things that are known with their truth, 508e and gives the knower his proper capacity to know, this you can say is the form of the good itself.[444] You should certainly think of it as something that is known; but as cause of knowledge and truth, however beautiful both of these may be, you need to think of the good as different from and still more beautiful than they are. And just as in the parallel case we had to treat 509a light and sight as resembling, but not as actually being, the sun, so here we need to treat knowledge and truth as resembling the good, but neither of them as *being* the good, because what the good is, in itself, is to be valued even more than they are.'

'An inconceivable beauty it must have,' he said, 'if it gives us knowledge and truth, and itself outdoes them in beauty. It certainly can't be pleasure you're talking about!'[445]

'Please! What are you suggesting?' I replied. 'But let's take an even closer look at this image of ours.'

'How?'

509b   'In the case of things that are seen, I think you'll say that the sun is cause not only of their being seen, but of their coming-into-being, their growth and their sustenance – even while not itself *being* coming-into-being.'

'How would it be?'

'Just so, in the case of things that are known, you need to say not only that their being known comes from the good, but that their very being – what they are – comes from it, even while the good is not itself being, but is even beyond being, superior to it in dignity and in power.'[446]

509c   To which Glaucon responded to quite comic effect: 'Apollo! A super superiority that will be!'[447]

'You made me do it,' I said, 'twisting my arm like that, and making me say what I think about it.'

'And don't you stop, either,' he said. 'Give us more on the image with the sun, if nothing else; anything you may be leaving out.'

'There's a whole lot I'm leaving out,' I said.

'Well don't,' he said; 'not even a little bit.'

'I think it'll be more than a little,' I said. 'But anyway, I shan't willingly omit anything that can be covered now.'

'Please don't,' he said.

509d   'Well then,' I said, 'keep in your mind that there are these two things, as we're saying, the good and the sun, one of them ruling over a kind of things, and a region, that are known to intellect, the other over what I would call the heavenly scene, if only I didn't want to seem to be playing clever games with words.[448] Anyway, you've got hold of these two distinct kinds, the visible and the intelligible?'

'I have.'

'So take a line, cut into two unequal segments, one representing the first category, the other the second; then cut each of these again, in the same proportion. The cuts represent differences in relative clarity and obscurity: thus the lower part of the segment representing the visible contains mere images, these being first of all shadows, then what appears to us on the 510a surfaces either of liquids or of anything that's solid but smooth and bright – everything like that; you know what I mean.'

'I do.'

'The other part of the visible segment should be taken as representing what the images in the first are images of, namely, ourselves and other animals, all types of plants and the whole family of manufactured objects.'

'Done,' he said.

'Would you be willing to say about this segment', I asked, 'that in terms of truth and the lack of it image stands to original in the same proportion as what is believed does to what is known?'[449]

'I would,' he said; 'very much so.'   510b

'Now see how the intelligible segment has to be cut.'

'And how's that?'

'Like this: in the lower part of it, the soul now uses as images the very things that were the originals in the visible segment, and is compelled to make its investigations on the basis of hypotheses, not moving up to a first principle but down to a conclusion; whereas in the upper part it moves up from a hypothesis to a non-hypothetical first principle, without the images it used in the previous part, and operating with those "forms"[450] alone, nothing else.'

'I haven't understood what you're saying,' he replied. 'Put it to me again.'

'I shall,' I said;[451] 'now that I've said what I have, you'll be in 510c a better position to understand. I think you do know that when people occupy themselves with things like geometry, or arithmetic, or anything else like that, they start by hypothesizing the odd, the even, the various figures, three kinds of angles, and so on, and parallel things in other disciplines, depending on which one they're in; and then they go on to behave as if they know about them, having introduced them as hypotheses, and they don't think it necessary to give any further account of them, either to themselves or to anyone else, on the grounds 510d that they're obvious to anyone.[452] Proceeding to the rest of their argument from these beginnings, they finish whatever investigation it is that they're embarked on in a similarly hypothetical mode.'

'Absolutely,' he said; 'that much I do know.'

'You'll also know that they make use of kinds of objects that belong to the visible sphere, and construct their arguments about these, when it's not actually these they're thinking about, but rather the things that these resemble: their demonstrations 510e are aimed at the square itself and the diameter itself,[453] not the one they're drawing, and similarly with everything else. The very things they make or draw, that cast shadows and give off reflections in water and so on, these they in turn use as images, 511a when in fact their aim is to see those very things one cannot see except with the mind.'

'True,' he said.

'This is a kind of thing I included in the intelligible, but with two provisos: first, that the soul was compelled to investigate it by means of hypotheses, and because it was unable to rise above the hypothetical it failed to go up to a first principle; second, that it used, as images, the very things that were themselves the originals for the images below them, and were esteemed and honoured as clear in comparison with these.'

'I understand', he said, 'that you're talking about what hap- 511b pens in geometry and things like that, other related sorts of expertise.'

'So understand me as saying that the other part of the intelligible segment of the line represents what reason itself grasps through the power of dialectic, treating its hypotheses not as first principles but strictly as hypotheses, like underpinnings, or steps on a ladder, in order to pass beyond the hypothetical to the first principle of everything, and after having grasped it, to reverse its progress, holding tight to what leads down from that 511c true starting-point, so that it reaches a conclusion without using anything perceptible at all, only forms, themselves by themselves, to reach forms – and ends with forms.'

'I do understand', he said '– not well enough, because what you're describing seems to me a major task, but I do see that you want to mark off the way that dialectical expertise looks at what is,[454] and the intelligible, as clearer than the way it's looked at by those engaged in other kinds of so-called expertise, which treat hypotheses as first principles; although they do see something, and must necessarily have used thought rather than sensations to see it, still, because they don't investigate by 511d rising up to the true first principle, only by using hypotheses, they seem to you not to have an intelligent grasp of the things they're looking at. And I think you're calling the state of geometrical and other similar experts thoughtful rather than truly intelligent, thoughtfulness being something in between belief and intelligence.'

'You've grasped the point very adequately. Do please take me as assigning these four states of mind to the four segments of the line: intelligence to the highest, thoughtfulness to the sec- 511e ond – then, to the third, assign conviction, and conjecture to the last.[455] And arrange them in proportion to their clarity, taking degree of clarity as corresponding to the degree that the things they are assigned to[456] share in truth.'

'I understand,' he said, 'I agree, and I arrange them forthwith as you propose.'

Book VII begins [Book E] 'Next', I said, 'think of our nature in relation to edu- 514a cation, and the lack of it, in terms of the following image. Imagine human beings as if they were in a cave-like dwelling underground, with a broad opening to the daylight across the whole width of the cave. They have been there since childhood, chained not just by their legs but by their necks, so 514b that they can't move and can only look ahead of them – the neck-chain makes it impossible for them to turn their heads round. Light reaches them from a fire that burns way above and behind them; and in between the fire and the prisoners, high above, there is a path across the cave, beside which you need to imagine a little wall, built like those screens puppeteers

have in front of their audience so that they can show their pup-
pets above them.'

'Done,' he said.

515c   'Next, along this little wall, imagine people carrying a whole
collection of manufactured objects that stick up above it,
515a including human statues and representations of other kinds of
creatures fashioned out of wood and stone and all sorts of
other things; as you'd expect, some of the carriers are speaking,
others are silent.'[457]

'A strange picture', he said, '– and strange prisoners!'

'Ones that resemble us,' I said, 'since first of all do you think
people in that condition will have seen anything of themselves
or of each other except for their shadows, cast by the fire on to
the surface of the cave in front of them?'

515b 'How could they,' he asked, 'if they were prevented from
moving their heads even once in their whole lives?'

'And what about the things being carried along the wall?
Won't it be the same with them?'

'Of course.'

'So if the prisoners were able to have conversations with
each other, don't you think they'd label whatever they were seeing in front of them as what those things actually are?'[458]

'They'd have to.'

'And what if the prison gave off an echo from in front of
them? Whenever any of those passing along the wall behind them
said something, do you think the prisoners could suppose it came
from anywhere except from the shadow passing before them?'

'Zeus!' he exclaimed. 'I don't see how they could.'

515c 'So from every point of view,' I said, 'what people in that
situation would think of as the truth would be nothing but the
shadows of the manufactured objects behind them.'

'They couldn't avoid doing so.'

'Now think what it might be like for them to be released
from their chains and cured of their mindlessness. Suppose
something like this really happened: one of them was set free,
and was suddenly forced to stand up, twist his neck round,
then try to walk, and look towards the source of the light.

Given that he would be in pain as he did all this, and unable 515d
because of the glare to see the actual things that cast the
shadows he used to see, what do you think he'd say if someone
told him that what he saw before wasn't worth seeing anyway,
and that he was seeing better now because he was that much
closer to the truth of things, and turned towards things that
more truly are[459] – and then, to add insult to injury, pointed to
each of the things passing by along the wall and forced him by
question-and-answer to say what each of them was? Wouldn't
you expect him to be at a loss, and to suppose what he used to
see to be truer than the things now being pointed out to him?'

'Yes, much truer,' he said.

'And if this other person then also made him look towards
the source of the light itself, don't you suppose his eyes would 515e
hurt, and he'd turn round and try to bolt back in the direction
of the things he could see, thinking these really and truly clearer
than what was being shown to him?'

'Just so,' he said.

'What then if someone took hold of him', I said, 'and
dragged him bodily up from there, no matter how rough and
steep the slope, until finally he emerged into the light of the
sun? Don't you suppose he'd be suffering and complaining as 516a
he was dragged along, and that when he came into the light his
eyes would be filled with its beams, and he wouldn't be able to
see a single one of the things *now* called true?'

'No, he wouldn't, not immediately,' he said.

'He'd need time to adjust, I imagine, before he could see
things up there. First of all, he'd find it easiest to see shadows;
next it would be reflections of human beings and everything
else in water, then the things themselves; and from these he'd
move on to the heavenly bodies and the heavens themselves,
though he'd start by looking at them at night, gazing at the
light of the stars and the moon, because that would be easier 516b
than looking at the sun and the sun's light by day.'

'Of course.'

'Then finally, I imagine, he'd be able to catch sight of the
sun, not just reflected in water, or as it appears in any alien

location, but the sun itself, by itself, in its own place, and observe it as it is.'

'Inevitably,' he said.

'And after all of this, he would be able to reason to himself that it was *this* that not only provided the yearly cycle of the seasons and oversaw everything in the region of the seen, but was also in a certain way the cause of those other things he and the other prisoners used to see.'

'Plainly,' he said, 'that is the conclusion he'd come to.'

'And as he remembered the place he lived in first, what counted as wisdom there, and his former fellow-prisoners, don't you think he would call himself happy for his change of residence, and pity the others?'

'Indeed he would.'

'As for any honours and praises they heaped on each other, with prizes for the one who had the sharpest eye for the things passing in front of them, and could remember best which objects tended to come along earlier, or later, or together, so that he could predict on that basis which was going to come along next[460] – do you think our man would miss these rewards, and envy anyone honoured by the prisoners or holding princely power among them, or would he rather react, as Homer describes it, by much preferring to "work the fields above for someone else,/ A serf to a man with nothing",[461] or endure any fate rather than believe as they do and live like them?'

'I think the latter,' he said; 'he'd accept any fate rather than live like that.'

'Here's something else for you to think about,' I said. 'If someone in this situation went back down and sat down once more in his old seat, wouldn't darkness fill his eyes as he came down suddenly out of the sunlight?'

'It certainly would,' he said.

'And if he had to compete once more with the permanent prisoners at "discriminating" between those shadows of theirs, while his eyes were still not functioning properly, and hadn't yet had the not inconsiderable time they'd need to settle down in the new conditions, don't you think he'd make a laughing-stock of himself? It would be said of him, wouldn't it, that he'd only gone up to come back down with his eyes ruined, and that it wasn't worth even attempting the ascent? As for anyone who set about trying to release them and take them up there, if they could somehow get their hands on him and kill him, don't you think they would?'[462]

'Yes, very much so,' he said.

'Well, my dear Glaucon,' I said, 'this image then needs to be matched up as a whole with what we were saying before. The prison dwelling represents the seat of visual appearances, the fire in it the power of the sun; and if you think of that climb up to a view of things up above as standing for the ascent of the soul to the intelligible sphere, well, you won't be missing what I myself expect to be true, since that's what you're so anxious to hear. Whether it is actually true, I imagine only gods know. In any case, the way things appear to me is that in the sphere of the known what is seen last, and barely seen, is the form of the good, but that when it *is* seen, there can be only one conclusion – that it, in fact, is cause for everything of everything right and beautiful, as both progenitor of light and of the source of light in the sphere of the seen, and the source itself of truth and intelligibility in the intelligible sphere. It also seems to me that anyone who is to act sensibly, in private or in public life, must have had a sight of it.' 517b 517c

'I agree,' he said, 'at least to the extent that I can follow you.'

'Come on, then,' I said, 'agree with me on this further point: don't be surprised that those who have come this far are unwilling to involve themselves in human affairs, and their souls are constantly hurrying to spend time up above. I presume that's only too likely, if things really are as depicted in our image.' 517d

'Yes, it's likely enough,' he said.

'Nor is it any surprise, is it,' I asked, 'if someone moves from contemplating divine things to human ones, bad as they now seem to him, that he should cut a sorry figure – making a thorough fool of himself when, still blinking and not yet properly adjusted to the surrounding darkness, he's forced to compete in the lawcourts or elsewhere about the shadows of justice, or the statues that cast the shadows, and wrangle about the way 517e these are understood by people who have never yet caught sight of justice itself?'

'No surprise at all,' he said.

518a   'A person of any intelligence', I said, 'would remember that the eyes become confused in two ways, and for two reasons, namely, when their owners move from light into darkness, and when they move from darkness into light. Thinking that just the same will hold of souls, he wouldn't laugh when he observed one in difficulties and struggling to see, because that would be irrational. Instead, he'd look first to see whether it has come from a life of greater brightness, and is clouded by unfamiliarity with its new surroundings, or whether it's moving from a 518b   deeper ignorance to somewhere brighter, and it's the glare of the light that is dazzling it; and if it was in the first condition, he'd call it happy for the way it is, and for the life it's living, and if it was in the second condition, he'd pity it – or, if he did choose to laugh at it, it would be less ridiculous than laughing at a soul that has come down from the light above.'[463]

'That all sounds very reasonable,' he said.

'So,' I said, 'if this is true, our view on the whole subject should be this, that education is not what it's claimed to be by some of those who profess to provide it. What they claim is 518c   pretty much that if knowledge isn't present in a soul, they can put it there – as it were, putting sight into the eyes of the blind.'

'That is what they claim,' he said.

'Whereas', I said, 'our current argument indicates a different way of conceiving this capacity for learning we each have within our soul, and the instrument with which each of us learns. It is more like an eye that cannot be turned from the dark towards the bright unless the whole body turns with it; it must be turned round, together with the whole soul, away from changing things, until it becomes able to bear looking at 518d   what is,[464] and the most dazzling part of what is – and that, we say, is the good. Agreed?'

'Yes.'

'And for this', I said, '– this turning round of the soul – there will be a special kind of expertise,[465] which knows how the turning may be most easily and effectively achieved; and it

won't consist in putting sight into something, but rather of contriving it in something that already has it,[466] but has it incorrectly
aligned, and isn't looking in the right direction.'

'Yes, it seems so,' he said.

'So whereas the other so-called excellences of soul probably
have a kind of resemblance to bodily ones, since if they're not
already in a soul they can actually be brought about in it by
habituation and practice,[467] the particular excellence that wis-   518e
dom is really does seem, more than anything, to belong to
something diviner – which never loses its power, but becomes
useful and beneficial or useless and harmful according to which   519a
way it has been turned. Or haven't you noticed that if ever
there's someone people call a bad man, but "wise" nonetheless,
how keen-sighted his tiny little soul is, and how sharp at making out the things it's turned to? It's not that its sight is bad, just
that it's been commandeered in the service of badness, so that
the sharper its vision, the more bad it does.'

'Quite so,' he said.

'And yet', I said, 'if this element, in someone of that nature,
had been hammered into shape from childhood on, and had
had trimmed off from it the concomitants of change[468] that   519b
hold it down like lead weights, attached to it by gluttony and
other such pleasures of excess, that make the soul look downwards instead of upwards – if it had been freed from these, and
could turn towards things as they truly are, then the very same
element in the very same people would be as sharp at seeing
these as it is at seeing the things it's turned to now.'

'Yes, that's likely enough,' he said.

'And isn't it also likely,' I asked, 'indeed necessary, given
what we've said before, that neither the uneducated, with no
experience of truth, nor those permitted to spend the whole of   519c
their lives being educated, would ever have made adequate
governors of a city? The first, because they lack that single target they need to aim at when they do whatever they do, whether
in their private or their public roles; the second, because they
won't do it, voluntarily, thinking as they will that they've managed to decamp to the Isles of the Blest even before they're
dead.'

'True,' he said.

'So it's our job,' I said, 'as the founders, to force the best natures to come to what we said before was the most important subject of study, and get a sight of the good by completing that ascent we spoke of. When they've done that, and had sufficient sight of it, we mustn't permit them to do what is currently allowed.'

'And what's that?'

'To remain there,' I said, 'and refuse to come back down to those prisoners of ours and share in their labours and their rewards, whether of a more trivial or a more worthwhile kind.'

'We're going to treat them unjustly, then, are we,' he asked, 'making them live a worse life when they could be living a better one?'

'That's again to forget,'[469] I said, 'my friend, that it's no concern of the law to bring it about that any one group of people in a city does exceptionally better than the rest. No, the law's concern is to engineer well-being in the city as a whole, using a mixture of persuasion and compulsion to create harmony between the citizens, and ensuring that they share with one another whatever kind of contribution each group is capable of making to the common good. The law itself brings about people like that in the city, not in order to leave them free to turn in the direction each of them wants, but to use them for binding the city together.'

'True,' he said; 'I had forgotten that point.'

'Think, then, Glaucon,' I said: 'we won't in fact be doing anything unjust to these philosophers of ours; what we'll say to them, as we compel them to take care of the others, and guard over them, will actually be just.[470] We'll say this: "People who turn out like you in other cities quite reasonably don't take on their share of the labours in those cities – they spring up there of their own accord, despite the best intentions of the regime in force, and it's perfectly just, for something that's developed spontaneously and has nothing but itself to thank for nurturing it, not to fall over itself to pay back a debt it doesn't owe in any case. But in your case, it's *we* who gave birth to you, both for your own benefit and for that of the others, as leaders and kings, as it were in the hive,[471] better and more completely educated than the rest and more capable than they are of sharing 520c in both kinds of life.[472] So down each of you must go in your turn, to share their living space and become accustomed like them to observing things in the dark, because as you become used to it, having yourselves seen the truth about beautiful and just and good things you'll see a thousand times better than they do what each kind of shadowy image is, and what it is an image of. That way both we and you will have a city whose government is awake, and not in the dream state that now affects ordinary cities, governed as they are by people who shadow-box with one another and fight about who should 520d rule,[473] as if ruling were some kind of great good."[474] The truth, I presume, is this, that the city in which those who are to rule are least eager to do so must be the one whose government is the best, and least subject to faction; and the one that has acquired the opposite kind of rulers must be the opposite of that.'

'Quite so,' he said.

'So when they hear us saying this, do you think our nurslings will disobey us, and refuse to share in the labour of running the city, each in turn, while spending the greater part of their time in each other's company in the pure air above?'

'It's impossible that they would refuse,' he said, 'since they 520e are just, and so are the orders we'll be giving them. But quite certainly, each of them will approach ruling as something they can't avoid doing, which is the opposite of the attitude of those who presently rule in any city you care to name.'

'Yes, my friend,' I said; 'that's right. The fact is, you'll find that a well-governed city is possible only if you discover a life 521a better for your rulers than ruling, since only that kind of city will be ruled by those who are really and truly wealthy, not in gold, but in the wealth a person needs for happiness – a good and wise life. If public offices are occupied by beggars, people hungry for private goods, who think the good is something to be stolen from the public purse, then a well-governed city is impossible; for if ruling becomes something to be fought for, it spells destruction not just for the combatants but for the rest of the city too, because it is at war with its own and with itself.'

'Very true,' he said.

521b   'So,' I said, 'is there any other kind of life you can think of that looks down on political office, apart from that of true philosophy?'

'Zeus! No, I can't,' he said.

'But non-lovers of ruling must surely take it on, because if they don't, the rival suitors will start fighting one another for power.'

'Surely.'

'So whom else will you compel to take on the guarding of your city, if not those who not only have the greatest understanding of the things that make for the best government of a city, but have other rewards, and another, better life than that of running cities?'

'No one else,' he said.

521c   'So are you happy if we go on to consider how there will come to be such people in the city, and how one will lead them up into the light, like those legendary figures said to have gone up from Hades to the company of the gods?'

'Why wouldn't I be happy?' he asked.

'This won't, it seems, be a mere matter of the spin of a sherd,[475] but of the turning round of a soul from a day that is also somehow night[476] to true daylight – the very thing we'll claim to be true philosophy: an ascent to what *is*.'[477]

'Yes, quite,' he said.

521d   'So should we consider what kind of study has the capacity to do this?'

'Naturally.'

'Well, Glaucon, which subject of study will be the one to draw us away from the sphere of change to what is unchanging? A thought occurs to me as I ask the question: wasn't it as athletes for *war* that we were saying our people had to train when they were young?'[478]

'We were.'

'Then the subject we're looking for must possess another feature, alongside the other one.'

'What feature is that?'

'It must be of some use to men whose business is war.'

'Well, yes,' he said, 'if that really can be combined with the other feature.'

'But in our discussion earlier on we had them being educated through both physical exercise and music.'

'That's so,' he said.

'Physical training, I imagine, is preoccupied with what comes   521e
into being and perishes; after all, it presides over growth and decay in the body.'

'Evidently.'

'So this won't be the subject we're looking for.'

'No, it won't.'   522a

'Then will it be music – the part of it we described before?'

'But that,' he said, 'if you recall, was a counterpart of the guards' physical training, educating them through habit, and so far as harmony and rhythm were concerned merely giving them a kind of harmoniousness, not knowledge, and a good rhythm; and its words, too, whether they were in the form of stories, or more truth-like, conveyed other habits of behaviour close to these. There was nothing in it of the subject you're presently seeking that will lead to the kind of thing you're talking about.'

'Very much to the point,' I said, 'and thanks for reminding   522b
me – music really didn't contain anything of the sort we need. But for goodness' sake, Glaucon, where *will* we find what we need? All the ordinary kinds of skills appeared to us demeaning,[479] I think.'

'Of course they did! And yet, what is there still left, when you've taken out music and physical training, and the ordinary skills?'

'Come on,' I said; 'if we can't find anything outside these, let's take something that has a connection of some sort with all of them.'

'Like what?'

'Like what belongs in common to everything, whether skills   522c
or more thoughtful preoccupations, even branches of knowledge. It's one of the first things everybody has to learn.'

'And what *is* it?' he asked.

'This little thing,' I said: 'knowing your one, two and three – in short, number and counting. Isn't it the case that every skill and every kind of knowledge is compelled to involve itself with these?'

'Very much so,' he said.

'Expertise in war, too?' I asked.

'Yes, certainly,' he said.

522d   'Certainly', I said, 'in tragedies Palamedes is always showing up Agamemnon's complete hopelessness as a general. Haven't you noticed how he claims his discovery of number enabled him to set up the positions of the army at Troy, count the ships, and everything like that, as if they hadn't been counted before, and apparently – if he really couldn't count – Agamemnon didn't even know how many feet he had? What sort of a general do you think that makes him?'

'A pretty strange one, I think,' he said. 'If you believe the story.'

522e   'So,' I asked, 'we'll put down learning to calculate and count as a compulsory subject for a man who's going to be fighting wars?'

'Yes,' he said, 'that more than anything, if he's to understand the first thing about the positioning of troops. Or rather, if he's to be a human being at all!'

'And', I asked, 'are you noticing a feature of this subject that I'm noticing?'

'What's that?'

523a   'It's probably one of those subjects we're looking for, that naturally lead to intelligent thought;[480] it absolutely does have this tendency to draw us towards what is,[481] though no one in fact uses it like that.'

'How are you saying it does that?' he asked.

'I'll try to show you how at any rate it seems to me. If I go through the things I like to distinguish, in my own mind, as tending or not tending to lead in the direction we want, you can look at them with me and say whether you agree with me or not. Then we'll see more clearly if my guess is roughly right.'

'So show me,' he said.

'What I want to show you,' I said, 'if you can see it, is that some things in the sphere of the senses don't call out for intelligent thought to examine them, insofar as they're made out sufficiently well by perception itself; whereas others positively require thinking to intervene, because what mere perception does in these cases is quite unhealthy.' 523b

'You're clearly thinking about things seen from a distance,' he said, 'or the products of shadow-painting.'

'That's not quite what I had in mind,' I said.

'So what *do* you have in mind?' he asked.

'The cases that don't call for thought', I said, 'are those that don't result in an opposite perception at the same time; those that do turn out to require thought, I'm assuming, are those where perception no more indicates the presence of one thing than that of its opposite, whether we're looking from close up or from a distance. The following example will give you a clearer idea of what I'm saying. "These", we'll say, pointing, "are three fingers – little, second, middle."' 523c

'Quite so,' he said.

'Well, think of me as talking about them as seen from close up. Here's what I want you to ask yourself about them.'

'What's that?'

'Each of them equally appears as a finger, and in *this* respect there's no difference between it and the others, no matter whether you're seeing it in the middle or at either end of the row, whether as pale or as dark, fat or thin, or anything else like that. In no such case is the soul of any ordinary person forced to apply its intellect to the question of what a finger *is*; never in such a case does sight simultaneously indicate to it that the finger is the opposite of a finger.' 523d

'No indeed,' he said.

'So it's quite reasonable to expect', I said, 'that this sort of case won't call for intelligent thought, or arouse it.'

'Yes.'

'But what about the bigness or the smallness of the fingers? Does sight see these adequately, and does it make no difference to it whether one of the fingers is located in the middle or at one end? Similarly with fatness and thinness; or what about 523e

softness and hardness, in relation to touch? Don't all the senses
provide inadequate indications of such things? They're all as
524a bad as each other: first of all, the sense that's assigned to the
hard is compelled to do double duty and handle the soft as
well, with the result that it reports itself back to the soul as
perceiving the same thing as both hard and soft.'

'That's so,' he said.

'Well,' I asked, 'isn't it inevitable in such circumstances that
the soul should now be at a loss about what the *hard* this sense
is indicating can possibly be, if it's actually saying the same
thing is soft as well; and about what the light and the heavy
are, when something's perceived as light or as heavy and the
report comes back that actually the heavy is light and the light
heavy?'

524b 'Yes,' he said, 'these messages are pretty puzzling for the
soul, and need further looking at.'

'It stands to reason, then,' I said, 'that in situations like this
the soul will begin to summon up calculation and intelligent
thought, and try to examine whether the things being reported
back to it in each case are one, or whether they're two.'

'Of course.'

'And if they appear as two, each of the two will appear as
different and as one?'482

'Yes.'

'Now if each of them is one, and together they are two, then
524c if the soul is thinking of them as two it will be thinking of them
separately from one another. If it wasn't separating them, it'd
be thinking of them as one, not as two.'

'Right.'

'But now sight too, we say, saw big and small only as mixed
up together, not as separate – right?'

'Yes.'

'And in order to get clear about all this, intelligent thought
was needed to take a second look at big and small, not mixed
up but as separate – the opposite of the way sight looked at
them.'

'True.'

'Isn't it at some such point as this that it first occurs to us to ask ourselves, "So just what *are* bigness and smallness?"'

'Yes, absolutely.'

'And that's how we come to label one sort of thing as intelligible, another as visible.'[483]

'Absolutely correct,' he said.

'Well, this is precisely what I was trying to say just now, with 524d my distinction between things that tend to call out for thought and those that don't. The former, I'm saying, are the ones that impact on the senses along with their own opposites; those that don't affect the senses in this way don't tend to arouse intelligent thought either.'

'Well, now I do understand,' he said, 'and I agree.'

'So then, to which of the two kinds do number, and one,[484] belong?'

'I've no idea,' he said.

'Work it out from what we've just been saying,' I said. 'If *one* is well enough seen, or similarly grasped by some other sense, for what it is, by itself, then it won't be the sort of thing 524e that draws us to thinking about how things really are, as with the finger. But if some kind of opposite to it is always seen along with it, so that it appears no more as *one* than as the opposite, then there'll immediately be a need for a mediator, and a soul in this situation will inevitably be puzzled and forced into looking for answers, stirring itself to reflection and asking 525a what exactly oneness is, taken by itself – in which case learning about *one* will belong to those subjects that lead the soul, and turn it, towards looking at what truly is.'

'But that is, in fact,' he said, 'the effect seeing has; we see the same thing as one and as unlimited in quantity at the same time.'[485]

'And if *one* has this feature,' I asked, 'won't all number also have it?'

'Of course.'

'But calculation and arithmetic are all about number.'

'Quite so.'

'And they appear capable of leading us towards truth.'

'Superlatively so.'

525b   'Then it seems this will be one of the subjects of study we're looking for: it's needed not only by the war-expert, for the positioning of troops, but by the philosopher, because of the requirement on him to rise up out of what is changing to a grasp of things as they really are, if he is ever to become capable of true calculation, true reasoning.'[486]

'That's right,' he said.

'And our guard in fact is both war-expert and philosopher.'

'Indeed he is.'

'So it will be appropriate to include this subject in our legislation, Glaucon, and to persuade those who are going to share
525c   in the weightiest functions in the city to take up learning how to calculate, not just as a private hobby, but until they've got as far as looking at the nature of numbers by means of intelligent thought alone, not for the sake of buying and selling, as if they were practising to be merchants or shopkeepers, but in order to fight wars and to make it easier for the soul itself to turn away from what is changing towards truth, and towards what *is*.'[487]

'Very well said,' he replied.

'And it also occurs to me,' I said, 'now that we've talked
525d   about learning to calculate, just how subtle and versatile a tool it is for what we have in mind, provided it's deployed for the sake of knowing things and not for the sake of buying and selling them.'

'How so?' he asked.

'It has to do with what we were talking about just now – how effective it is in leading the soul upwards, as it were, forcing it to talk about numbers by themselves, and always resisting if anyone tries to offer it – the soul – numbers with visible or tangible bodies attached to them,[488] and talk about these. I imagine you're familiar with what the experts in this
525e   area do: if anyone tries to argue by dividing the one, taken by itself, they laugh and won't let him do it; if you do chop it into pieces, they'll multiply it, so anxious are they to avoid its appearing not as one but as many distinct parts.'[489]

'Very true,' he said.

526a   'So, Glaucon, what if someone asked them, "May we ask you splendid people which numbers it is you're talking about, where the one is as you think it should be, equal in each and every one of its occurrences, not differing by even a little, and not containing a single part?" How do you think they'd reply?'

'I imagine they'd reply that they're talking about those numbers that can only be grasped by thought, and can't be dealt with in any other way.'

'So you see, my friend,' I said, 'the subject in question is likely to be one we really can't do without, given the way it evidently forces the soul to use intelligent thought, itself, to get to the truth itself.'[490] 526b

'Yes,' he said, 'it certainly is very effective in that.'

'Here's another point for you to think about: those who are naturally good at numbers are naturally quick at learning practically anything, and even the slow ones, when they're trained and drilled in it, all tend to make progress and become quicker than they were, even if they get no other benefit from it.'

'That's true,' he said.

'And moreover, in my view you won't easily find subjects 526c that are more laborious to learn and practise at than this one is; there certainly aren't many.'

'Indeed not.'

'For all these reasons, then, we mustn't let this particular subject slip. The best natures must be educated in it.'

'I agree,' he said.

'So that will be one of the subjects we're looking for. As for the second, let's look at the one that follows on from this one, and see whether we find it appropriate at all for our purposes.'

'Which is that?' he asked. 'Are you talking about geometry?'

'Just that,' I said.

'Insofar as it has military applications,' he said, 'it clearly is 526d appropriate. When it comes to setting up camps, capturing strategic points, concentrating or spreading out one's forces, and all the other formations they use for armies either in actual battles or on the march, a man with an understanding of geometry will stand out above the same man without one.'

'Well, true,' I said, 'but actually just a small portion of geometry and calculation will suffice for things like that. What we

526e need to consider is whether the bulk of it, the more advanced part, contributes at all to that other goal, of making it easier to see the form of the good.[491] What contributes to this, we're saying, is anything that compels a soul to turn itself round, towards the location of that happiest of the things that are,[492] which it must catch sight of at all costs.'

'You're right,' he said.

'So if geometry makes us look at things as they are,[493] it's appropriate for our purposes; if it makes us look at things that change, it isn't.'

'Yes, that's what we're saying.'

527a 'Well,' I said, 'no one with the slightest acquaintance with geometry will dispute that this branch of knowledge is exactly the opposite of what's suggested by the way its practitioners talk about it.'

'How so?' he asked.

'The way they talk, I imagine, is quite ridiculous, though they can't avoid it; they talk as if they were *doing* things, and as if the aim of all their talk was something practical, all the time using terms like "squaring", or "applying", or "adding", and so on, when presumably the whole subject is in fact practised for the sake of acquiring knowledge.'

527b 'Absolutely,' he said.

'And can we agree on a further point about it?'

'What's that?'

'That it's for the sake of knowledge of what always is, not of what comes to be something at some point in time, and perishes.'

'That's easily agreed,' he said; 'geometrical knowledge *is* knowledge of what always is.'

'Nobly put, my friend. Then it will have the capacity to draw a soul towards truth, and bring about a philosophical cast of mind, directing upwards those elements in us that we now wrongly direct downwards.'

'So far as it possibly can,' he said.

527c 'So far as you can, then,' I said, 'you must make sure that your people in the City Beautiful[494] are under no circumstances

allowed to keep off geometry. In fact it has considerable side-
benefits too.'

'What are they?' he asked.

'Well, there are the ones you mentioned,' I said, 'the military
ones, and besides, we know, surely, that it makes all the difference in the world to a person's receptivity to any kind of
learning if he's already tackled geometry.'

'Zeus! All the difference,' he said.

'So are we to put this down as the second subject in our
young people's curriculum?'

'We are,' he said.

'What about astronomy as a third, do you think?'   527d

'That's certainly my view,' he said; 'having a better sense of
season, of months and of years, is appropriate for generals as
well as farmers and seafarers.'

'How disingenuous of you!' I said. 'It seems to me you're
afraid of what ordinary people will say if you prescribe useless
subjects. If truth be told, it's no mean feat at all, indeed it's very
hard, to put one's trust in the fact that when we study these
subjects a special instrument of the soul in each of us is cleansed
and has new fire breathed into it, when other pursuits corrupt   527e
and blind it, and when *it* is more worth saving than ten thousand eyes, because only with it do we see the truth. Those who
hear you saying such things, and already agree with you, will
find it absolutely and completely the right thing to say; but
those who have never recognized this element in their souls
will quite reasonably suppose you're talking nonsense, because
they certainly don't see any other benefit from subjects like this
that's worth speaking of. So you need to make up your mind,   528a
here and now, which of these two groups you're addressing. Or
perhaps you're not addressing either, but mainly saying what
you're saying for your own sake, even while you wouldn't want
to exclude others if they could derive something useful from it.'

'That's how I choose', he said, '– when I talk, or ask and
answer questions, it's mostly for my own sake.'

'So let's row back a bit,' I said. 'We're wrong about what
comes after geometry.'

'How did we get it wrong?' he asked.

'By making solids in rotation come after plane surfaces, before we'd taken solids in and by themselves. The correct 528b order is to go on from two dimensions to three, which presumably takes us to where we find cubes, and anything that has depth.'

'It does,' he said; 'but these, Socrates, are things that nobody seems yet to have found out about.'

'There are two reasons for that,' I said. 'One is that no city puts a value on such a subject, so that it's only feebly pursued, given its difficulty. The second reason is that researchers in this area need someone to direct them, because otherwise they won't find any answers, but in the first place it's hard to find anyone to fill the role, and in the second place, even if someone 528c were to be found, under current conditions those who would be able to do the research would be too independently minded to listen to him. But if a city as a whole acted as his co-director, and valued the subject, then they *would* listen, and given some continuous and intensive work the facts about it would be revealed; since even now, when it's devalued and put down by ordinary people, and by those who work in it when they can't explain the reason why it's useful, it has sufficient charm to force its way past all these obstacles and grow in stature, so that there'd be no surprise if it produced results in any case.'

528d   'Yes,' he said, 'it does possess quite exceptional charm. But please be clearer about what you were saying just now. I think you were taking the study of plane surfaces to be geometry.'

'Yes,' I said.

'And then', he said, 'you started by putting astronomy next, but a bit later you took that back.'

'I'll admit', I said, 'that by hurrying to get through everything quickly I'm actually slowing things down. Even though what came next was the study of three dimensions, the ridiculous state of research on the subject made me pass over it, and I started talking about astronomy, the study of the three-dimensional in motion, immediately after geometry.'

'Right,' he said.

528e   'So let's make astronomy our fourth subject for study, on the assumption that the neglected third will be available, once a city supports it.'

'A fair assumption,' he said. 'As for your rebuke to me just now, Socrates, on the subject of astronomy, for praising it in a vulgar way, I'm now going to praise it in line with your own approach. It's plain to everyone, I think, that *this* study compels a soul to look upwards, and guides it away from things here to things above.'   529a

'Probably', I said, 'it's plain to everybody but me. I don't think it is like that.'

'So how do you think it is?'

'Handled as it is by those who try to lead the way up to philosophy now,[495] I think its only effect is to make us look down.'

'Why do you say that?' he asked.

'Yours seems to me a very liberal view of what counts as the study of "things above",' I said. 'From what you're saying, someone would only have to try to learn something by bending his head back and gazing at decorations on a ceiling, and that'd be enough for you to count it as seeing in thought and not with the eyes. Well, maybe you're right, and I'm being simple-minded, but I can't think of any field of study as making a soul look upwards unless it is about what is, and what the eyes don't see. Where the objects of the senses are concerned, it doesn't matter whether someone tries to learn something about them by gawping upwards or by squinting downwards – I'll still deny he'll ever learn anything that way, because there is no knowledge in such things,[496] and I'll also deny that his soul is looking up – it's still looking down, even if he tries to learn by floating on his back on land[497] or in the sea.'   529c

'I've got what I deserve', he said, '– you're right to tell me off. But what was that you were saying, about our people having to study astronomy differently from the way it's currently studied, if it was to be useful for the purposes we have in mind?'

'It's this: the bodies that decorate our heavens adorn something that is seen. Thus while we are right to think of them as the most beautiful and most precisely drawn of their kind, all the same we must suppose them to fall far short of their true counterparts, that is, of the movements with which speed itself and   529d slowness itself[498] move in relation to each other, in turn carrying the things in them, measured by true number and conforming to all the true figures; all of which is to be grasped by reason and thought, and can't be grasped by sight. Or do you think it can?'

'Not for a moment,' he said.

'So,' I said, 'the decorations of the heavens should be used as paradigms, to help with the learning that leads to those other objects; it's just as if we happened to come across diagrams 529e exquisitely painted and worked by Daedalus, or some other craftsman or painter.[499] When an experienced geometer saw such pieces, I presume he'd thoroughly admire their workmanship, but would think it ridiculous to examine them in earnest 530a in the expectation of finding in them the truth about equals, or doubles, or any other ratio.'

'And it would be quite ridiculous,' he said.

'Don't you think the genuine astronomer will react in the same way,' I asked, 'as he looks at the movements of the stars? He'll suppose that the craftsman of the heavens put together both them and the things in them as beautifully as any such works could be composed, but as for the ratios of night to day, of night and day to month, of month to year, and of the move530b ments of the other stars to the sun's and the moon's and each other's, don't you think he will find it strange if someone imagines these as always staying the same and not deviating in any way at all, even though they're accompanied by body and are things we see, and will go on to seek in every way he can to grasp the truth about them?'[500]

'I do think so,' he said, 'now that I hear you saying it.'

'So it's by means of problems', I said, 'that we'll pursue the study of astronomy, as we do that of geometry, and we'll leave 530c the things in the heavens to one side, if we're truly going to use astronomy to transform from uselessness to use that element in the soul where wisdom by nature resides.'

'That's some role you're demanding for astronomy,' he said; 'a good many times greater than the one it has now!'

'And I think our demands will be similarly radical in other cases too, if we're any use as lawgivers. But anyway – is there any appropriate subject you'd like to add to our present list?'

'I can't think of one,' he said, 'not just like that.'

'But surely', I said, 'there are many different kinds of move- 530d
ment, not just one; at least I think there are. It'll probably take
a wise head to list them all, but at any rate there are two that
are obvious even to us laymen.'

'Which are they?'

'The one we've just been talking about,' I said, 'and its counterpart.'

'Which one is *that*?'

'Probably,' I replied, 'just as eyes are adapted to astronomy,
so ears are to harmonic movement. These are in a way sister-
sciences, as the Pythagoreans say, and you and I, Glaucon,
agree with them – or don't we?'

'We do,' he said.

'Well, since it's a big task to take on for ourselves, we'll ask 530e
them what they say on the subject, and whether they've anything else to add. But meanwhile, we'll be on our guard against
the thing that concerns us.'

'Which is?'

'That the people we're bringing up should ever try to get
away with an incomplete study of anything,[501] which fails – as
we were just now saying present-day astronomy does – to
arrive consistently at the point all need to reach. I'm sure you're
aware that experts in harmonics make the same sort of mistake 531a
as the astronomers, and labour away just as uselessly as *they*
do, measuring the relationships between audible concordances
and sounds.'

'Ye gods! They do,' he exclaimed, 'and it's quite ridiculous!
They invent what they call "dense" intervals, putting their ears
up close as if they were eavesdropping on the neighbours – and
then some of them claim they can still hear a sound in the middle, so that *this* is the smallest interval, and the standard unit,
whereas others dispute that, denying that it's really a different
sound at all, and both sides let ears lord it over intelligent 531b
thought.'

'No,' I said; 'you're talking about the ones who cause trouble
for the lyre-strings, torturing them by racking them on the
pegs – I could go on and talk about the plectrum beating, or

rather plucking, answers out of the strings, and the strings refusing to speak or saying too much, but that would be over-stretching the image, so I'll let it go. Let me simply say that the people you refer to aren't the ones I have in mind. It's rather the very people we were just saying we'd consult on the subject of harmonics, because they make the same mistake as the astron-531c omers: they look for the numbers to be found in these perceived concordances of theirs, and they won't move up to the level of problems and ask which numbers are in themselves concordant and which not, and why they are so or not.'

'That's a superhuman task you're talking about!' he said.

'Useful, all the same,' I said, 'towards the search for the beautiful and good; useless if it's pursued for any other pur-pose.'

'Yes, probably,' he said.

'And my view is', I said, 'that if the study of all the subjects 531d we've talked about reaches as far as those aspects that unite them and make them akin, and is able to infer just what their affinities are, then engagement with them does contribute to the goal we're proposing and isn't labour in vain; if it fails to reach that point, it's all in vain.'

'That's my guess too,' he said. 'But it's a huge undertaking, Socrates.'

'Undertaking the preliminaries, are you saying,' I asked, 'or what? We're aware, aren't we, that all of this is a prelude to the main theme, what *really* needs to be learned? I don't suppose you think cleverness at these things makes people experts in dialectic.'

531e   'Zeus! No,' he said, 'though I may have come across some very rare exceptions.'

'But', I said, 'exceptions or not, does it seem to you that they will ever know any of the things we say they need to know, without the capacity for the give and take of argument?'

'To that, too,' he said, 'the answer is certainly no.'

532a   'And isn't *this*, Glaucon, the main theme-tune, the one that dialectic performs – one that, while it belongs to the intellect, finds its counterpart, in that image of ours,[502] in the capacity of sight, at that very stage at which it tries to turn itself to living

creatures themselves, to the stars themselves, and finally to the
sun itself? Just so, when someone tries to make his way by
means of dialectic, setting out after each thing as it really is, in
itself, through argument and without any of the senses,[503] and
not giving up until he grasps what good really is, in itself,   532b
through the use of intellect by itself, then it is that he finds himself at the furthest limit of the intelligible, as our escaped
prisoner found himself at the limit of the visible.'

'Yes,' he said; 'quite so.'

'So you'll label this journey "dialectical"?'

'Naturally.'

'And the prisoner's release from his chains,' I said, 'his turning away from the shadows, to the images and the firelight that
cast them, his climb up from under the earth into the sun, his
inability still to look at the living creatures there, or the plants,   532c
or the sunlight, his focus now on divine reflections in water,
shadows of real things, not shadows of mere images, and cast
by a light no more real than they are, by comparison with the
light of the sun – that engagement with the subjects we've
described has the power, we're saying, to bring it all about, and
lead what is best in the soul to a sight of what is best among the
things that are, just as in our image the element of the body
that has the most clarity was led to the sight of what is bright-   532d
est in the region of the bodily and visible.'

'Speaking for myself,' he said, 'I do accept all of this. But it
still seems to me very hard to accept, even if in another way it
seems hard *not* to accept it. Nonetheless, since we mustn't
allow this to be our only opportunity to hear you on the subject, and we'll have to come back to it on many future occasions,
let's take it for now that things are as we're saying, and get on
to the theme of dialectic itself, going through this just as we've
gone through the prelude to the theme. So go on, tell us what
kind of capacity it is, this dialectic of yours – how it is divided   532e
up, and down what roads it leads, since evidently these will be
the ones that take the traveller to a resting-place, as it were,
that will bring an end to his journeying.'

'My dear Glaucon,' I said, 'you'll not be able to follow any   533a
further – although that wouldn't be for any lack of eagerness

on my part, and it wouldn't any longer be a mere image you'd see of the thing we're talking about, but the thing itself as it truly is – or at any rate that's how it appears to me. As to whether it would really be so or not, that's not something one should insist on from where we are now; but what we may properly insist on is that there is something for us to see, of the sort we're referring to. Isn't that so?'

'Certainly.'

'And shouldn't we also insist that it is the capacity of dialectic alone to reveal it, to someone experienced in the things we've been talking about, and that it's impossible for it to be seen by any other route?'

'That too', he said, 'we'll properly insist on.'

533b   'At any rate,' I said, 'no one will dispute our claim that achieving a methodical grasp of the real nature of each and every thing belongs to a separate kind of inquiry. All other sorts of expertise are oriented towards human beliefs and desires, or making things and putting them together, or else looking after what's made or put together; as for the remaining ones, like
533c   geometry and so on, which we said had some sort of contact with what truly is, we see that while they do dream about what is, it's impossible for them to see it with open eyes, just so long as they keep using hypotheses and leaving them in place because they're unable to give an account of them. If your starting-point is what you don't know, and you weave your end-point and the steps in between out of what you don't know, how on earth, for all that it hangs together, could it ever turn into knowledge?'[504]

'Impossible,' he said.

'Isn't it dialectical inquiry alone', I asked, 'that proceeds in the way required and does away with hypotheses, moving on
533d   to the true starting-point[505] and finding confirmation there? Finding the eye of the soul dug deep down in some kind of alien slime, it gently draws it out and guides it upwards, employing the kinds of expertise we've talked about as co-workers to help bring it round. These we've frequently labelled as branches of knowledge, out of habit, when actually they require a different name, one that groups them together as something more dis-

criminating than belief, dimmer than knowledge – I think we
went for "thoughtfulness" before.[506] But when the questions at
issue are as important as those that presently lie before us, I
don't imagine anyone's going to quarrel about a name.'

'No indeed,' he said.[507]   533e

'So we're content', I said, 'to go on calling the first segment
of the line knowledge, the second thoughtfulness, the third   534a
conviction, the fourth conjecture, with the latter two constitut-
ing what we're calling belief, the former two intelligence; belief
being concerned with what changes, intelligence with what
is, so that intelligence is to belief as what is, truly, is to the
changing, and knowledge is to conviction, thoughtfulness to
conjecture as intelligence is to belief. The relation between the
things these are assigned to,[508] and the division into two of each
of the two sets of things in question – what is believed and
what is grasped by intelligence – we'll set to one side, Glaucon,
to prevent its costing us many times the number of words we've
used in discussing the preceding topics.'

'Well,' he said, 'I certainly agree with you about the rest,   534b
insofar as I'm able to follow.'

'And will you also give the name "dialectician"[509] to someone who gets hold of an account of what each thing is?
Correspondingly, will you assert that just insofar as someone
isn't able to give such an account of it either to himself or
to anyone else, to that extent he lacks intelligent understanding
of it?'

'I could hardly say he had it,' he replied.

'And won't it be the same with the good? If someone isn't
capable of giving an account of the form of the good, one that
sets it apart from everything else, and of surviving all chal-   534c
lenges, like some kind of fighter, eager to test what he's saying
not by reference to belief but to how things truly are, and coming through all of this with his account still standing – if he
can't do all of this, your claim will be, won't it, that he has no
knowledge either about the good itself or about any other
good, and that if he is managing to get a hold on some kind of
shadowy image of it, it's through belief and not through knowledge? He's dreaming and dozing away his present life, you'll

534d say, and will get to sleep properly in Hades before he ever wakes up here?'

'Zeus!' he exclaimed. 'I'll definitely say all of that!'

'And what's more, those children of yours that you're talking about bringing up and educating – if you ever found yourself actually bringing them up, I imagine you'd not let them rule in the city and take charge of the things that matter most if they had as little account to give of themselves as geometers do of their lines.'[510]

'I certainly would not,' he said.

'You'll legislate, then, for their taking part, above all, in the kind of education that will make them able to ask and answer questions in the most expert way?'

534e 'I shall,' he said, 'but not without you.'

'So,' I asked, 'do you think we now have dialectic sitting over and above the subjects for study in general, like a coping-stone,

535a so that none could any longer be slotted in above it? In short, is our treatment of what is to be studied now complete?'

'I think it is,' he said.

'You still have the question of how to allocate them', I said, '– deciding who we're going to give these subjects to, and under what conditions.'[511]

'Clearly so,' he said.

'Do you remember the selection we made earlier, for our rulers, and the kind of people we selected?'

'Of course,' he said.

'Well,' I said, 'take it that in most respects we'll have to select the very same natures, preferring those specimens who are the most stable and the most courageous, so far as possible

535b the best looking,[512] and so on. But we need to add to this list: the people we're looking for mustn't just be upstanding and enterprising characters, they'll also need to possess the natural traits that are conducive to the kind of education we're talking about.'

'Which ones would you single out?' he asked.

'What else, dear Glaucon, but that they need to be keen on

their studies, and not find learning difficult? Souls are much readier to back off, I tell you, from studying hard subjects than from hard exercise, because the pain is much more their own – a private pain, not one the soul shares with the body.'

'True,' he said.

'And we must also look for a good memory, single-minded- 535c ness and a total devotion to hard work. How do you suppose anyone will be willing, otherwise, to go through with so much learning and practice on top of all that hard physical labour?'

'No one would,' he said, 'unless he had all the gifts nature could give him.'

'The problem nowadays, in any case,' I said, 'and the reason why philosophy is in such disrepute, is as I said before,[513] that the people who get involved in it aren't the ones it deserves – what philosophy needs, we said, is genuine practitioners, and it gets spurious ones instead.'

'What is your point?' he asked.

'In the first place,' I said, 'if someone's going to take up with 535d philosophy, his enthusiasm for hard work mustn't be lame on one side, so that he loves working at half of what he has to do and not at the other half. That's what you get when someone is devoted to training and hunting and happily works himself to the bone when it comes to anything physical, but is no lover of learning, doesn't listen, isn't inclined to ask any questions of his own, and actually hates working at anything like that; and it's equally one-sided if his enthusiasms are the other way round.'

'Very true,' he said.

'And in respect of truth, too,' I said, 'won't we declare a soul 535e disabled in just the same way if it hates voluntary falsehoods, can't bring itself to tell them and over-reacts when other people do, but happily puts up with the involuntary sort[514] and isn't upset by being caught out as ignorant in this or that, wallowing in beast-like ignorance as contentedly as any pig?'

'Yes, absolutely,' he said. 536a

'And there's a need to be particularly on the watch', I said, 'when it comes to moderation, and courage, and high-mindedness, and all the other parts of excellence, to ensure that spurious examples don't pass themselves off as genuine. If ever there is less than a complete understanding of how to look for things like this, whether on the part of an individual or a city, then without our knowing it we start employing lame counter-feits in relation to any of the things in question,[515] whether it's as friends or as rulers.'

'Very much so,' he said.

536b   'Then we must be very careful about all of this,' I said. 'If the individuals we introduce to such important learning and train-ing are sound in both limb and mind, justice itself will find no fault with us, and we'll keep the city and its institutions intact. But if we bring in other sorts of people, we'll achieve exactly the opposite, and expose philosophy to even greater floods of laughter.'

'It certainly wouldn't reflect well on philosophy,' he said.

'Quite so,' I replied. 'But the way I'm now behaving myself looks a bit ridiculous.'

'How so?' he asked.

536c   'I forgot for a moment that we were only playing,[516] and spoke too intensely. The fact is that as I was speaking I glanced at philosophy, and seeing it undeservedly trampled over, I think I became upset, and spoke out against those responsible like someone in a rage, and more earnestly than I should have done.'

'Zeus, no!' he exclaimed. 'At least it didn't seem so to me, listening to you.'

'Well, it did to me, as the one who said it,' I replied. 'Any-way, let's not forget that when we were previously selecting the rulers[517] we were for singling out old men, and this time round

536d   we can't do that. We mustn't believe Solon[518] when he tells us old age brings the ability to learn many things – actually, it will sooner make us able to run; if there's ever any heavy work to be done, and lots of it, it's for the young.'

'That must be so,' he said.

'So things like calculation and geometry, and all the prelim-inary study that prepares the way for the study of dialectic, need to be put before our people while they're still children, though without teaching it in the form of a compulsory subject.'

'Why is that?'

'Because a free person should never learn anything under the condition of slavery. A body that's forced to work hard is never the worse for it, but a lesson forced on the soul is never retained.' 536e

'True,' he said.

'So,' I said, 'my friend, as you bring up these children of yours in their various subjects, best not to do it using force, but in the form of play, so that you can also see more clearly what their nature fits them for.' 537a

'That's reasonable enough,' he said.

'Do you remember something else we said', I asked, '– that the children should be taken to war on horseback as observers, and where it was safe should be brought close to the action and taste blood, like young hunting-dogs?'[519]

'I do,' he replied.

'Well,' I said, 'whichever of them reliably appears able to cope exceptionally well with all these things – the hard physical labour, the studying, the dangerous situations – he needs to be put on a special list.'

'At what age?' he asked.

'At the end of their period of required physical training. That will last two or three years,[520] during which any other kind of activity is more or less ruled out; working out and sleeping aren't conducive to studying. At the same time their performance in physical training will be a significant test in itself.' 537b

'Of course it will,' he said.

'Following this period,' I said, 'the selected twenty year olds on our list will be given greater privileges than the rest, and at the same time they'll have to bring together the subjects that were presented to them higgledy-piggledy in their education as children, in order to gain a synoptic view of the relatedness of these subjects, both to each other and to the nature of things as they truly are.' 537c

'It's only that sort of learning that sticks, certainly,' he said, 'if people can manage it.'

'Yes,' I said, 'and it's the best way of finding out if someone is naturally suited to dialectic or not, because if you're not capable of a synoptic view of things, you can't be good at dialectic.'

'I agree,' he said.

537d   'So,' I said, 'you'll have to look and see which of our young people are most like this, and which of them also show the most staying-power, in their studies, in war and in everything else that's laid down for them; then as they pass the age of thirty you'll pick these out, from what is already a select group, award them still greater privileges, and put them to the test, through the power of dialectic, to discover which of them is capable of letting go of his eyes and his other senses, and moving on, with truth as his companion, to the forms of things themselves. And here, my friend, you'll have to be particularly on your guard.'

537e   'How so, exactly?' he asked.

'You're not aware, then,' I said, 'just how much harm is done because of the way dialectic is currently practised?'

'What harm?' he asked.

'I think it encourages people to reject authority,' I said.

'It certainly does,' he said.

'So do you think that's at all surprising?' I asked. 'And don't you feel for them?'

'Why exactly should I?' he replied.

'Imagine', I said, 'that someone was substituted for another
538a   child, was brought up surrounded by great wealth, a great and numerous family, and an equally great number of flatterers, but then on reaching manhood realized that the people claiming to be his parents weren't his real parents, and couldn't find his real ones. Can you guess at how he'd be, towards his flatterers and towards those who were happy to make the substitution, whether during the time he didn't know about it or during the time he did? Or shall I tell you my guess?'

'Please do,' he said.

'Well,' I said, 'my guess is that during the time he didn't
538b   know about it he would pay more respect to his supposed father and mother and other relatives than those who were flattering him – he'd be less likely to allow them to go short of anything, less likely to do or say anything to them that went against the law, and less likely to disobey them when it came to the important things.'

'That's likely enough,' he said.

'And when he recognized how things really were, I'm guessing he would go the other way. The respect and attention he'd given them would slacken, and would be transferred to the flatterers; he'd listen to these much more than he did before, and take them as his new pattern for living, associating with them quite openly, not caring a hoot for that "father" of his and the rest of his supposed family, unless he was naturally a thoroughly decent person.' 538c

'All of that's likely enough,' he said; 'but how is this image of yours relevant to the case of our beginners in dialectic?'

'Like this. I imagine that from our childhood on there are things we believe about what is just and beautiful; beliefs we're brought up with, so that we listen to them and respect them like parents.'

'Yes, that's so.'

'And there are also other, opposite ways of behaving that come with pleasures attached, able to flatter a soul and draw us to them. But if people have even a touch of restraint, they resist, and go on respecting and listening to the beliefs that have been handed down to them.' 538d

'That's right.'

'So', I asked, 'what if someone in the latter condition finds himself faced with the question "The beautiful – what is it?", and he gives the answer he learned from the lawgiver; and then argument refutes that, and by doing the same many times over in a variety of ways finally reduces him to believing that what he'd thought the beautiful to be was actually no more beautiful than it was ugly – and similarly with the just, and the good, and all the things he used to respect most? What do you think will happen after that to his respect and readiness to listen to them?' 538e

'Inevitably,' he said, 'they'll be weakened.'

'So then', I asked, 'when he no longer relates to these beliefs of his or gives them respect as he used to do, and at the same time isn't discovering what the beautiful or the just truly are,[521] what kind of life will he be more likely to move on to than the one that flattered and pleasured him?' 539a

'It'd have to be that one,' he said.

'The result, I imagine, is that he'll seem to have changed from being law-abiding to rejecting authority.'

'Inevitably.'

'Isn't all this just what you'd expect if people begin studying dialectic this way; and don't they deserve a lot of sympathy, as I was suggesting just now?'

'Yes,' he said, 'and pity as well.'

'So to avoid your having to pity your thirty year olds like this, mustn't you be careful about the way you introduce them to dialectic?'

'Very careful,' he said.

539b   'And if there's one thing you need to be especially careful about, it's letting them get a taste of it while they're still young – right? I think you'll have observed that when young teenagers have their first taste of dialectical argument, they treat it as a form of play, just as a way of getting people to contradict themselves;[522] they mimic people who refute them by trying to do the same to others, happily tugging away like little puppies at whoever comes near them, and verbally shredding them.'

'Yes,' he said; 'they enjoy it no end.'

539c   'And when they've often refuted others, and been often refuted themselves, they rapidly and emphatically descend into disbelieving everything they thought before. The result is that both they and philosophy generally get a bad name with everybody else.'

'Very true,' he said.

'Whereas an older person', I said, 'wouldn't want any part in craziness of that sort. The people he'll imitate will be those who choose dialectic in order to investigate the truth, rather than those who play at it for the sport of contradicting each 539d   other; he'll be more balanced about it himself, and he'll bring credit to what he's doing rather than discrediting it.'

'You're right,' he said.

'What we said in introducing this whole subject, about the need to allow only the naturally balanced and steady to participate in dialectic, not anyone and everyone, as now, however unsuitable – all of that, too, was designed with a view to caution.'

'Yes, absolutely,' he said.

'Is it enough for them to stay with the study of dialectic –
continuously and intensively, with no other activity distracting
them – stretching themselves mentally for twice the number of   539e
years they'll have spent exercising their bodies?'

'Are you making that six years,' he asked, 'or four?'[523]

'It doesn't matter,' I said. 'Make it five, because after that
you'll anyway have to move them back down into that cave of
ours, and make them take up military offices and any others that
are suitable for the young, so that they gain as much practical
experience as anyone else. You'll also have to test them, under   540a
these new conditions, to see if they stand up to being pulled this
way and that, or whether they show any sign of losing their grip.'

'How long are you giving for that?' he asked.

'Fifteen years,' I replied. 'And when they've reached the age
of fifty, those that have stayed the course and met the highest
standards in everything they've had to do or learn must now be
led to the end-point of their journey, and compelled to lift the
eye of the soul,[524] directing it towards the very thing that illuminates everything else, the good itself, so that once they have
seen it they can use it as a paradigm[525] for ordering city, citizens   540b
and themselves. For the rest of their lives they must take turns
at this, devoting the greater part of their time to philosophy,
but submitting themselves to political labours when their turn
comes and ruling, each for the city's sake, not because it's a fine
thing to do but as something that has to be done.[526] And then,
having educated others like themselves to take their place as
city-guards, succeeding generations of them will go off to
inhabit the Isles of the Blest, while the city sets up memorials
and sacrifices for them at public expense – as demi-gods, if the   540c
Pythia[527] agrees, or if not, as divinely happy individuals.'

'You're like a sculptor, Socrates – making these ruling men
of ours such paragons of beauty!'

'Yes, and the ruling women, too, Glaucon,' I said; 'don't
imagine I've been talking the slightest bit more about men than
about any women there turn out to be in the city with the
appropriate natural endowment.'

'Right,' he said, 'if they really are to share equally with the
men in everything, in the way we described.'[528]

540d   'So now', I said, 'do you agree that the city and its institutions as we've described them are not mere wishful thinking,
and that what we've described may be difficult to realize, but
is nevertheless possible, in a way – that is, in just the way we
indicated: if true philosophers, whether one or more than one,
should come to power in a city, dismissing as illiberal and
worthless the rewards people now aspire to, making it their
first priority to get things right, with the rewards that come
540e   from that, and treating what is *just* as the greatest and most
indispensable thing, all the time putting themselves at its service and making it grow as they put that city of theirs in due
order?'

'How will they do that?' he asked.

541a   'By sending everyone in the city who is more than ten years
old out into the countryside,' I said, 'and isolating their children, away from the current ways of doing things, which are
their parents' ways too, so as to bring them up in *their* preferred
ways and under *their* laws, which will be as we have described.
This is the quickest and easiest way, don't you think, that the
city and the institutions we've talked about will be established,
so providing happiness for the city itself and bringing the greatest benefit to the people among whom it comes about?'

'It would, very much so,' he said; 'and as to how it would
541b   come about, if it really ever did, Socrates, your account seems
to me a good one.'

'So,' I asked, 'have we now let our twin treatments run on
long enough, of this city of ours, and of the individual resembling it? It's clear by now, I imagine, what sort of person we'll
say he must be.'[529]

'Yes, it is,' he said; 'and as for your question, I think we're
done with those subjects.'

543a   'So there we are. We're agreed, then, Glaucon, that a   Book VIII
city with the top arrangements for government will be   begins
one in which women are shared, children are shared, and so are
all stages of their education, as well as the prescribed activities

in war and in peace; kingship being assigned to those who have turned out best both in philosophy and in relation to war.'

'That is agreed,' he said.

'We also agreed that when the rulers are in place, they will 543b take the soldiers and house them in the way we described before,[530] that is, so that none of them has any private facilities, but all are shared. And as well as their housing, if you recall, I think we settled on rules governing their acquisition of property.'[531]

'I do recall,' he said. 'Our thought was that none of them should own any of the things people own nowadays; rather, as the athletes for war and city-guards that they are, they should 543c each year receive pay for their role in the form of the maintenance required for that role, devoting their efforts to taking care of themselves and of the rest of the city.'

'That's right,' I said. 'But come on – now that we've finished with all this, let's recall where we first started on this sidetrack, and rejoin the path we were following before.'

'That's not hard,' he said, 'because you were talking then pretty much as you're talking now, as if you'd finished talking about our city – saying that you proposed to take as models the kind of city you'd described by that point, and the individual resembling it, even while it seems you had an even more beau- 543d tiful model to bring in, both for a city and for an individual.[532] 544a Anyway, you were saying that other sorts of cities were mistaken, if this one was correct,[533] and you claimed, as I remember it, that apart from this one there were four types of regime[534] that it would be worth our looking at, to observe their shortcomings, and also to get a picture of the individuals resembling them. The idea was that when we'd surveyed all of them, and agreed which was the best individual type and which the worst, we'd then determine whether the best was happiest and the worst the most miserable, or whether the truth was different. I'd just asked you which four regimes you had in mind, when 544b Polemarchus and Adimantus broke in – and that's how you came to take up your argument again,[535] and how we come to be where we are now.'

'Quite correct,' I said; 'well remembered!'

'So offer me the same hold again, as if we were wrestlers, and if I ask you the same question again, try and answer it in the way you were about to back then.'

'I will if I can,' I said.

'And actually,' he said, 'I am anxious, myself, to hear what these four regimes you had in mind are.'

544c   'That I can tell you easily enough,' I said. 'The ones I'm talking about are the ones that have distinct names. First there's the one praised by most people, the one they call Cretan or Spartan.[536] Second, and second too in terms of the praise that's accorded to it, is the one they call oligarchy, a real Pandora's box of a regime; then hard on this one's heels, and permanently at odds with it, there's democracy. And finally there comes tyranny, in all its nobility, the fourth and last of the diseases that affect a city, and in a class of its own.[537] Or can you think
544d   of another variety of regime, clearly distinct in type from these four? Rule that's passed down through a family, kingships that are bought, and other regimes like that will, I imagine, fall somewhere in among the four – you'll find them as much among non-Greeks as among Greeks.'

'There are certainly lots of strange regimes that people talk about,' he said.

'And you recognize', I said, 'that there must be as many types of human beings as there are of regimes? Or do you suppose that political regimes come somehow "from oak or
544e   rock"?[538] Don't they rather come from the traits that characterize a city, and give it a particular slant, as it were, pulling everything else after them?'

'Yes,' he said, 'I don't suppose there's anywhere else they could come from.'

'So if there are five types of cities, individuals' souls will come arranged in five different ways too.'

'Of course they will.'

'Well, we've already described the individual who resembles the aristocratic type of regime[539] – the person we're correctly describing as good and just.'

545a   'We have.'

'So should we next describe the inferior types – the type that loves winning, and honours,[540] who corresponds to the Spartan regime; then the oligarchic type, the democratic and the tyrannical? Once we've observed the most unjust of them, we'll be able to contrast him with the most just, and so complete our investigation into how justice unmixed compares with unmixed injustice when it comes to the happiness or misery of their possessors. Then we can decide whether we should listen to Thrasymachus and pursue injustice, or go with the argument that's emerging now, and pursue justice.'   545b

'That's exactly what we must do,' he said.

'So how should we proceed? We started by looking at character-traits at the level of regimes before we looked at them in individuals, on the grounds that things would be clearer there; shall we do the same here, and look at the honour-loving regime first? The only name I know that's used for it is "timocracy" – or else we could call it "timarchy".[541] In connection with that, anyway, we'll consider the corresponding individual; then we'll go on to oligarchy and the oligarchic individual, take a look at democracy and observe democratic man, then move on to the fourth regime-type, a city under a tyranny, and again look at the soul corresponding to that – after all of which we'll try to reach a good enough judgement about the matters we've put up for debate.'   545c

'That would certainly be a reasonable way of looking at everything, and reaching our decision,' he said.

'So come on,' I said, 'let's try to say how a timocracy might come about from an aristocracy. Or perhaps there's a simple rule, that any change of regime in a city begins with the element in it that holds the offices of power, when faction takes hold in that. If it's of one mind, however small it may be in numbers, it's impossible to move it.'   545d

'Yes, that's so.'

'So how, Glaucon,' I asked, 'will movement come about in our city? How will our auxiliaries and rulers come to fall out with each other and with themselves? Perhaps we should do as Homer does and pray to the Muses to tell us "how first it befell" them to fall out,[542] and declare, as they do so, that for   545e all their lofty, tragic style[543] they're playing with us, not serious, teasing us as if we were children?'

'How will their story go?'

546a   'Like this, I suppose. "Hard though it is for a city like yours to be moved, put together as it is, still, since everything that has come into being must also perish, even a thing so well constructed will not last for ever. It will fall apart, and the manner of its fall will be this. Not only among plants in the earth but among creatures upon it, soul and body bear or fail to bear fruit as the seasons for each complete their cycles, which are brief in the short-lived, longer in the long-lived. In the case of

546b   your species, those you have educated to be leaders of the city – for all their wisdom, and for all that they combine observation with calculation – will fail to hit upon the proper moments for reproducing and for abstaining from reproduction; these will pass them by, and they will sometimes cause children to be produced when they should not. The cycle for divine birth is captured by a perfect number, whereas for mortal birth the number is that in which the controlled potencies of growth first realize the three dimensions, and four limits, of the things that bring about likeness and unlikeness, and growth and decay, in

546c   such a way as to render everything mutually translatable and rational; of which a base of four over three, combined with five and raised to the fourth power, offers two harmonious figures, the first with two sides equal, taken a hundred times over, the second having one side equal but the other longer, and consisting of a hundred times the square on the rationalized diameter of a square with side five, less one, or the square on the irrational diameter less two, and a hundred times the cube on side three.[544] All of this constitutes a geometrical number[545] governing the sort of thing in question, namely, whether the new generation

546d   will be better or worse, and if ever the guards' ignorance of this causes them to have brides cohabit with bridegrooms out of due season, the resulting offspring will not be well endowed by nature, nor fortunate. Certainly, it will be the best of these that their predecessors set up as rulers, but they will be unworthy of it all the same, and when the time comes for them to assume their fathers' powers, in the first place they will

begin to neglect us, the Muses, by assigning too little importance to our sphere, and then by down-grading physical
education too, so that your young people become less musical
than they should be. From these will be established rulers who   546e
do not have quite what guards need, if they are to assess to   547a
which of Hesiod's races, or of yours, a person belongs, whether
gold, silver, bronze or iron.[546] When iron is mixed up with silver and bronze with gold, dissonance and imbalance will
replace harmony in the city – and once these arrive, no matter
where, they always beget war and enmity. 'For those of such
birth',[547] we declare, faction is their birthright, wherever and
whenever they are born."'

'Yes, and we'll declare that they're right,' he said.

'They'd better be,' I replied, 'seeing that they're the Muses.'

'So what', he asked, 'do the Muses have to say to us next?'   547b

' "Once faction had set in," ' I said, ' "then it was[548] that each
pair of elements pulled in their own direction, the iron and
bronze[549] towards making money and acquiring land and property, gold and silver, and the other pair, the gold and silver, since
they were not poor, but were possessed of riches in their souls,
tried to lead the way to excellence and the old order of things;
and as they struggled and strained against each other, they
agreed on a compromise: that they should distribute the land
and the houses to be held privately, and rob of their freedom   547c
those they used to guard and protect, their former friends and
providers, turning them into subjects and slaves, while occupying themselves with war and a different kind of guarding." ' [550]

'I think this is where the change starts,' he said.

'And wouldn't this regime be somewhere in the middle
between aristocracy and oligarchy?'

'Absolutely.'

'So that's how the regime will change; once changed, how
will it be governed? Or is the answer already clear enough – in   547d
some respects it will follow the example of its predecessor, in
others that of oligarchy, since it's in between the two; but it will
also have some peculiar features of its own.'

'Just so,' he said.

'The respect it accords to those in office, the abstention of its fighting element from farming, the crafts and money-making activities in general, the provision of common messes, the attention it gives to physical training and to competing in war – in all such respects it will imitate its predecessor, won't it?'

'Yes.'

547e   'On the other hand, its fear of giving power to the wise, because those it has of this kind are of mixed quality, no longer possessing the simple, single-minded wisdom of old; its tendency to favour more spirited and simple-minded individuals

548a   who are born to be more focused on war than on peace, and to give pride of place to military stratagems and devices; the fact that it occupies itself day in and day out with making war – in most cases these will be features peculiar to it?'

'Yes.'

'But such people will have an appetite for money,' I said, 'like those who live under oligarchies, and they'll nurture a savage, secret preference for gold and silver, because they'll have the store-rooms and private treasuries to put it all in and hide it, all within the protecting walls of their houses, literally

548b   private little nests for entertaining women and anyone else they fancy and spending lavishly on them.'

'Very true,' he said.

'They'll also be mean with their own money, because they value it so much and can't amass it openly, but appetite will make them love spending other people's, enjoying their pleasures secretly, hiding from the law like boys running away from a father. They've had to be forced into their education rather than being talked into it, because they've neglected the true

548c   Muse, who works with argument and philosophy, and made the gymnasium a higher priority than music.'

'The regime you're describing there is certainly a mixture,' he said, 'of bad and of good.'

'Yes, it is a mixture,' I said, 'but there's just one single feature of it that is really distinctive, which comes from the dominance in it of the spirited element: the love of coming out on top, and of being honoured.'

'Very much so,' he said.

'This, then,' I said, 'is how a regime of that general sort

would come about, and what it would be like. We've only given
an outline sketch of it, not gone into all the details, because
even sketches will suffice for what we need, to identify the most
just and the most unjust individuals, and anyway it would be
an impossibly long undertaking to go through all types of
regimes and dispositions without leaving anything out.'

'Quite right,' he said.

'So what about the man corresponding to the regime? How
would he come about, and what would he be like?'

'Well, *I* think', said Adimantus, 'he pretty much resembles
Glaucon here, at least so far as the love of winning is concerned.'

'Maybe,' I said, 'in that respect; but in other respects I think
his nature will be unlike Glaucon's.'

'What are these?'

'He'll have to be rather obstinate,' I said, 'and also somewhat on the unmusical side, even while still a music-lover, and
someone who loves listening, but is no speaker. Rather than
merely looking down on slaves, as someone with a proper education will, he'll tend to be savage with them, while he'll be
gentle with the free-born; he'll be highly deferential to officials, but set on office and honours for himself, basing his
claims not on what he has to say, or anything like that, but on
what he does, whether in war itself or the activities surrounding it, being the sort of person who loves physical exercise and
hunting.'

'Yes,' he said, 'because that's the character of the regime in
question.'

'Won't it also be true of this type of person', I asked, 'that
while he's young he'll look down on money, but the older he
gets the fonder he'll be of it, because he has that element of the
money-lover in him, and isn't single-mindedly set on excellence, having been deprived of what is best able to guard that?'

'Which is what?' asked Adimantus.

'Reason,' I said, 'mixed in with music. This alone guarantees
the excellence of its possessor, once it is present and takes up
lifelong residence in him.'

'Well said,' he replied.

'So that's the young timocrat for you,' I said; 'just like the timocratic city.'

'Absolutely.'

549c 'And his origins are something like this. Sometimes he'll be the young son of a good father who lives in a city that is not well governed, avoids honours, offices, lawsuits and all that meddling with other people's business, and is happy to accept a loss of status in order to live a quiet life –'

'So how does the son turn timocrat?'

'When first of all he hears his mother being upset that her 549d man isn't one of the ruling group,' I said, 'and that she's losing status among the other women because of it. She sees that he's not over-concerned about money, and doesn't fight or exchange insults, either privately in the lawcourts or on the public stage, but takes a casual attitude towards everything like that; he's always turned in on himself, she notices, and neither exactly respects nor disrespects her. The son hears her being upset by all of this, and telling him his father is no man at all, too easy-going, and using all the other sorts of refrains one hears from wives with husbands like that.'

549e 'Yes, there's a whole assortment of them,' said Adimantus, 'as you'd expect.'

'And you'll be aware', I said, 'that sometimes in such house-holds the slaves too, or the ones that are supposed to be well meaning, whisper similar things in the sons' ears, and if they notice anyone owing the father money, or treating him unjustly in some other way, and the father not making anything of it, 550a they tell the son that when he grows up he'll have to punish the lot of them and prove himself more of a man than his father is. Then if he goes out of the house and hears and sees the same sorts of things happening – those who don't get involved in the city being called simple-minded and held in low esteem, and respect and praise being accorded to those who do – well, when he hears and sees all that sort of thing, and he's also hearing what his father is saying, and seeing his father's life from close 550b enough to compare it with others', he is pulled in opposite directions: by his father, watering the rational element in him and making it grow, like a plant, and by everybody else doing the same to the appetitive and the spirited in him. Because he's not naturally a bad person, and has just fallen into bad company, the pull from the one side cancels that from the other, and he ends up in the middle, handing rule within himself over to his own middle element, the spirited element that loves to win, thus becoming that proud individual, the lover of honour.'

'I think you've certainly captured his origins,' he said.

'Then we have our second regime in the bag,' I said, 'and our second individual type.'   550c

'We have,' he said.

'So shall we follow Aeschylus, and talk of "another man, disposed before/ Another state"[551] – or rather, according to our agreed procedure, the state before the man?'

'Yes,' he replied, 'absolutely.'

'And I imagine the sort of regime that comes after the last one will be oligarchy.'

'What kind of set-up are you calling oligarchic?' he asked.

'The kind that's based on property qualification, where the rich rule, and a poor man is excluded from ruling.'

'I'm with you,' he said.   550d

'So we need to say how the change from timarchy to oligarchy begins?'

'Yes.'

'Well,' I said, 'even the blind can see how the change occurs.'

'How?'

'What destroys a timarchy', I said, 'is that store-room each has for himself and keeps filling with gold. First of all they invent new ways of spending their money, and bend the laws to that purpose by refusing to obey them; their wives refuse too.'

'Very likely,' he said.

'Next, I imagine, each looks at what his neighbours are doing, and tries to emulate them, so that before long they've made most of their group behave like themselves.'   550e

'Very likely.'

'And after that,' I said, 'as they move ever further into money-making, the greater the value they give to that the less value they attach to excellence and goodness. Isn't that the nature of the difference between excellence and money, that they are as it were on opposite sides of a balance, each always tipping it the opposite way?'

'Very much so,' he said.

551a   'So the more that wealth and the wealthy are valued in a city, the less a city will value goodness and good people.'

'Clearly.'

'Whatever we value at any time, we recognize in our practice; whatever we don't value is passed over.'

'Just so.'

'Thus instead of loving to win, and be honoured, they end up becoming lovers of money-making and of money. They praise the wealthy man, they admire him, they install him in office; the poor man they disbar.'

'Quite.'

'And that's when they establish a law that will define the
551b   regime as an oligarchy, fixing the amount of money – a larger amount where it's more oligarchic, smaller where it's less so – that a person will need in order to hold office, proclaiming that anyone possessing less than the required amount of property is excluded. Either they put this through using force of arms, or else they'll have terrorized everyone into accepting this sort of regime already, and not have to use actual force. Isn't that how it happens?'

'Indeed it is.'

'So that's roughly how an oligarchy comes about.'

'Yes,' he replied. 'But how does this kind of regime operate? And what are the failings we were attributing to it?'[552]

551c   'First of all, think of the very feature that defines it. Imagine what would happen if ships' steersmen were appointed like this, on the basis of property qualifications, and a poor man wasn't allowed to steer even if he happened to be better at it.'

'I imagine', he replied, 'that all concerned would have a bumpy voyage.'

'And will it be the same with steering or controlling anything?'

'Yes, I think so.'

'Except a city?' I asked. 'Or do you include running a city too?'

'That more than anything else', he replied, '– much more, given how extraordinarily hard, and important, a task it is to govern a city.'

'So that's one important failing that an oligarchy will have.'   551d

'Evidently.'

'What about the next one – is it any less important than the last?'

'Which one?'

'That a city with that kind of regime will inevitably be two cities, not one: a city of poor people and a city of rich ones, all living in the same place and continually plotting against one another.'

'Zeus!' he exclaimed. 'That's certainly just as important a failing as the first.'

'And it's hardly to be recommended that they won't be able to wage a war, either, because that would force them either to arm the general population, and end up more in fear of them than of the enemy, or else not to arm them, in which case they'll   551e be truly oligarchs when it comes to the battlefield;[553] and matters will be made worse by their reluctance, as money-lovers, to contribute to any war-chest.'

'Hardly to be recommended.'

'And what about that aspect we were so rude about earlier on,[554] people's meddling in lots of different things – farming,   552a making money, fighting wars, all at the same time – as they will do under this kind of regime? Or is it all right for them to do that?'

'Absolutely not.'

'See now if you think this regime won't also be the first to introduce something worse than anything we've so far talked about.'

'What's that?'

'Making it perfectly permissible for someone to sell everything he has, and for someone else to acquire it, and then for the seller to live on in the city without fulfilling any of the roles that go to make up a city, whether it's making money, working at one of the crafts or serving as a cavalryman or hoplite; all   552b he'll be is a pauper, labelled "without means".'

'Oligarchy will be the first to permit that,' he said.

'At any rate this sort of thing won't be prohibited under oligarchies, because if it were, one group wouldn't be super-rich, another absolutely impoverished.'

'Right.'

'Now consider this point: was this person actually of any more use to the city, in the respects we've just mentioned, when he was still wealthy and spending?[555] Or did he merely appear to be one of those ruling the city, when he was really neither ruling nor serving it, just consuming whatever resources he had to hand?'

552c   'That's right,' he said; 'it was only an appearance – he actually did nothing better than spend and consume.'

'So shall we compare him to a drone emerging in his cell among the honey-bees, a bane to the hive – a drone in his own little house, a bane to the city?'

'Yes, Socrates,' he said, 'absolutely.'

'Well, Adimantus,' I said, 'there's this difference: the gods made winged drones stingless, whereas only some of the footed
552d   variety are like this – some have a terrible sting. They all develop into beggars, but only the stingless ones stay that way into old age; from the ones with stings you get the whole of what is labelled as the criminal class.'[556]

'Very true,' he said.

'Clearly, then,' I said, 'wherever you see beggars in a city, somewhere in the location there will be thieves, purse-snatchers and temple-robbers hidden away – specialists in all sorts of crimes like that.'

'Clearly,' he said.

'Well, don't you see beggars there in oligarchic cities?'

'Pretty well everywhere,' he said, 'outside the ruling class.'

552e   'Don't we conclude, then,' I said, 'that such cities also con-tain lots of criminals, complete with their stings, which the city's officers will devote attention to keeping forcibly under control?'

'That is the conclusion,' he said.

'And won't we say that this type of person emerges there as a result of a failure of education, a bad upbringing, and the way the regime is constructed?'

'We will.'

'In any case, that's roughly what a city under oligarchic rule will be like, and we've listed the bad things about it, but there are possibly more.'

'They're pretty much as we've said,' he replied.

'Then we're done with this regime too,' I said, 'the one   553a
people call oligarchy, and ruled on the basis of property qualifications. Next let's consider the origins of the individual
resembling it, and what he's like when he's emerged.'

'Yes, absolutely,' he said.

'Well, doesn't the change from timocratic to oligarchic man
take place essentially like this?'

'Like how?'

'When the timocratic man has a son, the son at first emulates
his father and follows in his footsteps; and then he sees him
suddenly wrecked by his city, like a ship on a reef, and being   553b
thrown overboard with all his possessions. He's served as a
general, or in another high office of state, but then he gets
embroiled in the courts, damaged by the evidence of professional informers,[557] and ends up executed, or in exile, or
deprived of citizenship and with all his property confiscated.'

'Yes, that sounds a likely sequence,' he said.

'Yes, my friend – and when the son has seen all this, been
through it and lost everything he owned, I imagine he's afraid,
and immediately dethrones that spirited element that used to   553c
reign in his soul along with a love of honour, throwing it out on
its head; humbled by poverty, he turns to making money, and
through determination, saving every little bit and working at it,
he actually gets some together. Don't you think someone in
these circumstances, who behaves like this, is giving the throne
in him to the appetitive and money-loving element, making
that his Great King, and dressing it up in diadems and necklets
and exotic little swords?'[558]

'I do,' he said.

'As for the rational and spirited elements, meanwhile, I   553d
imagine he makes *them* sit on the ground below the king, to its
left and its right, as its slaves. The rational element he forbids
to calculate, or inquire into, anything except how to turn less

money into more, while the spirited element is forbidden either to admire or honour anything except wealth and wealthy people. The single thing it can pride itself on is acquiring money and anything that contributes to that.'

'There's no other way,' he said, 'so swift or so certain, of
553e changing a young man from loving honour to loving money.'

'So is this our oligarchic man?' I asked.

'Well, at any rate, when he started he was like the regime that changed into an oligarchic one.'

'So let's see if he'll resemble an oligarchy.'

554a '
'Let's.'

'Won't he do so, first of all, by the fact that he attaches most importance to money?'

'Of course.'

'And also by his working away, and scrimping and saving, and the fact that, of the desires and appetites he has, he only satisfies the necessary ones, and refuses to spend money on anything else, keeping those other desires of his under lock and key on the grounds that there's no point to them.'

'Absolutely.'

'Given how squalid he is,' I said, 'making a surplus on everything to add to his pile, which is what most people even approve
554b of, won't he be the one that resembles the regime in question?'

'It seems so to me,' he said; 'at any rate money is what both the oligarchic city and he honour most.'

'That, I imagine, is because education has passed this sort of person by.'

'I think so,' he said; 'otherwise he wouldn't have chosen a blind leader for his chorus,[559] and be honouring him above all else.'

'Well said,'[560] I replied. 'Think of it this way: shouldn't we say that, because of his lack of education, drone-like desires
554c emerge in him, some of them merely begging for attention, others actively criminal, which he forcibly keeps under control because of his general carefulness?'

'Yes, we certainly should,' he said.

'And do you know where to look,' I asked, 'in order to observe the crimes someone like this commits?'

'Where's that?' he asked.

'His guardianship of orphans, and any other situation that offers him the same opportunity to behave unjustly and get away with it.'

'True.'

'Doesn't this make it clear that when in his ordinary business dealings someone like that acquires a good reputation by appearing to be just, some element of decency in him is enabling him to keep other, bad desires that he has in him forcibly under control? He doesn't persuade them that they should behave, and he doesn't use reason to tame them; it's plain compulsion and fear, because he's afraid of putting the rest of his possessions at risk.' 554d

'Yes, quite so,' he said.

'And – Zeus!', I said, '– my friend, once it's a matter of spending other people's money and not their own, you'll soon find at least most of them do possess those drone-like desires.'

'Yes indeed,' he said; 'very much so.'

'So this sort of man won't be free from internal faction. Instead of being one person, he'll in a way be two, though for the most part the better desires will win out over the worse ones.' 554e

'That is so.'

'That makes him more respectable-looking than many, I imagine. But he'll fall a long way short of the true goodness of a soul, when it is at one and in harmony with itself.'

'I think so.'

'Moreover, his parsimony will make him a poor contestant 555a when it comes to winning individual prizes or other marks of distinction in the city, and unready to spend money for the sake of reputation and competitions like that. He's afraid to wake up those spendthrift desires of his, and bring them in on the side of his ambitions, so he puts only a few of his resources on the line, in true oligarchic style,[561] losing most of the time but staying rich.'

'Indeed so,' he said.

'So is there any longer doubt', I asked, 'that the thrifty money-maker belongs with the oligarchic city, in terms of 555b resemblance?'

'No doubt at all,' he said.

'Democracy, then, seems to be what we need to look at next – both how it comes into being, and what it is like when it has, the object being, again, to recognize the characteristics of the corresponding individual and judge him in comparison with the others.'

'That will certainly be in keeping with what we've done before,' he said.

'So,' I asked, 'has the way oligarchy changes to democracy something to do with the excessive pursuit of the goal that's been set, of having to make oneself as wealthy as possible?'

'How so?'

555c   'Ruling as they do on the basis of their great wealth, I imagine the rulers are unwilling to place legal curbs on young people who lose their self-restraint, and prevent them from spending and losing their property. They want to be able to buy it or lend money on it themselves, in order to add still further to their own wealth and prestige.'

'That's what they want,' he said, 'more than anything.'

'So isn't it already evident that in any city, giving pride of place to wealth is incompatible with the acquisition by its citi-
555d   zens of a proper moderation? One or the other has to go; you can't have both.'

'That's pretty clear,' he said.

'In fact this sort of neglect, in oligarchies, which allows people to throw off any restraint, sometimes drives men of no little quality into penury.'

'It certainly does.'

'And there they sit, these people, with weapons for stings, some of them debtors, some of them disfranchised, some both,
555e   hating and plotting against those who have what is theirs, and against the rest, lusting for revolution.'

'That's right.'

'Meanwhile the money-makers, their gaze fixed downwards, seeming not even to see the others, insert the fatal sting of their money into any survivor that fails to resist them, reaping inter-
556a   est many times what they put in, and simultaneously creating a large class of drones and beggars in the city.'

'Yes, it's bound to be large,' he said.

'And they're unwilling to douse this kind of trouble as it spreads, either in the way we mentioned, by passing a law that stops people doing what they like with their money, or by applying a second kind of legal solution.'

'What would that be?'

'It would be a second-best to the other one, but it would compel citizens to pay attention to goodness. If there were a law that made entering into voluntary contracts normally at 556b the individual's own risk, there would be less unscrupulous money-making in the city at large, and it would find itself incubating fewer of the problems we were talking about just now.'

'Many fewer,' he said.

'But as it is,' I said, 'and for all the sorts of reasons we've given, the rulers in oligarchies bring about the condition we described in their subjects. As for themselves and their own, don't they make the young ones fond of luxury and unused to exerting themselves either physically or mentally, too soft to 556c stand up to pleasures and pains, and just plain lazy?'

'No question.'

'Turning themselves, meanwhile, into people who have neglected everything but making money, and have paid no more attention to goodness than the poor have.'

'No indeed.'

'If that's the condition they're in, what do you suppose happens when rulers and ruled come into contact, on journeys or in some other shared activity, whether it's attending a religious festival or serving on campaign together, on board ship or on the field, and they look at each other, even at moments of dan- 556d ger, and the poor suddenly find they're not the slightest bit inferior to the wealthy – often, indeed, the poor man, lean and sunburnt, stationed in battle beside a wealthy one, shade-reared and with rolls of excess flesh, will observe him hopelessly wheezing and helpless. Do you imagine he doesn't draw the obvious conclusion, that people like this are only wealthy because he himself is a coward? Or that when he and his like get together in private, they don't pass on the message, "They're ours for the taking; they're nobodies!"'

556e

'Yes,' he said, 'that is the reaction – I'm well aware of it.'

'Just as a sickly body requires only a little push from outside to tip it into actual illness, and is sometimes in conflict with itself[562] even without external influences, so it only takes a small event – one side trying to bring in allies from an oligarchic city, or the other from a democratic one – to tip an already sickly city into illness and internal fighting; and sometimes it, too, needs no external factors to split it into contending factions.'

557a   'Very much so,' he said.

'And democracy, I think, comes about when the poor win, kill some of the other side, exile others and then give everybody who is left an equal share in constitutional power, public offices being mostly distributed by lot.'[563]

'Yes,' he said, 'this is how democracies are set up, whether it's through the actual use of armed force or only the threat of it, causing one side to withdraw.'

'So how do these people run their lives?[564] And what will
557b   this sort of regime be like? Clearly the corresponding individual will turn out to be somehow democratic.'

'Clearly,' he said.

'First of all, aren't they *free* – doesn't the city come to be full of freedom, and freedom of speech? Isn't there licence there for anyone to do as he wishes?'

'That's certainly what they say,' he replied.

'And where such licence exists, clearly each individual will proceed to make his own private arrangements for running his life, as he pleases.'

'Clearly.'

557c   'Under this sort of regime, then, I imagine, more than any other, you'll find people of all sorts.'

'Obviously.'

'Possibly', I said, 'it's the most beautiful of regimes. It's like a many-coloured cloak, embroidered with every flower there is, but with character-traits for flowers, and looking just as beautiful; and maybe,' I said, 'like children and women when they see brightly coloured things, many would actually judge it the *most* beautiful.'

'Yes indeed,' he said.

'And what's more, my friend,' I said, 'it's a delightfully convenient place for us to go looking for a constitution.'

'Why is that?'   557d

'Because, thanks to the licence it gives its citizens, it contains every kind of regime within it. Anyone who wants to put a city together, as we were doing just now, ought to visit a city governed by a democracy and pick out whatever kind of arrangement pleases him – it's like going to a universal store of regimes: you just make your selection, and found your city accordingly.'

'There'd certainly be no lack of models on display,' he said.

'The absence from this kind of city of any compulsion on a   557e citizen to rule, even if he's qualified to do so, or to *be* ruled, either, if he doesn't want to, or to go off to war when there's a war on, or be at peace when everybody else is, if peace isn't what he wants; the fact that, if there's some law prohibiting him from taking office or sitting on a jury, he'll take office and sit on the jury anyway, if he feels like it – isn't all that a marvel-   558a lously pleasant way of doing things, in the short term?'

'Perhaps,' he said; 'in the short term.'

'And what about the calmness of some of those convicted in the courts? Isn't it exquisite? Or haven't you seen people who have been condemned to death or exile under this kind of regime, and yet still stay on in the city and move about in public – how someone like that can walk around like the returned ghost of a hero without anybody either caring or noticing?'[565]

'I've certainly seen many like that,' he said.

'And the tolerance of the democratic city, its utter lack of meticulousness, its contempt for all those high-minded things we   558b said when we were founding our city, about how only someone born with an utterly exceptional nature could ever become a good man, if from earliest childhood his play was not surrounded by beauty, and all his pursuits and activities likewise – how high-mindedly it tramples over all of this! It doesn't care a bit what kinds of things a person did before he entered politics and started running things, and gives him respect on the sole condition that he declares himself well disposed towards the people.'

'Truly noble!' he said.

558c   'So these will be the characteristics of democracy,' I said,
'and others related to these. It's an attractively anarchic and
colourful regime, it seems, according a sort of equality to equals
and unequals alike.'

'As we all know only too well,' he said.

'So now,' I said, 'think what the corresponding individual
will be like. Or as with the regime, should we rather ask first
how he comes about?'

'Yes,' he said.

558d   'Isn't it like this? Our thrifty, oligarchic man will, I suppose,
have a son that's been brought up under his father's rules and
in his father's ways.'

'Of course.'

'So he too will exercise a rule of force over the pleasures in
him that involve spending and not making money – the ones
that are called unnecessary.'

'Clearly,' he said.

'To make sure we can see what we're talking about,' I said,
'do you want us to start by defining necessary and unnecessary
desires?'

'Yes,' he said.

'Aren't the ones that would justify being called necessary the
558e   ones that we wouldn't be able to turn away, and those whose
completion benefits us? Our very nature, after all, makes it
necessary for us to seek both of these types. Right?'

'Very much so.'

559a   'So we'll be justified in attaching the label "necessary" to
them.'

'Indeed.'

'And what about the desires that can be got rid of, if one
works at it from a young age – whose presence also does us no
good, and in some cases does us harm: wouldn't we be right in
calling these unnecessary?'

'We would, yes.'

'So let's choose an example of each kind, to give ourselves a
rough idea of what we're talking about.'

'Let's do that.'

'Well, won't one necessary desire be for eating just so much

as we need for health and well-being – the desire for food itself,   559b
and for cooked food?'

'I think so.'

'The desire for food, I suppose, being necessary for both
reasons, both because it brings benefit and because it can stop us
from living if we don't satisfy it.'

'Yes.'

'Whereas the desire for cooked food will be necessary just
insofar as it brings benefits in terms of well-being.'

'Quite so.'

'What about the desire that goes beyond these, for other
sorts of food, one that is capable of being removed from most
people if it's suitably restrained and educated from childhood
on, and is harmful not only to the body but to the soul and its
acquisition of wisdom and moderation? Wouldn't that rightly   559c
be called an unnecessary sort of desire?'

'Absolutely right.'

'So shall we also label these as desires that spend and don't
make money, and the others as ones that do, because they're
useful when it comes to getting things done?'566

'Certainly we shall.'

'And shall we take the same line with sex and everything
else?'

'We shall.'

'That drone figure of ours, then – it's these sorts of pleasures
and desires we were saying he was full of, the unnecessary ones;
they're what he's ruled by, whereas the individual ruled by the
necessary ones is the thrifty oligarchic type.'

'Of course, yes.'

'So,' I said, 'let's go back to saying how the democratic type   559d
develops out of the oligarch. The typical way it happens seems
to me like this.'

'How?'

'When a young person who's been brought up in the uneducated and thrifty way we were just describing gets to taste the
honey, like the drone he is, by associating with a set of flashy,
clever creatures able to furnish him with a whole range of pleasures, of every variety and kind – that's the sort of situation you   559e

need to think of as marking the beginning of a change from the oligarchic regime in him to a democratic one.'

'It's quite inevitable,' he said.

'So just as the city started to change when an alliance from outside intervened to support one part of it, like supporting like,[567] doesn't the young person in our case change when one of two warring elements in him receives outside support from a type of desires akin to and resembling itself?'

'Absolutely.'

'And presumably if some counter-alliance comes in to support the oligarchic element in him, from the direction of his father, perhaps, or else his other relatives, remonstrating with him and castigating him, then there's faction and counter-faction and a battle in him against himself.'

'Naturally.'

'What happens then, I presume, is that the democratic element yields to the oligarchic, some of his desires are either killed off or go into exile, and as a sort of sense of shame establishes itself in the young person's soul, order is restored.'

'That does sometimes happen,' he said.

'But then presumably other desires akin to the ones that went into exile are quietly brought up in their place, through the father's ignorance of what a proper upbringing is, and they grow numerous and strong.'

'That's certainly what tends to happen,' he said.

'The result is, isn't it, that they draw him back into the same bad company, coming together secretly and giving birth to a whole rabble inside him?'

'Of course it is.'

'And finally, I presume, they capture the acropolis of the young person's soul, having seen it unoccupied by any studies or fine pursuits or words of truth, which make the best watchmen and guards in the minds of men loved by the gods.'

'Much the best,' he said.

'So then false words and beliefs, swindlers all, presumably rush up and take the place in his soul that should be occupied by the true ones.'

'Very much so,' he said.

'And then back he goes to those Lotus-eaters and lives openly among them; and if some detachment arrives from his family to support the thrifty element in his soul, those swindling words bar the gates of the royal walls in him,[568] not just preventing the relieving force itself from getting through, but not giving a hearing, either, to embassies sent by older and wiser individuals.[569] Instead, they fight for control of him and take it. They call a sense of shame silliness, deny it its rights, push it out into exile; moderation they label as unmanliness, trample it into the mud, then throw it out too. As for reasonable behaviour and orderly expenditure, these they persuade him to regard as boorish and illiberal, joining with a crowd of useless desires to drum them out of town.'

'Very much so.'

'And when they've somehow removed these, quite purged them, from the soul of the person they're occupying and initiating with their own great rites, the next thing is for them to bring back arrogance, anarchy, profligacy and shamelessness, in all their glory, with a large retinue and covered in garlands, singing their praises and giving them pretty names – arrogance becoming a sign of culture, anarchy freedom, profligacy magnificence, shamelessness courage. Isn't it in this sort of way', I asked, 'that while still young he'll exchange an upbringing among necessary desires for the liberation and release offered by unnecessary and useless pleasures?'

'Quite evidently so,' he said.

'And after that, I imagine, someone in this situation ceases to make any distinction in his life between necessary and unnecessary pleasures, spending money, effort and time on both alike. But suppose that he's lucky, and doesn't get carried away too much: when he's a bit older and the great commotion in him has passed, perhaps he'll receive back parts of what was previously exiled, and won't surrender himself wholesale to the invaders. Then he starts to operate by assigning a kind of equality to pleasures, handing rule over himself to whichever pleasure happens to turn up, as if chosen for the position by lot, so that when *one* is satisfied he turns himself over to another, and then another, looking after all of them equally and giving each its proper turn.'

'Quite so.'

'And', I said, 'he doesn't listen to a word of truth, or give it entry to his guardhouse, should any tell him that some pleasures belong to the kind of desires that are fine and good, others to bad ones, and the first sort need to be taken up and respected, the second restrained and put in chains. He shakes his head at anything like that, declaring that there's no difference between them and all must be given equal respect.'

'That's very much how he is,' he said, 'and how he behaves.'

'So that', I said, 'is how he lives from day to day, pandering to each desire as it rolls up. Now you'll find him under the influence of drink and pipe-players, now on a diet of bread and water; now he's exercising in the gymnasium, next he's lazing around and neglecting everything – and the next moment he's spending time at what he says is philosophy. Often he plays the politician, leaping up and saying or doing whatever comes into his head. If there are some military figures he happens to admire, he rushes off in that direction; or else it will be business types, and off he goes that way. There is no order in this life of his, nothing to constrain it; and to him it is simply delightful, the life a free man should live – blest, even, and he'll stick to it through thick and thin.'

'That's absolutely the life of the equality-monger,'[570] he said.

'And I think it's a life full of colour,' I said, 'containing a greater variety of traits than any. This is the individual we're after, with the same beautiful range of hues that the corresponding city had. Many men, and women, will aspire to his way of living, containing as he does so many different models for regimes and ways of life within him.'

'Yes,' he said, 'he's our man.'

'So we'll be right, then, to call him democratic man, and we can take him as corresponding to the democratic city?'

'We can,' he said.

'So,' I said, 'it only remains for us to describe the most

beautiful of all regimes, and the most beautiful of all individuals: tyranny, and the tyrant.'

'For sure,' he said.

'So come on, dear friend, tell me – what kind of thing does
tyranny turn out to be? That it comes about from democracy is
pretty clear.'

'It is.'

'And is the way in which tyranny comes from democracy in
one respect the same as the way democracy comes from oligarchy?'

'How so?'

'Think about what they put forward as the good', I said,   562b
'– what we said brought about the establishment of oligarchy.
That was wealth – right?'

'Yes.'

'And then, when their desire for wealth became insatiable,
and they neglected everything else, that was what we were saying brought oligarchy down.'

'True,' he said.

'Well, similarly, isn't what destroys democracy the insatiable
desire for what *it* defines as the good?'

'And what are you saying that is?'

'Freedom,' I said. 'I think you'll hear it said in a democratic
city that this is its prize possession, making it the only sort of   562c
city worth living in if you're by nature free.'

'Yes,' he said, 'it's something that's very often claimed.'

'So,' I said, 'to return to what I was going to say just now: is
it the insatiable desire for this sort of good, to the neglect of
everything else, that undermines this regime too, and prepares
the demand for tyranny?'

'How so?'

'I think, when a democratic city, thirsty for freedom, gets   562d
wine-pourers in charge that are no good, and drinks more than
it should of freedom unmixed, then unless the rulers are entirely
mild-tempered and offer it ever larger doses of what it wants, it
punishes them and accuses them of being disgusting oligarchs.'

'They do that,' he said.

'And what's more,' I said, 'they walk all over those who do as they're told by those in office, calling them volunteers for slavery, mere nobodies, and they give public as well as private approval and recognition to office-holders who behave like ordinary citizens and ordinary citizens who behave as if they were in office. How can a city like that avoid going all the way, and realizing complete freedom in everything?'

562e 'It can't.'

'No less surely, my friend,' I said, 'it seeps down, this anarchy, into individual households too, until finally it infects even the animals.'

'How are we claiming it does that?' he asked.

'We're saying, for example,' I replied, 'that a father gets into the habit of behaving like a child, and stands in fear of his sons;

563a sons become used to behaving like fathers, and feel no shame or fear before their parents – all in the name of freedom. Resident aliens are treated like citizens, citizens like aliens; and it's the same with foreigners who aren't resident.'

'Yes, that does happen,' he said.

'It does,' I said; 'and here are some other trifling things that happen in this sort of case. Teachers fear and fawn on their pupils, pupils despise their teachers and overseers[571] alike; in every context, the young behave like their elders, competing

563b with them in everything they say and do, while the old stoop to putting on shows of wit and playfulness and mimicking the young, for fear of being thought unattractive, or autocratic.'

'Quite so,' he said.

'But, my friend,' I said, 'freedom extends still further in this kind of city – to the point where even those who've been bought in the market-place, men or women, are no less free than those who bought them. And I almost forgot to mention how equal and free wives become in relation to husbands, and husbands to wives.'

563c 'So shall we get on and say, as Aeschylus has it, what "just now came to our lips"?'[572]

'Certainly,' I said. 'What I'm saying is this – that no one would believe, unless he saw it for himself, how much more freedom domestic animals have here than in other cities. Bitches literally *do* become just like their mistresses, as the saying has it; horses and donkeys are in the habit of parading the streets with total freedom and an air of importance, bumping into anyone they happen to meet if he doesn't get out of their way, and all the other animals become similarly puffed up with freedom.'

'Tell me something I don't know,' he said; 'it happens to me 563d all the time when I go out into the country.'

'And the net effect of all this,' I said, 'when it all comes together, is the sensitivity one readily observes in the souls of the citizens, which makes them angry and unable to put up with it if anyone tries to tie them down in the slightest respect. The final stage I think you'll recognize: a disregard for the very laws themselves, whether written or unwritten, to make quite sure nobody lords it over them, in any way at all.'   563e

'I recognize it all too well,' he said.

'So those, my friend, in my view,' I said, 'are the beginnings – so fine, so vibrant – from which I think tyranny is born.'

'Vibrant indeed,' he said. 'But what happens next?'

'The same sickness that took hold of oligarchy and destroyed it takes hold of democracy too, only in a more widespread and virulent form, because of this licence people have; and in the end it is completely in control. The fact is that whenever something is overdone it tends to produce a great shift in the opposite direction – in the seasons, in plants, in our bodies, and not least 564a in the case of political regimes.'

'That's likely enough,' he said.

'Certainly an excess of freedom seems always to give way to an excess of slavery, whether it's individuals we're talking about or cities.'

'Probably so.'

'Probably, then,' I said, 'it's from democracy, not from any other sort of regime, that tyranny develops – the most extended and savage form of slavery, I suppose, from freedom in its most developed form.'

'Very likely,' he said.

'But I don't think that was your question,' I said. 'What you

564b wanted to know was what kind of sickness it is that takes hold
of democracy as it does of oligarchy, and finally reduces it to
slavery.'

'That's right,' he said.

'Well,' I said, 'what I had in mind was that lazy, spendthrift
class of men, the most courageous among them in the lead, the
least manly following; we're comparing them to drones, some
of them with stings and some without.'

'And rightly so,' he said.

'These two types, then,' I said, 'cause trouble wherever they
564c arise, under any regime. They're like phlegm and bile[573] in the
body, which the good doctor – the lawgiver, in the case of the
city – needs to look out for well in advance, like any good bee-
keeper; the chief aim will be to prevent them from emerging at
all, but if they do emerge, then they'll need to be cut out, cells
and all,[574] as quickly as possible.'

'Zeus! Yes,' he said, 'that they must.'

'So to give us a better chance of seeing clearly what we're
after, let's proceed like this.'

'Like how?'

564d 'By dividing the democratically run city into three parts,
which is how it actually is. The first part, presumably, will consist of the kind of people we've just been talking about, which
because of the licence given to everybody will certainly grow
no less freely than in the oligarchic city.'

'That is so,' he said.

'But it is much more aggressive under a democracy than
under an oligarchy.'

'How so?'

'Under an oligarchy, because it is accorded no respect, and is
excluded from power, it cannot flex its muscles or gain any
strength; whereas under a democracy, barring a few exceptions, it is probably the dominant class. Its most aggressive
members do the talking, and the acting, while the rest of them
gather buzzing around the speaker's rostrum and won't put up
564e with any dissenting voice. And the result is that this sort of person governs everything, or almost everything.'

'Very much so,' he said.

'And then there's another class of people that is always distinguishable from the mass.'

'What is that?'

'Presumably, when everybody is trying to make money, it's those who are naturally the most orderly that generally acquire the most wealth.'

'Very likely.'

'That's where the most honey is for the drones, then, and where it's easiest for them to extract.'

'Yes,' he said; 'there's not much to be extracted from people who don't have it to start with.'

'With that kind of wealth, I imagine, the drones will call them their special feeding-ground.'

'Pretty much,' he said.

'And the third class will be the "people", comprising all 565a those who work for themselves, mind their own business and don't own very much; they're the most numerous, and the most powerful when they're gathered together in one place.'

'That's true,' he said, 'but they're not often willing to do that, unless they get a share of the honey.'

'And don't they always get it,' I asked, 'to the extent that the dominant group manage to combine taking wealth away from those who have it, and distributing it to the people, with keeping the largest share for themselves?'

'Yes,' he said, 'that's how this third class gets its share.' 565b

'And so those who are having their wealth taken away from them are presumably forced to defend themselves, by making speeches in the assembly and taking any action that is open to them.'

'Naturally.'

'And so now, even if they have no desire for revolution, the other side can charge them with plotting against the people and having oligarchic tendencies.'

'Of course.'

'So finally, when they see the people setting out to do them an injustice, not intentionally, simply out of ignorance, because they've been led astray by all the slanders, there comes a point 565c when they truly do become oligarchic types, whether they like it or not; it's not by choice, simply another part of the harm done by that drone-type, using his sting on them.'

'Exactly so.'

'So then both sides start launching impeachments, suits, court-cases.'

'Very much so.'

'And whenever that happens, don't the people tend to set up one individual as their champion, feeding him and lifting him up above them?'

'That is what they do.'

565d 'This much is clear, then,' I said: 'if ever a tyrant is born, at the root of it is this role of people's champion; nothing else.'

'Absolutely clear.'

'So how does this change begin, from popular champion to tyrant? Isn't it, obviously, when this "champion" starts acting like the character in the story about the sanctuary of Lycaean Zeus[575] in Arcadia?'

'Which story is that?' he asked.

'The one where a single piece of human innards gets chopped up among those from other sacrificial animals, and the person 565e who tastes that one piece – so the story goes – is turned by fatal necessity into a wolf. You've not heard the tale?'

'I have, yes.'

'And isn't it just like that with anyone who has become people's champion, who has found a compliant mob to follow him and for whom the blood of his own kind means nothing – who brings unjust charges, as people will,[576] goes to court and blithely commits murder, wiping out a man's life, defiling 566a tongue and mouth with a kinsman's blood? Banishing, killing, hinting at abolition of debts and redistribution of land? Isn't what inevitably comes next for such a person – his destiny – either that he dies at the hands of his enemies or that he rules as tyrant, his change from man to wolf complete?'

'It's quite inevitable,' he said.

'This', I said, 'will be the man who stirs up trouble against the possessors of wealth.'[577]

'He will.'

'And then, if he's forced into exile and returns despite the best efforts of his enemies, won't he come back the finished tyrant?'

'Clearly.'

'And if they're unable to throw him out again or have him executed by attacking him in the assembly, then they start plot- 566b ting a violent death for him by secret assassination.'

'That's certainly what tends to happen,' he said.

'Anyone who's reached this stage of the process then invents the plea you'll find on the lips of all tyrants in such a case – that the people need to provide a small bodyguard to keep the people's helper safe, for their own sake.'

'Absolutely,' he said.

'And they give it to him, I suppose, because they're fearful for him, and quite unworried about their own prospects.'

'Absolutely.'

'When he sees all this, the man who has money, and a repu- 566c tation as a people-hater as well as the money – well, at that point, my friend, in the words of the oracle given to Croesus, he "takes off to many-pebbled Hermus –/ Flees, and does not stay, nor fears the shame of cowardice." '[578]

'Right,' he said, 'because he won't be getting a second opportunity to fear it.'

'And presumably,' I said, 'if he's caught, death awaits.'

'Inevitably.'

'Meanwhile, that champion of the people clearly doesn't himself lie prostrate, a "great man greatly fallen",[579] but rather 566d kills off lots of others and stands tall in the city's chariot, now the completed product: no longer champion, but tyrant.'

'He's bound to,' he said.

'So,' I asked, 'shall we enumerate the blessings that accrue both to man and to city – any city where such a person comes about, mere mortal that he is?'

'By all means,' he said.

'In the early days and weeks', I said, 'he has a smile and a friendly greeting for anyone he meets. He denies he's a tyrant; 566e he makes lots of promises, privately and in public, annuls debts, distributes land to the people and to his own associates, and pretends to be gracious and gentle to everyone. Right?'

'Inevitably,' he said.

'But when he's neutralized his enemies in exile, coming to terms with some and destroying others, I imagine the first thing you'll notice about him is that he's always stirring up some war or other, to make sure the people need a leader.'

'Very likely so.'

567a 'And also to impoverish them, through having them contribute to the war-effort, so that they're forced to concentrate on their daily needs and are that much less likely to plot against him.'

'Clearly.'

'And again, he'll have a pretext for destroying anyone he suspects of free-thinking and resistance to his rule, by handing them over to the enemy. For all these reasons, mustn't a tyrant always be provoking a war?'

'He must.'

'And in doing so, mustn't he be ready for the citizens' hatred of him to grow?'

'Of course.'

567b 'Inevitably, even some of those who helped install him and are now in power with him will speak their minds, whether to him or to one another, criticizing what is happening – or at least that's what the really most courageous among them will do.'

'Probably.'

'So the tyrant will have to take all of these individuals out, if he is to rule, until he has no friend or enemy left who's of any use at all.'

'Clearly.'

'He needs a keen eye, then, to pick out the courageous, the 567c high-minded, the sensible and the wealthy; so blest with happiness is he that whether he likes it or not he must be the enemy of all of these, and actively plot against them, until he has quite purged the city clean.'

'And what a fine sort of purge it is,' he said.

'Yes,' I said; 'the opposite of the sort doctors give our bodies – they clean out the worst to leave the best, and the tyrant does the reverse.'

'As it seems he must,' he said, 'if he is to rule.'

'In which case he's bound by a happy necessity either to 567d
spend his life among people most of whom are worthless, and
being hated by them, or not to live at all.'

'That is his happy fate,' he said.

'And the more the citizens hate him for doing what he does,
won't he need a larger and more loyal bodyguard?'

'Of course.'

'So who will be loyal to him? Where will he summon up
such people from?'

'Lots will come flying to him of their own accord, so long as
he pays the right money.'

'By the Dog!' I exclaimed. 'I think you're talking about
drones again – foreign ones, from wherever it may be.' 567e

'You think right,' he said.

'What about domestic ones? Mightn't he perhaps propose
depriving the citizens of their slaves, freeing these and adding
them to the detachment round him?'

'Certainly,' he said; 'because I warrant you these will actually be the most loyal to him.'

'What a blessedly happy thing this tyranny business is,'
I said, 'if these are the men he relies on for friendship and 568a
loyalty, having destroyed their predecessors.'

'These are certainly the sort he relies on,' he said.

'And these friends of his even admire him; enjoying their
new status, they seek out his company, while decent citizens
hate and avoid him.'

'Naturally.'

'It's not for nothing', I said, 'that tragedy as a whole is
thought a wise thing, and Euripides its foremost exponent.'

'How so?'

'Because among all his utterances, deriving from deep
thought, he gave us this pearl: really, "tyrants are wise", he 568b
says, "by keeping wise men's company."[580] Clearly it's the
people we're talking about that he had in mind as "wise men".'

'And he also describes tyranny as "godlike",' said Adimantus, 'and calls it by lots of other flattering names – and it's not
just him; other poets do it too.'

'That's exactly why,' I said, 'given that wisdom of theirs, the tragic poets don't hold it against either us or those whose approach to government is close to ours, when we refuse to allow apologists of tyranny like them into our regimes.'[581]

568c 'They don't, I think,' he said; 'the smart ones among them, anyway.'

'But they travel around to other cities, I think, gathering the crowds and putting their lovely voices out to hire, loud and persuasive enough to draw the regimes in those cities towards tyranny and democracy.'

'Yes, indeed.'

'And on top of that don't they get paid and honoured for it, particularly by tyrants, as one would expect, but also by democracies? The higher they go up the ladder of regimes, the

568d fainter the respect they receive, like a climber failing to make headway from lack of breath.'

'Absolutely.'

'But we've digressed here. Let's get back to that splendid, numerous, multifarious and ever-changing private army of the tyrant: how will he support it?'

'Clearly,' he said, 'if there are temple treasuries in the city, he'll plunder those – and he'll make the general public con-

568e tribute less wherever there's sufficient money coming in from people who've sold up and moved out.'[582]

'And what about when these sources run dry?'

'Clearly he and his fellow-drinkers, and his male and female friends, will be supported from the patrimonial funds.'

'I see what you're saying,' I replied: 'that the people, who spawned the tyrant, will support him and his friends.'

'They'll have no alternative,' he said.

'What are you saying?' I asked. 'What if the people become upset, and say that it's contrary to justice for a grown-up son to be supported by his father? Rather, it should be the other way round, and the son should be supporting the father – and any-

569a way, they didn't bring him into the world and set him up so that as soon as he was big enough *they* should find themselves slaves to their own slaves, supporting him, and the slaves,[583] along with a miscellaneous collection of others. What they had in mind was their own freedom: liberation from the rule of the wealthy and the so-called fine and good, with him as their champion. And now they tell him to get out of the city with his friends, like a father driving his son out of the house along with a raucous rabble of drinking-partners. What then?'

'Zeus!' he exclaimed. 'That's the moment the people will 569b realize what they've done, and what kind of beast they were spawning when they opened their arms to him and encouraged him to grow. Too late they see it's a case of weaker trying to drive out stronger.'

'What's that?' I replied. 'Will the tyrant dare to raise his fists to his father, and beat him if he fails to do as he's told?'

'Yes,' he said, 'after he's removed his father's weapons.'

'Your tyrant is a parricide, then,' I said, 'and a cruel nurse for the old. This, it seems, will be an acknowledged tyranny, and the people will have exchanged the proverbial smoke for the fire – enslavement to free men for domination by slaves; 569c instead of that excessive and ill-judged freedom they had before, now they have trapped themselves in the cruellest and bitterest kind of slavery, slaves themselves to slaves.'

'That is very much what happens,' he said.

'Well then,' I said, 'won't it be fair to say that we've described well enough how tyranny evolves from democracy, and what it's like once it has come about?'

'Yes,' he said, 'our description is entirely sufficient.'

Book IX   'It remains for us to look at the tyrannical individual: 571a
begins   how he develops from the democrat, what he is like when
[Book F]   he's emerged and whether the life he lives is wretched or
blessedly happy.'

'Yes, there's still him,' he said.

'Do you know what I still miss?' I asked.

'What's that?'

'I don't think we've yet properly distinguished the number of types of desires there are.[584] If we don't fill this gap in our account, the outcome of the investigation we're conducting will be less clear than it might be.'

'It's not too late to do it now, surely,' he said.   571b

'No indeed. Here's the further point about desires I want us
to see. Among the unnecessary pleasures and desires there seem
to me to be some that are contrary to any sort of law. They
probably come about in anybody, and if they're kept down by
the laws and by the better desires, along with reason, in the
case of some people they can probably either be eliminated
571c   entirely or significantly reduced in number and strength; but in
some cases they remain stronger and more numerous.'

'Which are the desires you have in mind?' he asked.

'The ones that are aroused in the context of sleep,' I replied,
'when the rest of the soul – the rational, gentle element that
rules over the other – is dormant, allowing the beast-like and
savage element, fuelled by food or wine, to skip away, push
sleep aside and look to realizing its own true character. In such
a situation, cut loose from any sense of shame and without wis-
571d   dom around to bother it, you'll agree there's nothing it won't
do. Without a moment's hesitation it sets to copulating – so it
thinks – with mother, and anyone or anything else, human,
divine or animal; no murder is too foul for it, no flesh too horrible to eat – in short, it exhibits a perfect mindlessness and
lack of shame.'

'Very true,' he said.

'But I think it's a different matter when a person has a
healthy control over himself, and goes to sleep after arousing
the rational element in him, and feasting it on fine words and
571e   fine subjects for thought. This sort of individual has reached an
accommodation with himself, having neither starved nor sated
his appetitive element, so that it is lulled to sleep, and instead of
572a   causing trouble, with its pleasure or its pain, for the better
element in him, allows that better element to investigate purely
on its own, to reach out beyond itself and see what it does not
know, whether something past, present or future.[585] In the same
way he will also have calmed the spirited element in him, and
won't go to sleep after an angry quarrel with someone, passion
still blazing. So when he takes his rest he'll have quietened both
these two elements and roused the third, where thinking takes
place; and that way, you'll agree, not only will he be in the best

position to apprehend the truth, but the visions that appear to him in his dreams will be least likely to be lawless.'

'I think that's absolutely right,' he said.   572b

'Well, this has taken us a bit far away from our immediate subject, but what we need to appreciate is that in each of us, even in some who appear entirely decent people, there really is a fearsomely savage and lawless type of desires like this, as revealed by what happens in sleep. See if you think I'm talking sense, and you agree with me.'

'I do.'

'Now remember what we said the democratic individual   572c was like.[586] I think we said he grew up from an early age under the guidance of a thrifty father who only approved of the money-making desires, and devalued the unnecessary ones targeted at amusement and showing off. Right?'

'Yes.'

'But then he got together with more sophisticated people, full of the desires we've just been describing, and came to hate his father's parsimony, so launching himself in the direction of the total excess that distinguishes these new desires. But because he had a nature superior to that of his corruptors, he was still   572d drawn in the opposite direction too, finally settling down in the middle between their ways and his father's, and through what he saw as a decent combination of the advantages of both, managed to live a life that was neither unsuitable for a free man nor outside the law – so completing the transition from the oligarchic to the democratic type.'

'That was and is our view of this sort of person,' he said.

'So now imagine such a person grown old,' I said, 'and with a young son brought up, in his turn, in his father's ways.'

'Done.'

'And imagine the same things happening to the son as hap-   572e pened to his father. He is drawn to complete lawlessness, or complete freedom, as it is called by those who try to lead him on, and meanwhile his father and his other relatives support those middling desires of his just as his corruptors support the others. Finally, when these clever magicians and tyrant-makers

see no other way of capturing the young man, they contrive to
573a implant in him a special, ruling passion, champion of all those
idle, spendthrift desires of his: a special kind of drone, winged
and powerful.[587] Or do you have some better way of describing
the passion for such things?'

'No,' he said; 'that's the right description.'

'And when those other desires buzz around him, full of the
promise of incense and myrrh, and garlands and wine, and all
the wild pleasures of such partying, they bring the drone on
and nurture it to the limit, creating in it the sting of perpetual
573b yearning; and then it is that this new champion of the soul
acquires a bodyguard of madness and frenzy, so that if it
catches any beliefs or desires in the man with a reputation for
worthiness and still with a trace of shame in them, it kills them
off and pushes them out, until it has purged him of moderation
and filled him with an alien madness instead.'

'That quite describes the origin of the tyrannical individual,'
he said.

'And isn't this in fact the sort of reason why Eros has always
been called a tyrant?' I asked.

'Probably,' he replied.

573c   'A drunken man, too, my friend,' I said, 'has something of
the tyrant about him, doesn't he?'

'Yes, he does.'

'Again, the madman, the man who has lost his mind, asserts
himself over gods as well as men, thinking it's in his power to
control them.'

'Indeed so,' he said.

'The upshot is, my fine friend, that a man becomes tyrannical precisely when either through his nature or behaviour, or
both, he comes to combine the features of drunkenness, lust
and madness.'

'Absolutely.'

'That's how the man comes about, it seems, and what he's
like. So what kind of life does he lead?'

573d   'As people say when they're telling jokes,' he replied, 'I don't
know – you tell me!'

'I shall,' I said. 'I imagine the next thing is for someone like that to go in for feasting, carousing, revelling, whoring – all the sorts of activities one expects from people in the grip of a tyrannizing passion that governs everything in their soul.'

'Inevitably,' he said.

'And don't lots of terrible new desires sprout up alongside that governing passion, every day and night, each with its own numerous requirements?'

'Lots.'

'So any sources of revenue there may be are soon exhausted.'

'Naturally.'

'Next comes borrowing, and drawing on capital.'   573e

'Of course.'

'And when it all dries up, isn't there an inevitable outcry from the desires, vigorous as they are, and packed tightly together in the nest? Their owner is driven on as if by stings, especially from the master-passion itself, but with all the other desires following its lead like loyal bodyguards; and finally he is forced into a frenzied reckoning: who has something he can take from them, through deception or by open force?'   574a

'Very much so, yes,' he said.

'So then he must get what he needs from no matter where, or else be gripped by tearing pains and agonies.'

'He must.'

'Just as the new wave of pleasures flooded out the old, and took what was theirs, won't the embryo tyrant think it his right to usurp his father's and his mother's place, despite his young age, and take from them, helping himself freely to the family's wealth when he's already used up his share?'

'Surely,' he said.

'And if they don't let him do that, won't he begin by stealing   574b
from them – deceiving his own parents?'

'Absolutely.'

'But if he found he couldn't do that, the next step would be robbery with violence.'

'I imagine so,' he said.

'And if the old couple resisted him and fought back, what then, my fine friend? Would he be careful about not behaving like a tyrant to them?'

'I'm not too optimistic about his parents' prospects in that situation,' he said.

'Zeus! Adimantus, do you really think he'd prefer a new
574c mistress he doesn't need to the old mother he's always loved and couldn't ever have done without? Or the latest darling boy he doesn't need to the father he does, wrinkles and all, most ancient of all those he loves? Would he really rain blows on his mother and father? Make them the slaves of the newcomers, if he brought his new darlings under the family roof?'

'Zeus! Yes, he would!' he exclaimed.

'What a delightfully happy event it seems to be,' I said, 'to spawn a tyrannical son.'

'Delightful,' he said.

574d   'And what happens when this sort of person finds his father's and his mother's resources beginning to run out, and the pleasures now collected within him are swarming in numbers? Won't he begin by breaking into someone's house, or finding someone out late at night and grabbing his cloak; then graduate to stripping bare a sanctuary? In all of this, the beliefs he has had since childhood about what is fine and shameful, the ones that count as just, will be overpowered by others, newly released from slavery to act as agents and bodyguards of his ruling passion. Previously these were only let loose when he
574e was asleep, in dreams, in those days when there was still democratic rule in him, under the laws and his father, but now that he is tyrannized by passion, what he occasionally became in his dreams he now is, in every minute of his waking life. No mur-
575a der, no food, no action will be too horrible for him.[588] The tyrant-passion in him will live in perfect anarchy and lawlessness, being itself sole ruler, and will impel him, like a tyrant in a city, to any kind of outrage that will feed both itself and the clamouring mob around it – part of which has come in from outside, from his keeping bad company, and part is homegrown, given its head and set free because he has behaved in the same way himself. Isn't that the kind of life someone like this will live?'

'Indeed it is,' he said.

575b   'Now if there are only a few people like this in a city, and the majority of the citizens behaves with good sense, they emigrate and become bodyguards to some tyrant elsewhere, or sign up as mercenaries if there's a war on somewhere. But if they develop in a time of peace and tranquillity, then they stay on in the city and do all sorts of minor damage.'

'Like what?'

'Robbery, house-breaking, purse-snatching, clothes-stealing, temple-robbing, kidnapping, that sort of thing. Sometimes, if they're plausible speakers, they become professional informers, giving false evidence and taking bribes.'

'Minor stuff, yes,' he replied; 'so long as there are only a few of them.'

'Yes,' I said, 'because the minor is minor in relation to the 575c major; and none of these things comes within shouting distance, as they say, of the damage and misery involved in the case of tyranny. When there come to be a lot of people like this, along with their fellow-travellers, and they see how numerous they are, these are the ones who then go on – with the help of a mindless general population – to spawn that tyrant of ours, who will be whichever one of them stands out as having the biggest tyrant in him, with the greatest power over his soul.'

'That's likely enough,' he said; 'after all, he'll know more 575d about tyranny than anyone.'

'If people submit to him and don't resist, that's that, but if the city won't have any of it, then, if he can, he'll dole out the same punishment to the country that gave him birth as he did to his mother and father, bringing in new friends and repaying the "motherland", as the Cretans call it, the fatherland he once loved, by keeping it in slavery to them. That will be the goal of 575e such a man's desire.'

'Yes,' he said, 'just that; absolutely.'

'And I'll tell you how such people behave in private life even before they're in power. First of all, they'll not spend time with anyone unless he flatters them and is ready to do anything for them; or if they need something from someone, they'll degrade 576a themselves with fawning shows of friendship, then behave like strangers once they've got what they wanted.'

'Yes, very much so.'

'They live their whole lives, then, without ever being friends with anyone – always either lording it over someone or behaving as someone else's slave. Freedom and true friendship the tyrannical nature will never taste.'

'Absolutely.'

'And won't we be right in calling such people untrustworthy?'

'Of course.'

'And unjust too – as unjust as he could possibly be, if we were right in agreeing what we did before about the nature of justice.'[589]

'And we were right,' he said.

'So let's sum up the worst type of individual. I think he's the waking version of what we made the stuff of dreams.'

'Absolutely.'

'And this worst type emerges when someone highly tyrannical in nature acquires sole power; not only that, but the longer he lives as tyrant, the more like this he becomes.'

'Inevitably,' said Glaucon, taking over the argument.

'So is it the case', I asked, 'that whoever is shown to be worst will also be shown to be most miserable? And that whoever is the greatest tyrant, and for longest, is truly most miserable and for the longest time? Among ordinary folk, of course, there are as many views as there are of them.'

'That much', he said, 'is bound to be true.'

'So,' I asked, 'does the tyrannical individual compare in terms of likeness to the city ruled by a tyranny, the democratic individual to a democratically run city, and the other types likewise?'

'Surely.'

'As city is to city, then, in terms of its goodness and happiness, so too individual to individual?'

'Of course.'

'So how does a city under a tyranny compare in goodness to one under a kingship of the sort we described earlier?'

'It's the complete opposite,' he said; 'one is best, the other worst.'

'I shan't ask you which is which,' I replied, 'because it's obvious. But do you make the same judgement about their happiness and unhappiness, or a different one? And let's not be blinded by looking at the tyrant on his own, or him and a few individuals around him. We need to go into the whole city and look at 576e that, giving our view only when we've slipped in and observed it all together.'

'That's the right proposal,' he said. 'And anyone can see that there's no more miserable city than one ruled by a tyranny, and none happier than one ruled by kings.'

'So now would it be right for me', I asked, 'to make this same proposal in the case of the two individuals as well, 577a namely, that the only proper judge in these matters is the one who can think his way into an individual's character, and get a proper view of it from the inside – not looking at tyrannical types from the outside, and being dazzled like a child by the display they put on for an external audience, but so far as possible seeing through all that? What if I thought we should all listen to the person who not only has this capacity to judge, but has actually lived under the same roof as a tyrant, and witnessed both how he behaves at home, towards his family and friends, where he's most easily seen stripped of the costumes he 577b dons for his public performances, and how he responds to the perils of life out in the city – since our reporter will have seen all this, should we ask him to report to us how the tyrant compares to the other individuals we've described in terms of happiness and misery?'

'That's an absolutely right proposal too,' he said.

'So,' I said, 'should we now pretend that we'd be capable ourselves of forming a judgement, and that we've actually met tyrannical types like this, so that we can have someone to answer our questions?'[590]

'Certainly.'

'Then here's how I'd like you to approach the subject. Keeping in mind the resemblance between city and individual, go 577c through the features of each, looking first at one, then the other.'

'Which features do you have in mind?' he asked.

'First of all,' I said, 'as cities go, will you say that the one under a tyranny is free, or in a state of slavery?'

'In the most complete state of slavery possible,' he said.

'And yet you can make out masters in it, who are free.'

'Yes,' he said, 'I see a small element of that; but the whole that is contained in it, broadly speaking, and the most respectable elements, are reduced to a dishonouring and miserable slavery.'

577d 'If individual resembles city, then,' I said, 'mustn't the same state of affairs exist in him too? Mustn't his soul be groaning with wholesale enslavement and loss of freedom, the parts that used to be the most respectable now serving as slaves, and a small part, the worst and the maddest, now its master?'

'It must,' he said.

'So which would you say a soul in this kind of state was – enslaved, or free?'

'I'd certainly call it enslaved.'

'Again, doesn't a city enslaved under a tyranny least do what it wants to do?'

'Much the least.'

'In that case, the soul that's under a tyranny will similarly
577e least of all do what it wants to do, that is, if we're talking about the soul as a whole. Perpetually driven this way and that by the violent sting of desire, it will be full of confusion and remorse.'

'Surely.'

'And must the city run by a tyrant inevitably be rich, or poor?'

'Poor.'

578a 'Then a tyrannical soul, too, must always be needy and unsatisfied.'

'Just so,' he said.

'What about fear? Mustn't a city in this condition be full of it, and the corresponding individual likewise?'

'Inevitably.'

'Lamentation, groaning, wailing, anguish in general: do you think you'll find it in any city more than in this one?'

'Surely not.'

'And do you suppose there's more of this sort of thing in any individual than there is in our tyrannical one, driven mad as he is with desires and passions?'

'How could there be?'

'It was all these factors, I imagine, and others like them, that 578b caused you to adjudge[591] the city, at any rate, most miserable, among cities.'

'And wasn't I right?' he asked.

'You certainly were,' I replied. 'So what's your verdict on the tyrannical individual, in view of these same factors?'

'That he's more miserable, by a long way, than any other individual type,' he said.

'Here', I said, 'I'm afraid you're wrong.'

'Why so?' he asked.

'I don't think he is yet the most miserable.'

'So who is?'

'Well, here's someone I imagine you will count as more miserable.'

'Who is that?'

'Someone who conforms to the tyrannical type,' I said, 'and 578c doesn't live out the life of a private person, but is unfortunate enough to be provided, by some mischance, with the opportunity to become an actual tyrant.'

'From what we've said before,' he replied, 'I take it you must be right.'

'Yes,' I said, 'but it shouldn't be just a matter of what we think in such cases. We need to examine them very thoroughly, using the kind of argument I'm going to suggest. After all, what we're looking into is the greatest of all questions – how to live well or badly.'

'Quite right,' he said.

'So see if you think the following makes any sense. It seems 578d to me that our inquiry needs to start with a parallel case.'

'Which is?'

'Any and every private person in a city who is wealthy and

owns many slaves. They have this much in common with tyrants, that they rule over a large number of people, though the number in his case is larger than in theirs.'

'Indeed it is.'

'You recognize, don't you, that they aren't in any state of fear; they're not afraid of their slaves?'

'What is there for them to be afraid of?'

'Nothing,' I said, 'but do you see the reason?'

'Yes,' he said; 'it's because the whole city is there to back up every individual private citizen.'

578e   'A good answer,' I said. 'Imagine an isolated person who owns fifty or more slaves. What do you think his state of mind would be if one of the gods lifted him and his wife and children up out of the city, and set him down along with all his possessions, slaves included, in some remote spot where no free person would come running when he needed help? Just think how terrified he'd be of being slaughtered by the slaves – not just himself, but his children and his wife too.'

'Absolutely terrified, I should think,' he said.

579a   'At that point he'd be forced, wouldn't he, to start currying favour with some of the slaves, even, making them lots of promises, freeing them when they'd done nothing to deserve it – courting the very people who should be serving him?'

'He'd have to,' he said; 'it'd be either that or be killed.'

'What if the god also settled lots of neighbours all round him, who won't stand for anyone's claiming the right to treat others as slaves, and will inflict the severest penalties on anyone they catch doing it?'

'With nobody but enemies around him, and watching his
579b every movement, I imagine he'd be even more in trouble – every kind of trouble.'

'So the tyrant lives in a prison of his own making, does he not, brimming as he is with the many and various fears and passions we have described? Avid though he may be for seeing new things, he alone in the city is debarred from travelling anywhere, and from viewing the sights other free men want to see. More often than not he lives like a woman, hidden in the

recesses of his house, and envying other citizens if any of them 579c
should go abroad and see something good.'

'Absolutely,' he said.

'Aren't things like this a measure of the greater miseries
reaped by the tyrannical type – the one you just now judged
most miserable merely because of the poorness of the government within him – if he comes to live out his life no longer a
private citizen, but forced by some turn of fortune to become a
real tyrant, trying to rule others while not even being in control
of himself? It's like asking someone who is physically ill and 579d
not in control of his own body to spend his life competing in
the games or fighting instead of staying quietly at home.'

'Very true, Socrates,' he said; 'a very apt analogy.'

'Isn't this an absolutely miserable situation to be in, my dear
Glaucon?' I asked. 'Isn't the life lived by the actual tyrant truly
harsher even than that of the man whose life you judged
harshest?'

'Yes, surely,' he said.

'In truth, then, even though some deny it, the actual tyrant
stands revealed as actually a slave, of the most fawning kind, a 579e
toady to the very worst; as failing – to anyone who knows how
to observe a soul as a whole – even to begin satisfying his
desires; needier, then, than anyone, and truly poor; brimming
with fear throughout his life, full of convulsions and agony – if
there really is a resemblance between his state and that of the
city he rules, which there is. Right?'

'Very much so,' he said.

'And in addition to all this we need to give him all the 580a
features we talked about before. We said that inevitably, and
more and more with each passing day, his power will make him
envious, distrustful, unjust, friendless, impious, host and nurse
to every kind of badness, and for all these reasons bringing
misfortune, to himself most of all but to anyone near him as well.'

'No one with any sense will argue with you,' he said.

'So now imagine that you were judging in some sort of com- 580b
petition,' I said, 'and the final decision was down to you. Tell
me here and now who in your view comes first in the happiness

stakes, who second, and so on, among the five contenders: the kingly person, the timocratic, the oligarchic, the democratic and the tyrannical.'

'The decision is easy,' he said. 'In terms of their goodness and badness, and happiness and its opposite, I'll rank them like choruses on the stage.[592] My ranking follows the order in which they appeared.'

'So should we hire a herald,' I asked, 'or shall I make the announcement myself: "This is the verdict of the son of Ariston: the best and most just[593] individual is happiest, and he is the one who is most kingly and king over himself; the worst and most unjust is the most miserable, and *he*, in truth, is the most tyrannical, tyrant to the furthest degree possible over both himself and his city."'

580c

'Count the announcement as made,' he replied.

'And should I then add a rider,' I asked: "whether their respective conditions go undetected or not, by all men and all gods"?'[594]

'You should,' he said.

'Fine,' I said; 'so that's one demonstration we have in the bag. Here's a second one – see what you think of it.'

580d

'What's this new one?'

'The fact', I said, 'that the soul of every person is divided into three kinds, just like a city,[595] will I think give us another way of demonstrating our point.'

'What way?'

'It's this: there being a threesome in the soul, it appears to me there'll be three kinds of pleasures too, one peculiar to each of the threesome; and similarly there'll be three kinds of desires and of rule within the soul.'[596]

'How so?' he asked.

'There's one bit of the soul, we're claiming, with which a person learns, one with which he gets angry, and a third which took on so many forms that we had no name for it that would pick it out uniquely – so we named it after the most important and strongest element in it, labelling it "appetitive" because of the intensity of the desires or appetites concerned with food, drink, sex, and everything of that sort; and we also called it

580e

"money-loving" because money is the chief means of bringing   581a
such desires to completion.'

'And we were right,' he said.

'So if we said that what it took pleasure in and loved, too,
was profit, would that be indicative enough, as summing up
this part of the soul, to justify our calling it the "money-loving"
or "profit-loving" part?'

'It seems so to me,' he said.

'As for the spirited part, we're surely saying, aren't we, that
its whole impulse is always towards coming out on top, win-   581b
ning and gaining recognition?'

'Very much so.'

'So it will be appropriate to call it ambitious and honour-
loving?'

'Yes, indeed.'

'As for the part we learn with, it's obvious to anyone that *it*
is always wholly intent on knowing what the truth is, and is the
least interested of all three parts in money and reputation.'

'Much the least.'

'So it will be in order to designate it as loving learning, and
wisdom-loving – philosophical?'

'Of course.'

'And', I asked, 'are some souls ruled by this part, others by   581c
whichever of the other two it happens to be?'

'That's so,' he said.

'Which is why we say that there are three fundamental types
of people too: lovers of wisdom, lovers of winning and lovers
of profit?'

'Surely.'

'And three kinds of pleasure too, one underlying each?'

'Absolutely.'

'Well,' I said, 'I'm sure you'll recognize that if you tried asking representatives of each of these three types in turn which of
these lives is most pleasant, each of them will give the highest
praise to his own. The money-maker, for example, will claim   581d
that the pleasures of winning honours, or of learning, are
worthless in comparison with profit-making, if there's not some
sort of financial return from them.'

'True,' he said.

'And what about the honour-lover?' I asked. 'Doesn't he think of the pleasure that comes from money as somewhat vulgar, and of any pleasure taken from learning, if the learning brings no prestige, as insubstantial rubbish?'

'Quite so,' he said.

'And the lover of learning, the philosopher – what are we to suppose he makes of the other pleasures in comparison with 581e that of knowing what the truth is, and of being permanently in some such condition as that, as he learns? Won't he think them far behind his own pleasure, and label the others as literally "necessary", on the grounds that he would do without them altogether if there were no compulsion on him to have them?'

'We can be certain of that,' he said.

'So now', I asked, 'when the pleasures, and the whole lifestyle, of each of the three types of individual are subject to disputes like this, not only about which is the finer or more shameful, or worse or better, way to live, but about which is 582a simply more pleasant and more painless, how will we tell which of them is telling the most truth?'

'I've absolutely no idea,' he said.

'Try thinking what the requirements are for making good judgements about the future. We'll need experience, won't we, and wisdom, and argument – will there be any better means of judging than these?'

'Hardly,' he said.

'So think: of the three men we have before us, which is most experienced in all the pleasures we referred to? Does the profit-lover seem to you to have more experience of the pleasure that comes from knowing, by learning about the nature of truth 582b itself, than the philosopher has of the pleasure that comes from turning a profit?'

'There's a big difference,' he said. 'One of them can't avoid tasting the other sort of pleasures, from childhood on, whereas there's no necessity for the other type, the profit-lover, when he learns about the nature of things, to taste the sweetness of such learning, or become experienced in it – in fact, it's not easy for him even if he's keen.'

'The philosopher, then,' I said, 'is far ahead of the profit-lover when it comes to experience in the pleasures of both types.'

'Yes, far ahead.'

'And how does he compare with the honour-lover? Is he more inexperienced in the pleasure that comes from being honoured and respected than the honour-lover is in the pleasure that comes from wisdom?'

'No,' he replied. 'If any of the three accomplishes what he's set out to do, honour follows. The rich are honoured by many, as are the courageous and the wise. So the pleasure that comes from being honoured is one that all the different types have experience of, whereas it's impossible for anyone but the philosopher to have tasted the kind of pleasure that comes from the sight of things as they truly are.'[597]

'So far as experience goes, then,' I said, 'he's the one in the best position to judge.'

'Much the best.'

'And moreover, he's the only one whose experience will have been accompanied by wisdom.'

'Of course.'

'But again, when you think about the very tool that's needed for judging, that doesn't belong to the profit-lover, or the honour-lover; it belongs to the philosopher.'

'What tool is that?'

'I think we were saying that judgements should be reached by means of arguments. Right?'

'Yes.'

'And arguments are more the tool of the philosopher than of anyone else.'

'Of course.'

'Now if wealth and profit were the best means of deciding what had to be decided, wouldn't what the profit-lover said by way of praise or disparagement necessarily be truest?'

'It would have to be.'

'And if it were honour, and coming first, and courage, wouldn't pride of place go to the judgement of the honour-lover, the lover of winning?'

582c

582d

582e

'Clearly.'

'But now that the best means of deciding is through experience, wisdom and argument?'

'It must be the judgement of the philosopher, the lover of argument, that's truest,' he replied.

583a 'Of the three kinds of pleasure, then, it's the one that belongs to the learning part of the soul that will be most pleasant, and the most pleasant of the three kinds of life will be the life of the person in whom this part rules.'

'It must be so,' he said; 'the wise person is the one with the authority, at any rate, when it comes to praising one's own life.'

'And to which life, and which kind of pleasure, does the judge award second place?' I asked.

'To the pleasure of the military type, the honour-lover, since that's nearer to the philosopher than the pleasure the money-maker gets.'

'So last place, it seems, goes to the pleasure of the profit-lover.'

'Of course,' he replied.

583b 'So that's two calls, two throws in succession for the just person over the unjust; and for the third, Olympic-style, in honour of Zeus of Olympus and Saviour,[598] I want you to see that the pleasure of the others is not even wholly true, or pure, as the wise person's is; it's a kind of shadow-painting of pleasure, as I think I've heard some clever person say.[599] This, I'm telling you, would be the greatest and most decisive throw of all.'

'It would indeed. So what do you have in mind?'

583c 'I'll find out,' I said, 'if you answer my questions as I search.'

'Ask away,' he replied.

'So tell me,' I said: 'don't we say pain is opposite to pleasure?'

'Indeed we do.'

'And do we also say that there's such a thing as having neither pleasure nor pain?'

'We do.'

'Something in the middle between the two, a kind of resting of the soul in relation to both?'

'Just so,' he said.

'Do you recall the things sick people say, when they're ill?'

'Like what?'

' "There's really nothing more pleasant than being in good health," they say; "I just didn't notice how pleasant it was until I was ill!" '   583d

'I do recall.'

'And don't you also hear people saying, in the grips of some agonizing pain, that there's nothing more pleasant than having the pain stop?'

'I do.'

'And I think there are lots of other situations like this. When people are in pain, what they praise as most pleasant isn't enjoying themselves – it's just *not* being in pain, and the peace and rest such a state brings with it.'

'Yes,' he said, 'at the time that probably is pleasantly appealing.'

'Equally, then, when a person stops having pleasure,' I said, 'resting from the pleasure will be a painful thing.'   583e

'Probably,' he said.

'So what we were claiming just now to be in between both things, pleasure and pain, namely being at rest, will in some cases actually *be* both.'

'It seems so.'

'Is it really possible for something that is neither of them to turn into both of them?'

'I don't think so.'

'And actually, when pleasure occurs in the soul, and when pain does, they're both motions – right?'

'Yes.'

'But didn't we just find that what is neither pain nor pleasure is actually a matter of resting in between them?'   584a

'We did.'

'So how is it right to think not being in pain pleasant, and not enjoying pleasure painful?'

'It can't be.'

'It isn't like that, then,' I said; 'it merely appears so. To have peace and rest appears pleasant, at the time, in comparison with pain, and painful compared to pleasure; but there's nothing sound about any of these appearances in relation to true pleasure – they're like an illusionist's tricks.'

'That's what the argument indicates, certainly,' he said.

'So now', I said, 'you need to look at pleasures that don't 584b come from pains, in case the present turn in our argument starts you thinking that maybe this really is how things are, and pleasure is the cessation of pain, and pain the cessation of pleasure.'

'Where do I look?' he asked. 'Which pleasures do you have in mind?'

'Well,' I said, 'there are others we could talk about, but I'd like you to think especially about the pleasures surrounding smells. These can be amazingly powerful, and they occur suddenly, both without any preceding pain and without leaving any pain behind after them.'

'Very true,' he said.

'So we shouldn't persuade ourselves that pure pleasure is 584c release from pain, or pain release from pleasure.'

'No, we shouldn't.'

'But now take the so-called pleasures that extend through the body to the soul: pretty much the largest number and the greatest among these are somehow or other of this type, relief from pain.'

'They are.'

'And doesn't the same apply to the anticipatory pleasures and pains that precede them and occur because we're expecting them?'

'It does.'

584d   'So do you recognize what sort of thing they are,' I asked, 'and what they most resemble?'

'What's that?' he asked.

'Do you believe there's such a thing in nature as an up, a down and a middle?'

'I do.'

'Well, when someone is travelling from down to middle, he surely thinks he's travelling up – right? – and when he's standing in the middle, and seeing where he's travelled from, he'll imagine he's up, if he hasn't seen what's truly up?'

'Zeus!' he said. 'Under those circumstances I imagine he couldn't think anything else.'

'And actually,' I said, 'if he travelled back to where he'd come from, he'd think he was travelling down, and that would 584e be true.'

'Obviously.'

'And won't this all be because of his lack of experience in the true up, middle and down?'

'Clearly.'

'So will it come as any surprise to you if inexperience of the truth causes people to have unhealthy beliefs about lots of other things – in particular, if their relationship to pleasure and pain and what lies in between the two is such that, when they move towards what's painful, they get things right, because 585a they really are in pain, but when they move from pain to the middle state, they don't? They may strongly believe they're reaching fulfilment and pleasure, but actually they're being misled into comparing pain with absence of pain because they've no experience of pleasure. It's as if they had no experience of white, and started comparing black with grey instead.'

'Zeus! No surprise at all,' he replied. 'I'd be much more surprised if it wasn't like that.'

'Well, look at it this way,'[600] I said. 'Aren't hunger, thirst and things like that emptyings, as it were, of our bodily state?'   585b

'Surely.'

'And aren't ignorance and stupidity similarly an emptiness of our mental state?'

'Very much so.'

'And won't there be filling up in both cases – in the person getting nourishment, and in the person possessing good sense?'

'Of course.'

'Is the filling truer if it's with what is less whatever it is, or if it's with what is more?'[601]

'Clearly the latter.'

'So which do you suppose are the things that share in a purer

kind of being? Things like food, drink, food that's cooked, or
585c any sort of nourishment you like? Or the kind of things that
includes true belief, knowledge, intelligence, or indeed excellence of any sort? You need to decide which you think has more
to it: the kind of thing that's associated with what is always
alike, and immortal, and with truth, insofar as not only is it
like that itself but it comes about in the context of such things;
or the kind that's associated with what is never alike, and
merely mortal, both being a thing of that sort itself and coming
about in the context of things of that sort?'[602]

'What's associated with what is always alike wins hands
down,' he said.

'And does anything share more in being what is always alike
than knowledge does?'[603]

'Surely not.'

'Or share more in truth?'

'Not in truth either.'

'And if something shares less in truth, won't it also share less
in what is?'[604]

'It must do.'

585d   'So, to put the point generally, the kinds of things involved
in looking after the body have a smaller share in truth and
being than the corresponding kinds of things involved in looking after the soul?'

'Much smaller.'

'And don't you think the same holds of body itself as compared to soul?'

'I do.'

'So something that is filled with things which have a greater
share in what is, and has a similarly greater share itself, is more
truly filled than something that is filled with things which have
a lesser share, and itself has a lesser share?'

'Naturally.'

'In which case, if being filled with what belongs to our nature
585e   is pleasant, then what is more truly filled, with more substantial things, will more really and truly cause us pleasure, and a
pleasure that is true; whereas what shares in less substantial

things[605] will be less truly and reliably filled, and share a pleasure that is less trustworthy and less true.'

'That's quite inescapable,' he said.

'So it looks as if people who have no experience of wisdom 586a and excellence, and who are engaged the whole time with feasting and the like, travel down and then as far back again as the middle, wandering like that their whole lives through, and never rising further – never yet having looked up, to the true up, beyond the middle, let alone travelled there, or been really and truly filled with things of substance, or tasted a pleasure that is sure and pure. Instead they look permanently down, as if they were cattle, heads down to the ground – or rather the table – grazing away, alternately fattening themselves and copulating, kicking and butting each other with iron hooves and 586b horns to get more of the same, and finally doing one another to death, from frustration, because they're filling themselves with nothing substantial, they're not filling the substantial part of themselves, and they're not even filling the part of themselves that contains it.'

'That's quite an insight you have there, Socrates,' said Glaucon, 'into the lives of ordinary people – what a prophet you are!'

'And won't they inevitably be involved in pleasures mixed with pains, illusions of true pleasure, shadow-paintings that 586c take their colour from the juxtaposition of the two, pleasure and pain, so that both appear intense – engendering mad passions for themselves among the mindless, who then fight over them as Stesichorus says the heroes at Troy fought over the phantom of Helen, because they didn't know the truth?'[606]

'Inevitably, yes,' he said, 'it must be something like that.'

'What of the spirited element? Mustn't the same sort of thing inevitably occur when someone follows its projects?[607] When he's driven either by envy, because of his love of honour, or by compulsion, because he so loves to win, or by an anger born of a bad temper, and sets out to fill himself full of honour, victory 586d and spirit without reasoning or intelligence?'

'Yes, the same sort of thing must happen in this case too,' he said.

'So,' I said: 'may we confidently assert, in respect of those desires associated with these two elements in the soul, the one that loves profit and the one that loves winning, that some of them,[608] if they follow knowledge and reason, if they pursue their pleasures in the company of these, and if they then take those to which wisdom leads them, will be achieving the truest

586e pleasures, or the truest possible for them, because they are following truth, and also the pleasures proper to them, if what is most proper to each thing is what is best for it?'

'Which it certainly is,' he said.

'If the whole soul follows its wisdom-loving, philosophical part, then, and is free from internal faction, the result is that each part is just, performing its proper role in all respects, and

587a capping it all by reaping the pleasures that belong to it, the best it has, the truest of which it is capable.'

'Exactly so.'

'But when one of the other parts gains control, the result is that it not only fails to discover its own pleasure, but forces the others to pursue a pleasure alien to them, and untrue.'

'Right,' he said.

'Wouldn't the elements standing furthest from philosophy and reason be the ones that would be most responsible for that?'

'Much the most.'

'And won't what stands furthest from reason be what is furthest removed from law and due order?'

'Clearly so.'

587b   'Wasn't it the passionate, tyrannical desires that we found clearly fitting this description?'

'Yes, they much more than the others.'

'And least removed from reason were the orderly desires of the king.'[609]

'Yes.'

'So it's the tyrant, I think, who will stand at the furthest remove from true pleasure, and from his own;[610] the king will be closest.'

'That follows.'

'The tyrant's life will also be the least pleasant, then,' I said, 'and the king's the most pleasant.'

'That absolutely follows.'

'So do you know', I asked, 'just how much less pleasant the tyrant's life is?'

'I'll know if you tell me.'

'There being three kinds of pleasure, one genuine and two counterfeits, it seems the tyrant has gone beyond even the counterfeits – setting himself outside law and reason altogether, 587c with only slave-like pleasures left to guard him and keep him company. Just how much worse off this makes him, it's not at all easy to say, but we might try it this way.'

'Which way is that?'

'I believe the tyrant was at the third remove[611] from the oligarchic type, the democrat coming in between them.'

'Yes, he was.'

'And if what we said before is true, won't the pleasure he lives with, illusion that it is in relation to true pleasure, be similarly at three removes from the oligarch's own illusory pleasure?'

'Just so.'

'But the oligarchic type is again at third remove from the kingly, if we merge aristocratic[612] and kingly into one.' 587d

'Third it is.'

'Measured numerically, then,' I said, 'the distance of the tyrant from true pleasure is three times three.'

'Apparently.'

'Then,' I said, 'the illusion that is tyrannical pleasure, measured spatially, will be a square.'[613]

'It certainly will.'

'And if you cube that square, it becomes clear just how far removed the tyrant is.'

'Yes,' he said, 'if you're a mathematician.'[614]

'So to put it the other way round, if you try to state the distance separating the king from the tyrant in terms of the truth 587e of his pleasure, when you've finished the calculation you'll find the king's life is seven hundred and twenty-nine times more pleasant than the life of the tyrant.'

'An unbelievable torrent of calculation!' he exclaimed. 'So *that*'s the difference between the two men, the just and the 588a unjust, in relation to pleasure and pain.'

'And what's more, the number it gives is a true one,' I said, 'that fits a life – if days and nights and months and years do.'[615]

'And they certainly do,' he said.

'And if that's the margin of the good and just person's victory over the bad and unjust one in terms of pleasure, when it comes to decency of life, beauty and goodness, won't the margin of victory be quite unbelievably greater?'

'Zeus, yes! Unbelievably greater,' he said.

588b 'Very good,' I said. 'Now that we've reached this point in the argument, let's go back to the claim that has brought us here – the original one. I think the claim was that it pays for a person to act unjustly, if he's perfectly unjust but has a reputation for justice. That was the claim, wasn't it?'

'It was,' he said.

'So now let's talk it through, given that we've agreed about acting unjustly and acting justly, and what effect each has on us.'

'How shall we proceed?' he asked.

'By moulding a verbal image of the soul, so that the person who is making the claim in question knows just what he's doing.'

588c 'What sort of image?' he asked.

'It'll be one that resembles the sorts of creatures talked about in the old stories, like the Chimaera, or Scylla, or Cerberus – and there are lots more cases, where different life-forms are supposed to have grown together and become one.'

'Yes, that's the story,' he said.

'So for the first of your life-forms, start by moulding a complex and many-headed beast, with a ring of heads both from tame beasts and from wild ones, all of which bits it can change or sprout at will.'

'It'll be a clever craftsman who can do that,' he said. 'Still,
588d words are easier to mould than wax and things like that, so count it done.'

'Next mould me another single life-form – a lion, and then a third: a human being. Of the three, the first should be by far the largest, the second the second largest.'

'These are easier,' he said. 'They're done.'

'Now join the three of them into one, keeping them separate but so that they've grown together somehow.'

'Done.'

And then all round the outside of them mould me the image of one of the three, the human being, so that to anyone who 588e can't see what's inside, and only sees the outside cover, it all looks like a single creature – a human being.'

'Done.'

'So if our man claims that it pays this human being to act unjustly, and that it's not in his interests to do what is just, we'll say this amounts to claiming that it actually pays him to feast the complex beast in him and make it strong, along with the lion and everything the lion brings with it, while starving and 589a weakening his inner human being – so that the human being is dragged along in whichever direction either of the others may take it, and does nothing to get them used to each other, and make them friends, but simply leaves them to bite and fight amongst themselves and devour one another.'

'That's exactly what the person praising injustice will be saying,' he replied.

'Whereas the person who claims that it pays to act justly will be saying that what needs to be done and said will be determined by what renders the inner human being most in control, 589b so that it looks after the many-headed creature like a farmer, feeding and nursing the domesticated bits and stopping the wild ones from sprouting, and makes an early alliance with the lion and his kind – in short, so that it nurtures both the others, publicly taking charge of their care and making them friends with each other and with itself?'

'That's surely what the person praising justice is saying, too.'

'From every point of view, then, the one singing the praises of just behaviour will be saying what is true and the one prais- 589c ing injustice will be saying what is false. In relation to pleasure, in relation to reputation, and in relation to the benefit justice brings – in all these respects its supporter is a truth-sayer, while its opponent not only says nothing sound but lacks all knowledge of what he's opposing.'

'It seems to me he has no knowledge of it at all,' he said.

'Well, let's try some gentle persuasion on him; he's not getting it wrong because he wants to. Let's say to him: "Splendid!" and ask: "But won't we want to say that even the things that are conventionally counted fine and shameful are so for the same sort of reason – fine things being those that put the animal-like aspects of our nature under the human – or maybe it's the divine? – in us, shameful those that put the tame at the mercy of the savage?" How will he respond? Will he agree?'

'He will if he listens to me,' he said.

'By this reckoning, then,' I asked, 'who can it conceivably profit to take money unjustly, given that by doing so a person is in effect enslaving the best part of himself to the worst? It wouldn't pay him to take it, however much it was, if it meant his son or daughter being enslaved – and to a band of malignant savages at that; so if he mercilessly subjects the most divine aspect of himself to the most godless and vicious, isn't misery the only result? Isn't his money-taking more horrible, more destructive than Eriphyle's? No gold necklace for him, in exchange for a husband's life and soul,[616] but gold for the ruin of his own soul.'

'Much more horrible,' said Glaucon; 'I'll answer you on his behalf.'

'And don't you think this is the sort of reason why lack of restraint has always been condemned, namely, that it allows that fearsome creature, the great multiform beast, more freedom than it ought to have?'

'Clearly,' he said.

'And aren't people condemned for obstinacy and bad temper when the lion-like, or snake-like, element in them increases disproportionately in size and intensity?'

'Absolutely.'

'And for luxury and softness when loosening and slackening in this same element make it cowardly?'

'Surely.'

'Toadying and illiberality: that's what you get when someone makes this element, the spirited one, subject to the mob-like beast, and accustoms it to being trampled over, from childhood

589d

589e

590a

590b

on, for the sake of the money needed for the insatiable beast, making the lion into a monkey?'

'Yes indeed,' he said.

'And why do you suppose demeaning, manual occupations 590c attract reproach? Won't we claim that it's because they indicate that the best element in a person is too weak for him to be able to rule over the animal natures in him, only to serve them, and too weak for him to be capable of learning anything except how to fit in with them?'

'Very likely,' he said.

'So if someone like this is to be ruled over in a manner similar to that in which the best person is ruled, we declare that he must be a slave to that same best person, who has the divine element 590d ruling within himself; and we say this not with the purpose that he be harmed by such slavery, which was Thrasymachus' view of being ruled,[617] but because we suppose it better for everyone to be under divine and wise rule. It will be best if he has that divinity and wisdom within him, but failing that it will need to be set over him from outside, so that all may so far as possible resemble each other and enjoy mutual friendship, insofar as they are all ruled by the same thing.'

'Yes, and rightly so,' he said.

'And it's clear that the law has this same purpose in view,' I 590e said, 'insofar as it is the ally of everyone in the city without distinction; as does the way we control our children, by not allowing them their freedom until we've established a kind of regime within them, as in a city, using the best element in us to 591a foster their best element, so that when we've set up a guard and ruler in them similar to our own we can then safely set them free.'

'Yes, that's clear enough,' he said.

'So how on earth can we say, Glaucon, and by what argument can we justify saying, that it pays anyone to act unjustly, or behave without restraint, or do anything shameful, if the result is to make him a worse person,[618] only with more money or some extra bit of power?'

'There's no way we can,' he said.

'And how can we say it pays to act unjustly and not be
591b   detected and punished? Won't escaping detection mean that a
person gets even worse? Whereas if he is detected, and punished, the beast-like element in him is calmed and tamed, the
tame element freed, and the whole soul restored to its nature at
its best, as it acquires moderation and justice, together with
wisdom – so attaining a condition more valuable than strength
and beauty, and health, in a body; more valuable, that is, by the
same degree that soul is more valuable than body.'

'Absolutely,' he said.

591c   'So won't the intelligent person live with all his resources
focused on this? Won't he first of all value the sorts of learning
that will put his soul in this condition,[619] and dismiss any other
sort?'

'Clearly,' he said.

'And next,' I said, 'so far as concerns the condition and nurture of the body, not only will he not turn that over to beast-like
and unreasoning pleasure, and direct his life accordingly, but
he won't live with an eye on health, either, or make it his priority to be strong, or healthy, or beautiful, unless it helps to make
591d   him a more moderate person as well. He'll always be seen fine-
tuning his body for the sake of a finely tuned soul.'

'He certainly will,' replied Glaucon, 'if he's going to be a
true musician.'

'And won't he bring the same order and harmony to the
acquisition of money? He won't be thrown off track, will he,
by ordinary people's ideas about happiness, and go on end-
lessly piling more and more on his heap – trouble as well as
money?'

'I think not,' he said.

591e   'No,' I replied; 'his basis for running things, when it comes
to adding to or spending his resources, will be so far as possible
to keep his eye on the regime within him, and guard against
disturbing any of the elements in it by having either too many
resources or too few.'

'Of course,' he said.

592a   'And he'll use the same criterion in relation to honours. With
some of them, he'll willingly accept his share, or try them, if he

thinks they'll make him a better person; others, if he thinks
they'll upset the disposition of things within him, he'll run
away from, whether it's a matter of private or public life.'

'He won't want to go into politics, then,' he said, 'if his pri-
orities are as you say.'

'By the Dog!' I exclaimed. 'He certainly will, in the city that
belongs to him,[620] though probably not in the place he was
born, unless by some divine piece of good fortune the two coincide.'

'I understand,' he said; 'you're saying he would go into politics, in the city we've described and founded – one that exists
in words, only, since I don't imagine it's to be found anywhere
on earth.'

'No,' I said, 'but perhaps it is set up as a paradigm in the   592b
heavens,[621] for anyone who wishes to see it, and found himself[622]
accordingly. But it makes no difference whether it actually exists
anywhere or will exist; only in this city's affairs will he take a
part, and no other's.'

'Very likely,' he said.

Book X   'Now there are many reasons I have in mind', I said, 'why   595a
begins   our city was founded in absolutely the right way, but not
the least of those reasons is the way we treated *poetry*.'

'In what respect?' he asked.

'In that we refused in any way to admit poetry that works
through imitation.[623] The absolute necessity of barring it is
even more apparent, it seems to me, now that the different   595b
kinds that belong to the soul have been distinguished from each
other.'[624]

'How so?'

'Well, to be frank with you all – because you won't go off to
the poets of tragedy, and all those other imitation-producing
types, and inform on me – everything like that seems to corrode
the minds of the audience, or those of them who aren't pro-
tected by knowing the truth about the things they're hearing.'

'What do you have in mind?' he asked.

'I have to come clean,' I replied. 'And yet I'm held back by a

595c love and respect I've had for Homer since boyhood. It seems he was the first to teach all these beautiful things tragedy offers us – he started it all. But it's respect for the truth and not for a man that should come first, so as I say, I have to come clean.'

'You certainly do,' he said.

'So listen up – or rather, answer me a question.'

'Ask away.'

'Can you tell me what the production of imitations is, in general? I ask because I'm not entirely clear in my own mind what it thinks it is.'

'As if I'm going to be clear about it', he said, 'if you aren't!'

'There'd be nothing strange in that,' I said. 'People who
596a don't see so well often see things before the sharper-sighted.'

'That's so,' he said; 'but if anything does occur to me, with you here I certainly won't be rushing to say so. You do the looking!'

'Well, should we start our inquiry where we usually start? What we usually do, I think, is to posit each form as a single item, relating in each case to a plurality of things to which we attach the same name as we do to the form.[625] Do you follow me?'

'I do, yes.'

'So let's do it now, with any plurality you want. Take couches,[626] if you like, or tables – I imagine there are many of both of these.'

'Obviously.'

596b 'But as for forms, in relation to these products,[627] I take it there are just two, one of couch and one of table.'

'Yes.'

'And aren't we also used to saying that it's by looking to the relevant form that the craftsman of either product makes what he makes, namely the couches or the tables we actually use, and similarly in other cases? I take it none of the craftsmen crafts the form itself.'

'How could they?'

'They couldn't. But there's another kind of craftsman too – see what name you're going to give to him.'

596c 'What kind of craftsman is that?'

'One who makes everything each individual craftworker makes.'

'What an amazingly clever man he is!'

'Wait – he's even cleverer than that. This very same crafts-man, with his own hands, isn't just able to make manufactured items. Everything that grows from the earth, he makes; every living creature he fashions, including even himself. And on top of all that he does earth, heaven, gods, the things in the heavens, things in Hades under the earth – he fashions it all.'

'What know-how!' he said. 'Utterly amazing!'   596d

'You don't believe me?' I asked. 'Tell me, do you deny that such a craftsman could exist at all, or do you think there could be someone who made all these things, in a way, but in another way not? Can't you see you could make them all yourself, in a certain way?'

'What way is that?'

'It's not difficult,' I said; 'in fact there are many forms of this sort of making, all of them quick. The quickest way is probably for you to carry a mirror around with you everywhere – in a   596e flash you'll make the sun and all the things in the heavens, you'll make the earth, you'll make yourself and other living creatures, manufactured things, plants; everything we were just talking about.'

'Yes,' he said, 'as they appear to be; not, I take it, as they truly are.'

'Good,' I said. 'You're getting the point that matters. Crafts-men of this sort, I think, will include the painter – right?'

'Of course.'

'But I think you'll claim that the things he makes are not true.[628] Still, in a certain way the painter too does make a couch, doesn't he?'

'Yes', he replied, '– but again, what he's making is something as it appears to be.'

'What about the couch-manufacturer? Weren't you just say-   597a ing that he doesn't make the form we identify as "what a couch is";[629] he just makes a couch?'

'That is what I said.'

'If he isn't making what a couch is, then he won't be making the real thing, will he – just something that is like the real thing, without actually being it? If someone claimed that the product of the couch-manufacturer, or of any other craftsman, was something that *is*, perfectly,[630] he'd probably not be telling the truth.'

'No,' he said; 'at any rate, that's the way people familiar with this sort of discussion[631] will think.'

'Let's not be at all surprised, then, if even the craftsman's couch really is a bit ill-defined by comparison with the true couch.'

597b '‘Let's not.'

'So,' I asked, 'do you want us to use all this to find the type we're looking for,[632] the producer of imitations?'

'If you want,' he replied.

'These couches of ours, then – there turn out to be three of them, don't there, in a way? First, there's the one that's there in nature, which I imagine we'll say was fashioned by god – who else?'[633]

'Nobody.'

'Then there's the one fashioned by the carpenter.'

'Yes,' he said.

'And then the one fashioned by the painter. Right?'

'Let's take it to be so.'

'So we have painter, couch-manufacturer, god: three makers overseeing three kinds of couches.'

'Three, yes.'

597c '‘Now as for the god, whether out of choice, or because there was some constraint on him not to fashion more than one "couch in nature", in any case he made just that one – the couch itself, what a couch *is*; two or more couches like that were not planted by the god nor will they ever spring up.'

'Why so?' he asked.

'Because if he made two,' I replied, 'each by itself, once more a single one would appear whose character *they* would possess, in their turn; and it, not they, would then be what a couch is.'

'Correct,' he said.

'The god knew this, I think, and because he wanted to be the

true maker of the *truly* true couch, not just of some couch or   597d
other, as if he were any old couch-manufacturer, he engendered
it with uniqueness as part of its nature.'

'Very likely.'

'So do you want us to call him its plantsman,[634] or something like that?'

'That seems to fit,' he said, 'given that it's through nature
that he has made both this and everything else he has made.'

'What about the carpenter? Won't we call him a craftsman
of couches?'

'We will.'

'And the painter – will we call him a craftsman and maker of
the same sort of thing?'

'Certainly not.'

'So how will you describe his relationship to a couch?'

'It seems to me most reasonable to designate him a producer   597e
of imitations of the thing the others are craftsmen of.'

'Very good,' I said; 'so it's the one whose offspring is two
removes from nature that you'll call a producer of imitations.'

'Yes, absolutely,' he replied.

'Then that's what the maker of tragedies will be too, if he's
someone producing imitations – at two removes or so[635] from
the king and from the truth, by his very nature, along with all
other such producers.'

'Very probably.'

'So we're agreed about what it is to produce imitations. But   598a
now answer me this about the painter: do you think he tries to
imitate that very thing itself, in each case, as it is in nature, or
the products of the craftsmen?'

'The products of the craftsmen,'[636] he said.

'Make this more precise – as they are, or as they appear?'

'What's your point?' he asked.

'This: if you look at a couch from the side, or from the front,
or from wherever you like, is it any different in itself? Or does
it merely *appear* to vary, while actually being no different at all;
and similarly with everything else?'

'The latter,' he said. 'It appears different, but isn't.'

'So here's the point – how is painting done in each case: with   598b a view to imitating what a thing is, as it is, or to imitating what appears, as it appears? Is the product of its imitation appearance, or truth?'

'Appearance,' he said.

'So imitation-producing turns out to be a pretty long way away from the truth; and the reason, it seems, why it can fashion everything is because it gets only a small hold on anything, and an illusory one at that. Thus our painter, for example, will paint a shoemaker, a carpenter or any other craftsman without knowing anything about any of these crafts; yet all the same, if he was a good painter he'd be able to paint a carpenter and fool children and people with no sense into thinking it was a real one, if he showed it to them from suitably far away.'

'Of course.'

'In any case, my friend, our attitude in all such matters should be this: if someone ever reports to us that he's encountered a man who's an expert in all the crafts, and in every other kind of specialist knowledge, and that there's nothing he doesn't know more exactly than anyone, we need to think of him as a simple-minded sort of person, who has apparently encountered some kind of sorcerer or producer of imitations and been fooled into supposing him the smartest person around, because of his own inability to test for knowledge and its absence, and the imitation of it.'

'Very true,' he said.

'So then,' I said, 'our next task must be to examine the tragedians, mustn't it, along with their leader, Homer? Because we hear it said by some that they actually do know everything, not just the arts and crafts, but all things human, as these relate to goodness and badness, and even things divine; for they say that any good poet, if he's going to compose well on the subjects he's composing about, must actually know about them, or not be able to compose at all. So what we need to look at is whether it's imitation-producers of the sort in question they've encountered, and been fooled by – whether they've seen their products and simply failed to grasp that they're twice removed from the real thing, and quite easily put together by anyone who doesn't know the truth, just because they're producing appearances and not the real things; or whether there is actually something in the claim, and good poets really do know about the things ordinary people suppose them to get right.'

'We must certainly put that to the test,' he said.

'Well, if someone could make both things – both what was going to be imitated and the illusion of it – do you think he'd seriously give himself over to the crafting of illusions, and make that govern his own life, as the best thing he had going for   599b him?'

'I certainly don't.'

'If he were really and truly knowledgeable about the things he is imitating, I imagine he would much sooner busy himself with doing rather than imitating. He'd try to leave behind him lots of fine works of his own, for people to remember him by, and be keener to be the object of encomia than to be the one giving them.'

'I think so,' he said. 'In terms of honour and benefits received, there's no comparison.'

'Well, on some subjects we needn't bother challenging Homer, or any other poet. We don't need to ask if any of them   599c actually knew anything about medicine, rather than just being good at imitating the things doctors say. We don't need to ask what patients any poet, old or new, is ever said to have made healthy, in the way Asclepius is, or what students of the medical art any of them left behind them, as Asclepius did in his successors. And we'll not ask them about other kinds of expertise either; those we'll leave aside. But when it comes to the finest and most important subjects Homer attempts to talk about, like wars, or generalship, the government of cities, or   599d how to educate a person, then it is surely in order to question him. "Homer, dear friend," we'll say to him, "if you're really not two removes from the truth on the subject of goodness, and you're really not a craftsman of illusion, which is how we've defined producers of imitations – if that's not what you are, and you're really just once removed from the truth, so that you'd be able to recognize the sorts of things people do that will make them better or worse people, whether in private or in public life, do please tell us which city was governed better

because of you. Lycurgus improved Sparta, and many others
599e have improved their cities, great and small; what about you?
Which city credits you for having been a good lawgiver and
brought it benefits? Italy and Sicily have Charondas, we have
our Solon; which city has you?" Will he be able to name one?'

'I don't think so,' said Glaucon; 'at any rate, none is talked
about even by the Homeridae themselves.'[637]

600a   'Well, is any war in Homer's time remembered for being well
conducted through his leadership or advice?'

'No.'

'What about the many ingenious ideas wise men are said to
have – new ways of doing things in technical and other practical spheres, of the sort we associate with Thales the Milesian,
or the Scythian Anacharsis?'

'Nothing whatever of that sort.'

'Well, if he contributed nothing to public life, maybe he
made up for it in private? Perhaps there are reports of Homer
himself having been a leader in education during his lifetime,
whose disciples so loved to be with him that they then passed
600b on a peculiarly Homeric way of life to later generations – in the
same way that Pythagoras was loved by *his* disciples, and their
successors even now stand out among their contemporaries for
what they call a "Pythagorean" mode of living?'

'Nothing of that sort is reported either,' he said. 'In fact,
Socrates, Homer's associate Creophylus would look an even
more comic example of education than his name suggests,[638]
600c if the stories about Homer are true, since it's said that
Creophylus singularly neglected him while he was alive.'

'That's certainly the story,' I replied. 'But, Glaucon, if Homer
had really been able to educate people and bring improvement
to them – if he had the capacity not just to imitate in this sphere
but to *know* – don't you think that lots of people would have
joined his group, and that he'd be honoured and loved by
them? Protagoras of Abdera, Prodicus of Ceos,[639] and a whole
600d host of others manage to talk privately to their contemporaries
and impress on them that they won't be able to run either a
household or a city unless they put *them* in control of their education; their disciples love them so passionately for this wisdom

of theirs that they practically carry them around on their shoulders. Are we really to suppose, if he had a genuine ability to help people towards goodness, that Homer's contemporaries would have allowed him, or Hesiod for that matter, to travel round performing their poetry, and wouldn't have clasped them closer to themselves than they would their gold? Wouldn't they have forced them to stay at home with them, or, if that 600e didn't work, chaperoned them on their travels until they'd had enough of an education from them?'

'I think that's absolutely true, Socrates,' he said.

'So is our position to be that all those who go in for poetry, starting from Homer, are imitators who produce mere illusions of goodness and the other subjects they make their poems about, and have no hold on the truth – just as we were saying the painter who has no knowledge of shoemaking will make 601a something other people think *is* a shoemaker, so long as they have no knowledge of shoemaking either, and simply go by the colours and shapes?'[640]

'Absolutely.'

'The poetic type of maker, I think we'll say, similarly colours in the various kinds of expertise, as it were, through his words and phrases, not knowing anything himself except how to produce imitations good enough to make him seem to others like him, who go just by the words, to be saying all the right things, whether he happens to be talking – in metre, with rhythm, and suitable arrangements of musical notes – about shoemaking, or generalship, or anything else. Such is the power of enchant- 601b ment these products of theirs naturally have. Yet when they're stripped of their musical colouring, and spoken just on their own, well, I think you know the sorts of things the poets produce. I'm sure you've seen them.'[641]

'Indeed I have.'

'Isn't it a bit like seeing the faces of the young but not beautiful when they've lost even that youthful bloom?' I asked.

'Absolutely,' he replied.

'Now consider this point: this producer of illusions, we're saying, the imitation-maker, knows nothing of the real thing, 601c only of appearances. Right?'

'Yes.'

'Well, let's not leave things only half said; let's look at them properly.'

'Go on,' he said.

'The painter, we're saying, will *paint* a horse's reins, and the bit in its mouth.'

'Yes.'

'Whereas *making* them belongs to the leather-worker and the metal-worker?'

'Quite.'

'So does the artist know what sorts of things reins or bits need to be? Does even the maker – the leather- or metal-worker – know? The only person who knows, surely, is the one who knows how to use them – the horse-expert.'

'Very true.'

'And won't we say the same thing holds true in every case?'[642]

'How?'

601d   'For every object, we'll say, there are probably these three kinds of expertise: one in using it, one in making it and one in producing imitations of it.'

'There are.'

'And isn't the measure of the excellence, beauty and correctness of any manufactured item, any living creature, any activity none other than the use for which each is made or born?'[643]

'Quite so.'

'So there's no escaping the fact that it's the user who has the most familiarity with any object; he's the one who can tell the maker how well or how badly the thing he's using performs in 601e   use. For example, the pipe-player presumably reports back to the maker which pipes do what he wants them to do, and will tell him which ones he should make; the maker will then do as he's told.'

'Obviously.'

'Then one of them knows which ones are good and which bad and says so; the other will trust him and make his pipes accordingly.'

'Yes.'

'In respect of one and the same object, then, the maker will have a correct conviction about its beauty or its badness, from being with the person who knows, and being compelled to 602a hear from the person who knows; the user will have knowledge.'

'Absolutely.'

'What about our producer of imitations: will he have the user's knowledge about the beauty and correctness or otherwise of whatever things he may be painting, or will he have correct belief through being compelled to be with someone who knows, and told what sorts of thing to paint?'

'He'll have neither.'

'Then the imitation-producer won't either know, or have correct beliefs about, how whatever it is he's imitating stands in relation to beauty or badness.'

'It seems not.'

'What a charming relationship with wisdom our poetic imitator will have, about the subjects of his compositions!'

'It's not charming at all.'

'But he'll still carry on imitating all the same, not knowing 602b how any particular thing is bad or good. What he'll imitate, it seems, is the sort of thing that appears beautiful to ordinary people who know nothing about it.'

'What else?'

'So this much, it appears, is pretty well agreed between us. The imitative type knows nothing worth mentioning about the things he's imitating – imitation is a form of play, and not to be taken seriously; and those who engage in tragic composition, in iambics or in hexameters,[644] are imitators to the highest possible degree.'

'Absolutely.'

'Zeus!' I exclaimed. 'This business of imitation, then – it's 602c concerned with something actually *two* removes from the truth? Is that right?'

'Yes.'

'So what sort of element in us does it relate to, and have the capacity to affect?'

'What sort of thing are you talking about?'

'Something like this. If we rely on our sight, I think we find the same magnitude appearing to differ in size when we see it close up and when we see it from a distance.'

'We do.'

'And the same things appear both bent and straight, if we look at them first under water and then out of the water – both concave and convex, too, because of the way our sight vacil-602d lates about colours, and clearly every sort of confusion is present there by itself[645] in the soul. It's this aspect of our nature that shadow-painting exploits as effectively as any sorcery; conjuring, too, and all those other kinds of trickery.'

'True.'

'And don't measuring, counting and weighing provide most welcome protection against this sort of thing, preventing our being ruled by what merely appears larger or smaller, or more, or heavier, and allowing what has actually done the calculations and the measurements and the weighing to rule instead?'

'Of course.'

602e   'But that will be a function of the calculating element in the soul.'

'It will indeed.'

'Often, though, when this has done its measuring, and is signalling that one set of things is larger or smaller than, or the same size as, another, simultaneously the opposite appears to it to be true, of the very same things.'

'Yes, it does.'

'And weren't we saying that it's impossible for the same person to make opposite judgements about the same things at the same time?'[646]

'We were, and correctly so.'

603a   'The element of the soul that's judging contrary to the measurements won't then be the same as the one that's judging in accordance with them.'

'No, it won't.'

'But the element that trusts in measurement and calculation will be the best element in the soul.'

'Of course.'

'So then the element opposing it will be one of the inferior elements in us.'

'It must be.'

'This was what I wanted us to agree about when I was saying of painting, and the production of imitations in general,
that if the product it fashions is far removed from the truth, the   603b
element in us that it talks to, dallies with and befriends – for no
sound purpose, or any true one either – is itself no less far
removed from wisdom.'

'I agree absolutely,' he said.

'It's an inferior thing, then, this production of imitations,
that mates with another inferior thing and spawns inferior offspring.'

'It seems so.'

'Does this hold only in the case of visual imitations,' I asked,
'or does it apply to ones we can hear – the ones we call poetry?'

'Very probably it applies there too,' he replied.

'Well,' I said, 'let's not rely simply on a probable analogy
with painting. Let's turn directly to this very element of the   603c
mind we're saying the imitative art of poetry talks to, and see
whether it really is an inferior thing, or to be taken seriously.'

'Yes, that's the thing to do.'

'So let's propose the following: imitative art, we say, imitates
human beings performing actions that are forced or voluntary,
thinking that they've done either well or badly out of those
actions, and all the while experiencing either pain or pleasure.
Am I missing anything?'

'No.'

'Now in all this, is a person at one with himself? Or is it the   603d
same with actions as it is with vision? In relation to vision, we
found a person splitting into factions, and making room in himself for opposite views about the same things at the same time. Is
he split and in conflict with himself about his actions too? Actually, I recall that we've no need to agree about this now, because
we reached a perfectly satisfactory agreement about it all earlier
on in our discussion. There are tens of thousands of oppositions
of this sort within us; our souls are teeming with them.'[647]

'That's quite correct,' he said.

'Indeed it is,' I said. 'But there are some things we missed   603e
out back then that I think we need to discuss now.'

'What, exactly?' he asked.

'When a good man meets with misfortune, for example when he loses a son, or something else that he values very highly, I think we also said before[648] that he has a greater ability to endure it than anyone else.'

'Absolutely.'

'But now let's ask ourselves whether he'll not be distressed at all, or whether that's impossible, and he'll somehow manage a measured response to the pain.'

'Rather the latter,' he said, 'if we're to tell the truth.'

604a   'Now answer me this question about him: do you think he'll be more inclined to resist, and fight against the pain, when he's being observed by his peers, or when he's alone, just by himself, in solitude?'

'Much more when he's being observed,' he replied.

'Whereas when he's on his own, I imagine, he won't hold back; he'll utter lots of things he'd be ashamed of if anyone heard him, and do lots of things he wouldn't wish to be seen doing.'

'That's right.'

'And telling him to resist are reason and law; pulling him back to his pain is the misfortune itself?'

'True.'

604b   'Since there is this opposite and simultaneous pull in the man, connecting to the same thing, our claim is that there must be two distinct elements to him.'

'Of course.'

'One of which is ready to obey the law, and follow the law as its guide.'

'How so?'

'I think the law declares[649] it best to be as calm as possible in misfortune and not be upset, on the grounds, first, that it is not yet clear whether such things are good or bad; second, that taking them hard makes things no better for the future; third, that

604c   nothing in human affairs is worth serious attention; and fourth, that grieving impedes the very thing whose presence such conditions require as quickly as possible.'

'And what's that?' he asked.

'Reflection,' I said; 'reflection about what has happened, so that one can respond to the fall of the dice, as it were, and dispose one's affairs in the way that reason decides would be best, instead of behaving like children who have fallen over, wasting one's time howling and clutching whichever part is hurt. What is needed is always to accustom the soul to attend as quickly as it can to healing, and to righting what has fallen over or become 604d sick, effacing lamentation with a doctor's skill.'

'That will certainly be the right way for a person to approach the turns of fortune,' he said.

'So is it the best element in us that we say wants to follow this calculation?'

'Clearly.'

'And what pulls us towards dwelling on what happened to us, and wailing about it, and never has enough of either, that we shall proclaim to be irrational, shall we not, and lazy, and hand in hand with cowardice?'

'We certainly will.'

'One of these elements, the upsettable one, surely offers 604e plenty of colourful possibilities for imitation. The wise and quiet disposition, by contrast, because it is always much as it always was, is neither easily reproduced by the imitative arts nor readily understood when it is, especially not by a large collection of people, when all sorts are gathered together in the theatre. After all, what is being presented before them is pretty much alien to them.'

'Absolutely.'   605a

'So the imitative poet clearly has no natural connection with this kind of element in the soul, nor is this what his wisdom is designed to appeal to, if he is to gain a reputation among ordinary people. His connection is rather with the upsettable, colourful disposition, because it's so easy to imitate.'

'Clearly.'

'We're justified, then, surely, in singling him out for criticism, and in making him the counterpart of the painter. He already resembles the painter in the inferior nature of what he produces, compared to the truth – and the way he talks to an element of the soul that's also inferior, rather than to the best

605b element, that's something he has in common with the painter too. That is justification enough for our refusing to admit him into any city, if it is to be well governed, because by rousing, nurturing and strengthening this element of the soul he corrupts the element of it that reasons; it's like handing over a city to people of inferior quality, and putting them in charge while destroying the better sort. That's just what we'll say the imitative poet is doing, installing a bad regime in the private confines of each individual soul, gratifying the mindless element in it 605c that doesn't make a distinction between larger and smaller things, but thinks the same things now large, now small. He's an illusionist, producing nothing but illusions, standing altogether far removed from the truth.'

'Absolutely.'

'And yet we still haven't brought our most important charge against this kind of poetry. What is truly terrifying about it is surely its capacity to cause damage even to good people – all but a very few.'

'Of course, if that's what it really does.'

'Here's what I'm saying; you see what you think. When we're listening to Homer or one of the other tragic poets imi-605d tating one of the heroes in a state of grief, and he's stretching out a long wailing speech, or even breaking into song and breast-beating, I think you'll recognize that the best of us surrender ourselves to the pleasure of it, and follow the hero's lead, sharing his suffering with him and earnestly praising as a good poet any who is especially able to make us do that.'

'Of course I recognize it!'

'But if one of us suffers a personal loss, you notice that we pride ourselves on the opposite – on our ability to keep our peace, and endure. We think of that as a manly response, and 605e the other, the one we praised in the other context, as a woman's.'

'I have noticed,' he said.

'So is such praise fitting?' I asked. 'Surely when one sees a man being as one doesn't expect oneself to be, and would be ashamed to be, the appropriate thing is to be disgusted, not to enjoy and praise it?'

'Zeus! No,' he replied; 'that looks quite unreasonable.'

'Yes,' I said; 'certainly if you think of it like this.'   606a
'How?'

'Just think of the fact that what is being fed by the poets, and enjoying being fed, is the very element that is kept forcibly down in the context of personal misfortunes, and starved of the full quota of weeping and wailing it would need to satisfy its natural desires. Meanwhile, because the best element in us has not been fully educated through reasoning, or through habit, it relaxes its guard over this other, plaintive element, because after   606b all it's another man's sufferings it's watching, and there's nothing for *it* to be ashamed of if someone else claiming to be good grieves when he shouldn't, and so it praises and pities him. Why not? It thinks the pleasure involved is sheer profit, and it wouldn't want to miss out on that by turning up its nose at the whole poem. There are few people, I think, who are able to reason out how what we reap from others' lives inevitably affects ourselves; if we feed up our pitying element on the suffering of others, it is not easy to hold it down in the context of our own.'

'Very true,' he said.   606c

'And doesn't the same argument apply to what we laugh about? If there are jokes you hear reproduced on the comic stage or even in private company that you'd be ashamed to make yourself, and instead of loathing them as bad you heartily enjoy them, you're doing the same as with the things we pity. You were keeping down the element in yourself that wanted to make the jokes, for fear of being thought a buffoon; now you're releasing it, and once having given it its head there, before you know it you'll start getting carried away when you're on your own and becoming a comic poet yourself.'

'Very much so,' he said.

'And it's the same with sexual desire too, with anger, and   606d with everything in the soul that relates to appetites and pain and pleasure, the very things we're saying accompany all our actions[650] – poetic imitation has this sort of effect on us, feeding and watering these things when they should be left to wither, and causing them to rule in us when they ought to *be* ruled, so that we can become better and happier instead of worse and more miserable.'

'I can't disagree with you,' he said.

606e   'So, Glaucon, when you encounter admirers of Homer claiming that this is the poet who has educated Greece, that he deserves to be taken up and studied both for the management of human affairs and for an education in them, and that everyone should arrange and live his own life in accordance with the
607a   guidance this poet gives – well, you should love and cherish them, for doing the best they can, and concede that Homer is indeed most poetic, first among tragic poets, but recognize nonetheless that the only kinds of poetry that can be admitted to the city are hymns to the gods and encomia to the good. If you admit the seductive, saucy Muse, whether she works in lyric or in epic verse, you'll find pleasure and pain kings in your city, in the place of law and that reasoning which is on any occasion by common consent agreed to be best.'[651]

607b   'Very true,' he said.

'So let that be our defence, now that we've gone back to the subject of poetry: since that is what she is like, it was perfectly reasonable to propose banishing her from the city. Our argument would allow us to do nothing less. And let's further say to her, in case she accuses us of a certain austerity and boorishness, that a quarrel between philosophy and poetry is nothing new:[652] that "yelping bitch" that "bays against her master",[653]
607c   "chief in the empty chatterings of fools", "the ruling mob of the very wise",[654] those "refined thoughts" leading to "empty bellies" – they're just some of the countless signs of a longstanding opposition between the two. Despite all that, for our part let it be said that if poetry that aims at pleasure through imitation could put forward an argument to show that she should be part of a well-governed city, we would be delighted to receive her back, because we're aware of the enchantment she works on us too. But it is impiety to betray what one thinks
607d   to be true. She enchants you too, my friend, doesn't she – and especially when you're seeing her through Homer?'

'Yes, very much so.'

'So she's entitled to come back in if she can defend herself, in lyric or one of her other metres?'

'Absolutely.'

'Presumably we'd also allow any supporters of hers that love poetry but aren't good at it themselves the chance to make a case for her in prose, and show that she isn't merely pleasing but also beneficial for the government of cities and human life in general. We'll be a well-disposed audience, because presumably it'll be to our advantage if she does turn out not just to be enjoyable but beneficial into the bargain.' 607e

'It most certainly will,' he said.

'But if they can't do that, my dear friend, then we must behave like people who have fallen in love but don't think it's good for them, and have to force themselves to hold back. Imbued as we are with a love of such poetry, by being brought up under these fine regimes of ours, we're disposed to find her as good and true 608a as she could possibly be; but so long as she is unable to marshal a defence, as we listen to her we'll chant our argument against her to ourselves, like a kind of charm, to prevent us from relapsing into the childish love most people have for her. In any case, we see that this sort of poetry must not be taken seriously, as having any kind of serious grasp on the truth. We see instead that the listener must beware of her, out of fear for the regime in 608b himself; he must believe the things we've said about poetry.'

'I absolutely agree,' he said.

'Yes, because the contest matters, my dear Glaucon,' I said, 'more than we think, this contest of ours to become good or bad – too much for it to be worth our being lured by honour, or money, or any sort of power, or indeed poetry, into a neglect of justice and the other parts of excellence.'

'I agree with you,' he said, 'given everything we've talked about, and I think anyone else would too.' 608c

'And yet', I said, 'we haven't even talked about the biggest rewards of excellence, the biggest prizes it has to offer.'

'They must be incredibly big,' he said, 'if they're bigger than the ones we've mentioned.'

'What is there', I asked, 'that can ever be big in a small space of time? Certainly the whole of this time of ours, from childhood to old age, will be small when compared to all time.'[655]

'A mere nothing,' he replied.

'Then do you think something that is immortal should be serious about so short a span of time, and not about all time?'

608d   'I think you're right,' he said. 'But why do you say this?'

'Have you not noticed', I asked, 'that our soul is immortal, and never perishes?'[656]

Glaucon looked at me astonished, and said, 'Zeus! No, I haven't, myself; you're able to say it is, are you?'

'I certainly should be able to,' I said, 'and I think you should be too. It's not hard.'

'It is for me,' he said. 'Please tell me what you're saying "isn't hard".'

'I will,' I said.

'Just do it!' he replied.

'There's something you call good,' I asked, 'and something you call bad?'

608e   'There is.'

'And do you have the same notion of them as I do?'

'What's that?'

'That what destroys and corrupts is always the bad, and what preserves and benefits is always the good.'

'I'm certainly with you there.'

'And do you agree that there's a bad, as well as a good, 609a   specific to each individual thing? Ophthalmia for the eyes, for example; disease, for the body as a whole, mildew for grain, rot for wood, rust for bronze and iron – what I'm saying is, don't you think practically everything has its own congenital badness, some disease, so to speak, peculiar to it?'

'Yes, I do.'

'And when that comes to affect it, it makes what it's affecting bad too, and ultimately breaks it down and destroys it?'

'Surely.'

'Then it's the bad that's congenital to each thing, and the badness it causes in that thing, which destroys it; or, if this isn't 609b   going to destroy it, there's nothing else that will – the good will certainly never destroy anything, and neither will the neither-good-nor-bad.'

'No; how would it?' he replied.

'So if we find anything in existence that is made bad by its own specific form of badness, and this – its specific badness – is unable to break it down and destroy it, we'll already know that nothing could ever destroy something of that nature?'

'That's reasonable enough,' he said.

'What about the soul?' I asked. 'Is there anything specific to it that makes it bad?'

'There certainly is,' he replied. 'It's all the things we were talking about just now, injustice, lack of restraint, cowardice and ignorance.'

'So do any of these break it down and destroy it? And be 609c careful: we don't want to be misled by the idea that being destroyed by injustice, the soul's specific badness, is simply a matter of the unjust and stupid person's being caught out doing something unjust. Rather, think of it as you would in other cases: for example, the specific badness of a body, disease, dissolves and destroys it by reducing it to a state where it's not actually a body at all; and similarly with all the other examples we mentioned just now – their destruction by their particular forms of badness, when these have attached themselves and 609d are present in them, is a matter of their passing into non-existence.[657] That's right, isn't it?'

'Yes.'

'Now try thinking about the soul in the same way. When injustice and the other forms of badness are present in it, does their presence in it, and attachment to it, destroy it by making it waste away, until they bring it to the point of death and separate it from the body?'[658]

'They certainly never do *that*,' he said.

'And yet it's unreasonable to suppose', I said, 'that a thing could be destroyed by something else's badness, but not by its own.'

'Yes, that would be unreasonable.'

'Yes, Glaucon, because if you think about it, we don't even 609e insist that a body is destroyed by the badness specific to foods – whether staleness, or rottenness, or whatever it may be; rather, when the badness specific to foods themselves brings about the specific badness of a body, in a body, then we'll say that the

body has been destroyed because of them, but actually *by* its
610a own badness, disease. We'll never expect the body, which is
one thing, to be destroyed by the badness of another set of
things, foods, unless this badness, the one that doesn't belong
to it, has first brought about in it the badness that does.'

'You're absolutely right,' he said.

'By the same argument,' I said, 'unless the badness specific to
the body can bring about the specific badness of a soul, in a
soul, let's not expect a soul ever to be destroyed by a badness
that doesn't belong to it – that is, in the absence of its own, one
thing being destroyed directly by the badness of another.'

'Yes, that's reasonable,' he said.

'Either, then, we must refute these claims of ours or, for so
610b long as they remain unrefuted, I propose we refuse to accept
that soul is destroyed by fever, or disease generally, or by a
slash to the throat, or even if someone cuts the whole body into
the smallest possible pieces – none of these things will alter the
case in the slightest degree, unless and until someone proves
that because these things are happening to the body the soul
becomes in itself more unjust and more impious. That the badness specific to one thing can ever cause the destruction of
something else by transferring to that thing, without that
610c thing's own specific badness coming to be in it, is a claim we
shan't put up with from anyone.'

'But that', he said, 'is something no one will ever show – that
death makes the souls of the dying more unjust.'

'And', I said, 'if anyone has the nerve to confront our argument head on, in order to avoid being forced to agree that our
souls are immortal, and tries to claim that the dying person
actually does become worse and more unjust, then I presume
we'll conclude that if this claim is true, then injustice is some-
610d thing fatal to its possessor, like a disease, and that it's a born
killer, killing[659] anyone who catches it – more quickly in the
case of those that have it worst, in a more leisurely fashion if
someone has it more mildly; it won't be like now, when injustice brings death to the unjust only because others apply it to
them as a punishment.'

'Zeus!' he exclaimed. 'Injustice won't turn out to be so terrible after all, if it's going to be fatal to those that catch it; it will be a way out of their troubles. My own view is that it will turn out to be exactly the opposite – it's others it kills, if that's 610e really possible, not its possessor. In fact it makes its possessor pretty lively, and alert as well as lively. I think it looks that far from being fatal; its pitch is quite different.'660

'You're right,' I said. 'When the soul's own badness, the bad that peculiarly belongs to it, lacks the power to kill or destroy it, the bad that's assigned to destroying something else will hardly destroy it, or indeed anything but the thing it's assigned to.'

'Hardly,' he said, 'as probabilities go.'

'And if it's not destroyed by anything bad whatsoever, whether belonging to it or to something else, mustn't it clearly 611a be something that always is661 – and if it's something that always is, then clearly immortal too?'

'It must be,' he replied.

'Then let's take it to be so,' I said. 'And if it is, you notice the consequence, that there will always be the same souls. After all, if none is ever destroyed, they presumably can't become fewer; and neither can there come to be more of them, since if any-thing immortal did increase in number, you recognize that the increase would come from the mortal, and everything would end up being immortal.'

'True.'

'But let's not imagine that would happen,' I said, 'because reason won't allow it; and particularly let's not imagine that 611b soul is the kind of thing, in its truest nature, to brim over with variety and dissimilarity and difference in relation to itself.'662

'What's this you're saying?' he asked.

'It's not easy for something to be timeless,' I said, 'if it's a composite of many elements and they haven't been put together in the most beautiful way, which is what appeared to us to be the case with the soul.'

'No, probably not easy.'

'Well, that the soul *is* immortal will follow both from our argument just now, and from other arguments;663 but as for seeing the kind of thing it truly is, one mustn't look at it as we are looking at it now, crippled by its association with the body 611c and other things that harm it. Rather, we must use rational reflection to examine it properly, as it is when it's purified from such things, and if we do so sufficiently well, we will find it to be something far more beautiful, and gain a far clearer insight into things like justice and injustice, and everything else we have talked about on the present occasion. As it is, what we have said about it describes truly enough the way it presently appears; yet to have viewed it in that condition makes us like people who see the sea-dwelling Glaucus:[664] they see him, but 611d can't any longer easily make out his original nature – the old parts of his body have been broken off or been worn away by the waves, mutilated out of all recognition, while others have attached themselves in the form of shells and seaweed and rocks, so that he resembles any kind of beast more than he does his old natural self. That is the condition in which we're seeing the soul, too, beset by countless sources of harm. But we must turn our gaze elsewhere, Glaucon.'

'Where?' he asked.

'To the soul's love of wisdom – reflecting on the things it 611e touches on, the sorts of company it strives for, akin as it is to the divine and immortal, that which always is,[665] and what it might become if the whole of it applied itself to such things, and this impulse lifted it clean out of the sea in which it is now, 612a breaking off the rocks and shells that currently cling all around it, because it feasts on earth; a wild profusion of earth-bound, rocky growths from all the feasting that people describe as happiness. Then one would see whether its true nature is to contain many kinds within it, or only one,[666] or exactly how it may be. But I think we've described well enough what happens to it, and the kinds it contains, in the context of a human life.'[667]

'Absolutely,' he said.

'So hasn't our argument done all the things we promised for it – in particular, by not adducing the rewards for justice, or the 612b reputation it brings, in the way you were claiming Hesiod and Homer did?[668] Haven't we discovered that justice really is, in and by itself, what's best for the soul, in and by itself, so that a soul should do what is just whether or not it has Gyges' ring, or a ring like that *and* the cap of Hades too?'[669]

'We certainly have,' he said.

'So, Glaucon,' I asked, 'will anyone now be able to reproach us for taking the next step, and restoring to justice and the other parts of excellence all the various rewards they offer the soul, whether from men or from gods, both while a man is still alive and when he dies?'[670]   612c

'Absolutely not,' he said.

'Then will the two of you give me back what I loaned to you for the duration of the argument?'

'What was that, exactly?'

'I conceded to you that the just person should be thought to be unjust, and the unjust person to be just, because both of you asked me to;[671] even if these things couldn't in fact be hidden from the gods, you thought it should be conceded for the sake of the argument, so that justice and injustice could be judged against each other in and by themselves. Or don't you recall, Glaucon?'   612d

'It'd be a crime if I didn't!' he exclaimed.

'So now that judgement has been passed on them,' I said, 'I demand back from you on behalf of justice the good reputation she in fact enjoys, not just among gods but among men. It is time for us to agree that she is well thought of; time for her to come up and receive the prizes[672] she bestows on those who possess her merely from being *thought* to do so, since now we know that she is no deceiver, and that if people truly take her to themselves, she truly does bestow on them the blessings that come from *being* just.'

'Just demands indeed,' he said.   612e

'So,' I said, 'will you first grant me that the gods – being gods – are well able to recognize each of them, the just and the unjust, for what he is?'

'We will,' he said.

'But if that's so, then they'll love the one and hate the other, as we agreed at the start.'[673]

'True.'

'And won't we agree that for someone who is loved by the gods, everything that comes from them, at least, is as good as it could possibly be, unless he is already unavoidably damaged in some way from a previous mistake.'[674]   613a

'Absolutely.'

'This, then, is how we should think about the just man, should he ever come to be poor, or ill, or any of the other things that are reputed to be bad: for him, such things will end in some good, during his lifetime or even after his death. For the gods, being gods, surely never neglect anyone who can commit himself to becoming just and, through the practice of excel-
613b lence, as like god as it is possible for a human to be.'

'One would certainly expect that sort of person not to be neglected by his like,' he said.

'And should we think the opposite of all this about the unjust person?'

'We certainly should.'

'These, then, are the sorts of prizes the gods award to the just person.'

'I certainly think so,' he said.

'And what about the prizes he'll receive from men? If we're to set things out as they really are, the position is surely this: clever, unjust people perform like runners who run the first leg
613c well but not the leg back – they bound keenly off at the start but become figures of fun by the end, running away from the track with no wreath and their ears drooping to their shoulders; meanwhile, the real runners make it to the end, receive the prizes and carry off the wreaths. Isn't that how it mostly turns out for the just, too? Don't they make it to the end of every action, of every shared enterprise, of their whole life with a good name and any such prizes men have to offer?'

'Indeed so.'

'Then will you allow it if I now say about them what you
613d were saying[675] about the unjust? I'm going to say that when the just become older, they hold office in their own city if they wish, take a wife from whichever family they wish, give their own children in marriage as they wish – everything you said about the unjust, I now say about the just. And on the subject of the unjust, I say that even if they get away with it in their youth, at the end of the race most of them are caught making fools of themselves, and when they're old, miserable souls,

they're trampled over by strangers and citizens alike, whipped and – well, they have happen to them all the things you rightly described as sounding crude;[676] imagine you've heard me listing   613e them too. Well – *will* you allow it?'

'Certainly,' he said; 'you're saying only what's just.'

'So these', I said, 'will be the sorts of prizes and rewards and gifts, from gods and from men, that accrue to the just person   614a while he is still alive, over and above the benefits we said justice itself bestows.'

'And very fine and secure those prizes are,' he said.

'Well, they are nothing', I said, 'in number or magnitude, when compared to those that await the just and the unjust after death. We need to hear about these too, if either of them, just or unjust, is to be paid back the full description the argument owes him.'

'Please describe them,' he said; 'there are not many things   614b one would rather hear about.'

'I have to tell you, my tale won't be on an Odyssean scale,' I said. 'Nonetheless it is the story of a brave man, Er, son of Armenius, a Pamphylian.[677] Once upon a time this Er died on the battlefield, and when on the tenth day the corpses were picked up they were all decomposed – except for Er's, which was picked up intact. He was taken home, and on the twelfth day he was lying on his pyre, ready for his funeral, when he suddenly revived, and having done so was able to report what he had seen in that other place.[678]

'He said that when his soul exited himself,[679] it journeyed in the company of many others, and together they arrived at a   614c miraculous place where there were two openings in the earth, side by side, and other openings in the heavens opposite and above them. In between these openings judges were sitting, and as they reached their decisions, they ordered the just to take the path leading to the right and up through the heavens, with tokens fixed round the front of them to show what had been decided about them, while the unjust they ordered to the left and down; they too wore tokens, this time on their backs, recording everything they had done. But when Er came forward, they told   614d him he was needed as a messenger to mankind, to tell them about what went on there. They instructed him to listen to and observe everything in the place.

'What he saw there, he said, was souls departing, when judgement was passed on them, through one of the openings in the heavens and one in the earth; as for the other two, from the one in the earth souls were coming up parched with thirst and covered in dust, while from the other were descending other 614e souls, pure and clean from the heavens. As they kept arriving, they appeared to him as if they'd been on a long journey, so glad were they to make their way out to the meadow and encamp there as if at some festival. They greeted one another, if they found someone they knew, and pressed each other for information; souls that had come up out of the earth wanted to know how things were up above, souls down from the heavens how things were down below. And as they told their stories to 615a each other, the first group did so wailing and weeping, as they recalled all the terrible things they had suffered and seen on their journey under the earth – a journey, Er said, that lasted a thousand years. The souls from the heavens, meanwhile, told of pleasures enjoyed and sights of unbelievable beauty.

'To tell you all the many details, Glaucon, would take a long time. But the nub of it, he said, was this: however many injustices anyone had ever done, and to however many victims, he had paid the penalty for all of them in turn, tenfold for each – that is, with payment arranged in periods of a hundred years, 615b this being the measure of a human life, to make it ten times the offence; so that, for example, if anyone had caused many deaths, perhaps by betraying a city or an army, and throwing them into slavery, or else had shared in some other atrocity, then for all these things their reward would be ten times the pain for each death – and equally, if anyone had done good deeds, and become just and pious, they received the reward they deserved, in the same measure.

'There were other things he said that weren't worth record- 615c ing, about infants who died at birth or lived only a short time; he also described even greater punishments and rewards for impiety and piety towards the gods and towards parents, and for murdering one's kin. In this connection, he said he was there when one person was being asked by another where the great Ardiaeus was. This Ardiaeus had become tyrant of some city or other in Pamphylia exactly a thousand years before, having killed off his old father and elder brother and, so it was 615d said, done many other sorts of impious things too. Well, according to Er the person who was asked the question replied, "He hasn't come, and he won't be coming here at all. This was actually one of the terrible sights we saw. We were close to the mouth of the opening and about to emerge, after everything we'd been through, when suddenly we caught sight of Ardiaeus and others, pretty much the majority of them tyrants, though there were some private citizens, too, who had themselves committed major crimes. Just when they thought they were going 615e to make it up through the opening, the mouth would not let them through, and gave out a bellow if ever anyone tried to pass through when he was so incurably bad, or hadn't been punished enough. And there were men there standing by," he said, "savage men with a fiery look to them, who understood the sound, and they'd immediately seize some of these people and take them away. But Ardiaeus and others they chained 616a hand, foot and neck, threw them to the ground and flayed them, then dragged them off the path to tear their flesh on the thorn bushes,[680] all the while indicating to those passing by why they were dragging them off and where – to be hurled into Tartarus."[681] Many and various their fears might have been before, this man said, but a new one now exceeded them all – that they would hear that sound when *they* tried to go up through the mouth, and it was with the greatest relief that each went through and no sound came.

'The penalties and punishments Er described, then, and the benefits corresponding to them, were something like that. 616b Now after seven days had passed for the groups in the meadow, he said that on the eighth they had to get up and move on. After three days' march, they arrived at a vantage-point from which they saw a shaft of light, like a pillar, stretching from above down through the whole of the heavens and the earth – it most resembled the rainbow, he said, only it was brighter and

purer than that. Another day's march took them to it, and there
616c in the middle of the light they saw stretching from the heavens
the ends of the ties that bind them – for the light, he said, is
what binds the heavens together, cradling them like the under-
girding of a trireme. Stretching from the ends is the spindle
of Necessity, whose turning causes all the rotations in the
heavens;[682] and the shaft and hook of the spindle are of
adamant, the whorl[683] partly of adamant and partly of other
kinds of stuff.

616d   'The nature of the whorl was like this. In shape it resembled
an ordinary spindle, but from what Er said we need to think of
it as like one large whorl, hollow and scooped out all the way
through so that another, smaller one can fit snugly inside it, in
the way nested jars fit into each other, and then a third, and a
fourth, and so on, until there are eight whorls in all, each lying
616e successively in the next, leaving their rims visible as circles at
the top and so forming a continuous surface, as of a single
whorl around the shaft; and the shaft drives straight through
the middle of the eighth. The circle formed by the rim of the
first and outermost whorl he said was the broadest, that of the
sixth second broadest, that of the fourth third; the circle
of the eighth came next, then that of the seventh, that of the
fifth, that of the third, and finally, narrowest of all, there came
the circle of the second. The circle of the broadest and first of
the rims was spangled, that of the seventh was brightest, while
617a the circle of the eighth had its colour from the seventh's shining on it;[684] the second and the fifth were similar in colour to
each other, but yellower than the eighth and seventh, the third
was the whitest, the fourth reddish, the sixth second whitest
after the third. The spindle as a whole turned in a circle with
the same movement, but within the whole, as it turned, the
seven inner circles, from second to eighth, turned gently with
the opposite movement.[685] The innermost of these, the eighth
617b circle, travelled fastest, the seventh, sixth and fifth, keeping the
same speed as each other, second fastest; third fastest was the
fourth, turning with a movement that to them, Er said,
appeared to circle back on itself; the third circle came in fourth
fastest, the second fifth.

'The spindle, he said, turned in the lap of Necessity, and on top of each of its circles was mounted a Siren,[686] each turning along with her circle and emitting a single sound, a single musical note; all eight together sang in single harmony. Roundabout, 617c and equidistant one from another, sat three more female figures, each on her throne – daughters of Necessity, the Fates, clad in white and with garlands on their heads: Lachesis, Clotho and Atropos, singing to the accompaniment of the Siren harmony. Lachesis sang of things past, Clotho of the present, Atropos of the future; at intervals, Clotho helped turn the spindle's periphery with a touch of her right hand, Atropos its inner circles with her left, Lachesis now the inner, now the outer, now with her left 617d hand, now with her right.

'As for Er and his group, well, as soon as they arrived, they had to go before Lachesis. A priest or spokesman then began by arranging them all in an orderly line, after which he took from her lap some lottery-tokens, along with models of different kinds of lives, and mounting a lofty platform proclaimed: "This is the word of Lachesis, maiden daughter of Necessity: 'Souls that live for a day: once more the cycle begins for your mortal kind; once more will it end in death. No divine guide 617e will be allotted to you; the choice of guide will be your own.[687] Let the one who draws the first lot be the first to choose a life, and his choice will be irrevocable. Excellence knows no master; as each honours or dishonours her, so will his share of her grow or diminish. The blame is the chooser's, not god's.'"

'With these words, the priest threw the lots down among them all, and each picked up the one that fell beside him – except for Er himself, because he was told not to; and as they 618a did, each saw which number he had drawn. The next thing was that the priest laid out the models of different kinds of life on the ground before them. There were far more than there were people present, and they were of every conceivable variety, including all the different forms of animal life and, of course, all human lives. There were tyrannies among them, some of them lasting the course, some of them interrupted midway and ending in poverty, exile and beggary. There were lives of distinguished men – some distinguished for their looks and beauty,

618b or strength and prowess of some other physical kind, others for
their birth and the qualities of their forebears; equally, there
were lives of men undistinguished in any of these ways. Wom-
en's lives too, of both sorts, distinguished and undistinguished,
and by the same criteria. Any ordering of the soul[688] was not
included in them, because of the inevitable truth that the kind
of soul a person has is determined by his choice of life; but all
the other things[689] were there, Er said, combined with each
other and with wealth and poverty, sometimes with sickness in
the mix, sometimes with health and sometimes with these
things in balance.

'It is here, then, my dear Glaucon, that all the danger seems
to lie for a human being. This is why we must devote our atten-
618c tion above all to ensuring that each of us dismisses every other
subject of study and becomes someone who searches for and
studies this one subject, namely, whether he may be able to discover, from whatever source he might learn it, just who it is
that will make him skilful and knowledgeable enough to distinguish a good life from a bad one,[690] and always, wherever he
is,[691] to choose the better life out of those that he could live –
reckoning up all the things just mentioned, and assessing the
difference they make to the goodness of a life by being combined or kept apart: for example, what effect[692] beauty will
have for bad or good when mixed with poverty or wealth, and
618d in company with what kind of disposition of the soul; being
well or low born, being a private citizen or holding office, being
strong or weak, being quick or slow at learning, or having any
such natural attribute of mind, or indeed any acquired one –
what effect these things have when mixed together with each
other: all of this needs to be calculated, so that we are able to
make a reasoned choice between the worse and the better life,
618e judging worse and better by reference to the nature of the soul,
and calling "worse" the life that will lead to our soul's becoming more unjust, "better" the life that will lead to its becoming
more just. Everything else we shall ignore, because we have
seen that whether a person is alive or dead, this is the most
619a important of all choices he has to make. He must go to Hades
with this belief in him as strong as adamant, so that there too

he may remain undazzled by wealth and other sources of harm, and not fall headlong into tyranny or other such forms of activity that will cause irremediable harm to many and even greater harm to himself, but rather know always to choose the life that has a middling share in wealth and the rest, avoiding the extremes in either direction both in this life, so far as he can, and in every life to come.[693] For that is how a human being 619b comes to be happiest. In fact our messenger from the other place reported the priest on that occasion saying, "Even the person who comes up last, if he has chosen intelligently, can look forward to an acceptable life, not a bad one, if he lives it with determination. Let not the first be careless in his choice; let not the last despair of his."

'After the priest had spoken, Er said, the person who had drawn the first lot immediately came up and chose the greatest tyranny available. Stupidity and greed prevented him from 619c checking all the details properly before making his choice, so he failed to notice that it destined him for eating his own children and other horrors; when he took the time to look more closely, he beat himself and wailed about his choice, in clear contravention of the priest's warnings, since instead of blaming himself he blamed chance, the gods, anyone rather than himself. Now he was one of those who had come down from the heavens, having spent his previous life under a well-ordered constitution,[694] and his excellence derived from habit unsupported by philosophy, and in fact, generally speaking, those 619d who had come down from the heavens were no less likely for that to find themselves caught in this kind of situation, because they were untrained in suffering; most of those who had come up out of the earth, by contrast, had suffered themselves and seen others suffering, and so did not make their choices in a rush. Because of this, and because of the way the lots chanced to fall, most souls actually found their situations, bad or good, reversed. In fact, if on arriving in life here a person is always 619e healthily engaged in philosophy, and the fall of the lot hasn't put him among the last to choose, the likelihood is – to go by Er's report from that other place – not only that he will be happy here, but that his journey from here to there and back again will not be rough and under the earth, but smooth and heavenly.

620a   'That was a sight worth seeing, Er said – the way different souls made their choices; a cause of wonder, at once pitiable and comic. For the most part, they chose in line with what they were used to in their previous life. Thus Er saw what had once been Orpheus' soul choosing the life of a swan, out of hatred for the female sex, because after dying at the hands of women he had no wish to be born into the world from one; he saw Thamyras'[695] soul had chosen a nightingale's life, and he saw a swan changing its choice to that of a human life, and similarly

620b   other musical animals. The soul that went twentieth chose the life of a lion – and it was the soul of Ajax son of Telamon, avoiding human life because it remembered the decision over Achilles' arms.[696] Next up was another whose sufferings made it hostile to the human race, Agamemnon's,[697] and it went for the life of an eagle instead. Somewhere in the middle was the soul of Atalanta:[698] once it had caught sight of the great honours attaching to a male athlete's life, it could not resist, and

620c   had to take it; after which, Er saw the soul of Epeius, son of Panopeus, taking on the nature of a female craftworker.[699] And far off, among the last, he saw the soul of the buffoon Thersites[700] taking on the skin of a monkey. But by chance it was Odysseus' soul that went up the very last of all to make its choice. Because it remembered the sufferings of its previous life, it had got over any love of honour it had before, and went round for a long time looking for the life of an ordinary man who minded his own business. He had difficulty finding it; it

620d   was lying around somewhere, neglected by the others, and when he saw it he chose it gladly, saying that he would have done the same if he had had the first choice instead of the last. Similarly with other animals – they made the change into humans or each other, the unjust into the savage and the just into the tame; all sorts of mixings took place.

'In any case, Er said, when every soul had made its choice of life, they approached Lachesis in the order assigned to them by the lottery, and she sent them off, each of them, with the guide

620e   they had chosen, to guard over their lives and bring the things

they had chosen to fulfilment.[701] The guide took each soul first
before Clotho, beneath her hand as it turned the revolving
spindle, to ratify the destiny[702] its lot had allowed it to choose;
then, when it had claimed its destiny, he led it on to where
Atropos was spinning, so that of the threads now spun over it
there could be no unspinning, and from there it passed beneath
the throne of Necessity; and there was no turning back.[703]   621a
When it had passed through, and the others had done the same,
all of them journeyed to the plain of forgetfulness[704] through
terrible, suffocating heat, for the place was empty of trees and
all the things the earth gives rise to; and they camped, as evening came on, beside the River Careless, whose water no vessel
can hold. All of them were required to drink a measure of the
water, but those who had no wisdom to save them drank more   621b
than the measure; each as he drank forgot everything. When
they had gone to sleep and it was the middle of the night, there
was thunder, the earth shook, and they were suddenly carried
up and away to be born, each to his own destination, with the
speed of shooting stars. As for Er himself, he said he was
stopped from drinking any of the water, but he still had no idea
how he got back into his body. He just looked up suddenly and
saw it was dawn and he was lying on the pyre.

'And that, Glaucon, is how the story was saved for us instead
of coming to an untimely end; it will save us too, if we believe   621c
in it, and we shall cross the river of forgetfulness in good shape,
with our souls undefiled.[705] And if we're to follow my own
advice, we'll believe the soul to be immortal, capable of with-
standing all kinds of harm and all kinds of blessing, and keep
always to the upward path, doing everything we can to practise
justice with wisdom. That way we shall not only be friends to
ourselves but loved by the gods, both while we remain here and
when we carry off the prizes of justice, gathering them in like   621d
victors at the games; and both here and in the thousand-year
journey we have talked about, we shall fare well.'

Notes

Unless otherwise stated, references to 'Slings' are to the new Oxford *Republic* (Oxford Classical Texts, 2003).

1. *a prayer to the goddess ... just as fine*: The Athenians had recently imported the cult of the Thracian goddess Bendis; perhaps Thracians resident in the city had set out to show the locals how things should be done.
2. *it really is ... from a whole collection of slave-masters*: Omitting *esti* in d2.
3. *Sweet hope ... ever-shifting thought*: A fragment of a lost poem.
4. *this is not what constitutes justice*: Or 'this is not what marks off justice', its *horos*, *horos* being in origin the boundary of something, or a boundary-stone; the term becomes standard for 'definition'.
5. *board-game*: Specifically, the game called *petteia* (see n. 55).
6. *hoplite*: 'Hoplites' were the heavy-armed infantry, the mainstay of the army.
7. *outshone ... oath-breaking*: Homer, *Odyssey* 19.395–6.
8. *canine goodness*: Or 'canine excellence', or 'canine virtue'. 'Goodness', 'excellence' and 'virtue' are all possible renderings of the Greek noun *aretê*, which corresponds to the adjective *agathos*, 'good'. What is at issue in the present context, and in the *Republic* generally, is simply what makes a particular thing good at doing what that kind of thing characteristically does, or is for – and while Socrates will claim that what makes human beings good are what we generally call 'virtues', we are much less likely to talk about the 'virtue' of a dog. So *aretê* needs to be either 'excellence' or 'goodness'; and 'goodness', here at least, makes it much easier to follow the thread of Socrates' argument.
9. *Periander ... who thinks he has great power*: The four men named were actually very rich, in money terms, and would be thought by any ordinary person to have great power; for Socrates, no one has real power unless he knows how to use it – as

these four will not, if they think themselves powerful just because they are rich (cf. section 4 of the Introduction, and n. 15 below).

10. *if I hadn't seen him . . . struck dumb*: The reference is to a superstition about wolves.

11. *seek out for each*: Each *expert*, that is, taken simply as an expert in the field – though Thrasymachus, to judge from his answers to Socrates' next questions, is still tempted to think in terms of what (according to him) is in the interests of each *individual*, taken as an individual person rather than as an expert.

12. *what is actually just . . . in his own interests*: That is, insofar as he stops everyone else maltreating each other (making them behave justly), while actually maltreating everyone else (behaving unjustly) himself.

13. *other forms of rule*: I.e., things like medicine or steersmanship, which also involve someone's giving orders.

14. *as others do . . . in terms of conventional thinking*: One such person is Polus in Plato's *Gorgias*; and Socrates' response to Polus is precisely framed 'in terms of conventional thinking'.

15. *to outdo*: Or 'to have [or get] more than' (*pleon echein*). The same expression, and a variant of it (*pleonektein*), will recur, with the same apparent variation of sense, several times in the following argument. This shifting between 'outdoing' and 'having/getting more than' has often been seen as damaging to Socrates' argument; but it may be more important to keep in mind the difference between what will count as 'outdoing' or 'having more than' someone for Thrasymachus (having more power, money . . .) and what will count as such for Socrates (having more of the things that are, for him, truly good, i.e., wisdom, and everything that flows from wisdom).

16. *No, not even the just action*: I.e., let alone the unjust one (reading *oude tês dikaias* rather than Slings's *oude tautês*, in the new Oxford text).

17. *intelligent and good*: 'Good', perhaps, precisely because 'intelligent' (on which see following note). Socrates here underlines Thrasymachus' general claim that injustice is thoroughly to be *admired*.

18. *And in the respects . . . he's bad*: Socrates is presumably here picking up on Thrasymachus' own pairing of 'intelligent' (*phronimos*) with 'good' (348d, 349d). The term *phronimos* is normally, in Plato, scarcely distinguishable from *sophos*, 'wise' (or 'expert'), at least when the latter term is used without irony – and in fact 'wise' will shortly be substituted for 'intelligent' in the present argument.

19. *a soul*: 'Soul' is both 'mind' and (as we will immediately learn)

what makes us alive, the principle of life – which presumably our 'mind' is not.

20. *And we agreed*: See 350d. The soul wasn't in fact mentioned there, but Thrasymachus' latest answers hardly indicate that he would wish to quarrel with the idea that people are called 'just' or 'unjust' by virtue of the state of their souls.

21. *the feast of Bendis*: See 327a–b, with n. 1.

22. *does make a person happy*: The jump here from '354c' to '357a', and similar jumps elsewhere, are explained in the Note on the Text and Translation.

23. *healing other people ... money-making*: Evidently Glaucon has either not absorbed or not accepted Socrates' attempt to separate money-making as an art or activity separate from others (341c–342e, 345c–d); but after all, as he has just indicated, he has not been persuaded by Socrates' case as a whole.

24. *the kind ... blessed with happiness*: In particular, perhaps, because – as Glaucon has proposed – this kind includes intelligence. An attachment to intelligence, or wisdom (*sophia*), is a condition of being a philosopher, and philosophy, for Socrates, is the key to life.

25. *his desire to have more*: The Greek term here, *pleonexia*, is the noun corresponding to the verb translated 'outdo' in Socrates' argument with Thrasymachus back in 349b–350c; in contexts like the present one, it has clear connotations, not just of wanting to have more, but of overreaching, wanting to have too much (from other people's point of view); i.e., simple greed.

26. *the ancestor of Gyges the Lydian*: This is a somewhat odd expression, insofar as it seems to suggest that the audience already has reason to know this unnamed ancestor of Gyges. If the text translated here actually represents what Plato wrote, just possibly he is covertly acknowledging a borrowing from Herodotus, who relays a similar but less exotic story about Gyges himself (Herodotus, *Histories* I.8–13). At 612b, Socrates refers to him simply as Gyges.

27. *with an impunity the equal of a god's*: The gods in Homer typically (a) do whatever they want, and (b) are invisible except when they choose not to be, and even then usually appear only in disguise.

28. *As he follows the furrow ... fruits of wisdom won*: Glaucon here quotes the two lines, from Aeschylus' *Seven Against Thebes* (593–4), that follow the one he first paraphrased back in 361b ('the just man desires not to be thought good but to be good').

29. *Bear acorns . . . fleecy sheep*: Hesiod, *Works and Days* 232–3.
30. *As when a king . . . offers him fish*: Homer, *Odyssey* 19.109–12.
31. *'behind him leaves' children and children of children*: The allusion is to a source unknown to us.
32. *they bury . . . in some sort of slime*: As Socrates himself does (or applauds others for doing), at *Phaedo* 69c.
33. *force them to carry water in a sieve*: Again, Socrates does the same (see *Gorgias* 493a–c). In effect, he is being asked to improve on his defence of justice in other dialogues too.
34. *The ways to be bad . . . we must sweat our way*: Hesiod, *Works and Days* 287–9.
35. *Our prayers move the gods . . . overstep the mark and err*: Plato is here modifying Homer, *Iliad* 9.497 ff. (or else had a somewhat different text from ours).
36. *'Will straight justice . . . shield me through life?'*: Another fragment from a lost poem.
37. *as revealed . . . by the wise*: Simonides (from another lost poem).
38. *Archilochus' wise old fox*: The reference is once again to fragments. Archilochus flourished in the early seventh century, a century and a half before his fellow lyric-poet Simonides (331e). 'Shadow-painting' refers to a technique, especially used for scenery in the theatre, which creates an illusion of depth.
39. *soothing vows*: Quoted from 364e.
40. *overstep the mark and err*: Cf. 364e (Homer).
41. *children's children*: Adimantus echoes his (poetic) phrasing at 363d.
42. *ordinary discussions*: See 363e–364a.
43. *each of us . . . his own best guard*: The theme of guards and guarding will become an important one later in the *Republic*; this is its first significant occurrence (the actual terms, *phulax* and *phulattein*, appeared first at 333e–334a, where they were translated in terms of 'keeping safe').
44. *the battle of Megara*: Probably one that took place in 409.
45. *to act as her bodyguard*: The verb used here, *epikourein*, is related to the noun (*epikouros*) that will be used for the soldier-class in the good city.
46. *the character of the smaller*: Or 'the form [even 'the look'?] of the smaller' (the Greek term is *idea*).
47. *it'll be no small undertaking*: After all, it involves creating a whole *city*.
48. *we gather many . . . calling this shared habitation a 'city'*: There

may be a play in the Greek (hardly translatable into English) on 'city' (*polis*) and 'many' (*polloi*).

49. *a system of tokens*: I.e., a currency (omitting *nomisma* from the Greek text, as a copyist's gloss – as Slings suggests in the new Oxford text).

50. *their beloveds*: The reference is apparently to an idealized symposium, in which each adult (male) symposiast is paired off with his young (male) 'beloved', or *paidion*. (Alternatively, and as most translators propose, the sense is 'themselves and their *children*'.)

51. *rhapsodes*: Specialist performers, and interpreters, of poetry, like Ion in Plato's dialogue *Ion* (who confesses to specializing exclusively in Homer – he has nothing to say even about Hesiod, who works within the same genre of epic).

52. *Child-overseers*: I.e., *paidagôgoi*, who among other duties would have taken boys to school.

53. *Then we'll need swineherds . . . on top of everything else*: No doubt the main point here is that we didn't need swineherds because there were no pigs (the only animals in the 'healthy' city were to be ones that were needed for purposes other than to be eaten (370d–e) – though no doubt they would be eaten, e.g., after sacrifices to the gods: what else to do with the meat?); now, in the 'feverish' city, there are pigs, as part of an expanded and more luxurious diet, so that there will have to be swineherds too. But might Socrates here be raising a more subtle issue: would the 'healthy' city, which Glaucon equated with a city *of* pigs, need a swineherd to run it? (Would *that* city even need any running?)

54. *if we . . . lived as before*: I.e., if we have the luxurious diet proposed, rather than the one 'we' had in the 'healthy' city.

55. *a decent petteia-player*: *Petteia* was a board-game. We know little about the rules; what we do know suggests that there is no modern equivalent – chess might come close in complexity, and *petteia* may have a piece called 'king', but there, more or less, the similarities seem to have ended.

56. *hoplite fighting*: See n. 6.

57. *the function of our guards is more important than anyone else's*: So far, the 'guards' (*phulakes*) simply represent the city's fighting force. But their role will gradually be expanded, and then split into two: the 'guards' proper will be the rulers, 'guarding' the city's well-being, while 'guards' as described in the present context will become the rulers' 'auxiliaries' (*epikouroi*).

58. *which natural dispositions ... they belong to*: There follows what will turn out to be the first of three sketches of the qualities required for 'guarding a city', as the detailed specifications for this role are gradually filled in. In 412c–414b Socrates will describe how the 'guards' will be divided into those with a ruling function and those without (see preceding note); then, in 503b, when 'the complete and finished guards' (414b) have been revealed as *philosophers*, he will begin giving his fullest description of the qualities required – that is, just for that small proportion of the guards being described in the present passage who will join the ruling group.

59. *when it comes to being a guard ... a young man of good breeding*: The translation here does not reproduce the pun present in the Greek, on *phulax*, 'guard', and *skulax*, 'puppy' – which is what evidently sets up the whole analogy Socrates now launches; and so far, in fact, the role of the 'guards' hardly extends beyond that of watch-dogs, however much it will be expanded in what follows.

60. *spirited*: The term used here, *thumoeidês*, will later be employed to refer to one of the 'parts' of the soul – the 'part' in virtue of which, when it is in the right condition, a soul and a person will be courageous: see esp. 439e–442c (specifically, a person will be courageous if the 'spirited' part retains what it has been told, in the course of its training, about what is and is not to be feared: 442b–c). In the present context, however, the reference seems to be to a more basic kind of 'spiritedness', namely, one that is shared with animals, and a natural rather than an acquired attribute; and even though Socrates has just suggested a link with courage, and made courage a requirement for 'guards', he will in a moment (and for now) insist only that they must be 'spirited'.

61. *what their souls must be like*: Or, as we might prefer to say, 'in relation to their mental attributes'. As before, however, it is probably helpful, especially in light of later developments in the *Republic*, not to assimilate Plato's body/soul contrast too easily to our contrast between body and mind.

62. *both to one another and to the other citizens*: Reading *allêlois ... kai tois allois politais* (the text is corrupted).

63. *And how wouldn't it be a sign ... knowledge and ignorance?*: All of this is surely meant to be a bit of a stretch, and it is tempting to write it off just as a way of including a 'philosophical' disposition among the requirements for the 'guards', who will eventually provide the pool from among whom the future

philosopher-rulers will be selected. There may, however, be more
to it than that (and more than Glaucon can possibly know), for
in the *Lysis* – apparently written before the *Republic* – Plato has
Socrates seeking to identify what is truly loved, and truly good,
precisely with 'what belongs to one' (*to oikeion*, the phrase used
here; cf. also 375c), and suggesting that it takes true wisdom to
learn what that is. In other words, the strained analogy with
guard-dogs perhaps includes a covert reference to the *Lysis* –
simultaneously taking us forward to that moment in the
Republic when the key feature of the philosopher-rulers is
revealed as their understanding of the good itself.

64. *It must be ... that's for sure!*: Glaucon's response here must
surely be sardonic; it is hard to suppose him to be agreeing with
genuine enthusiasm to something so obviously obscure.

65. *being philosophical – loving wisdom*: These four words translate
just two in the Greek, i.e., *(to) philosophon*. To be *philosophos*,
or a *philosophos*, in Greek, is to love (*philein*) wisdom (*sophia*).

66. *how shall we have these people ... educated?*: The signs are that
'these people' will be the 'guards' rather than the citizen body as
a whole (see 378c, 383c, 398b). However, the controls required
for the guards' education, to shield them from the wrong influences, will turn out to affect the city as a whole (see esp. 399e).

67. *I certainly expect ... will help*: Neither Adimantus nor anyone
else tells us how it will. But in fact the kind of upbringing and
education that will be described will include, as its major com-
ponent, an education in excellence or virtue; in this sense we
shall actually be observing justice and the other excellences as
they 'come into existence in a city.'

68. *a somewhat lengthy investigation*: As indeed it turns out to be;
it will not end until 412b.

69. *how to educate our men*: Socrates specifically says 'men'. Much
later on, he will introduce a policy of including women among
the 'guards' as well as men – a proposal that his interlocutors
initially greet with amusement, and a long argument is required
to silence their laughter; for the moment, evidently, he prefers to
hold his fire, taking one step at a time.

70. *If we look at the grander stories ... the less grand ones too*:
Which of course is the kind of thing they are already doing, in looking at justice in the city in order to find justice in the individual.

71. *not a pretty one*: I.e., ugly.

72. *Uranus ... Cronus ... his son*: Uranus (Heaven), Hesiod tells us,
tried to prevent his own children being born, from Earth, until

one of them, Cronus, responded by castrating him; Cronus then went one better than Uranus by eating his offspring, until he was outwitted by Zeus, who then replaced him as king of the gods.

73. *wouldn't be doing anything . . . gods themselves did before them*: As Euthyphro suggests to Socrates, at *Euthyphro* 5e–6a.

74. *embroidered images of gigantomachies*: The most famous image of a gigantomachy, or battle between giants and gods, was on the great ceremonial robe of Athena that was brought out on the occasion of Panathenaic festivals.

75. *that's the sort of thing . . . from the beginning*: So some of what Adimantus complained doesn't happen in today's society (367a) *will* happen in the city that Socrates, Glaucon and he are designing. But see 392a–c.

76. *son . . . father*: Hera's son is the craftsman Hephaestus himself (who apparently trapped his mother in a specially designed throne); his father is Zeus. The story in question is told at *Iliad* 1.593–626.

77. *the battles between the gods in Homer's poem*: See *Iliad* 20.1–74, 21.385–513.

78. *for the encouragement of excellence*: Evidently, then, story-telling will be one of the ways in which we will see 'justice coming into existence' (369a) in the city, along with the other excellences.

79. *if someone were to ask us once again*: Once more, Adimantus wants specific details (see 377e).

80. *the gods*: I.e., any or all of them. Here and in what follows Socrates uses the singular, 'god' (*theos*), with or without the definite article, because he is talking about the gods in general. It is tempting, then, to translate with 'god', used generically (much as we use 'man' for mankind), but this is awkward, at least in part because even with a lower case initial letter 'god' will tend to suggest a singular god (or God), when throughout Socrates is talking about either any or all of the gods – and by the time we reach 381c, 'god' becomes an impossible translation, since Socrates switches in the same sentence from 'god' to 'each one of them'.

81. *not only are the gods . . . in fact good*: As this suggests, the goodness of gods is axiomatic for Socrates – and evidently also for Adimantus, since he immediately assents to Socrates' proposition here.

82. *'two jars' . . . corners of the fair earth*: Plato here selects from and adapts *Iliad* 24.527–32.

83. *'lord high steward' . . . all alike*: Socrates is here perhaps adapt-

ing Homer, *Iliad* 4.84, which has Zeus as 'steward' specifically of war.

84. *Pandarus' oath-breaking . . . truce*: Another episode in the *Iliad* (4.30 ff.).

85. *Themis*: Goddess of due order, of things in their right place.

86. *as Aeschylus says*: In his *Niobe*, now lost.

87. *what happened to the offspring of Pelops*: I.e., Atreus and Thyestes, cursed as a result of Pelops' causing death by cheating in a chariot-race; Atreus served up his brother's sons to him for dinner.

88. *now actually . . . changing their appearance*: Reading *gignomenon kai allattonta*.

89. *from this point of view*: I.e., if we're talking about change brought about by external factors.

90. *the gods . . . city streets*: Homer, *Iliad* 17.485–6.

91. *Proteus or Thetis*: Both gods were (according to the poets) habitual shape-shifters.

92. *'the life-providing sons of Inachus, Argive river'*: Evidently from a lost play of Aeschylus.

93. *here's the other possibility*: See 380d.

94. *nobody who's out of his mind . . . is loved by the gods*: Because the very fact of their being mad or out of their minds would be a sign of divine disfavour?

95. *no divinity or god . . . with falsehoods*: The Greek phrase rendered here as 'no divinity or god', *to daimonion te kai to theion*, recalls the similar phrase Socrates uses at *Apology* 31c–d, *theion ti kai daimonion*, to describe the divine 'sign' (*Apology* 40b) or 'voice' (*Apology* 31d) which intervenes with him from time to time, and whose authority he accepts unquestioningly.

96. *the signs they send*: See preceding note.

97. *as the second of our outlines*: See 380c–d.

98. *having Zeus send that dream to Agamemnon*: *Iliad* 2.1–34. The dream promises Agamemnon victory over the Trojans if he launches an immediate attack; but Zeus' real plan is a Greek defeat.

99. *in his play*: The play is now lost.

100. *my son*: Achilles, killed by an arrow shot by Paris but guided by Phoebus Apollo.

101. *refuse to give him a chorus*: I.e., not let him put his play on (a chorus being an essential requirement of any tragedy).

102. *What about . . . courageous?*: Socrates' description of the formation of 'guards' of the new city has from the beginning been in terms of what should and should not be allowed 'if they are

going to' have the qualities they'll need; there is no suggestion that merely hearing the right things said will be enough by itself – even, perhaps, if they already have the right natural qualities.

103. *I'd rather work the fields ... assembled here*: The dead Achilles' response to Odysseus, when the latter tries to console him by talking of his glory in the world above (*Odyssey* 11.489–91).

104. *The halls ... gods themselves*: Iliad 20.64–5 (the gods are facing each other across the battlefield, and the god Hades fears the consequences).

105. *Alas ... all mind and thought bereft*: Iliad 23.103–4 (in a dream, Achilles has just tried to embrace the 'shade' of his beloved Patroclus).

106. *Alone ... passing shadows*: Odyssey 10.495 (said of the prophet Tiresias, to whom Persephone granted the unique privilege of keeping his mind even when dead).

107. *Straight off ... manhood gone*: Iliad 16.856 (of Patroclus' death); 22.382 (of Hector's).

108. *Like smoke ... was gibbering gone*: Iliad 23.100–101 (Patroclus slips from Achilles' grasp).

109. *As when ... gibbering, together*: Odyssey 24.6–10 (the 'shades' are those of Penelope's suitors, who have been killed by Odysseus on his return home).

110. *Cocytus and Styx*: Cocytus, like Styx, River of Loathing, is a river of the underworld – the River of Lamentation.

111. *send a shiver through anyone who hears them*: Omitting two words in the Greek (*hôs oietai*) which make no sense and are not readily emended to anything that does.

112. *we say*: The 'we' in this case seems to be Socrates and his interlocutors, in their role as legislators for the new city.

113. *Lying now on his side ... unforgiving sea*: Iliad 24.10–12, with the last line apparently adapted (Achilles, son of the sea-goddess Thetis, mourns his dead comrade Patroclus).

114. *with both hands ... down from his head*: Iliad 18.23–4 (Achilles hears the news of Patroclus' death).

115. *rolling there ... appealing to them one by one*: Iliad 22.414–15 (Priam, descended from Zeus, pleads with his people to be allowed to ransom his son Hector from Achilles).

116. *Oh! What a wretch ... best of sons*: Iliad 18.54 (Thetis feels for Achilles' grief at Patroclus' death).

117. *Alas, dear man ... grieves within*: Iliad 22.168–9 (Zeus on seeing Hector pursued by Achilles).

118. *Ah me! ... tamed and killed*: Iliad 16.433–4 (Zeus grieves at the imminent death of one of his own sons).

119. *And now there rose ... through the hall*: Iliad 1.599–600 (Hephaestus is a god, but lame, and on both counts unsuited to wait on table; but it successfully distracts the quarrelling gods).

120. *If what we were saying just now is right*: See 382c–d.

121. *the rulers of our city*: This is the first time rulers have been mentioned; Socrates will later bring them centre-stage.

122. *tells or acts out a falsehood*: This wider sense of *pseudesthai* – wider, that is, than mere 'lying' – was well prepared for in the previous discussion of falsehood (377a–386c), but is in any case surely implied by the present context.

123. *those who work their craft ... working of wood*: Odyssey 17.383–4.

124. *moderation*: I.e., *sôphrosunê* (as at 364a), which often used to be translated, unhelpfully, as 'temperance'; etymologically, the term is closer to 'sound-mindedness', but in the present context 'moderation', and/or 'moderateness', generally fits better. It is in any case one of the four main virtues or excellences that Socrates will discuss and eventually define, the others being justice, courage and wisdom.

125. *The chief elements of moderation ... food*: See 430c–432b, where 'being rulers of their own desires' will provide the basis of an analysis of moderation/moderateness 'in the city' in terms of obedience to rulers.

126. *Sit, my friend ... listen hard to what I say*: Iliad 4.412 (Diomedes rebukes Sthenelus).

127. *on went the Achaeans ... captains' wrath*: Actually a combination of two widely separated part-lines in our text, Iliad 3.8 and 4.431. The 'Achaeans' are the Greek army.

128. *You wine-sack ... the heart of a deer*: Iliad 1.225 (Achilles to the Achaean/Greek commander-in-chief, Agamemnon).

129. *there beside us ... fills the waiting cups*: Odyssey 9.8–10, apparently in modified form, and torn from its proper context – Odysseus is actually talking of the delights of listening to a singer at a feast. In Homer, Odysseus probably is 'wisest'; by Plato's time, his name is at least as likely to be associated with trickery and treachery.

130. *To die of hunger ... meet one's doom*: Odyssey 12.342 (one of Odysseus' crew, shipwrecked, is persuading the others to eat the Sun-god's sacred cattle – with fatal results for the crew).

131. *when first they used to come ... their dear parents all-unknowing*: Socrates here recites phrases from Homer's telling of the story (*Iliad* 14.294–391). Zeus and Hera were hardly an ordinary courting couple, nor were their parents particularly 'dear'. (For Zeus' and Hera's relationship with their father Cronus, see 377e–378a.)

132. *Hephaestus' entrapment of Ares and Aphrodite*: *Odyssey* 8.266–366 (Hephaestus literally traps his wife Aphrodite in bed with Ares, and shows them off for the amusement of the other gods).

133. *He smote his breast ... you bore than this*: *Odyssey* 20.17–18 (Odysseus hears the sounds of his maidservants going off to cavort with his wife's suitors, and holds himself back from slaughtering them – just yet).

134. *Gifts sway ... respected kings*: Possibly a line from Hesiod.

135. *the advice Achilles' tutor Phoenix gave him ... if they didn't*: *Iliad* 9.515–23.

136. *or ... in return for payment*: That is, Hector's corpse, to Priam (*Iliad* 24.501–2, 552–62, 592–5).

137. *Far-shooter ... pay you back in full*: *Iliad* 22.15, 20

138. *This hair ... as his spoils*: *Iliad* 23.151.

139. *war-prisoners*: That is, Trojans who had been taken prisoner in battle rather than killed. The two episodes referred to are in *Iliad* 24.14–21 and 23.175–6 respectively.

140. *grandson of Zeus ... Chiron*: Peleus' father was Aeacus, son of Zeus; Chiron is a Centaur who – this story is not in Homer – literally brought the infant Achilles up in the wild. Homer recognizes Chiron mainly for his knowledge of medicine.

141. *those terrible abductions*: Of Helen, from Sparta, and of the goddess Persephone from Hades (a failed attempt). These stories were evidently to be found in other, non-Homeric, epics, and in tragedies.

142. *son of a god, or hero*: In this context, as in many, the two expressions are virtually synonymous.

143. *Those close to Zeus ... potent in their veins*: Socrates cites again from Aeschylus' lost play *Niobe*.

144. *a ready ... acceptance of badness*: And in particular, presumably, of a lack of moderation/moderateness, the excellence or virtue on which the discussion has been focusing.

145. *the subject we were discussing all along*: I.e., the benefits of justice. In talking about 'how gods should be talked about, and demi-gods, and heroes, and the underworld' (392a), Socrates and his interlocutors have actually managed to give at least a partial

account of how two of the excellences – courage and moderation – might come about in a city, suitably organized. However,
talking about how poets and others do, and should, talk about
men and about human life inevitably takes us back to the terms
of Adimantus' original challenge: people actually do tell us that
happiness comes from injustice, and who's to say they're wrong?
And, as Socrates will immediately point out, to meet that challenge he still needs to define justice first (after all, he and
Thrasymachus were evidently in complete disagreement about it,
and nothing has yet been done to put that right). So though we
might have expected a sketch of justice here to parallel those of
courage and moderation, we can't have one. Instead, Socrates
will push ahead with his description of the education of the
guards in the new city. When the broad outlines of that city are
finally completed, Socrates will propose that it is a good one, possessing all the excellences, and will instigate the awaited search
for justice (and, in a very preliminary way, wisdom) within it.

146. *his god*: Apollo.

147. *and he beseeched . . . leaders of their peoples*: Iliad 1.15–16.

148. *dithyrambs*: A type of wild choral lyric originally associated with
Dionysus.

149. *from what we said before*: See 369e–370c, 374a–d.

150. *it's my impression . . . comedy and tragedy*: Socrates does not
here rule out the possibility that the ideal comic writer might be
identical with the ideal tragic writer (a possibility he floats at the
end of the *Symposium*).

151. *imitate a woman . . . in labour*: These, and the items that follow,
are all actual or possible examples of what tragic and/or comic
poets in particular might portray to an audience. It gives special
point to Socrates' argument that all the actors in the theatre
would be male.

152. *appropriate arrangement of notes . . . musical mode*: Here and in
what follows, 'arrangement of notes' and 'mode' translate the
same Greek term, *harmonia*. Socrates will move on to music
proper, and the actual 'modes' or styles of Greek music, in a
moment; for now he is talking only about the analogues to
musical arrangements (modes) and rhythms in speech.

153. *the political arrangements we . . . are proposing*: I.e., our regime,
or 'republic', *politeia*.

154. *At this point . . . how it is to be said*: See 392c.

155. *Marsyas and his*: One story is that Athena invented the kinds of
instruments that Socrates and Adimantus have just discarded,

and threw them away in disgust because they distorted her face. The legendary human musician Marsyas found them and challenged Apollo, master of the lyre, to a competition.

156. *By the Dog!*: A favourite oath of Socrates'; at *Gorgias* 482b, he swears 'by the Dog, the god of the Egyptians'.

157. *This city of ours that we were calling 'luxurious'*: See 372e.

158. *we're actually giving it a thorough cleaning up*: And so, perhaps, making it more like the kind of city that Socrates called 'true' and 'healthy' (372e again) and Glaucon likened to a city of pigs (372d), though it will evidently remain larger and more complex. We should also remember that the very requirement for 'guards' grew out of the expansion of the city to accommodate the kind of spice and variety that Glaucon suggested would be necessary for any decent city of men; nor have we yet been told anything about the way of life of those inhabitants of the new city who are *not* guards. Providing the right environment for the guards will have a 'cleansing' effect on the whole city, but we have not so far been given grounds for supposing – despite that talk of a 'thorough cleaning up' – that Socrates would give it a totally clean bill of health.

159. *a well-balanced ... life*: I.e., presumably, a life exhibiting the two chief excellences or virtues that have been the focus of the discussion so far, moderation and courage.

160. *when we've spotted them*: Reading *idontas* for the manuscripts' (and Slings's) *idonta*.

161. *forms*: See n. 170.

162. *What I can say ... that I can't tell you*: Whatever may have been the forms of rhythm and musical arrangement Glaucon has in mind, their relevance to the present context is not obvious – which may be the point. On the three forms of rhythm, see n. 164.

163. *when we're with Damon*: Damon is a famous musical expert; but as inventor of the relaxed Lydian mode (398e), he might not actually be too welcome in the new city.

164. *rhythms ... as the foot rises and falls*: The dactylic foot, the basic building block of epic verse, consists of one long (syllable) plus two shorts (e.g., *seminal*), where the latter can be replaced by a second long, giving a spondee (e.g., *spondee*) in place of a dactyl. Socrates seems to be poking gentle fun at the idea that shorts can 'become' longs, and vice versa. The 'equal', as in dactyls and spondees, is probably one of the three forms of rhythm Glaucon refers to at 400a, while iambs and trochees (short-long, e.g., *belief*,

and long-short, e.g., *vivid*, respectively) exhibit a second form, the 'double', one part of the foot being 'double' that of the other; the third form, the 'cretic', long-short-long (e.g., *germinal*, pronounced as in French), is represented by the ratio 3:2.

165. *'But then'*: Glaucon here mimics Socrates.

166. *the disposition of the soul*: Or 'the soul's ethos (*êthos*)'.

167. *fineness in speech*: Cf. 401a.

168. *he more than anyone . . . affinity to himself*: I.e., he will welcome the right kind of speech, because it will be telling him to do what he is already inclined to do in virtue of his musical training.

169. *by the gods!*: The exclamation reflects Socrates' awareness of just how much knowledge his proposals about music will presuppose: see following note.

170. *the forms of moderation . . . everywhere around us*: Socrates does not seem to be referring here to different forms (*eidê*) of moderation, courage, and so on, quite in the way that he referred, e.g., to the different forms (*eidê*), i.e., kinds or types, of rhythm at 400a. 'Recognizing the form of moderation (etc.)' here seems rather to be a matter of recognizing moderation (or whatever it may be) for what it is, i.e., as instantiated in, or shared in by, sensible things, especially flesh-and-blood individuals ('as we encounter them . . . around us') – which is actually the kind of task Socrates, Glaucon and Adimantus are presently embarked upon, in their search for moderation, courage, wisdom and justice in city and individual.

171. *the most beautiful*: Or 'the finest'. The Greek adjective has both connotations, but 'beautiful' is required by the next turn in the argument.

172. *if someone were out of tune*: I.e., with 'the things I just mentioned' – 'the forms of moderation, courage . . .'.

173. *makes one lose one's mind*: Glaucon here plays on the *phron*-root of *sôphrosunê* – 'sound-*mind*edness' as well as 'moderation' (see n. 124).

174. *lack of moderation*: Or 'lack of restraint' (*akolasia*).

175. *for fine ends*: I.e., fine-and-beautiful (*kala*) ones (see n. 171). For an example of what these ends might be – improvement of the beloved, and progress towards truth about beauty and goodness on the part of the lover – see Diotima's account of the ascent of love in the *Symposium* (207c–212a).

176. *After . . . its physical counterpart*: See 376e.

177. *the mind*: 'Mind' (*dianoia*) here seems barely distinguishable from 'soul', *psuchê* (our 'psyche'); that is, what it refers to

appears to be what Socrates up till now has been content to call 'soul'.

178. *One thing we said*: See 389e ff.

179. *Corinthian girls*: I.e., saucy prostitutes, to be taken with dinner?

180. *the songs and tunes . . . every rhythm*: See 399c–d.

181. *sons of Asclepius*: Asclepius is the legendary founder of the art of medicine; calling contemporary doctors his 'sons' – in fact a normal honorific title for members of the medical profession – doubles the irony already present in the description of them as 'clever' or 'subtle' (*kompsoi*).

182. *the woman who gave. . . Pramnian wine*: In the text of the *Iliad* as we have it (at 11.624), one Hecamede pours Pramnian wine, during an episode when Eurypylus has been wounded; either Plato had a different text, or he is embellishing – or misremembering – the story.

183. *Phocylides' advice*: Phocylides was a sixth-century poet from Miletus in Asia Minor.

184. *Let's not get into a fight with him about it*: And after all, there might well be a question about exactly when 'a man has enough to live on'; from the perspective of the notoriously frugal Socrates, though evidently not from Glaucon's, 'enough to live on' might be almost nothing.

185. *it puts a complete block . . . tested in this way*: Socrates here seems to refer, somewhat obliquely, to the development of the special excellence of *wisdom* – of which, in the 'guards', hardly anything has yet been said, and in fact will not be said until much later on, when the philosopher-rulers – to be selected from the guards whose education is currently being discussed – have been introduced as the true 'guards' of the city. (Slings, 2003, marks a minor lacuna near the beginning of this sentence, suspecting the omission of 'I said'; I record the fact without thinking it necessary to mark it in the translation.)

186. *They sucked . . . soothing balms*: Based on Homer, *Iliad* 4.218.

187. *any more than they did for Eurypylus*: See 405e.

188. *in accordance with what we said before*: See the 'outlines' of what may and may not be said about gods at 379a–383c.

189. *And won't a truly musical person . . . and capture it at will*: Socrates here returns to two points he made in introducing the subject of physical training, namely (1) that physical training will be closely related to its musical counterpart (404b), and (2) that he and Glaucon won't need to go into the details (403d–e).

190. *the spirited aspect of his nature*: Socrates has already talked about this, or at any rate the requirement for the guards to be 'spirited', back at 375a–376c – a passage to which he will shortly explicitly refer back.

191. *they have ... for the sake of the soul*: Typically, Plato attributes to people – here, any educators who either have proposed or will propose an education based on music and physical training – the motives he thinks correct, rather than those they actually had, or have.

192. *isn't it ... will bring gentleness?*: In 375a–376c, it was suggested that gentleness (there *praotês*; here the term for 'gentle' is *hêmeros*, 'tame') required the kind of 'philosophical' quality possessed by the best kind of guard-dogs, i.e., the ability to distinguish friend from enemy. That Socrates has that passage in mind is confirmed by what he says next.

193. *we say*: As indeed 'we' actually said at 375a–376c.

194. *crude*: Or 'rustic'; cf. the reference to 'boorishness' (*apeirokalia*) at 403c.

195. *'softest of spearsmen'*: Apollo's taunt to Hector at *Iliad* 17.588.

196. *or give its perceptions the thorough cleansing they need*: This looks like another brief and elusive anticipation, as at 407b–c, of the subject of the wisdom of the philosopher-rulers. (True philosophy, and true wisdom, will turn out to be, among other things, a matter of rising above the apparent evidence of our senses.) A further such anticipation will follow shortly, in 412a–b, itself followed immediately by the question about who will rule the city – but without any explicit mention of the requirement that the rulers be philosophers. That will be introduced as a quite separate step, after the main business presently in hand (i.e., the search for a definition of justice) has been completed.

197. *the gods*: Socrates actually uses the singular; but see n. 80.

198. *appropriate degrees of stretching and slackening*: Cf. 410d–412a.

199. *its arrangements*: Its *politeia*, its 'constitution', which will include the laws it has governing education.

200. *of course it's ... not a detailed treatment of the subject*: Much more will be said about it when Socrates finally makes his radical proposal that the rulers should be *philosophers* – of which we (and Glaucon) have so far only had hints, for example in the brief reference at 412c to the requirement for 'intelligence' in the business of 'guarding'.

201. *those falsehoods ... when the occasion required it*: See 389b–c.

202. *but if not*: Is this perhaps a further reference forward to the introduction of philosopher-rulers? After all, it is hard to see

how *philosophers* could be brought to believe the sort of story Socrates will now propose (which he himself will say 'would take a lot of persuading to make people believe').

203. *something with a Phoenician flavour*: The reference may be to the story of Cadmus the Phoenician, founder of Thebes, who peoples the new city by sowing a dragon's teeth. Stories about men born from the earth – a literal version of autochthony – were not unusual; Plato himself makes use of them several times for his own purposes.

204. *bringing them up and educating them*: That is, presumably, 'the rulers and the soldiers', at least in the first instance; the proposed education system has for the most part explicitly been restricted to the 'guards'.

205. *That we shouldn't insist on, my dear Glaucon*: And there will in fact be a further excursus, on the education of the rulers, later on (beginning at 521c).

206. *hired auxiliaries*: The emphasis here is on 'hired'; Adimantus' question is how the life and function of Socrates' 'auxiliaries' will differ from those of plain mercenaries.

207. *won't get pay . . . as ordinary people would*: In fact, under ordinary circumstances the only people likely to work in return for food alone would be slaves.

208. *Our thought was*: See 369a.

209. *shortly . . . opposite kind of city*: See 449a (though actually the subject will then be put off for some considerable time).

210. *reclining on couches, left to right*: I.e., arranged in due order as at a symposium or drinking-party, of the sort usually reserved for the rich.

211. *compelling . . . guards of ours*: I.e., perhaps, using a combination of force (through the law) and persuasion. The 'guards' in this case are presumably those of the original guards selected as rulers (the 'complete and finished guards' of 414b).

212. *the best . . . specific function*: Socrates called them 'true craftsmen of freedom for the city' (395c).

213. *it must be . . . by its nature*: I.e., perhaps, there will be a kind of happiness that belongs to craftsmen, and another to each of those two superior kinds of 'craftsmen', the auxiliaries and the guards.

214. *bad at what they do*: The term Socrates uses here, *kakoergos*, in its usual Platonic spelling, *kakourgos*, is associated with a different kind of 'bad-working'; *kakourgoi* are 'malefactors', 'rogues' or 'criminals'.

215. *they themselves . . . athletes in the business of war*: Cf. 403e.

216. *it's like one of those puzzles . . . to play with*: As in, 'When is a city not a city?'

217. *the proverbial one big thing . . . rather than just big*: The proverb is about the fox, who knows a lot of things, and the hedgehog, who knows one big thing (how to escape the fox). Thus the point of Socrates' qualification ('or perhaps . . .') is to allow the possibility that there are other things more important than the one 'big thing' he is talking about now, i.e., the upbringing and education of the young guards, crucial though these may be.

218. *that would be best*: It is not clear whether Adimantus is referring here specifically to the subject of women, marriage and children, or to the general proposal that the guards, if well educated, can be left to sort out this and other matters for themselves. In any case, it seems unlikely that he has any idea how radical Socrates' proposals about women and the family will be. At 449c–d Adimantus will complain about Socrates' cavalier treatment of the subject here, and insist on his being more specific. (Socrates obliges.)

219. *a kind of circle*: That is, as we might say, a virtuous one.

220. *the song . . . the more*: In the Greek text this is almost two complete lines, corresponding roughly to our text of Homer, *Odyssey* 1.351–2.

221. *Damon*: See 400b, with n. 163.

222. *the gods*: The Greek (as so often before) uses the singular, collectively.

223. *four cubits tall*: I.e., something under two metres tall (or six feet – by ancient Greek standards, tall but not too tall).

224. *the head of a Hydra*: The hydra was a many-headed monster faced by Heracles; if he cut off one of its heads, two or three would grow in its place.

225. *our previous recommendations*: See 422a, 423c, 423c–d, 423e ('the one big thing').

226. *on the navel-stone at the centre of the earth*: I.e., at Delphi. In iconography, at least, a stone in the shape of a convex navel is Apollo's seat.

227. *you said*: I.e., at 368b–c.

228. *our city . . . is completely good*: This comes as something of a surprise, given that Socrates has just suggested that *in*justice as well as justice might be found in it. Perhaps what he has in mind is that, if the city has been set up properly, it will possess all the relevant species of goodness or excellence – which is the only point that he will actually infer from its 'complete goodness'. It

will still remain a possibility that not all its *inhabitants* will be perfectly good; after all, if they were, why would the 'guards' need to be assigned the role of an internal police force? And we also know, from the discussion about how the rulers will be chosen (412c–414b), that some of the guards will be better than others. (See also 420b: our aim is 'to achieve happiness *so far as possible* for the city as a whole.')

229. *Then take any four things . . . the one that was left*: None of this seems obviously to apply in the present case, where any number of things might in principle be mistaken for 'the thing being looked for', i.e., justice, or indeed any of the other three. But the second of the two scenarios described corresponds pretty well with what will actually happen: having 'discovered' where wisdom, courage and moderation are to be found in the city, Socrates will find himself in a position to identify its justice, too, as 'what's left': see esp. 433b–c.

230. *these rulers of ours . . . complete guards*: See 412c–414b.

231. *dispensing with it*: Socrates explained the idea – and the causes – of people's 'dispensing with' beliefs at 412e–413c.

232. *pleasure, more fearful . . . than any*: Socrates ends the sentence in impassioned (and rhetorical) mode. 'Chalestrian lye' was known as a particularly powerful detergent.

233. *this*: I.e., clearly, the educated sort of correct belief about what is and is not to be feared.

234. *civic courage*: In the first instance, this will be courage as it belongs to the city; but it will also be the courage of the *citizen*, as distinct from the so-called 'courage' we attribute to animals and slaves – and also from another, still higher, variety of courage, to be attributed to the philosopher-rulers (this may well be what Socrates is referring to in the next sentence: see 486a–b). 'Civic' courage, in this respect, seems to belong to the category of what Socrates will call 'demotic', i.e., ordinary (and non-philosophical) goodness or excellence: see 500d.

235. *moderation, or moderateness*: I.e., *sôphrosunê*; its opposite is *akolasia*, 'lack of restraint' (see 431b).

236. *it looks more . . . the previous two did*: Socrates makes it sound here as if he was expecting at least one of the four excellences to be associated with 'concord or attunement'; and given the prominence of music in the educational programme for the new city, that is not perhaps so surprising.

237. *rulers and ruled . . . should rule*: See 389d–e, where Socrates

introduced obedience to rulers as one of the 'chief elements' in moderateness, alongside control of one's desires.

238. *and point it out*: Reading *phrasêis* (Slings, 2003, has *phraseis*).

239. *have often said ourselves*: That is, perhaps, in the course of ordinary conversation.

240. *what's left, in our city*: I.e., evidently, what's left of the relevant items in it – presumably salient features that might plausibly be identified with/as the city's excellences or virtues.

241. *the three things we've looked at*: Adding the words *triôn hôn* between *tôn* and *eskemmetha*, as suggested (but not printed in the text) by Slings, 2003.

242. *what makes it possible . . . is present*: 'Makes it possible', i.e., as the 'universal rule' that 'each individual should practise the single role', etc. (433a) may be presumed to do: see 374a–e (where the rule is first introduced), then 395b, 406c, 421a. To understand what this has to do with justice, we have only to think back to Thrasymachus' proposal (see esp. 338e–339a) that laws – and so justice as conceived in legal terms – will always serve the interests of the rulers, the implication being that ruling goes hand in hand with exploiting the ruled; contrast what Socrates will immediately say about the function of the law in the new city.

243. *we did say*: I.e., at 427e–428a.

244. *Will you . . . judging legal disputes?*: Evidently, then, making legal decisions will be a part of the function of ruling.

245. *and everything else . . . accordingly*: I.e., probably, so that the new carpenter-shoemaker had the tools and social positions/roles ('honours') belonging to both roles.

246. *a natural craftsman or . . . money-maker*: Earlier, Socrates marked off money-making as a separate occupation of its own (separate from, e.g., medicine or shepherding: see esp. 341c–342e, 345c–e). He now treats all the producers, as a group, as opposed to the money-less soldiers and guards, specifically as 'money-makers', presumably insofar as they will all have to make money from, i.e., in addition to, being shoemakers, metal-workers, and so on; indeed, 'money-makers' will shortly become a shorthand name for them (434c), serving to separate them off from the two groups whose specific function is to care – in different ways – for the city as a whole, and whose needs are cared/catered for by the city in return.

247. *described . . . as criminality*: Cf. 422a, with n. 214.

248. *this pattern*: Or 'this form' (*eidos*).

249. *in respect of the form . . . they have in them*: For this way of talk-
     ing about properties (as we might call them) in things, compare
     esp. 402c. ('Form', here too, is *eidos*.)
250. *these same kinds*: 'Kind' here (i.e., kind of nature) is *eidos*,
     whereas in Socrates' last contribution it was *genos*; before that it
     was *genê phuseôn* ('kinds of natures'); very soon, 'kinds' will
     become 'parts' – and then 'kinds' again.
251. *it's another road . . . more challenging*: Cf. 504b–c.
252. *whether actions . . . will make no difference*: I.e., whether we're
     talking about actions in relation to others, or events internal to
     ourselves? 'Passions' translates *pathêmata*: some translators pre-
     fer to take the contrast as being between actions and *states* – which
     are certainly included within the range of the term *pathêmata*,
     but perhaps not when, as here, it is directly opposed to *poiêmata*
     (the basic contrast being between doing, *poiein*, and having
     something done to one, *paschein/pathein*).
253. *appetites*: The Greek term used here, *epithumia*, may also serve,
     in Plato, as a general term for desire or wanting of any sort, but
     in the present context it refers primarily to what he consistently
     treats as the bodily desires.
254. *a distinct category*: I.e., of desire (see preceding note). Part of the
     basis for treating the bodily desires as a special category is hinted
     at in the next part of the sentence, namely, that they have a par-
     ticular capacity for making their presence felt.
255. *one could perhaps think this objector had a point*: The imagined
     objection is in fact one that Socrates himself might have raised,
     since one of the key tenets with which he is associated is precisely
     that all desire, always, is for the good. See section 2 of the Intro-
     duction to this volume, on 'Socratic intellectualism', and also
     505e, where Socrates will explicitly say that 'every soul pursues
     [the good]', and that it is 'the very thing for the sake of which
     [every soul] does everything it does'. (This is, however, a contro-
     versial passage – as indeed is the present one.) If, as argued in the
     Introduction, the intellectualist viewpoint is actually incorpor-
     ated into the *Republic* itself, we shall need to ask whether there
     is any way in which the perspective of 'this objector' might sur-
     vive alongside the position Socrates is now arguing for. In any
     case, for the moment, he makes clear that he does not see the
     objection as fatal to that position.
256. *or whatever we should suppose it is of*: It is as difficult in Greek
     as it is in English to find a general word for the correlate of
     knowledge, taken just *as* knowledge (i.e., knowledge without

qualification or specification). 'Learning', *mathêma*, here is a mere stand-in for this (later, however, Socrates will introduce something he calls the 'greatest *mathêma*', or 'greatest object of knowledge': the 'form' of the good).

257. *the things that drag ... the soul in such directions*: That is, the appetites; see esp. 442a, with n. 268.

258. *either through ... sickness*: Examples of the two types of case Socrates has in mind might be perhaps (for the first type) someone suffering from thirst because of extreme summer temperatures – in a location where, say, the only available water-supply was polluted; and (for the second) a habitual, or pathological, drunkard or glutton.

259. *spirit ... we get angry with*: Socrates here implicitly refers back to earlier discussion of the requirement for spiritedness – properly controlled, of course – among the guards (375a–376c, 410b–411e); at the same time he connects spirit with the ordinary emotion of anger, which is clearly what leads Glaucon at first to locate it with the 'appetitive' element.

260. *Leontius, son of Aglaion*: Otherwise unknown to us.

261. *distinct from this too*: I.e., as it is evidently distinct from the appetitive element.

262. *the different elements ... were three*: See 435b (there it was 'kinds of natures', *genê phuseôn*; here it is simply *genê*, 'kinds' – that is, of elements – on its own, but the reference is clearly the same).

263. *soldiering*: I.e., the *epikourêtikon* element, the *epikouroi* or 'auxiliaries'.

264. *the same phenomenon in animals*: I.e., presumably, the presence of spirit without reason.

265. *the verse we cited in that other context*: See 390d, with n. 133.

266. *the same kinds of elements ... in the city*: That is, presumably, in the city Socrates and his interlocutors have described – but also, perhaps, insofar as this city is a model for others, in any city, to the extent that it resembles the model. 'Kinds of elements': the Greek here has only 'kinds', but it is clear enough what Socrates is referring to – different 'somethings' ('kinds of natures', as he called them back at 435b; in the present translation they are typically 'elements', used as one way among several of reproducing Greek constructions using the neuter of the definite article with a participle, or a clause introduced by a neuter relative pronoun – 'what we calculate with', 'what we experience anger with', etc.).

267. *as we said*: See esp. 411e–412a.

268. *which is the . . . most insatiable when it comes to money*: Socrates refers here to the numerousness of our appetites, which makes them directly analogous to the masses who make up the third 'kind' in the city (cf. 431a, 'the sheer mass of the worse [element]', along with 437d–438a, which immediately multiplied the appetites by insisting, e.g., that desire for a cold or a hot drink must be broken down into a desire (1) for a drink, (2) for cold or hot), and also creates a direct analogy with the third and lowest 'kind of nature' in the city, i.e., the money-makers. The reasoning and spirited elements in themselves require little by way of financing; the sheer number of the appetites, combined with the fact that they contain no mechanism in themselves – 'by [their] nature' – to limit them, in principle makes them actually 'insatiable' in their demands for the money needed to satisfy them.

269. *this part of him*: This is the first time in the discussion of the different 'elements' of the soul that Socrates has used the term 'part'; see 429b–c for the treatment of the corresponding 'part' of the city, on which the present context implicitly depends.

270. *the spirited . . . words it has heard*: The words in question are presumably the same as the 'beautiful words and beautiful lessons' referred to at 442a. Instead of *hupo tôn logôn*, 'by the words', later manuscripts read *hupo tou logou*, 'by reason', which would tend to imply that the reasoning element/part in the individual himself determined what was and was not to be feared; but up to this point that role has been consistently assigned to the legislators and/or to story-tellers rather than to reason in individual souls. Thus the city was courageous 'by virtue of having in [its fighting] part the capacity to preserve under any circumstances the belief that the things that are to be feared are the very same or of the same sorts that the *lawgiver* told them about in the course of their education' (429b–c) – a passage that provides the basic model for the present sentence, with the notable omission of the reference to belief (beliefs, one imagines, would naturally belong to the reasoning element – even though both spirited and appetitive parts will shortly be said to 'share the belief' with the reasoning part that the latter should rule: 442d). At the same time, Socrates is happy to attribute knowledge to both city (428b–429a, on the basis that it is able to make good decisions) and individual (in what he will next say, here in 442c), as he probably must, if they are to be called wise. (Wis-

dom, presumably, would be expected to involve at least some sort of knowledge.) The question is, where they will get that wisdom from; so far, rulers and auxiliaries have only been assigned a fairly basic musical and poetic education, along with physical education. Later on Socrates will add a whole new dimension to the rulers' education, which will turn them into *philosophers*, capable of reasoning, and reaching truths, for themselves; but we are not there yet.

271. *it too will have knowledge*: I.e., like the city (428b–429a).

272. *we've so often talked about*: Most recently at 441d–e (one role for each person/element/part).

273. *if anything . . . disputes the conclusion*: I.e., if we still have any doubts, and/or if any element/part of the soul thinks it deserves more.

274. *element*: Or 'kind' (*genos*).

275. *becoming a friend to himself*: The unjust person, Socrates claimed at 352a, was 'the enemy both of himself and of the just'.

276. *along with any others . . . between*: Evidently, then, there may be more than three elements/parts to the human soul; Socrates is not committing himself.

277. *enslaving the kind whose nature is to rule*: The text is mangled here, but the general sense is clear enough.

278. *to inquire whether . . . by being punished*: I.e., to answer the original question that Socrates undertook to try to answer, in response to challenges from Glaucon and Adimantus, back in 367e–368c.

279. *the very thing that gives us life*: Or 'the very thing with which we live' (the soul).

280. *'aristocracy'*: Socrates here appropriates the term 'aristocracy', *aristokratia* – rule by the best, *hoi aristoi* – for rule by the people who, according to his argument, will actually be the best, both in themselves and at the job.

281. *men*: Socrates here uses the masculine plural in a way that could, in principle, include women. But Glaucon, at least, will assume that it is just men, and male rulers, that Socrates is talking about; the possibility of female rulers is something that needs to be, and will be, specifically argued for.

282. *well, obviously . . . 'what friends have, they share'*: See 423e–424a.

283. *Adrasteia*: A close relation of the more familiar Nemesis.

284. *because I really do suppose . . . in matters of justice and law*: If this looks a strange idea, it is perfectly compatible with a

recurring idea in Plato, that death is of no great importance to us, at least by comparison with intellectual error – one of the greatest such errors being to think that death is something to be afraid of. 'In matters of justice and the law': Socrates' proposals, after all, would be enshrined in law in the new city. (The text seems to be corrupt here; as usual, I read the text preferred, and defended, by Slings in the new Oxford *Republic*.)

285. *women's roles . . . men's*: And/or 'the female drama' after the men's, with an implied reference to a form of drama – mime – in which the female (albeit with male performers) apparently did follow the male.

286. *when it came . . . riding horses*: I.e., serving as hoplites or in the cavalry.

287. *antilogic*: An expert in 'antilogic' would typically claim to lead a respondent who starts with one position, on anything whatever, into asserting the opposite of that position. See, e.g., *Phaedo* 101e, with 90b–c.

288. *dialectic*: 'Dialectic', or as Socrates sometimes calls it, 'the art of dialectic', is philosophical discussion or conversation of the sort that Socrates engages in (and is engaging in here).

289. *We're overly keen . . . pursuits*: That is, insofar as 'we' (Socrates and Glaucon) go along with our imagined opponents, who think that women and men have different natures – when 'we' actually started by proposing (451d–452e) that they should be treated identically, and haven't yet given up that position. For the logic of this difficult passage, see S. R. Slings, *Critical Notes on Plato's Politeia* (Leiden, 2005), pp. 81–2.

290. *What we were saying . . . the same nature*: The text here is clearly corrupt (Slings, in the new Oxford text, says 'hopelessly corrupt'); the translation adopted here follows the text proposed by Adam, i.e., *iatrikon men kai iatrikon tên autên phusin echein elegomen*, which omits three words transmitted by the main manuscripts, changes one, and may well not be exactly what Plato wrote, but seems to be roughly what the argument and the context require.

291. *In that case, my friend*: The 'friend' in question is presumably, in the first instance, the imaginary opponent; but he is barely distinguishable from Glaucon, who was the one who originally laughed at the proposal that the women should exercise naked with the men (452b), or – to be more generous – suggested that it might be laughed at 'at least from where we are now'. It is worth noticing that Socrates' and Glaucon's attention remains focused at least as much on *this* proposal as the apparently

rather more revolutionary idea that women should fight and perform the other functions of city-guards alongside the men – although of course in Socrates' eyes the two will in any case go together.

292. *The requisite natures ... both types of creature*: Socrates seems to draw this conclusion directly from the claim that there are no woman-only pursuits (of a relevant kind), only pursuits available to both sexes, and in which both can compete. The inference is supported by his assumption that women are born to do things other than merely bear children – an assumption confirmed by his discounting of differences in reproductive roles at 454d–e.

293. *a natural wisdom-lover*: I.e., a natural lover of *sophia*, a philosopher.

294. *to live ... with men of the same sort*: 'To live with', *sunoikein*, as used of a woman or a man, suggests marriage rather than mere cohabitation; as we shall see, in the present context it hovers between, or combines, both senses.

295. *back to where we were before*: See 451e.

296. *harvests laughter's fruit 'by wisdom unmatured'*: Socrates adapts an evidently well-known saying of Pindar (known to us only as a fragment: 'harvests the unripe fruit of wisdom'), originally aimed at philosophical speculations of his day.

297. *surviving this first wave, as it were*: The metaphor of swimming was first introduced back at 453d – where Socrates pictured himself and his interlocutors out in the open sea.

298. *the previous ones*: See 421b–c, e, 423c, c–d.

299. *if those serving as their auxiliaries are worthy of theirs*: The title 'auxiliaries', *epikouroi*, can be translated more literally as 'helpers'.

300. *not by the laws of geometry ... but by the laws of sexual attraction*: And so, in reality, not strictly necessary at all.

301. *it wouldn't be just*: That is, presumably, according to the agreed definition of justice, in terms of the principle one man/woman, one job (unregulated sexual activity, in particular, might distract guards from guarding).

302. *I believe we said ... the category of medicine*: See 389b.

303. *hymns suitable for the matings that result*: Ordinary marriage hymns would celebrate permanent unions; the unions in the new city, being temporary, would presumably require celebration in a different way.

304. *either a big city or a small one*: On the criteria for 'bigness' and 'smallness' in a city, see 423a–b.

305. *And the young ones . . . why that should be so*: Socrates will say more about this a few pages later (468b–e).

306. *they'll hide away . . . not to be divulged to anyone else*: Many, perhaps rightly, have seen this as proposing infanticide; but if so, it is unclear why Socrates should not spell this out. (Relevant passages for comparison are *Republic* 372c, 410a, 415a–b, 459e, 461c; *Theaetetus* 149a–151d, esp. 151c; and *Timaeus* 19a.) In any case – and this is what matters for the argument – the children in question will be removed from the group to which they were born.

307. *from the time his 'sprinter's edge' is past its sharpest*: I.e., from the age of twenty-five. Socrates seems to be quoting here, perhaps from a poet celebrating a victory at the games.

308. *the prime for both . . . in body and in mind*: That may be Glaucon's view; Socrates will later imply a different view about when both men or women are in their mental prime.

309. *together with a fearsome lack of restraint*: 'Lack of restraint' may be either cause or consequence here – or both (see 443c–444a).

310. *to 'marry'*: The verb is *sunoikein* (see n. 294).

311. *the Pythia adds her consent*: Socrates perhaps recurs here to the point that mating will take place at religious festivals, which will presumably be established, along with other forms of 'service to the gods', under the guidance of Delphic Apollo (the 'Pythia' being his priestess and mouthpiece). See 427b–c.

312. *'rulers'*: Or just 'officers' (at Athens, 'archons', i.e., *archontes* – as it happens, the same term that Socrates uses for 'rulers' generally).

313. *helpers*: And 'auxiliaries' (*epikouroi*: see n. 299). The second-tier guards, the soldiers, are of course in the first instance auxiliaries to/helpers of the first-tier ones, the 'real' guards, and rulers.

314. *pay them and keep them fed*: That is, pay them by keeping them fed (being their 'rearers', *tropheis*: the image of the guards as watch-dogs lives on); see 464b–c.

315. *'sharing' women and children*: Socrates refers back here to Adimantus' original challenge to him, at 449c–d, to say what sort of 'sharing' he had in mind; his explanation is now complete.

316. *we're also agreeing with what we said before*: Such agreement being part of what Socrates said they had to show (461e).

317. *the so-called blessed life Olympic victors live*: Writers – including Plato – would typically use victory at the Olympic games to stand for the pinnacle of (ordinary) human achievement.

318. *their children*: I.e., presumably, their 'children' as previously
defined (a whole age-group, which will also include their children in the ordinary sense). Olympic victors might be awarded
free meals for life (cf. Plato, *Apology* 36e, where Socrates suggests that someone like him has a rather better claim to such
treatment), but probably not their children.

319. *someone complaining earlier – I don't know who it was*: See
419a–420a (Adimantus: 'So what will your defence be, Socrates,
if someone says . . .').

320. *the half is more than the whole*: Hesiod, *Works and Days* 40.

321. *the sharing of the women*: The phrase had a quite different sense
back at (say) 449d – there, women were being shared *in*, whereas
now it is they who are doing the sharing.

322. *must, surely, be . . . a farmer*: I.e., must be made to do the sort of
thing their behaviour on the battlefield will have shown to be
more suited to their capacities.

323. *That he should kiss . . . each of them*: And should go no further,
presumably at least so far as Socrates is concerned (see 403a–c:
there seems little reason why success on the battlefield should
trump the demands of the 'musicality' the guards learned in the
course of their education). Glaucon's response, however, seems to
throw some doubt on whether he is entirely with Socrates on this.

324. *That's fine . . . someone like that*: Despite his apparent approval
of Glaucon's suggestion ('That's fine'), the primary point of Socrates' response here is to remind him of the rules/laws already
laid down for sexual activity (and the discouragement of passionate love between the guards: 403a–c again), and for coupling
between the guards. Any such extra privileges, it turns out, will
be offered in contexts of a religious sort ('When there are sacrifices, and on all such occasions', 468d) – which will be either
adjuncts to the ordinary mating festivals, where partners are
chosen by the rulers rather than by the guards themselves (see
459d–460a), or actually these festivals themselves. Cf. 460b.

325. *'with the choicest cuts'*: Socrates here alludes to, and partially
quotes, a line in the *Iliad* (7.321).

326. *so that we can train our good men and women*: That is, presumably, in how to behave in relation to food, drink and sex. The
quotation – 'with the best seats . . .' – is from Homer (*Iliad*
8.162, 12.311).

327. *they belong to the golden race*: The reference here is not only to
Socrates' myth of the metals (gold, silver and iron in the soul),
back at 415a–c, but – as he will immediately suggest – to the

original myth that his own will have recalled, about successive races of man (golden, silver, heroic and iron), in Hesiod, *Works and Days* 106–201.

328. *holy demi-gods ... merely mortal men*: A version of Hesiod, *Works and Days* 122–3.

329. *the god*: I.e., Apollo (cf. 427b–c).

330. *when in fact the enemy in it has flitted off*: Probably a reminiscence of Homer – as, e.g., at *Odyssey* 11.222, where the soul of the dead person 'flits away like a dream'.

331. *a Greece*: A 'Greece' (*Hellas*), that is, consisting of numerous independent city-states.

332. *the first two waves that were threatening me*: See 457b–c.

333. *so unlikely sounding an idea*: I.e., the one Socrates is about to propose; evidently it is this, in itself, that constitutes the 'third wave', threatening to drown him – or rather, this together with the chorus of disbelief with which he expects it to be greeted.

334. *even if some deny it*: In the Greek context as much as in an English one, actions would generally be expected to speak louder than words.

335. *the things you yourself are prescribing*: I.e., for the establishment of the 'good city' – for the design of which Glaucon shares joint responsibility with Socrates, having gone along with him, at least in principle, every step of the way.

336. *more in tune with you than another person's might be*: Than Thrasymachus' might be, perhaps?

337. *to declare someone a lover of something*: As a 'philosopher' is a lover of wisdom (*sophia*).

338. *a wisdom-lover*: I.e., again, a *sophia*-lover, a philosopher.

339. *seeing sights*: Like, perhaps, the festival in the Piraeus Socrates had been attending at the very beginning of the *Republic*.

340. *every chorus that's put on*: To 'put on a chorus' is to put on a dramatic performance, especially at the festival of the Dionysia, of which there were city and rural versions.

341. *That's another right thing to say*: Cf. 449c.

342. *and so on with every kind of thing*: I.e., presumably, at least in the first instance, all cases where things similarly fall into opposing pairs.

343. *the nature of the beautiful by itself*: I.e., what that beauty is, taken in and by itself, that is in things like sounds and colours.

344. *going and seeing the beautiful by itself*: As the lovers of ordinary sights/spectacles go and see plays in the theatre; Socrates is still explaining the idea that Glaucon failed to understand at 475e,

that true philosophers are those 'who love the sight of truth'. Philosophers too, like ordinary 'lovers of sights' (*philotheamones*), 'love to spectate', only what they 'see' is different.

345. *if someone else tries . . . to a knowledge of it*: That is, probably, to recognizing it; the only difference Socrates has so far spelled out between true philosophers and mere sight- and sound-lovers is that the former acknowledge the existence of the thing in question while the latter do not. The root of the Greek term in question, *gnômê*, covers both 'knowing' and 'recognizing' (or 'acknowledging').

346. *something that's beautiful by itself*: I.e., in beautiful things (see 476a: 'each [kind of thing] is, by itself, one, but because they show up everywhere, by virtue of being associated with actions, and bodies, and each other, each of them appears many'); perhaps the *property* of beauty, taken by itself?

347. *And would we be correct . . . he merely believes?*: The 'latter person', i.e., the true philosopher, knows at least that there are such things as the beautiful/beauty by itself; the 'former', i.e., the sight- or sound-lover, merely believes whatever it is that he has in mind. Socrates seems not to suppose this kind of lover to be simply making a mistake, but rather to be partly right, partly wrong – right, perhaps, to the extent that beautiful things are *like* beauty itself (insofar as they are beautiful: they 'share in' beauty [itself]), but wrong insofar as they think that beautiful sights, sounds, etc., are all there is to beauty; or, as Socrates puts it, insofar as they think that these *are* beauty itself. (The reader should be warned that the 'merely' qualifying 'believes' here is supplied by the translator, to bring out the intended contrast between belief and knowledge; the text has 'on the grounds that he believes [and doesn't know]'.)

348. *concealing from him that he is not in a healthy state*: Because to reveal that to him would only serve to make him angrier – if he's one of those who 'isn't capable of following [even] if someone else tries to guide him' to knowledge (476c)?

349. *Something that is, or something that is not?*: 'Is' here – representing the Greek *on*, or *esti* – might be interpreted as 'exists'; it might also be the 'is' that appears in sentences of the form '*x* is *y*' (the 'is' of predication or identity); or else it might be 'is' in its veridical use ('is true', 'is the case'). None of these possibilities should be ruled out, at least for the moment, since (a) there is overlapping between them (so that, for example, a thing's existing may be understood in terms of its *being something*); (b) Socrates will go on to give

some specific indications of the kind of 'is' he ultimately has in mind; and (c), given Glaucon's answer to the question, on behalf of the sight- or sound-loving respondent, more or less any of the uses of 'is' just listed will somehow fit the present context and make at least reasonable sense (see following note).

350. *how could something that is not be known?*: One clearly couldn't know something that didn't exist, wasn't anything (at all) and wasn't true.

351. *that knowledge is for what is*: I.e., that knowledge is concerned with what is, as agreed just above – 'what is, entirely, is entirely knowable, whereas what is not in any way at all is wholly unknowable'. ('Is for' renders *epi* [+ dative] . . . *ên* [= 'is, as we agreed', the 'philosophical imperfect']. For a not dissimilar use of the same preposition, with the same grammatical case, see 341d and 345d, where the question is what some particular expertise will naturally be 'for', i.e., be concerned with.)

352. *non-knowledge*: I.e., apparently, the very opposite of knowing/ knowledge, in other words, a state in which the mind is simply blank; 'ignorance' of a particular kind. (Socrates employs an unusual word for 'ignorance' here, *agnôsia*, to point up the contrast with knowledge, i.e., here, *gnôsis*, but later in the sentence, and in what follows, he uses the more standard *agnoia*.)

353. *are assigned to different things*: 'Being assigned to' (*tetachthai epi*) seems to be exactly the same as 'being for' (see n. 351; and 524a, where the sense of touch is 'assigned to' perceiving both hard and soft).

354. *to knowing . . . what is, that it is*: Or, alternatively, 'to know-ing . . . what is, as it is'.

355. *my fine friend*: The 'friend' here is still the imaginary representative of the sight- and sound-lovers, for whom Glaucon is standing in.

356. *Knowledge . . . knowing, in relation to what is, that it is?*: Which is where we were already at 477b.

357. *Believing the same thing knowledge knows?*: The jury is still out on the question as to what exactly it is that is believed. But what we know for certain, because he's told us so, is that Socrates is setting out to show the sight- and sound-lovers that what *they* have is mere belief and not knowledge (476d–e); and that they suppose that beautiful things by themselves constitute beauty, without the need for 'a beauty existing by itself' (476c).

358. *to believe what is not*: That is, as Socrates goes on to suggest, for the believer to have nothing, i.e., what is not in any way at all, in his sights when believing.

359. *as it were*: The qualification is quite important, given the 'general rule' Socrates introduced at 436b, that 'the same thing won't act or be acted on in opposite ways simultaneously'. In effect, it recalls the rider he added to that rule at the time – 'at any rate in the same respect or in relation to the same thing'; and the things he has in mind will in fact turn out to 'be [whatever they are]' and 'not be' in different respects.

360. *nature*: Or 'character' (*idea*).

361. *that won't appear as ugly*: That is, presumably, in some (other) respect or other.

362. *the children's riddle . . . what it was sitting on*: The man who was no man (the eunuch) hit a bird that was no bird (the bat) sitting on a branch that was no branch (a reed, apparently) with a stone that was no stone (a pumice-stone).

363. *between being and not being*: That is, between being and not being beautiful, or whatever it may be, simultaneously (as it were); or, to put it another way, both 'sharing' and not 'sharing' in it – so that beauty both is, and isn't, in them.

364. *the many things ordinary people . . . and simply is*: It seems, then, that those 'lovers of sights and sounds' were all along stand-ins for 'ordinary people', people in general. It is people in general that identify beauty – or whatever else it may be: justice, perhaps – with what they see and hear on the stage (when in fact what they see or hear is somehow in between being and not-being what they think it is).

365. *aren't capable . . . lead them to it*: See 476c.

366. *philodoxers . . . philosophers*: I.e., lovers of belief, *doxa*, rather than of wisdom, *sophia*.

367. *Will they really be so very angry with us for saying so?*: Cf. 476d.

368. *if he has no paradigm . . . when it is laid down*: It is a *paradigm* for justice that Socrates was looking for, with Adimantus' and Glaucon's help, in the whole of 368d–444e – as he told us only a few pages ago, at 472d (using the same analogy with painting). What is now being demanded of philosophers is at the least that they should go through the kind of process that has been illustrated (i.e., in the case of justice). Socrates in fact suggested, at 472b, that he and his companions had perhaps not yet observed the paradigm 'as accurately as possible': '*if we do* discover the answer to our question about justice', he said (i.e., about 'what sort of thing it is'), which is hardly a ringing endorsement of the definition reached, and apparently confirmed, by 444e. And in fact, in what follows, a rather different, if related, notion of justice will emerge.

369. *in any other part of excellence*: I.e., any other than knowledge/ wisdom.

370. *when we were starting . . . the discussion*: I.e., at 474b–c.

371. *the kind of thing that always is . . . coming to be and passing away*: 'The kind of thing that always is' – or just 'the things that always are'. The Greek noun *ousia* in this context has a generic, or collective, sense (as, e.g., at *Phaedo* 76d, 78d, 92d–e), like 'god', as often in Plato's Greek, or 'man' in English. The translation 'essence', which used to be preferred, is not particularly helpful; what is in question, rather, is a collection of things that are themselves the 'essences' of things (what justice essentially is, what beauty essentially is, and so on). 'Not wandering this way and that', i.e., like the many things that attract the sight- and sound-lovers, which are now there, now not there, and/or now one thing, now another.

372. *the people we discussed before*: See 484c–485b.

373. *all there is*: That is, all *ousia* (see n. 371); but Socrates has just explicitly extended the philosopher's or wisdom-lover's concern to include things human as well as things divine – or in other words, to include things that are not exempted from coming to be and passing away as well as things that are deathless and immortal (485b). And after all, he has claimed that the philosopher will be passionate about every aspect of the truth, and it is clearly not his position that non-philosophers have no grasp on the truth *at all*. Their case – as illustrated by the sight- and sound-lovers – is for him more complicated than that.

374. *Well, is there any way . . . unjust?*: Along with a deepening idea of philosophical knowledge or wisdom, Socrates seems in effect – however inconspicuously – to be proposing new, philosophical versions of moderation, courage and justice; that is, as excellences deriving directly from the philosopher's total engagement with the truth.

375. *easily led . . . as it really is*: That is, to beauty as it really is (at least in the first instance) in the many beautiful things the sight- and sound-lovers believe in, to justice as it really is, and so on. The sight- and sound-lovers, for their part, were not capable of following even if someone tried to guide them to such things (476c, 479e).

376. *Momus*: Momus was the personification of fault-finding (*memphesthai*).

377. *when they're subjected to . . . treatment*: I.e., the one just described, at the hands of the expert in the 'newfangled kind of *petteia*', i.e., Socratic dialectic.

378. *'troubles won't cease for cities' until they're ruled by philosophers*: As Socrates declared at 473d.

379. *a verbal image*: I.e., a visual image or likeness (a 'picture'), but in words.

380. *And I suppose you never talk through images!*: Thus the analogy between city and individual began with an image (seeing the same thing in small and large letters); the 'guards' have repeatedly been compared with dogs (including bitches); and then there are those 'waves' that have threatened to overwhelm Socrates' argument, as well as the image of the 'stream' of desire in the soul.

381. *like the goat-stags ... pictured by painters*: The image that follows will be like a 'goat-stag' particularly, perhaps, insofar as it transfers what happens, according to Socrates, in one sphere (cities) into another (ships), where it would be at least unlikely to happen.

382. *The ship-owner*: In effect, the 'captain', insofar as he dictates the ship's destination; he represents the sovereign people, in a democracy, or whichever portion of the population holds the power in other regimes. The preceding reference to 'a fleet of ships' probably suggests that the image is intended to apply to all sorts of regimes, and not just (Athenian) democracy.

383. *as for his steering ... the art of steersmanship in the first place*: That is, presumably, they are unable to conceive of navigation except as conducted according to the wishes of one or another faction in the city. The idea of expertise as something impersonal is of course central to the whole image: a steersman who operated according to the whims of the crew would soon have his ship on the rocks.

384. *the genuine expert ... called a 'stargazer' and a 'babbler'*: As Socrates evidently was (cf. *Apology* 19b–c, referring to the comic poets, esp. Aristophanes; also *Theaetetus* 195b, *Sophist* 225d, *Statesman* 299b).

385. *that critic ... philosophers in cities*: See 487d. The 'surprise' is shared by Adimantus himself – surely they ought to be more respected, if they're capable of assuming power in the city?

386. *the wit who said otherwise was wrong*: The poet Simonides, it appears, proposed that it was better to be rich than wise, because the wise would gather round the rich anyway.

387. *when we were describing ... need to be born with*: I.e., in 485a–487a.

388. *what is*: I.e., with what things really are/things as they really are. See 507b, with n. 440.

389. *labelling the same things 'beautiful' and 'ugly' as they do*: We seem
to be back again with the sight- and sound-lovers of 475d–479e;
these were explicitly identified with the mass of ordinary people
at 479d.

390. *these educator-sophists*: I.e., roughly speaking, 'the people'.

391. *There is not . . . capable of countering theirs*: It is useful in this
context to know that ordinary, individual 'sophists' (professional teachers like Protagoras, on whom see n. 639) sometimes
did explicitly claim to be able to teach excellence ('virtue', *aretê*).
The present sentence thus, in effect, kills two birds with one
stone.

392. *the divine, as they say . . . divine dispensation*: There is here, presumably, the most discreet of references to Socrates himself – that
is, on Plato's part; *Socrates* cannot intend anything of the sort (at
least if he is the same person as he is in the *Apology*: see *Apology*
20c–23c, and esp. 23a–b, where he contrasts his own, purely
human, wisdom with the wisdom of gods).

393. *what was merely necessary . . . and the good*: The 'merely necessary' is what one can't do anything about, which in the present
context presumably refers primarily to the beliefs of 'the beast'.
'In nature', the necessary will be more like what we call 'brute
fact', which is for Plato to be sharply distinguished from the
good, although he suggests elsewhere that he thinks of the good,
on the cosmic level, as having a binding force of its own. See
Phaedo 97b–99d.

394. *it's as sure as sure can be*: The Greek talks about a proverbial
'Diomedean necessity'; even ancient commentators disagree
about what this referred to.

395. *recall what we said*: See 476b.

396. *And if someone . . . besetting him?*: No informed ancient reader
is likely to have missed the echoes, in the whole of 494b–e, of
Socrates' relationship with the colourful figure of Alcibiades –
the young, aristocratic politician and general who played so
important a role in Athens' disastrous decline to defeat and
humiliation by Sparta and her allies at the end of the fourth century. For Plato's own account of that relationship, see his
Symposium, which needs to be read against the background of
the charges that led to Socrates' execution, and above all the
accusation that he 'corrupted' the young.

397. *affinity for what is being said to him*: See 402a.

398. *if by chance . . . flowed that way*: For the figure, see 485d ('it's as
if a stream is being diverted off into another channel').

399. *and with no truth in it*: Cf. 490b.

400. *by many whose natures ... performance of their trades*: Quite who it is that Socrates means to pick out by this description is unclear; but see n. 402.

401. *had his chains taken off*: So, evidently, he's a metal-working slave (one who has made his own chains?).

402. *A few ... look down on them*: One example might be a shoe-maker called Simon, named as a friend of Socrates' by some ancient authorities (though not, as it happens, by Plato). Or is Simon, in Plato's view, rather, one of those 'whose souls are actually as broken and crushed by the physicality of their occupations as their bodies are deformed by the performance of their trades' (495d–e)?

403. *Theages*: Probably the son of one Demodocus, who had a distinguished public career; the son might have been expected to follow the father.

404. *my divine sign*: See n. 95.

405. *he is content ... kindness and good will*: As, according to Plato's *Apology*, *Crito* and *Phaedo*, Socrates himself lived and died.

406. *we did say even then ... laying down its laws*: See 412a–b.

407. *arguments*: I.e., presumably, what Socrates previously referred to as 'dialectic' (see 454a), about which we shall hear a great deal more.

408. *Heraclitus' sun ... kindled again*: For Heraclitus, the sun was new every day.

409. *roam free, like sacred animals*: And after all, Socrates has said that they may have something divine about them (497c).

410. *in that other place*: That is, in whatever place souls go to after separation from the body – traditionally Hades. We will hear about Socrates', and/or Plato's, distinctly untraditional conception of this 'other place' in the closing pages of the *Republic*.

411. *We're not going to give up ... encounter discussions like this again*: This whole little scene is reminiscent of the *Phaedo*, where Socrates tries to convince a similarly sceptical audience that the soul does not perish with the body, and that the philosopher will enjoy a better fate than his non-philosophical counterpart after ending his present life. He will come back to both themes at the end of the *Republic* itself.

412. *wordplay like that*: I.e., like 'seen realized'/'been theorized', which attempts to reproduce the more neatly repeated sound in the Greek, *genomenon/legomenon*; similarly 'rhyming' and 'chiming' just below, which tries to reproduce *parisômenon/hômoiômenon*

in the Greek, and 'in work and word' (*ergôi te kai logôi*). Plato's likely main target is the rhetorician Isocrates, and especially his *Panegyricus* and *Antidosis*, where he develops his own ideas for the improvement of man and society – mere words, according to Socrates' account here, prettified by laboured assonance.

413. *we'd justly . . . wishful thinking*: Cf. 450d.

414. *the Muse, herself*: I.e., presumably, the Muse of philosophy.

415. *giving different answers to your questions*: Reading *apokrineisthai* (Slings, 2003, despairs of the text here).

416. *perpetually directing . . . at individuals*: As Isocrates, in particular, targeted Plato.

417. *neither behaving unjustly . . . by each other*: Part of the point here is perhaps the contrast with the many beautiful things, good things, etc., that non-philosophical people believe in, insofar as these are always 'in conflict' with each other (see esp. 478e–479c).

418. *do you suppose . . . civic excellence as a whole*: That is, presumably, by helping to create or maintain a city that contained such excellence, like the one that Socrates, Adimantus and Glaucon have created. 'Civic', or 'demotic' (*dêmotikos*), excellence appears to contrast with the philosopher's own excellence, which derives directly from reason: see n. 374.

419. *when we say . . . the appropriate divine paradigm*: Cf. 484c–d. The 'divinity' of a city's laws – despite the acknowledged existence of human legislators – was evidently a common Greek notion. Normally, however, this would have been interpreted in terms of the laws' somehow being god-given, which is presumably how the ordinary people in the city of the *Republic* would be expected to understand it; given that they would still refuse to accept the existence of beauty itself, justice itself, and so on, they could have no real grasp of what precisely Socrates has in mind by a 'divine paradigm', i.e., a paradigm that shares the permanence of the immortal gods.

420. *and at what they are . . . accordingly*: The Greek text here is uncertain and contested. I have accepted Slings's solution, in the new Oxford text, which presupposes an anacolouthon (avoiding that in the translation by supplying the 'and' before 'fill in'). The kind of solution preferred by most others would give us 'and [glancing at the same time] at what they were trying to reproduce in human beings', which seems to make rather less good sense.

421. *the likeness of a man*: For the Greek term here, the rare *andreikelon* (possibly a Platonic coinage, based on the Homeric

theoeikelon, '[in the] likeness of a god', used in the next line), the standard lexicon gives 'flesh-coloured pigment'; that, of course, will be part of what Socrates has in mind, but hardly the main part.

422. *you claimed*: See 474a.

423. *a strange claim*: Because, again, a 'philosopher' is a 'wisdom-lover'; and would a lover of wisdom love what is *not* true?

424. *We ourselves . . . hard for them to survive*: See 495a–b.

425. *how . . . in the city*: That is, presumably, apart from the possibility, just discussed, that political power and philosophy might coincide in the real world, through the emergence of a paragon amongst the offspring of actual kings and princes.

426. *we said*: See 412b–414b.

427. *those to be appointed as the truest guards*: I.e., as the rulers ('the complete and finished guards', 414b).

428. *don't tend . . . would be needed*: The Greek text here is likely to be corrupt. Various solutions have been proposed; Slings, 2003, despairs; the translation offered tries to make the best of what the manuscripts give us.

429. *we said*: See 484d–485a.

430. *three kinds of element*: Or 'three forms' (*tritta eidê*).

431. *what we were trying to say*: I.e., at 435c–d.

432. *even though . . . to inquire any further*: Socrates is presumably referring here to what Adimantus just said ('It seemed to me . . .') – too indirectly, as it turns out, for Adimantus to notice.

433. *put every effort . . . unblemished as they can be*: I.e., as painters do with actual paintings.

434. *the form of goodness*: Or 'the nature of goodness'. For the moment at least, no more is in question than what goodness or the good ('taken by itself'), really is. Modern readers who have read other Platonic dialogues, e.g., *Lysis*, *Euthydemus* or *Symposium*, will themselves have 'heard often enough' that knowledge of the good is fundamental.

435. *This is one sphere . . . mere appearances*: 'Appearances' here translates *doxa*, which was also the term for 'belief' in the argument with the sight- and sound-lovers; there is more than likely a reference to that argument here.

436. *But what's your own view, Socrates?*: Adimantus is surely being provocative here; it is scarcely credible that he is not supposed to know Socrates' view on this central question (given how much else he is supposed to know, first hand, about the kinds of things Socrates says: 504e–505c). His next contribution shows what he

is about – Socrates should say what *he* thinks, not just criticize what others say.

437. *when you could be hearing . . . from others*: Another sideswipe, presumably, at rhetoricians like Isocrates.

438. *you'll have to make do . . . my 'offspring' of the good*: The Greek for 'interest' here is *tokos*, which is also 'child'.

439. *earlier in the present conversation*: See 476a.

440. *to which we apply the label 'what is', in each case*: That is, 'what beautiful/beauty (good/goodness, etc.) is', and/or 'what is beautiful (good, etc.)', namely, in the many beautiful (good . . .) things.

441. *there may be colour in them*: This perhaps implies a theory of vision that compares it to hearing – sound may travel to, even into, the ear, and still not be heard.

442. *the sun, which the good fathered*: The good, then, also has a cosmic role; cf. 493c, with n. 393.

443. *what is*: See 507b, with n. 440.

444. *the form of the good itself*: Or 'the character [*idea*] of the good'; what the good *is*, in its essential nature.

445. *It certainly can't be pleasure you're talking about!*: Among other things, Glaucon here reminds Socrates that he still hasn't said what *he* thinks the good actually is (see 506b).

446. *is not itself being . . . in dignity and in power*: The sense of these few words is one of the most contested issues in the whole of Plato. A crucial point to bear in mind is that 'beauty itself', for example, or 'the good itself', will be conceived as being cause of beauty/goodness in other things. By that token, 'being itself' (whatever that might be) would be cause of the being of other things. But now *the good* has been said to be cause of being in certain things, which raises the possibility, given the assumptions of the theory, that the good is the same as being. No, says Socrates, it is not; it's distinct from it, and is in fact the more prestigious and powerful of the two, because it does more than being does (being only causes being in things; good makes things not just good, but – somehow – also what they are, and knowable).

447. *Apollo! A super superiority that will be!*: 'Apollo!' is a kind of pun – Glaucon normally invokes Zeus, but for once prefers the Sun-god. The translation invents a different pun in what follows, as a way of representing the 'comic' tone. 'Super' is *daimonios*, which is typically 'divine', 'more than human'.

448. *what I would call . . . games with words*: The Greek words for 'seen' and 'heavens', as it happens, differ only by one or two letters.

('Heavenly scene' is Tom Griffith's way of conveying the pun, and could hardly be bettered: *Plato: The Republic*, ed. G. R. F. Ferrari, tr. Tom Griffith (Cambridge, 2000)).

449. *in terms of truth ... what is known*: What is being contrasted with what is known, as before, is what is *merely* believed (see 475d–480a, and esp. 478b).

450. *'forms'*: The Greek here, *autois eidesin*, clearly refers to the things Socrates has previously called *ideai* (also 'forms', in the present translation), giving them the general label 'what is' (507b). By this point, *eidos* and *idea* are firmly established as technical, or semi-technical, terms for those things we have come to know just as (Platonic) 'forms' – though Plato himself has plenty of other ways of referring to them. See Introduction, section 3. The 'intelligible region' (509d), according to Socrates' present account, would be one populated, not with particular examples of beauty, justice, etc., as the actual world is, or would ideally be, but with beauty, justice, etc., *themselves*. (These, of course, will be entirely real, according to Socrates; whether they would occupy real space, actually be located in some place, is another matter.)

451. *'Put it to me again.' 'I shall,' I said*: There are problems with the text here; as usual, I follow Slings's solution, in the new Oxford text.

452. *I think you do know that ... obvious to anyone*: Socrates will go on to explain this description of mathematicians, as merely using hypotheses, in a long and important passage on mathematics that begins at 524b (see esp. 525c–526b, with n. 490).

453. *the square itself and the diameter itself*: I.e., the 'form' of the square, the 'form' of the diameter, which tangible – manufactured or natural – squares or diameters are treated as 'resembling'.

454. *what is*: See 507b, with n. 440.

455. *then, to the third ... the last*: Glaucon suggested belief for the two lowest segments together; Socrates splits them, thus in effect introducing a further stage in the argument. Ordinary people see 'the many things' they believe (in) only as refracted, as it were, through the lens of poetry and the other arts, not as they are in themselves – which might include seeing them *for* what they are (i.e., mere images, as it were, of the corresponding originals). For 'conviction', cf. 505e.

456. *the things they are assigned to*: Or 'the things they are for'; the language is that of the argument with the sight- and sound-lovers in 475d–480a.

457. *as you'd expect ... others are silent*: If they were actual puppet-
     eers, one might have expected all of them to be speaking; but
     Socrates has a different sort of 'puppeteers' in mind – not all of
     whom use verbal forms of presentation/representation.

458. *they'd label ... what those things actually are*: I.e., they'd attach
     to mere shadows (even shadows of images) the kind of label
     philosophers attach to other things. The connection with the
     sight- and sound-lovers of 475d–479d is clear; in fact, these
     surely *are*, or at any rate are included among, the prisoners in the
     present image.

459. *things that more truly are*: I.e., as before, things that more truly,
     genuinely, fully are what they claim to be.

460. *could remember best ... come along next*: Thus having a purely
     empirical basis for any judgements – which would be true of
     anyone who only admitted the existence of many beautiful (just,
     good) things, not of a beauty (justice, goodness) itself.

461. *work the fields ... a man with nothing*: Part of a set of lines
     from the *Odyssey* already quoted more fully at 386c (Achilles is
     speaking).

462. *if they could ... don't you think they would*: Compare Socrates'
     reply, at *Phaedo* 115c, when Crito asks him what sort of burial
     he wants – 'Whichever you like ... that is, if you can catch me,
     and I don't get away from you'. Crito might be able to bury
     Socrates' body, but he won't be able to bury his soul, which he
     has just spent some hours trying to prove immortal.

463. *it would be less ridiculous ... from the light above*: That is, if
     either condition is comic, it's that of the soul that's blinded by
     the light because it's used to living underground, not that of the
     one that can't see in the dark because it's become used to the
     light (of truth).

464. *changing things ... what is*: The contrast, as always, is between
     looking at particular things (the many beautiful things, just
     things, good things . . .), which give us only a shifting and evan-
     escent idea of what beauty, goodness, etc., are, and looking at
     beauty, goodness, etc., themselves, and what they really *are*.
     'What is' (*to on*): or 'the things that are' (the 'forms').

465. *a special kind of expertise*: Presumably, dialectic (see, e.g., 511b–c).

466. *it won't consist in putting sight into something ... that already
     has it*: The 'something', presumably, is 'the instrument with
     which each of us learns' (518c), i.e., the reasoning mind.

467. *they can actually ... habituation and practice*: As courage, mod-
     eration and justice were in the ordinary guards.

468. *the concomitants of change*: I.e., what accrues to it (the reasoning element) as a consequence of being in something, i.e., a body, which is permanently changing, or always coming to be something else.

469. *That's again to forget*: See 419a–421c, with 465e–466c.

470. *will actually be just*: 'Just', that is, both according to ordinary ideas of justice, as a kind of reciprocity, but also, and perhaps especially, according to the definition of justice in the city as proposed at 432d–434c; in fact, the latter might be seen as justifying an appeal to reciprocity in this case.

471. *leaders and kings, as it were in the hive*: Even Plato's pupil Aristotle, the great biologist, thought queen-bees were king-bees. But at least, in the ideal city of the *Republic*, the presence of queen-bees is envisaged alongside the kings.

472. *both kinds of life*: I.e., the life of philosophy and the life of practical activity.

473. *whose government is awake . . . fight about who should rule*: For the contrast between waking and dreaming, see 476c–d; for civil strife and 'fighting about who should rule', see 488b.

474. *as if ruling were some kind of great good*: I.e., plainly, something that brought great benefit to *them*.

475. *the spin of a sherd*: I.e., of a painted, two-sided, fragment of pottery – like the toss of a coin.

476. *a day that is also somehow night*: There is presumably an allusion here to the earlier discussion of things that (somehow) manage both to be and not to be what they are supposed to be; there is possibly a pun on *nukterinos* = 'nightly', 'night-time' here, and *nukteris*, 'bat', recalling the riddle of the eunuch and the bat at 479b–c.

477. *what is*: See 518c–d, with n. 464.

478. *wasn't it as athletes for war . . . when they were young*: See 416d, 422b.

479. *All the ordinary kinds . . . demeaning*: See 495d–e.

480. *intelligent thought*: I.e., the use of 'intelligence' in the special sense given the term at 511d.

481. *what is*: Here *ousia* (equivalent to *to on* at, e.g., 518c–d and 521c).

482. *And if they appear . . . different and as one?*: Cf. 475e–476a, introducing the argument with the sight- and sound-lovers.

483. *And that's how . . . another as visible*: As in 508c–511e, then 517b–c.

484. *number, and one*: Socrates is presumably here thinking of number as countable, i.e., a collection of ones (cf. Euclid's definition

of number as 'a plurality of units'). 'One': or 'oneness'; compare the move from 'big' to 'bigness', 'small' to 'smallness', and so on. In the lines that follow, 'one' appears in italics simply to distinguish it from the indefinite pronoun.

485. *we see the same thing ... at the same time*: Thus Socrates, for example, will be both one (individual) and also any number of other things – snub-nosed, short, talkative ...

486. *true calculation, true reasoning*: Socrates here puns on *logistikos*, which refers both to *logistikê*, the 'art' of calculation, and to the reasoning capacity of the *logistikon*, or 'reasoning', element of the soul (as at 439d, 440e, etc.).

487. *towards truth, and towards what is*: I.e., as ever, what truly is. Socrates used identical phrasing at 508d, in the course of his comparison of the good with the sun.

488. *numbers with ... bodies attached to them*: As in 'one potato, two potato ...'; cf. n. 485.

489. *if anyone tries to argue ... many distinct parts*: This, it seems, is the response of expert mathematicians if anyone fails – if 'you', i.e., anyone not as expert as they are, fail – to distinguish between (a) one and numbers taken by themselves, and (b) one or plural *things*. The latter, being 'bodies', are divisible into parts; if one itself were divided, it would cease, impossibly, to be itself (being just what *one* forever is, or what is forever one). The mathematicians recognize this, but, crucially for Socrates, without recognizing that what they are dealing with are 'forms'; for them, 'one', i.e., 'the one [taken by] itself', 'two', and so on, are merely entities posited ('hypothesized', 510b–d) so that they can construct their arguments and theorems. This is the reason for the slightly comic tone of the present sentence, and the term Socrates chooses to refer to mathematical experts: they are 'clever', *deinoi*, at what they do – but, by implication, not clever enough.

490. *given the way ... to get to the truth itself*: I.e., as it forces the mathematicians to talk about the one itself, the two itself, and so on, even if they don't fully understand what they're doing (see previous note).

491. *the form of the good*: 'Form', again, in the special, semi-technical, Platonic sense – what the good, or goodness, really and truly is.

492. *that happiest of the things that are*: The good is 'happiest' of all 'forms', perhaps, in that it makes the person who has it, or 'shares in' it, happiest.

493. *things as they are*: Ousia again.

494. *the City Beautiful*: Or 'Callipolis'. A number of actual cities had such a name; Plato's Callipolis is another kind of city entirely.

495. *by those . . . philosophy now*: Isocrates is probably, again, the main suspect.

496. *there is no knowledge in such things*: I.e., there's no knowledge to be had just by looking at them (which is not the same as saying that there is no knowledge to be had *about* them).

497. *floating on his back on land*: This sounds odd, until one thinks of the opening of Aristophanes' *Clouds*, where the 'star-gazer' Socrates is suspended in a basket above the stage in order to give him a better view of the heavens.

498. *speed itself and slowness itself*: Or 'speed as it really is and slowness as it really is' (*to on tachos, hê ousa bradutês*); that is, the true 'forms' of speed and slowness. As this already seems to imply, the 'movements' in question will hardly be of any physical kind – indeed speed (itself) and slowness (itself) can hardly be unrelated to the only kind of movement that ought to be in question, i.e., 'intelligible' movement ('movement itself'). The closest analogy available might be with the formulae discovered by modern mathematical astronomers. However, this is a highly disputed passage, and is likely to remain so.

499. *some other craftsman or painter*: Socrates will go on immediately to talk about some putative 'craftsman (*dêmiourgos*) of the heavens' (530a); precisely such a craftsman makes his appearance in the account of the creation of the cosmos in Plato's *Timaeus*. Daedalus was a legendary architect, sculptor and inventor; his attempt at flight led to the death of his son Icarus, who flew too near to the sun.

500. *will go on . . . the truth about them*: Or '[and strange] to seek in every way he can to grasp the truth of them'.

501. *the people we're bringing up . . . incomplete study of anything*: See 504c.

502. *that image of ours*: I.e., the image of the cave.

503. *setting out . . . without any of the senses*: Inserting *te* between *aneu* and *pasôn*, after a hesitant suggestion by Slings, 2003.

504. *If your starting-point . . . turn into knowledge?*: Cf. 510c–511a, on geometry.

505. *the true starting-point*: I.e., presumably, 'the first principle of everything' (511b).

506. *we went for 'thoughtfulness' before*: See 511d–e.

507. *'No indeed,' he said*: In the manuscripts there follows a short

sentence, apparently attributable to Glaucon, which is pure gib-berish; wholesale surgery would be needed to give it any sense, but in any case, so far as one can tell, it would add little.

508. *the things these are assigned to*: See n. 456.

509. *'dialectician'*: I.e., 'expert in dialectic', as a mathematician is an expert in mathematics.

510. *as little account ... as geometers do of their lines*: The reference is perhaps punning – referring simultaneously to incommensurable lines in geometry, and to Socrates' treatment of mathematicians generally as dealing merely in hypotheses, i.e., things not properly understood or known (533c).

511. *You still have ... under what conditions*: See 502d.

512. *so far as possible the best looking*: For this specific (and, so baldly stated, surprising) requirement, see 403d.

513. *as I said before*: See 495c–496a.

514. *voluntary falsehoods ... the involuntary sort*: On these two dif-ferent kinds of falsehood, see 382a–383a.

515. *lame counterfeits ... things in question*: I.e., people who aren't what they claim to be, in relation to any of the excellences, because they're 'lame on one side', 'one-sided' (535d).

516. *we were only playing*: Because they're not *actually* constructing a new city?

517. *when we were previously selecting the rulers*: See 412c.

518. *We mustn't believe Solon*: Socrates refers to an evidently well-known fragment of verse from the sixth-century BCE Athenian lawgiver and poet ('I grow old forever learning many things').

519. *Do you remember ... like young hunting-dogs*: See 466e–468a.

520. *That will last two or three years*: Compare the two years' com-pulsory military training and guard-duty imposed in Athens on eighteen-year-old male citizens.

521. *when he no longer ... the just truly are*: I.e., in effect, when he's in between the states of the sight- and sound-lover and of the philosopher, as described in 475d–479d.

522. *just as a way ... contradict themselves*: I.e, as Socrates actually says, for 'antilogical' purposes (see 454a).

523. *six years ... or four*: See 537b, where two or three years was allocated for physical training.

524. *the eye of the soul*: Or 'the light/ray of the soul'. The term Soc-rates uses here is more typically used of the light of the sun (to which Socrates compared the orb of the eye, at 508a–b); but it is also a poetic word for the eye. (Cf. 'the eye [*omma*] of the soul' at 533d.)

525. *use it as a paradigm*: Cf. 484c.
526. *not because it's a fine thing . . . to be done*: Cf. 347b–d, 520c–e. 'Not because it's a fine thing to do': that is, by comparison with doing philosophy? Socrates noticeably does not say, as we might expect, 'not because it's a *good* thing', that is, for them (cf. 520d, where he is talking about people now, who fight over ruling 'as if ruling were some kind of great good'), because after all, according to 505d–e, everyone seeks the good in everything they do. In fact, all things considered, ruling will be the good, even the best, thing to do for the philosophers in the new city, if it's what is just; what it won't be is good for them in the sense of bringing them goods in the ordinary, crude, material sense.
527. *the Pythia*: I.e., Apollo's mouthpiece, in the temple at Delphi. For the idea of men as *daimones*, 'demi-gods', see 469a; the Greek puns on *daimones* and *eudaimones*, 'happy', 'blessed by the gods'.
528. *if they really are . . . in the way we described*: I.e., in 451c–466d.
529. *It's clear by now . . . he must be*: I.e., presumably, a philosopher, who exhibits the same kind of order as the city in which he or she will rule.
530. *in the way we described before*: See 415e–416b,
531. *we settled on . . . acquisition of property*: See 416d–417b.
532. *even while . . . both for a city and for an individual*: Thus, in a way, it was not a digression after all?
533. *you were saying . . . if this one was correct*: See 449a.
534. *regime*: Or 'constitution' (*politeia*).
535. *take up your argument again*: I.e., in order to introduce 'an even more beautiful model' of city and individual, having just appeared to finish with the subject.
536. *the one praised by most people . . . Spartan*: 'Most people', *hoi polloi*, here are perhaps thinking non-philosophers rather than the majority; most people in democratic Athens would scarcely have thought of Sparta – her long-standing enemy, and thoroughly elitist – as offering a model for government.
537. *in a class of its own*: This is a stab at what Plato might have written here; the text is evidently corrupted.
538. *'from oak or rock'*: Cf. *Apology* 34d (Socrates to the jurors at his trial), 'this is that saying of Homer's [e.g., at *Iliad* 22.126] – I'm not born "from oak or from rock", but from human beings, so that I do have relatives, and, yes, sons too . . .'
539. *the aristocratic type of regime*: See n. 280.
540. *the type that loves . . . honours*: The *philonikos* and *philotimos*, contrasting with the *philosophos* or lover of wisdom.

541. *'timocracy' ... 'timarchy'*: I.e., rule (*kratos, archê*) based on honour (*timê*), or rather the love of it.

542. *'how first it befell' them to fall out*: An allusion to Homer, *Iliad* 16.112–13.

543. *their lofty, tragic style*: 'Tragic' is here more or less synonymous with 'serious'. Homer will later be treated as leader of the tragic poets (595b–c, 598d).

544. *of which a base of four over three ... the cube on side three*: That is, it seems, $60^{4*} = 12,960,000 = 3,600^2 = (4,800^† \times 2700)$. For what it is worth, $12,960,000$ is also 100×360^2, i.e., the square of (roughly) the number of days in a human life multiplied by the number of years in that life (see 615a, where Socrates will use 100 years as some kind of measure of the human lifespan).

> *i.e. ($4 \times 3 \times 5$ [the sides of a 'Pythagorean' triangle]) 'raised to the fourth power' ('three times increased' in the Greek); † where $4,800 = (7 \times 7 - 1) \times 100$, or $(\sqrt{50^2} - 2) \times 100$, with 7 representing the 'rationalized' diagonal of a square side 5

545. *All of this constitutes a geometrical number*: This, i.e., apparently, 12,960,000 (with all its potentialities: see preceding note), is the notorious Platonic 'nuptial number', which has been and remains the subject of intense speculation. Whatever may, or may not, lie behind it in terms of serious mathematics (or, alternatively or additionally, mathematical mysticism), some general points are clear: (1) working out the number has to be difficult, since if it were easy there would be no reason for anyone to get it wrong, and the city could sail on undisturbed for ever; (2) the description as a whole is based on the mathematical construction of solids, as being what underlies the complex and changing world of the senses; (3) if the description ends up with *two* figures 'in tune' (literally, just 'attunements', *harmoniai*), that is no surprise if the number in question has to do with the regulation of sexual coupling; (4) the introduction of multiples of a hundred should perhaps be equally unsurprising, given that what is at issue is the regulation of coupling on a large scale; and (5) the number, whatever it is, clearly attempts to eliminate, or at least reduce, the element of irrationality in its constructions. 'Irrationality' here is, strictly speaking, incommensurability, or what cannot be expressed in terms of whole numbers. But in the context it will also, presumably, stand for irrationality in a wider sense, including and especially irrationality in human behaviour – so that if the mathematics of the

passage is obscure (and after all, the Muses are 'playing ... teasing us as if we were children'), its figurative sense is less so.

546. *gold, silver, bronze or iron*: See 415a–c.

547. *'For those of such birth'*: The Muses here echo themselves at Homer, *Iliad* 6.211 and 20.241 (both of them contexts where a hero is boasting of his ancestry).

548. *Once faction had set in ... then it was ...*: The following description is intended to have something of the feel of a summary of an epic narrative.

549. *the iron and bronze*: The bronze race in Hesiod is in fact a separate race of heroic warriors like those of the *Iliad* and *Odyssey*; thus the 'iron and bronze' now mixed in with the gold and silver in the rulers and auxiliaries itself acquires a somewhat ambiguous status (as, indeed, do Homer's heroes).

550. *a different kind of guarding*: I.e., against, instead of over, the rest of the population. As elsewhere in the context, Socrates here clearly alludes to actual conditions in Sparta. The true-blooded citizens, 'Spartiates', had perpetually to be on the watch against the subjugated population of Messenia on whose labour they depended.

551. *follow Aeschylus ... 'another man, disposed before/ another state'*: Socrates adapts, and puns on, two lines of Aeschylus' *Seven against Thebes* (451, 570), which describe one hero at each *gate*.

552. *we were attributing to it*: See 544c.

553. *they'll be truly oligarchs when it comes to the battlefield*: I.e., they'll have few, *oligoi* (even nobody, apart from themselves), to rule over/give commands to (*archein*) – a pun on *oligarchia*, which stands for rule *by* the few.

554. *earlier on*: See, e.g., 374b–c, 434a–b.

555. *was this person ... wealthy and spending?*: I.e., did he perform any useful role, as businessman, craftsman, soldier, or whatever it may be, even when he wasn't poor?

556. *what is labelled as the criminal class*: I.e., as opposed to those who commit crimes on a large scale – such as tyrants – and get away with it (cf. 344b–c; and also 422a, with n. 214)?

557. *professional informers*: I.e., 'sycophants', in the original Greek sense.

558. *diadems ... exotic little swords*: I.e., the sorts of emblems of wealth and power worn by the Great King of Persia, richest man in the world and sole ruler of a vast empire.

559. *a blind leader for his chorus*: I.e., Wealth, treated as a person, or rather, god: Plutus; often represented as blind, presumably because he distributed his favours so indiscriminately.

560. *Well said*: Reading *eu ge* (one of Slings's two suggestions, in the new Oxford text, for resolving a minor textual problem).

561. *in true oligarchic style*: Socrates uses the same pun here, on 'few' (*oligoi*), as at 551e (see n. 553).

562. *is sometimes in conflict with itself*: I.e., insofar as its different elements or 'humours' (see n. 573) are out of balance.

563. *public offices . . . distributed by lot*: A method of election, or selection, typically favoured by democracies like that at Athens.

564. *So how do these people run their lives?*: A somewhat pointed question, given that Socrates and his interlocutors are actually living under a democracy, as is Plato. But what follows, as Adimantus' next-but-one response probably indicates, is as much a theoretical reconstruction of a democracy, sometimes verging on caricature, as it is a description of democracy as it would be found in any actual city.

565. *how someone like that . . . without anybody either caring or noticing*: The text here is corrupt; I faithfully adopt, and make the best of, what Slings ultimately – after much hesitation – decided to print.

566. *So shall we . . . getting things done?*: For unnecessary desires as 'spending and not money-making', see 558d. Necessary desires 'make money', are *chrêmatistikai*, perhaps merely insofar as they are as *chrêsimoi*, 'useful', as unnecessary ones are wasteful (the etymological joke/pun in the Greek here is impossible to reproduce in English).

567. *just as the city . . . like supporting like*: See 556e.

568. *bar the gates of the royal walls in him*: I.e., stop any outside help from getting through to the ruling element in him, his reason.

569. *not giving a hearing . . . older and wiser individuals*: The English misses another pun, on *presbeis*, 'embassies', and *presbuteroi*, 'older [and wiser]'.

570. *the equality-monger*: I.e., the *isonomikos*, someone who likes equal distribution, *isa nemein*; a.k.a. the democrat.

571. *their . . . overseers*: I.e., their *paidagôgoi*, as at 373c.

572. *get on and say . . . what 'just now came to our lips'*: I.e., get round to explaining Socrates' casual remark about anarchy seeping down even to the household animals (562e). The quotation, which serves to soften Adimantus' implied rebuke, evidently comes from a play lost to us.

573. *phlegm and bile*: Two of the famous Greek 'humours', on the balance of which in the body human health is supposed to depend.

574. *cells and all*: See 552c.

575. *Lycaean Zeus*: 'Lycaean', *Lukaios*, is here derived from *lukos*, 'wolf'.

576. *as people will*: A covert reference to Socrates' own fate?

577. *This . . . the possessors of wealth*: See 565a.

578. *takes off . . . nor fears the shame of cowardice*: A fuller version of the oracle – given to Croesus, king of Lydia, when he asked the oracle how long he would reign – is given by Herodotus (I.55).

579. *a great man greatly fallen*: Homer, *Iliad* 16.776, describing the death of Cebriones, Hector's charioteer.

580. *tyrants are wise . . . by keeping wise men's company*: The same sentiment is elsewhere attributed to Sophocles.

581. *refuse to allow . . . into our regimes*: The fact that many 'tyrants' in tragedy are at least in principle benevolent evidently cuts no ice with Socrates. (On banning tragedy, cf. 394d.)

582. *and he'll make the general public . . . moved out*: The text here is uncertain; the translation offers the best that can be made out of what Slings prints in the new Oxford text (without any conviction on his part that it is right).

583. *the slaves*: Now freed; the new citizens of 567e–568a.

584. *I don't think . . . types of desires there are*: See 558d–559c.

585. *see what it does not know . . . past, present or future*: Socrates alludes here to the powers traditionally associated with the prophet or seer, hinting at an appropriation of those powers for the properly rational person.

586. *what we said . . . was like*: See 558d.

587. *a special, ruling passion . . . winged and powerful*: 'Passion' in this context translates *erôs*, a term normally used of the passionate love of one person for another, but also of any damaging and destructive preoccupation, like the English 'lust' (cf. 573b–c). Love is traditionally winged; here the wings serve to reintroduce the image of the drone.

588. *no food . . . too horrible for him*: Comic this may sound to us; not to an audience used to stories about gods, and men, eating their own children.

589. *if we were right . . . about the nature of justice*: In particular, presumably, in agreeing that justice consisted in a certain order between the different elements in the soul. The tyrant's soul, Socrates claims, is as far away from such order as it could possibly get.

590. *should we now pretend . . . answer our questions*: For Socrates and Glaucon it would have been a pretence, but by the time he

finished the *Republic* Plato had himself certainly spent time at the court of Dionysius II, tyrant/dictator of the Sicilian city-state of Syracuse. See Chronology.

591. *caused you to adjudge*: I.e., at 576e.

592. *like choruses on the stage*: Greek tragedies and comedies always had choruses; 'to rank choruses' is to rank the plays in which a particular chorus appeared, along with the main actors.

593. *This is the verdict ... most just*: The Greek here puns on the name Ariston, 'best' being *aristos*. The context recalls the original challenge mounted by Glaucon and Adimantus: see 367e–368a, where both were praised as 'Ariston's sons', and both at least implied to be *aristoi*.

594. *'whether ... all men and all gods'*: See 367e.

595. *divided into three kinds, just like a city*: See 435b–c – 'we shall expect the individual too to have these same kinds [or 'kinds of natures'] within his own soul' (that is, the same 'kinds' as had been discovered in a city), and so, of course, it turned out.

596. *three kinds ... of rule within the soul*: That is, as it turns out (581c), a soul may be ruled by any one of the three 'kinds' or elements in it.

597. *things as they truly are*: Or just 'what is', *to on*, referring to all those things to which the label 'what is' applies. See 507b.

598. *two calls ... Zeus of Olympus and Saviour*: Socrates alludes simultaneously to the wrestling competition at the Olympic games (held in honour of Olympian Zeus), which would be decided by three successful throws, and to the tradition of giving the third libation at a symposium to Zeus Soter, the saviour.

599. *heard some clever person say*: It is anybody's guess who the 'clever person' is. Sometimes (e.g., in 365c itself), Plato uses anonymous references like this to signal that he is actually not, or not wholly, in agreement with the 'expert' alluded to; but in the present case Socrates will himself conclude that the pleasure of the 'money-maker' is a 'shadow-painting' of the philosopher's (586b–c).

600. *Well, look at it this way*: Reading *g'oun*, and leaving aside the objections in Slings, 2003 (which also entail supposing a lacuna before the sentence).

601. *with what is less ... with what is more*: I.e., with the kind of thing to which the familiar label 'what is' – see 507b, with n. 440 – applies to a lesser extent, or the kind of thing it applies to more.

602. *decide which you think has more to it ... in the context of things*

of that sort: In the case in question, the decision might perhaps be between having a particular meal – which may or may not provide the right nourishment – and having a true belief or knowledge about what was truly nourishing.

603. *does anything . . . than knowledge does?*: Reading, and making the best of, the text proposed by Ferrari (see n. 448) here, i.e., *ê* [interrogative] *oun aei homoiou ousias ti mallon ê epistêmê metechei*. Slings despairs of the passage, and with some justification.

604. *if something shares . . . less in what is?*: Because whatever is less truly what it claims to be will be less easy to get hold of, as it were, *as* that thing?

605. *what is more truly filled . . . shares in less substantial things*: Presumably soul and body, respectively.

606. *because they didn't know the truth*: I.e., because they didn't know that the real Helen was elsewhere (actually, according to this story, in Egypt). Stesichorus was a lyric poet, born in Greek southern Italy in the second half of the seventh century BCE.

607. *Mustn't the same . . . follows its projects?*: I.e., mustn't his pleasures be mixed with pains in the same way?

608. *some of them*: Some desires, after all, have been declared to be utterly beyond the pale (571b–572b).

609. *the king*: I.e., the philosopher-king (or queen, presumably) who rules over Callipolis, the City Beautiful.

610. *and from his own*: I.e., from those he could have, if only he were a better and a wiser person.

611. *at the third remove*: For the Greeks, the next but one is third 'from' the one first thought of, as well as being third in order. Translating the idiom into English here, and making the tyrant only two removes from the oligarch, would spoil Socrates' sums (which appear to raise even more questions than his last excursion into mathematics, in 546b–c).

612. *aristocratic*: I.e., as before, in the sense of rule by the best.

613. *the illusion . . . will be a square*: And so, two dimensional, like a 'shadow-painting' (see 583b); the next move, cubing, will by the same logic give us the three dimensions of true pleasure.

614. *if you're a mathematician*: Which presumably Glaucon is not; but neither is Socrates, at least given the way he has just presented his 'argument'. (For a positive view of that argument, taking it as a compressed form of a more presentable one – reconstructed from elsewhere in Plato – see Robert D. Brumbaugh, 'Teaching Plato's *Republic* IX', in *The Classical Journal* 46 (1951), pp. 345–8.)

615. *if days . . . and years do*: That is, on the basis that the days and
     nights in a whole year together add up to (roughly) 729. The
     general idea, presumably, is that the king/philosopher has a
     whole lifetime of true pleasure, while the tyrant lives his life
     without experiencing true pleasure at all.

616. *No gold necklace . . . for a husband's life and soul*: In Greek
     mythology, Eriphyle was bribed with a gold necklace to per-
     suade her husband to go to war, and he was killed as a result.

617. *which was Thrasymachus' view of being ruled*: See 343b–c.

618. *a worse person*: And especially, according to the argument, a less
     rational person.

619. *the sorts of learning . . . this condition*: I.e., the sorts of learning
     that the guards were given in the City Beautiful (and presumably
     including, above all, philosophy)?

620. *the city that belongs to him*: I.e., the best one.

621. *perhaps it is set up . . . in the heavens*: Socrates' point here seems
     to be to emphasize that the city he, Glaucon and Adimantus have
     described is not to be taken merely as a 'city in words', but as a
     model to be followed.

622. *found himself*: I.e., as one would a city. The striking phrase – as
     peculiar in the Greek as it is in English – continues the analogy
     between cities and individuals.

623. *we refused . . . through imitation*: See 392c–398b.

624. *now that the different kinds . . . from each other*: The basic dis-
     tinction between the different 'kinds' ('parts', 'elements') of the
     soul was of course made much earlier in the conversation (435b
     ff.), after the treatment of the guards' education that provided
     the context for the original treatment of poetry. However, the
     long discussion of the different types of non-ideal individual,
     from the 'timocratic' to the tyrannical, has provided a far more
     detailed – and vivid – portrait of these 'kinds', and of the differ-
     ences and relationships between them. This now provides the
     basis for a more focused treatment of the problems Socrates
     thinks are posed by poetry for the best society.

625. *What we usually do . . . to the form*: See, e.g., 476b, 493c, 507b,
     510b, 511c. 'Each form': i.e., each form in the special Platonic
     sense. The word for 'form' in the Greek here is *eidos*; a few lines
     further down it will be *idea* – as usual, the terms are interchange-
     able. (The traditional translation of this sentence represents it as
     saying '. . . we habitually posit a single form in relation to each
     plurality of things to which we apply a common name', which
     would give us forms of any and every plurality. I am grateful to

David Sedley for finally persuading me that this traditional reading is wrong, both because it would require a different reference for the two occurrences of 'we' – members of the Socratic circle in the first case, Greek speakers generally in the second – and because of the run of the argument as a whole.)

626. *couches*: I.e., as used for eating on, or for drinking-parties.

627. *as for forms, in relation to these products*: Whether or not Plato was serious about positing 'forms' of manufactured objects is a question almost as old as the history of the interpretation of Plato itself. Socrates will say that the form of couch is somehow 'there in nature' (597b: so, perhaps, part of the world as it is constructed?), and surely couches and tables were invented by humans as well as manufactured by them? See 597b, with n. 633.

628. *But I think you'll claim. . . are not true*: Even though the painter is a craftsman, and is making something.

629. *the form we identify as 'what a couch is'*: This is one more case of 'apply[ing] the label "what is"'; see 507b, with n. 440.

630. *something that is, perfectly*: I.e., is, perfectly, what it claims to be (a couch). At 477a, Socrates contrasted 'what is, entirely' first with 'what is not in any way at all', then with 'what both is and is not'. The latter is the sort of category he has in mind here (an actual couch – as we would call it – certainly is a couch, but it will also be lots of other things: heavy or light, plain or ornate, and so on).

631. *people familiar with this sort of discussion*: I.e., presumably, people like Glaucon and Socrates. Glaucon here acknowledges that to most people it will be odd (to say the least) to claim that a couch you can recline on and have your dinner on is somehow less 'the real thing' than 'the couch itself', or 'what a couch is'.

632. *the type we're looking for*: See 595c.

633. *the one that's there in nature . . . fashioned by god – who else?*: But see next note.

634. *its plantsman*: I.e., *phutourgos*, 'gardener'. Socrates is playing on the root *phu-*, with its basic connotation of 'nature' (we have just had *phuteuein*, then *phuein* twice, first intransitively, then transitively: 'not *planted* . . . nor will they ever *spring up* . . . he *engendered* it'); as Glaucon goes on immediately to say, god, or the god, makes things 'through nature', i.e., presumably, by using natural processes as opposed to the artificial ones – carpentry, ceramics, metal-working, etc. – employed by human craftsmen. (For the idea that god 'makes' natural things, see esp. Plato, *Sophist* 265a–e.) But then one might say that the best kind of

couch, *klinê*, even in our familiar world, the world of the senses, is actually a natural one: a grassy bank, beside a stream, perhaps ('Most charming of all is the grass, growing on a gentle slope and thick enough to be just right to rest [*kataklinein*] one's head upon', Plato, *Phaedrus* 230c) – or 'palliasses strewn with yew and myrtle', as in the simplest kind of city Socrates described early on in the conversation, and contrasted with the couches used in the 'luxurious' and 'fevered' city (372b–e).

635. *at two removes or so*: 'Or so', because the next step will tend to put even more distance between 'imitation-producers' and the truth.

636. *The products of the craftsmen*: Certainly, asked to paint a picture of a couch, or a table, even an abstract painter would presumably start from the manufactured varieties.

637. *the Homeridae themselves*: The counterpart of Asclepius' successors (599c, often referred to as the Asclepiadae: see 405d, with n. 181), a kind of guild of performers and practitioners of epic poetry.

638. *an even more comic example ... than his name suggests*: 'Creophylus' – we know next to nothing about the man himself – perhaps suggests 'Creophilos', 'Meat-lover', which would certainly suit the comic stage.

639. *Protagoras of Abdera, Prodicus of Ceos*: Protagoras and Prodicus were both well-known professional educators (typically referred to as 'sophists'). Plato wrote a dialogue, *Protagoras*, in which Socrates is found in close conversation with Protagoras, among other things questioning his qualifications as a teacher. However, Plato seems generally to have taken him seriously, especially as a philosopher, and nowhere more so than in the dialogue *Theaetetus*, where Protagoras appears as a champion of extreme relativism. Prodicus is treated rather less seriously, chiefly as a specialist in fine distinctions between words.

640. *simply go by the colours and shapes*: Cf. 476b (the sight- and sound-lovers).

641. *I'm sure you've seen them*: That is, in the theatre/*theatron* ('you've seen' is *tetheasai*).

642. *in every case*: I.e., clearly, in the case of everything manufactured.

643. *And isn't the measure ... the use for which each is made or born?*: For the connection between excellence (or goodness) and function, see 335b, with note, and 352e–354a.

644. *iambics ... hexameters*: The basic metre of tragedy is iambic, while epic poets like Homer and Hesiod used hexameters. Socrates'

conflation of epic with the genre of tragedy began back in 595c. The relationship between the two is in fact close, particularly in terms of subject-matter: the fifth-century tragedians draw many of their characters, themes and plots from Homer and the other epic poets.

645. *is present there by itself*: I.e., spontaneously – our sight is something that is naturally confused.

646. *weren't we saying ... at the same time*: 'The same thing won't act or be acted on in opposite ways simultaneously ... in the same respect or in relation to the same thing', 436b.

647. *tens of thousands ... our souls are teeming with them*: See esp. 437b–d.

648. *I think we also said before*: See 387d–e.

649. *the law declares*: I.e., presumably, the law (*nomos*) as envisaged in Callipolis, the 'City Beautiful', itself. Alternatively, *nomos* here is to be taken as 'convention' rather than 'law' – in which case what it 'declares' is simply the first part of what follows, that one should meet misfortunes calmly. The grounds given for this are the very opposite of 'conventional'; indeed, almost anybody but Socrates, Plato and their circle would probably have laughed them out of court.

650. *the very things ... accompany all our actions*: See 603c.

651. *and that reasoning ... to be best*: If this is what Socrates has in mind, it would be an expansion of the simple 'reason and law' at 604a; the closest parallel in Plato would be at *Crito* 46b, where Socrates declares that he has never listened 'to anyone or anything, however close to me, except the one argument, whichever it is, that appears best by my reckoning'. Another possible, but perhaps less natural, way of understanding the Greek here translated would be something like 'and – what has been universally [?] agreed to be best – reason.'

652. *a quarrel between philosophy and poetry is nothing new*: I.e., as Socrates illustrates with the following snippets, taken from sources unknown to us, poets have been sniping at philosophers for years. In fact, though Socrates does not say so, philosophers before him gave as good as they got. But then elsewhere in Plato he is not much less rude about his philosophical predecessors than he is about the poets: take, for example, what he says about Anaxagoras at *Apology* 26d–e, or about cosmologists like Anaxagoras at *Phaedo* 97b–99c.

653. *that 'yelping bitch' that 'bays against her master'*: Plato's *Laws* (967c–d) talks of poets describing philosophers as 'bitches barking

at the moon' (Trevor Saunders, in the Penguin Classics translation of the *Laws*), evidently with the same passage, from the same unidentified poet, in mind. The sources of the following quotations are also unknown.

654. *the ruling mob of the very wise*: This translates the text printed by John Burnet and others, which includes the otherwise unattested word *diasophos* ('very wise'); Slings, 2003, probably rightly, doubts whether such a word ever existed, and despairs of restoring what Plato, and the poet, originally wrote.

655. *the whole of this . . . when compared to all time*: See 486a.

656. *Have you not noticed . . . never perishes?*: A strange-looking question, which certainly takes Glaucon aback. Socrates is of course pretending: no one could have 'noticed' that the soul was immortal, as if it were some quite ordinary fact of experience. He follows up with a fairly complex argument for his claim ('It's not hard', he says in the next breath, which – coming after 'Have you not noticed . . .?' – signals the exact opposite). Not many have found the argument persuasive, but its complexity makes it hard to dismiss out of hand.

657. *passing into non-existence*: I.e., into not being what they were before, like the body destroyed by disease.

658. *and separate it from the body*: The idea of death as the separation of soul, *psuchê* (psyche), from body was evidently standard in ordinary, non-philosophical Greek thinking, and does not in any way by itself prejudge the issue of the soul's mortality or immortality. Thus the 'soul' in Homer departs on death to the underworld, but as a mindless shadow-image of its former possessor. The whole question (as Socrates puts it in the *Phaedo*) is whether the soul survives as an intelligent entity.

659. *that it's a born killer, killing*: Reading *hup'autou, tou apokteinontos*, instead of Slings's *huph'hautou . . .*

660. *its pitch is quite different*: The verb in the Greek has the meaning of pitching [a tent].

661. *something that always is*: I.e., something that always is as, or what, it is; or, alternatively (or additionally), something that is always there, always exists.

662. *to brim over . . . in relation to itself*: That is, as the soul of the unjust person does?

663. *other arguments*: Like, for example, the four in the *Phaedo*.

664. *the sea-dwelling Glaucus*: A minor divinity, not to be confused with the Glaucus of the *Phaedo* (*Phaedo* 108d), who was apparently the inventor of welding.

665. *that which always is*: See 611a, with n. 661.

666. *whether its true nature . . . or only one*: Or simply, 'whether it is complex (*polueidês*) or uniform (*monoeidês*)'; but it is hard not to think that the question is meant to recall the one in 435b–c, as to whether the individual 'has these same [three] kinds (*eidê*) within his own soul', i.e., as the city has.

667. *in the context of a human life*: I.e., the life of an *anthrôpos*, a human being, understood as a composite of soul and body.

668. *in the way you were claiming Hesiod and Homer did*: See 363b–c.

669. *Gyges' ring . . . the cap of Hades too*: For Gyges' ring, see 359d–360d; the 'cap of Hades' (as worn by Athena at Homer, *Iliad* 5.845) was another device conferring invisibility.

670. *while a man is still alive and when he dies*: I.e., when soul and body are together and when they are separated ('man' = human being; cf. n. 667).

671. *both of you asked me to*: At 360e–361d and 367b–c respectively.

672. *prizes*: And they're first prizes, prizes for winning (*nikêtêria*).

673. *at the start*: See 363a–d.

674. *unless he is already . . . from a previous mistake*: Socrates seems here to be anticipating elements in the story he is about to tell – however *that* is to be interpreted – of the choices that will face us after the end of our present life and before we are reborn, into a new body.

675. *what you were saying*: See 362a–c.

676. *all the things you rightly described as sounding crude*: See 361e–362a.

677. *my tale . . . Er, son of Armenius, a Pamphylian*: 'Tale on an Odyssean scale' substitutes for 'tale of Alcinous' in the Greek. This expression had evidently become proverbial for a long tale; it refers to the story – occupying about one sixth of the *Odyssey* – that Odysseus tells Alcinous, king of the Phaeacians (Books 9 to 12). This story also happens to contain an account of Odysseus' own visit to the underworld, which provides the model for Er's. Part of Plato's point here is presumably to evoke this parallel, while also suggesting that his own – or the fictitious Er's – ambitions are rather smaller than Homer's (just as Er is a rather smaller figure than the great Odysseus). If so, it quickly becomes apparent that the suggestion is disingenuous; Plato's canvas is much wider, eventually including the whole universe. (The Greek also includes at least one untranslatable pun – on 'Alcinous' and *alkimos*, 'brave'.)

678. *in that other place*: I.e., wherever he – his soul – had gone after dying. 'The other place' would normally be Hades, or the

underworld; but the landscape that Socrates will report Er as describing is rather more complex than that of any Hades (or 'underworld') we encounter in Homer or elsewhere in Greek literature before Plato.

679. *exited himself*: I.e., left the Er composed of soul and body.

680. *threw them to the ground . . . on the thorn bushes*: If such details have too 'crude' a sound about them to be mentioned in the context of actual physical punishment (613d–e), Socrates perhaps finds them less objectionable as part of a metaphorical description of the punishment of disembodied souls. (All those being thrown to the ground, etc., here have left their bodies/corpses behind, just as Er has – though only for a brief time, in his case: 614b.)

681. *Tartarus*: Traditionally the deepest part of the underworld, and a place of punishment.

682. *all the rotations in the heavens*: That is, all the rotations of the heavenly bodies around the axis of the universe, as represented by the column of light (which in Plato's geocentric view will have to pass through the earth and out the other side).

683. *the whorl*: I.e., the weight at the bottom of the spindle; the hook is at the other end.

684. *The circle of the broadest . . . the seventh's shining on it*: The first circle, then, represents the fixed stars, the seventh carries the sun, the eighth the moon. The second, third, fourth, fifth and sixth circles respectively carry Saturn, Jupiter, Mars, Mercury and Venus.

685. *the opposite movement*: West to east, if the movement of the first circle, of the fixed stars, is – or appears to be, from a geocentric perspective – from east to west.

686. *a Siren*: In Homer (e.g., *Odyssey* 12.44 ff.), Sirens were creatures that lure sailors to their death by the sweetness of their singing; here they are elevated to a cosmic (and less sinister) role.

687. *No divine guide . . . will be your own*: According to the Socrates of the *Phaedo*, as it happens, each of us does have an appointed 'divine guide' (*Phaedo* 107d–e, 108b, 113d); but the kind of 'guiding' involved here in the *Republic* will turn out to be quite different: see 620d–e.

688. *Any ordering of the soul*: I.e., presumably, of its various elements (however many these may be – a question that Socrates appeared to reopen in 611b–612a).

689. *all the other things*: Presumably things like looks, strength, birth, etc.

690. *this one subject ... to distinguish a good life from a bad one*: To judge by Socrates' renewed attack on poetry before Er's story, an important part of 'this one subject' will be discovering who does *not* impart the knowledge in question.

691. *wherever he is*: I.e., in life or in death (see 618e, 619a).

692. *or kept apart: for example, what effect*: Omitting *eidenai*, as Slings (2003) suggests in his apparatus – if without sufficient confidence to omit it in the text he prints.

693. *in every life to come*: Or, possibly, 'in the whole of the life to come'; but actually, as we are about to discover, we – we middling sorts of people, at least – will have not just one life 'hereafter', but many.

694. *under a well-ordered constitution*: In a city with such a constitution, or with such a constitution in himself (or both)?

695. *Orpheus ... Thamyras*: Orpheus was torn to pieces by Maenads – worshippers of Dionysus – for preferring to worship Dionysus' saner rival, Apollo. Thamyras was a legendary singer, like Orpheus (and the swan and the nightingale); he was said to have been blinded by the Muses for challenging them to a competition.

696. *the decision over Achilles' arms*: Awarded after Achilles' death to Odysseus instead of Ajax, who went mad as a result and eventually killed himself.

697. *Next up ... Agamemnon's*: Agamemnon was killed by his wife in his bath with an axe.

698. *Atalanta*: Avoided marriage by challenging her suitors to a running-race, which she always won.

699. *Epeius ... female craftworker*: Epeius was designer of the device – the 'Trojan horse' – the Greeks used to sneak into Troy after having failed to get in by more conventional means.

700. *Thersites*: Probably the only ordinary soldier named in the *Iliad*, who speaks out of turn to his superiors and is finally put down by Odysseus.

701. *and she sent them off ... with the guide ... bring the things they had chosen to fulfilment*: So this is a very special kind of guide, and kind of 'guard', whose function is to keep the soul in his charge on the path it has chosen for itself in its new life. Divine this guide may be (the term in the Greek is *daimôn*), but he is no saviour. See 617e, with n. 687.

702. *destiny*: Or 'portion' (*moira*).

703. *he led it on to where Atropos ... no turning back*: The Greek here consists largely in a series of puns – Atropos is 'She who is

not for turning'; 'to spin over' (i.e., the threads of fate) is *epi-klôthô* (so Clotho has already done her spinning too); 'not to be unspun', *ametastropha*, is an adjective corresponding to the adverb *ametastreptei* ('without turning back'); and of course there could be no turning back of any kind if Necessity is involved.

704. *forgetfulness*: Here and in 621c Slings (2003) prints *lêthê*, 'forgetfulness', with an initial capital letter; the present translation assumes that it is not in fact a proper name in either case.

705. *in good shape, with our souls undefiled*: That is, perhaps, not defiled by drinking too much from the river of forgetfulness?

PENGUIN CLASSICS

CONVERSATIONS OF SOCRATES
XENOPHON

Socrates' Defence/Memoirs of Socrates/The Estate-Manager/The Dinner-Party

'He seemed to me to be the perfect example of goodness and happiness'

After the execution of Socrates in 399 BC, a number of his followers wrote dialogues featuring him as the protagonist and, in so doing, transformed the great philosopher into a legendary figure. Xenophon's portrait is the only one other than Plato's to survive, and while it offers a very personal interpretation of Socratic thought, it also reveals much about the man and his philosophical views. In 'Socrates' Defence' Xenophon defends his mentor against charges of arrogance made at his trial, while the 'Memoirs of Socrates' also starts with an impassioned plea for the rehabilitation of a wronged reputation. Along with 'The Estate-Manager', a practical economic treatise, and 'The Dinner-Party', a sparkling exploration of love, Xenophon's dialogues offer fascinating insights into the Socratic world and into the intellectual atmosphere and daily life of ancient Greece.

Xenophon's complete Socratic works are translated in this volume. In his introduction, Robin Waterfield illuminates the significance of these four books, showing how perfectly they embody the founding principles of Socratic thought.

Translated by Hugh Tredennick and Robin Waterfield and edited with new material by Robin Waterfield

PENGUIN CLASSICS

THE BIRDS AND OTHER PLAYS
ARISTOPHANES

The Knights/Peace/The Birds/The Assemblywomen/Wealth

> 'Oh wings are splendid things, make no mistake:
> they really help you rise in the world'

The plays collected in this volume, written at different times in Aristophanes'
forty-year career as a dramatist, all contain his trademark bawdy comedy and
dazzling verbal agility. In *The Birds*, two frustrated Athenians join with the birds to
build the utopian city of 'Much Cuckoo in the Clouds'. *The Knights* is a venomous
satire on Cleon, the prominent Athenian demagogue, while *The Assemblywomen*
considers the war of the sexes, as the women of Athens infiltrate the all-male
Assembly in disguise. The lengthy conflict with Sparta is the subject of *Peace*,
inspired by the hope of a settlement in 421 BC, and *Wealth* reflects the economic
catastrophe that hit Athens after the war, as the god of riches is depicted as a
ragged, blind old man.

The lively translations by David Barrett and Alan H. Sommerstein capture the full
humour of the plays. The introduction examines Aristophanes' life and times, and
the comedy and poetry of his works. This volume also includes an introductory
note for each play.

Translated with an introduction by David Barrett and Alan H. Sommerstein

PENGUIN CLASSICS

THE FROGS AND OTHER PLAYS
ARISTOPHANES

The Wasps/The Poet and the Women/The Frogs

> 'This is just a little fable, with a moral: not too highbrow for you, we hope,
> but a bit more intelligent than the usual knockabout stuff'

The master of ancient Greek comic drama, Aristophanes combined slapstick,
humour and cheerful vulgarity with acute political observations. In *The Frogs*,
written during the Peloponnesian War, Dionysus descends to the Underworld to
bring back a poet who can help Athens in its darkest hour, and stages a great debate
to help him decide between the traditional wisdom of Aeschylus and the brilliant
modernity of Euripides. The clash of generations and values is also the object of
Aristophanes' satire in *The Wasps*, in which an old-fashioned father and his loose-
living son come to blows and end up in court. And in *The Poet and the Women*,
Euripides, accused of misogyny, persuades a relative to infiltrate an all-women
festival to find out whether revenge is being plotted against him.

David Barrett's introduction discusses the Athenian dramatic contests in which
these plays first appeared, and conventions of Greek comedy – from its poetic
language and the role of the Chorus to casting and costumes.

Translated with an introduction by David Barrett

PENGUIN CLASSICS

LYSISTRATA AND OTHER PLAYS
ARISTOPHANES

Lysistrata/The Acharnians/The Clouds

> 'But he who would provoke me should remember
> That those who rifle wasps' nests will be stung!'

Writing at a time of political and social crisis in Athens, Aristophanes (*c.* 447–*c.* 385 BC) was an eloquent, yet bawdy, challenger to the demagogue and the sophist. In *Lysistrata* and *The Acharnians*, two pleas for an end to the long war between Athens and Sparta, a band of women and a lone peasant respectively defeat the political establishment. The darker comedy of *The Clouds* satirizes Athenian philosophers, Socrates in particular, and reflects the uncertainties of a generation in which all traditional religious and ethical beliefs were being challenged.

For this edition Alan H. Sommerstein has completely revised his translation of these three plays, bringing out the full nuances of Aristophanes' ribald humour and intricate word play, with a new introduction explaining the historical and cultural background to the plays.

Translated with an introduction by Alan H. Sommerstein

PENGUIN CLASSICS

HOMERIC HYMNS

> 'It is of you the poet sings ...
> at the beginning and at the end
> it is always of you'

Written by unknown poets in the sixth and seventh centuries BC, the thirty-three *Homeric Hymns* were recited at festivals to honour the Olympian goddesses and gods and to pray for divine favour or for victory in singing contests. They stand now as works of great poetic force, full of grace and lyricism, and ranging in tone from irony to solemnity, ebullience to grandeur. Recounting significant episodes from mythology, such as the abduction of Persephone by Hades and Hermes' theft of Apollo's cattle, the *Hymns* also provide fascinating insights into cults, rituals and holy sanctuaries, giving us an intriguing view of the ancient Greek relationship between humans and the divine.

This translation of the *Homeric Hymns* is new to Penguin Classics, providing a key text for understanding ancient Greek mythology and religion. The introduction explores their authorship, performance, literary qualities and influence on later writers.

'The purest expressions of ancient Greek religion we possess ... Jules Cashford is attuned to the poetry of the Hymns' Nigel Spivey, University of Cambridge

A new translation by Jules Cashford with an introduction by Nicholas Richardson

PENGUIN CLASSICS

MEDEA AND OTHER PLAYS
EURIPIDES

Medea/Alcestis/The Children of Heracles/Hippolytus

> 'That proud, impassioned soul,
> so ungovernable now that she has felt the sting of injustice'

Medea, in which a spurned woman takes revenge upon her lover by killing her children, is one of the most shocking and horrific of all the Greek tragedies. Dominating the play is Medea herself, a towering and powerful figure who demonstrates Euripides' unusual willingness to give voice to a woman's case. *Alcestis*, a tragicomedy, is based on a magical myth in which Death is overcome, and *The Children of Heracles* examines the conflict between might and right, while *Hippolytus* deals with self-destructive integrity and moral dilemmas. These plays show Euripides transforming the awesome figures of Greek mythology into recognizable, fallible human beings.

John Davie's accessible prose translation is accompanied by a general introduction and individual prefaces to each play.

'John Davie's translations are outstanding ... the tone throughout is refreshingly modern yet dignified' **William Allan**, *Classical Review*

Previously published as *Alcestis and Other Plays*.

Translated by John Davie, with an introduction and notes by Richard Rutherford

PENGUIN CLASSICS

ELECTRA AND OTHER PLAYS
SOPHOCLES

Ajax/Electra/Women of Trachis/Philoctetes

> 'Now that he is dead,
> I turn to you; will you be brave enough
> To help me kill the man who killed our father?'

Sophocles' innovative plays transformed Greek myths into dramas featuring complex human characters, through which he explored profound moral issues. *Electra* portrays the grief of a young woman for her father Agamemnon, who has been killed by her mother's lover. Aeschylus and Euripides also dramatized this story, but the objectivity and humanity of Sophocles' version provided a new perspective. Depicting the fall of a great hero, *Ajax* examines the enigma of power and weakness combined in one being, while the *Women of Trachis* portrays the tragic love and error of Heracles' deserted wife Deianeira, and *Philoctetes* deals with the conflict between physical force and moral strength.

E. F. Watling's vivid translation is accompanied by an introduction in which he discusses Sophocles' use of a third actor to create new dramatic situations and compares the different treatments of the Electra myth by the three great tragic poets of classical Athens.

Translated with an introduction by E. F. Watling

PENGUIN CLASSICS

THE GREEK SOPHISTS

'In the case of wisdom, those who sell it to anyone who wants it are called sophists'

By mid-fifth century BC, Athens was governed by democratic rule and power turned upon the ability of the individual to command the attention of the other citizens, and to sway the crowds of the assembly. It was the Sophists who understood the art of rhetoric and the importance of being able to transform effective reasoning into persuasive public speaking. Their inquiries – into the gods, the origins of religion and whether virtue can be taught – laid the groundwork for the next generation of thinkers such as Plato and Aristotle.

Each chapter of *The Greek Sophists* is based around the work of one character: Gorgias, Prodicus, Protagoras and Antiphon among others, and a linking commentary, chronological table and bibliography are provided for each one. In his introduction, John Dillon discusses the historical background and the sources of the text.

Translated by John Dillon and Tania Gergel with an introduction by John Dillon

PENGUIN CLASSICS

THE LETTERS OF THE YOUNGER PLINY

'Of course these details are not important enough for history ...
you have only yourself to blame for asking for them'

A prominent lawyer and administrator, Pliny (*c.* AD 61–113) was also a prolific letter-writer, who numbered among his correspondents such eminent figures as Tacitus, Suetonius and the Emperor Trajan, as well as a wide circle of friends and family. His lively and very personal letters address an astonishing range of topics, from a deeply moving account of his uncle's death in the eruption that engulfed Pompeii and observations on the early Christians – 'a desperate sort of cult carried to extravagant lengths' – to descriptions of everyday life in Rome, with its scandals and court cases, and of his own life in the country. Providing a series of fascinating views of imperial Rome, his letters also offer one of the fullest self-portraits to survive from classical times.

Betty Radice's definitive edition was the first complete modern translation of Pliny's letters. In her introduction, she examines the shrewd, tolerant and occasionally pompous man who emerges from these.

Translated with an introduction by Betty Radice

PENGUIN CLASSICS

NATURAL HISTORY: A SELECTION
PLINY THE ELDER

> 'The world is the work of Nature and,
> at the same time, the embodiment of Nature herself'

Pliny's *Natural History* is an astonishingly ambitious work that ranges from astronomy to art and from geography to zoology. Mingling acute observation with often wild speculation, it offers a fascinating view of the world as it was understood in the first century AD, whether describing the danger of diving for sponges, the first water-clock, or the use of asses' milk to remove wrinkles. Pliny himself died while investigating the volcanic eruption that destroyed Pompeii in AD 79, and the natural curiosity that brought about his death is also very much evident in the *Natural History* – a book that proved highly influential right up to the Renaissance and that his nephew, Pliny the younger, described 'as full of variety as nature itself'.

John F. Healy has made a fascinating and varied selection from the *Natural History* for this clear, modern translation. In his introduction, he discusses the book and its sources topic by topic. This edition also includes a full index and notes.

Translated with an introduction and notes by John F. Healy

PENGUIN CLASSICS

THE CAMPAIGNS OF ALEXANDER
ARRIAN

'His passion was for glory only, and in that he was insatiable'

Although written over four hundred years after Alexander's death, Arrian's *Campaigns of Alexander* is the most reliable account of the man and his achievements we have. Arrian's own experience as a military commander gave him unique insights into the life of the world's greatest conqueror. He tells of Alexander's violent suppression of the Theban rebellion, his total defeat of Persia, and his campaigns through Egypt, India and Babylon – establishing new cities and destroying others in his path. While Alexander emerges from this record as an unparalleled and charismatic leader, Arrian succeeds brilliantly in creating an objective and fully rounded portrait of a man of boundless ambition, who was exposed to the temptations of power and worshipped as a god in his own lifetime.

Aubrey de Sélincourt's vivid translation is accompanied by J. R. Hamilton's introduction, which discusses Arrian's life and times, his synthesis of other classical sources and the composition of Alexander's army. This edition also includes maps, a list for further reading and a detailed index.

Translated by Aubrey de Sélincourt
Revised, with a new introduction and notes by J. R. Hamilton